PHOTOGRAPHIC HANDBOOK OF THE

RARE BIRDS

of

BRITAIN AND EUROPE

PREFACE

No other aspect of ornithology provides such a potent combination of interest and excitement for so many birdwatchers as the study and pursuit of rare birds. There are many reasons why this should be the case – rare birds are unfamiliar, unpredictable, perhaps exotic in appearance, and sometimes from far-flung areas we rarely visit or know little about. Their identification is frequently challenging, and despite many years of systematic studies and field research, the reasons for their occurrence often remain perplexing. Yet, at a more basic level, perhaps it is simply the thrill of finding or seeing something so unusual that has made this facet of birdwatching so popular.

The enormous growth in birdwatching in general in recent years has been more than matched by an increase in interest in rare birds – so much so that they could now be described as a serious leisure pursuit in their own right. In Britain alone the appearance of one wayward vagrant can draw a crowd of hundreds, if not thousands, of birders. There are telephone answering systems, personal paging services, and magazines and journals largely or wholly devoted to the subject. Birders run competitive year-listing competitions and spend thousands of pounds twitching rarities the length and breadth of the country. The same is increasingly true for birdwatchers elsewhere in Europe, and with more information available on the identification and distribution of rare birds than ever before, this subject offers more than enough

interest and excitement to match any other.

We have aimed to capture some of that fascination with the publication of this handbook, which uniquely combines a comprehensive selection of photos of all of Europe's rare birds with species accounts which list in full or in summary their occurrences in every country of the continent. The assimilation of so much information and such an extensive collection of photos has been a long and involved task, and one made all the more frustrating by the knowledge that any work of this nature is destined to become out of date before it is even published. Old records of rare birds in Europe are constantly being reassessed by national committees; many hundreds – perhaps thousands – of recent rarity reports are likely to be under consideration across the continent at any one time, and new

species are being added to national lists somewhere in Europe almost every month.

As if to emphasise these points, news of a Cedar Waxwing in Britain broke just as the introduction to this handbook was being written – possibly the first wild occurrence in this country and, if accepted as such, only the second record for Europe. This provides a foretaste of the number of revisions which will be necessary in future to keep a handbook such as this up-to-date, and it also exemplifies the pace at which new or extremely rare species are being identified by birdwatchers in Europe. Nonetheless, the information in the pages that follow is as accurate and up-to-date as humanly possible at the time of writing, and we hope it will comprise an important and useful reference for every rare bird enthusiast for some time to come.

BIRD TOPOGRAPHY

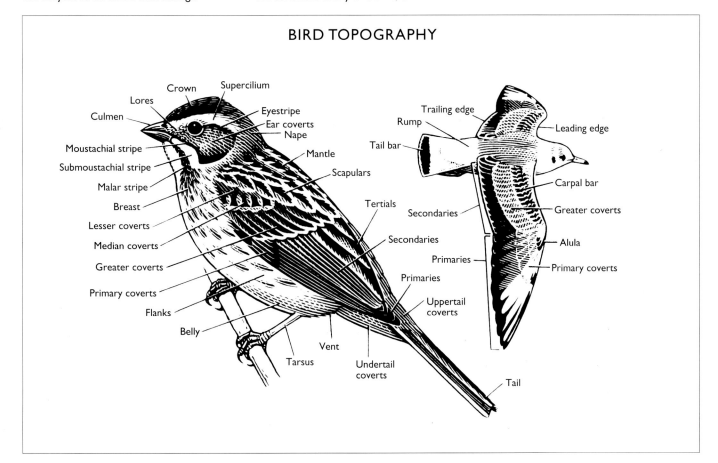

CONTENTS

INTRODUCTION

There have been many books covering Europe's birds, especially their identification, and it is probably true to say that European birdwatchers are better served with information than are any of their counterparts elsewhere in the world. Field guides remain the staple practical reference, but, with increasing attention being paid to the identification and occurrence of rare birds, a new demand has grown for more specialised information. In 1991, the publication of *A Field Guide to the Rare Birds of Britain and Europe* (Lewington *et al*) went a good way towards meeting that demand, but until now there has been no attempt to gather together in one volume both a full account of the documented records of Europe's rare birds and a complete photographic reference to them.

This handbook attempts to do just that: to provide a unique and up-to-date summary of the status of rare birds in the continent, and to assemble the most comprehensive collection of photographs of those species so far available. A significant amount of the material published – both records and photographs – has been gathered together in one volume for the first time, a feat made possible by the generous co-operation of rarities committees, national experts and individual birders and photographers across Europe.

Area covered
The area defined as Europe is, for the purposes of this book, that which extends from Britain and Ireland in the west to Poland, Romania and Bulgaria in the east, north to Iceland, the Faeroes and Norway (but not Svalbard), and south to the Mediterranean and the Balkans.

Turkey (including 'European' Turkey west of the Bosphorus) and Cyprus have been omitted, as both are more usually considered ornithologically part of the Middle East, and Malta and its neighbouring islands have also been excluded. Similarly, the geographically isolated archipelagos of the Canaries, Madeira and the Azores, while politically European, are not covered here, and, aside from the Baltic states which link Finland and Scandinavia with Eastern Europe, none of the republics which formerly comprised the Soviet Union is included.

At the time of writing, a number of the states comprising what was until recently known as Yugoslavia are still in disagreement over independent status and boundaries. Only Slovenia, the northernmost state, has so far gained a recognised new international identity, and is accordingly treated separately in the European Status sections; information for the other states appears collectively under the grouping of 'former Yugoslavia'.

The full list of countries and established European recording areas for which records information is given is as follows: Albania, Austria, Belgium, Britain (excluding Ireland), Bulgaria, Channel Islands, Czech Republic, Denmark, Estonia, Faeroes, Finland, France (including Corsica), Germany, Gibraltar, Greece, Hungary, Iceland, Ireland (comprising Northern Ireland and the Republic), Italy (including Sardinia and Sicily), Latvia, Lithuania, Luxembourg, Netherlands, Norway, Poland, Portugal, Romania, Slovakia, Slovenia, Spain (including the Balearic Islands), Sweden, Switzerland and former Yugoslavia (excluding Slovenia).

Species included
The main systematic list in this book deals with all rare species which have occurred in Europe in a live and truly wild state since 1 January 1958 – the year which saw the advent of 'modern' rarity-recording in Britain, and after which many other rarities committees became

established elsewhere in Europe. Although this may seem to be an arbitrary dividing line, the great majority of European records fall within this period, and the earlier absence of formal rarities committees and rigorous checking procedures – let alone the gaps in knowledge of distribution and especially identification – has in any event led to a significant number of older records (especially those without specimens) subsequently being reassessed and, in many cases, being deemed unreliable. For species which have been recorded since this date, all accepted records are given where known, including those before 1958; species recorded only before that date but not since are listed separately in Appendix 1. The main systematic list is at the time of writing complete up to 31 December 1994, though an unknown number of records from the latter part of this period are still likely to be under assessment.

Before getting into the detail of the contents of this handbook, it is necessary to define exactly what constitutes a rare bird in Europe. What might be an unusual species to a birder living in Britain could be a garden bird to someone in Finland or Greece, and arriving at a compromise which will suit every European country is therefore no easy task. The simple answer is that it is impossible to devise a set of hard and fast rules, but, for the purposes of this book, a line has been drawn to distinguish accidentals and rare or highly localised breeding species and visitors with the potential for vagrancy from the rest.

As a general rule of thumb, rare birds can in most situations be defined as falling into two main categories: vagrants to an area outside their established range; and rare but regular breeding, passage or wintering species. In this handbook there are few problems of definition for the first group, which comprises all those species whose normal range lies outside Europe (for example, American landbirds). The second is more complex: Steller's Eider and Rüppell's Warbler, for instance, would both be major rarities in most European countries, yet are regular species in significant numbers in very localised parts of the continent. How should such birds be treated in the context of their 'rarity' in Europe? Here, a rare bird is defined as either a true vagrant, or a species which occurs as a breeding, passage or winter bird either in very limited numbers or within a very restricted range in the continent. For species with a breeding distribution extending to at least a few countries, the typical cut-off point for inclusion

October on St Mary's in the Isles of Scilly, Britain – one of the best places in Europe to find rare vagrants.

is 250 pairs; for those with a more restricted distribution the threshold is much higher, as the species is likely to be rarer in a wider area of the continent. Hence, Long-legged Buzzard and Saker Falcon would be included in the first definition, and Brünnich's Guillemot, Rüppell's Warbler and Semi-collared Flycatcher among those in the second. There are occasional exceptions to this guideline, the most obvious being Eleonora's Falcon: this species has been included because, although breeding in thousands of pairs across the Mediterranean, it nests virtually nowhere else in the world and is therefore indisputably rare. By contrast, species such as Tengmalm's Owl and River Warbler, which are considered major rarities by birders in some parts of Europe but which breed widely in others, as well as in countries outside the region covered by this handbook, are not dealt with here.

Also excluded from the main systematic section are those breeding species which, although restricted in range or numbers, are by nature largely or entirely sedentary and unlikely to occur outside their normal range. Examples of this group include Small Button-quail (Andalusian Hemipode), Krüper's and Corsican Nuthatches, and Scottish Crossbill; such species are listed separately in Appendix 2.

Other species not covered in the main systematic list include vagrants of uncertain origin, feral birds, escapes or populations thought to originate wholly from escapes, releases and introductions; Appendix 3 contains brief details of some such species (notably vagrants of uncertain origin) and their occurrences. Similarly, subspecies or forms of species occurring regularly in Europe (for example Siberian Stonechat) are not treated separately here; it should, however, be remembered that this handbook largely follows the taxonomic view adopted in Britain, and that in other European countries a different judgement regarding the specific status of distinct forms of certain species may apply. Conversely, other forms regarded as subspecies in parts of Europe may be treated as distinct species in Britain, and therefore have separate entries in the systematic list.

THE SYSTEMATIC SECTION

This main section of the handbook comprises a systematic list with accounts which detail descriptions, vocalisations (where useful), habitat, distribution and European status of each of the 268 rarest species in the continent.

Systematic order

The order follows Beaman (1994). The English names used also generally follow Beaman except where these are clearly in conflict with those in current usage in Europe. Yellow-billed Loon, for example, may be a suitable English name for *Gavia adamsii* in a global context, but in Europe the English name widely used for this species is White-billed Diver. The same is true for Brünnich's Murre (Brünnich's Guillemot) and others, which are in any event identifiable by their scientific names.

Queuing for the boat to St Agnes, Isles of Scilly, in the hope of finding autumn rarities.

The species accounts

Description

The entry for each rare species features a brief text describing plumage, with supportive remarks on identification, behaviour and jizz as appropriate. In some instances comparison is made with more familiar European birds, and in a very few cases mention may be made of species not recorded in the continent. These accounts are, however, intended only to complement the status section and photographs, and not to act as 'stand-alone' guides to the identification of the species concerned: the information they contain has been compiled from a range of sources (see Bibliography, page 174), all of which should be consulted for further information. I am extremely indebted to the authors of the field guides, handbooks and other works which have been referred to for this purpose, all of whom have made a far more original contribution to knowledge of bird identification than is possible in a work of the present kind.

Voice

For those species for which vocalisations are of use in identification, notably waders and passerines, the descriptive text is followed by a brief summary of call and/or song. As with the descriptive texts, the information presented has been compiled from a range of relevant sources listed under Bibliography.

Habitat

A summary is also included of the typical habitat for each species in its home range. This can be of interest even for birds occurring as vagrants, which will typically attempt to seek out their preferred habitat wherever possible. Equally, however, many rare migrants may occur in atypical situations, an obvious example being Asiatic leaf-warblers on wind-blown European headlands and islands which are almost devoid of vegetation.

Distribution

This section summarises the species' world range, where appropriate often giving greater detail on areas close to Europe. For those species which normally occur in parts of the world remote from Europe, information is summarised more briefly. Distribution in Europe is mentioned in general terms, with country-by-country information being given in the following section.

European Status

This final section gives an up-to-date account of all known occurrences of the species as at 31 December 1994. This information has been compiled from a wide variety of sources (see Acknowledgements, Appendices and Bibliography), cross-checked and in almost every instance verified by an authority from the country concerned (the exceptions being Albania, from which no response was received, and former Yugoslavia, for which there currently appears to be no organised ornithological grouping).

Countries and established recording areas are, for ease of reference, listed in alphabetical order under each species, although the structure of this section depends on the status of the species concerned. Regular breeding, migratory and wintering ranges in Europe, for example, are always given first, with extralimital occurrences following after the summary phrase 'accidental elsewhere'. For those species which are purely accidental – that is, the true vagrants – status is summarised in an opening line based on the following definitions:

Extreme vagrant	1-5 records
Very rare vagrant	6-50 records
Rare vagrant	51-100 records
Frequent vagrant	100+ records

Occurrences are thereafter given in parentheses following each country name. The first figure is always the total number of records, whether 1 or 1,000, unless otherwise stated (in a few instances, the number of records and/or individuals is given). In cases where there have been five or fewer records, the dates are also given where known, though some may be incomplete (notably where older records are involved): for those with no date, the reason is usually given as 'date unknown' (where I have been unable to trace the date) or 'undated' (where no documented date for the occurrence apparently exists). In instances where more than one individual of the species has occurred on the same date, the number of individuals concerned (where known) is given immediately after the date; similarly, other details of the record, for example if the bird was collected, found dead or observed at sea, are also given where known.

The figure for the total number of records for each species refers to accepted records or, for those few countries without a formal committee system, documented occurrences, and not unsubstantiated reports. In a very few instances where notable and documented recent finds are still under consideration, these records have been included with the addition of an asterisk. In a handful of cases, records of particular note not fully adjudicated, not submitted, considered as possible or likely escapes or even rejected are also detailed and marked with an asterisk, for reasons of significance which will be obvious.

It has not always been possible to trace or give exact, or even any, details for some species in some countries. In such cases, the country name is listed but without additional information, so long as there are proven records in existence. Conversely, some species have occurred so frequently, even as vagrants, that it is not possible to calculate the exact number of records; this is often the case for vagrant wildfowl, which frequently return to the same wintering site in successive years and thereby confuse the picture in terms of numbers of individuals occurring. The same is also true for frequent 'accidentals' such as Richard's Pipit and Yellow-browed Warbler. Some such species might fairly be described as regular visitors as numbers reaching Europe are so great in some years, yet the individual birds involved are often apparently inexperienced first-years migrating in the wrong direction, and they occur in numbers which vary according to particular weather systems in place during migration times. In such instances, these more numerous species are for convenience termed 'frequent vagrant/visitor' in the text, and sample counts or trends may be given.

Interpreting the records

To arrive at the final totals of occurrences in each country, a wide range of bird reports, journals, magazines and books was researched (see Bibliography). The draft figures were then sent to rarities committees and other authorities throughout Europe for verification, with any required amendments to entries incorporated into the final version. This process has provided as accurate a collection

Rare birds attract large crowds: these British birders have successfully twitched a Black-faced Bunting at Pennington Flash, Greater Manchester.

of records for the continent as is possible, but the finished results should be interpreted within unavoidable constraints.

Firstly, most European countries now have rarities committees, but some have been established relatively recently and these have not always been able to review all of the historical data from their recording areas. In Hungary, for example, no screening of records took place between 1976 and 1987 except for species new to the country; the totals in such cases are therefore given either as a range of figures or should be viewed as the minimum number of records. Similarly, in Germany and Spain, where the rarities committees are also relatively new, only a proportion of records has been formally accepted but many earlier ones still stand or are deemed reliable; these have been included in the totals given. For those countries lacking official rarities committees, only fully documented or published occurrences have been used in the calculations.

Secondly, even in those countries where committees are established, the practice of submitting records is nothing like as well developed in some as it is in others. So, again using the Spanish example, some records for particular species are followed by indications of

other known occurrences which would be very likely to gain acceptance were they to be submitted.

Furthermore, national lists are maintained in ways that are often not directly comparable. The 'pending' file of category D in Britain, which includes records of species whose origin is uncertain, does not currently exist in some countries (for example in the Netherlands and Norway), and this can result in different treatments of the same species, and possibly even the same individual birds, in different countries; this is clearly a pitfall when interpreting, for example, records of 'vagrant' wildfowl on some lists, when those species are automatically disregarded on others. Similarly, individual records may come under review at any time, and even whole national lists fall under scrutiny, possibly altering the nature of information for particular species.

Additionally, not all rarities committees record information in a way that might be expected. The rarities committee in Britain, for example, currently publishes only totals of rarity occurrences which include the figures for Ireland, even though the latter country has its own rarities committee and publishes its records separately. There appears to be no list currently maintained of accepted records relating purely to Britain (England, Scotland, Wales and associated islands), and I have therefore had to calculate the figures given for Britain in the systematic list by deducting known Irish occurrences from the combined British and Irish totals; in some instances it is not possible to achieve an accurate figure by so doing, and approximate totals must suffice.

Any or all of the above factors, together with the fact that national lists are constantly being reviewed, mean that for some species the records totals presented here may differ slightly from those published elsewhere. This is especially likely in relation to countries such as Hungary and Spain, where the validity of older records has not always been adjudicated, and authors are obliged to form their own view.

One last cautionary note concerns the actual definition of a 'record'. Single-bird occurrences do not usually constitute a problem, but what of multiple occurrences of the same species at one site – perhaps even on one day? If birds return to the same site after an absence of days, weeks, months or even years, how can a rarities committee be sure of the number of actual individuals and/or 'records' involved? Different European countries may use different guidelines for dealing with such occurrences, and this may have knock-on effects in the totals listed here – for example, on the process of calculating the respective totals for Britain and Ireland from one original combined list. This should also be borne in mind when interpreting the figures given under European Status.

Finally, every effort has been made to ensure that the information contained throughout this handbook is as accurate and as up to date as possible. During the course of so much number-crunching and date-editing, however, errors will undoubtedly have crept into print, and the responsibility for these is mine alone. I would be delighted to receive comments, corrections or additional information for inclusion in future editions. These should be addressed to me, care of the publishers.

Dominic Mitchell

THE PHOTOGRAPHS

Comprising almost half of this handbook, the collection of photographs published here provides a unique photographic reference to rare birds which have occurred in Europe.

I have endeavoured to use, wherever possible, photographs actually taken in Europe to marry together details of occurrences featured in the text with individual birds in the photographs. In many instances, particularly for those species occurring more frequently (such as Buff-breasted Sandpiper and Richard's Pipit), there is no shortage of material from across the continent from which to choose. For other species, such as those which have occurred only once or on a handful of occasions, few or no photographs taken in Europe may exist; there are numerous examples of these, perhaps some of the most notable involving the rarer American wood-warblers. In such instances, I have of necessity used 'record' shots of poorer quality or included photographs taken after the period covered by this book (that is, since 1 January 1995), these latter photos being marked in their captions by an asterisk. (For the significance of an asterisk elsewhere in the text see page 10 on European status.) In a small number of instances, where there was no alternative, photographs taken in the species' natural range have been used. The latter are easily identifiable by their italicised captions which give more limited information.

I have also attempted to provide a range of images depicting various plumages (for example, male, female and juvenile) and 'poses' or settings (for instance, single-bird portraits, flocks, flying or feeding individuals, and so on). Again, the limitations of original source material meant that this has not always been possible, but the selection featured is the most comprehensive that could be compiled. The captions detail the species, age/sex where this information has been supplied or can be ascertained from the photograph, the date on which the photograph was taken, enabling photographs to be cross-referenced to records in the systematic section, and the location/country. In the case of the British Isles, to follow the systems of records assessment England, Scotland and Wales have all been included under 'Britain', and Northern Ireland and the Republic of Ireland treated together under 'Ireland'.

Finally, more species are being observed and photographed in Europe every year, and future editions of this handbook will aim to update material and include new images. Photographs for consideration will be welcome, and should be addressed to me, care of the publishers.

Steve Young

ACKNOWLEDGMENTS

A great many people contributed the benefit of their skills and experience in helping to take this work from inception to publication. Before thanking those individuals, however, we would like to record a special debt of gratitude to the many authors, illustrators and photographers whose work has been extensively referred to in the preparation of this handbook; their many individual contributions have provided an invaluable base on which to build the contents of this work. A full list of references can be found on page 173.

Many others directly contributed their time and expertise. The author is particularly grateful to Anthony McGeehan, whose comments on the species accounts greatly improved the original drafts, and also to David Christie, who brought his wide experience to bear in reviewing the completed text. Killian Mullarney graciously undertook the task of compiling information on ages and plumages for the photo captions, a time-consuming and laborious chore. Thanks also to Tim Harris, who made useful comments on parts of earlier draft accounts.

The information on rarity occurrences throughout Europe could not have been accurately compiled and verified without the kind help of the following, many of them acting in their roles as representatives of national recording bodies (see Appendix 5), others simply sharing their extensive knowledge of the status and distribution of birds in their countries or those that they know: Jánis Baumanis (Latvia); Pierandrea Brichetti (Italy); Andrea Corso (Italy); Helder Costa (Portugal); Josef Chytil (Czech Republic); Eduardo de Juana (Spain); Gunter de Smet (Belgium); Alan Dixon (Jersey, Channel Islands); João Carlos Farinha (Portugal); Annika Forsten (Finland); Gerard Gorman (Czech Republic, Hungary and Romania); Jørn R Gustad (Norway); Ricard Gutiérrez (Spain); George Handrinos (Greece); Erik Hirschfeld (Sweden); Sebastian Klein (Denmark); Yann Kolbeinsson (Iceland); Dr Gábor Magyar (Hungary); Dr Gintaras Matiukas (Lithuania); Dave McAdams (Ireland); Killian Mullarney (Ireland); Andrew M Paterson (Spain); Gunnlaugur Pétursson (Iceland); Andreas Ranner (Austria); Mike Rogers (Britain); Bob Scott (Bulgaria); Søren Sørensen (Faeroes); Tadeusz Stawarczyk (Poland); Dr Alfréd Trnka (Slovakia); Arnoud B. van den Berg (Netherlands); Bernard Volet (Switzerland); and Barry Wells (Guernsey, Channel Islands). In addition, Alan Knox and David Parkin (Britain), Dr Clive Finlayson and Ernest Garcia (Gibraltar) and Kieran Fahy and Oran O'Sullivan (Ireland) supplied helpful information on the national lists of their respective countries.

Special thanks must also be recorded to all of the many photographers, whose fine results, often achieved under difficult field conditions, speak for themselves. Without their images captured on film, this book would not have been published. For sourcing photographs and/or details of photographers in their respective countries, thanks go to Julian Bhalerao, Sheila Cobban, Dave Cottridge, Annika Forsten, Steve Gantlett, Hugh Harrop, Håkon Heggland, Jóhan Oli Hilmarsson, Erik Hirschfeld, Anthony McGeehan, René Pop, Tim Vaughan, Keith Vinicombe and Anders Wirdheim. A full list of photographic credits appears on page 174.

During her lengthy stewardship of what appeared at times to be an endless task, Jo Hemmings remained good-humoured and flexible as one deadline after another passed with still no light visible at the end of the tunnel. So too did our families who, in the front line of suffering throughout the course of this book and for many years previously, have put up with long absences in the field, piles of books, photographs and other tools of the trade creating chaos at home, and many hours of selfish slaving over words and pictures that would test the patience of a saint. Our special thanks to Hazel and Eddie, and to Isobel, David, Nicky and Holly.

WHITE-BILLED DIVER

Gavia adamsii L 75-90 cm (c 30-36 in)
DESCRIPTION Larger and thicker-necked than Great Northern Diver; powerful pale yellow bill (brighter in summer, upslanted at tip) is most obvious feature in all plumages. Adult summer very similar to Great Northern, but with purplish head sheen, fewer dark bars on narrower white neck patch, and fewer, broader white 'chequers' on dark upperparts. In winter, all plumages correspondingly browner and paler than equivalent in Great Northern; diagnostic differences from latter include paler, almost fawn-grey neck sides with uneven darker smudging. In particular, has more distinct smudge on lower cheek (below ear-coverts) and wholly pale, almost translucent bill tip. In spring, beware moulting adult Great Northern Diver, which may acquire mostly whitish bill.
HABITAT In breeding season inhabits tundra lakes in high Arctic; otherwise in coastal waters.
DISTRIBUTION Breeds from north-west Russia (sparsely) and north Siberia to Alaska and arctic Canada, migrating to winter as far west as northern Scandinavia; some also reach southern Scandinavia, the North Sea and the Baltic.
EUROPEAN STATUS Regular in winter and on passage in Norway (has probably also bred) and Sweden (724); increasingly recorded Finland (140 up to 1984; no longer an official rarity). Accidental elsewhere: Austria (5: 1840; Dec 1884; 16 Jan 1955; 8-9 Apr 1984; 29 Oct-14 Nov 1988); Britain (159); Belgium (2: 22 Dec 1979; 3 Mar-7 Apr 1987); Czech Republic (4: 8 Jan 1935; 28 Jan 1942; 25 Dec 1942; 10-17 Feb 1976); Denmark (227); Estonia (8); Faeroes (3: 1 June 1976; 5 June 1982; 7 June 1988); France (10); Germany (22); Ireland (4: 3 Feb 1974; 28 Jan 1977; 16 May 1979; 2 Feb-late Mar 1986); Italy (3: 2 Dec 1902; 19 Dec 1902; 7 May 1989); Netherlands (28); Poland (13); Slovakia (1: 25 Nov 1884); Slovenia (2: 13 Nov 1982; 23 Jan 1986); Spain (2: 14 Dec 1985, two; 20 Feb 1994*); Switzerland (3: 2 and 6 Dec 1973; Jan-Mar 1982; 12 Dec 1994-28 Feb 1995).

PIED-BILLED GREBE

Podilymbus podiceps L 31-38 cm (12.5-15 in)
DESCRIPTION Compact, chunky grebe, resembling large Little Grebe with bigger head, short, thick hen-like bill, longer neck and whitish undertail-coverts in all plumages. In breeding plumage, head dark brown with blackish forehead; upperparts dark brown, contrasting with rufous-brown flanks, grey-brown foreneck and conspicuous 'blunt' rear end. Bill is bluish-white with broad black subterminal band in summer and plain horn-coloured in winter, when black patch on chin and throat also absent; non-breeding birds have plain-faced appearance which is reinforced by dark eye and pale eye-ring. First-winters occasionally retain traces of stripy head pattern of juvenile plumage (pure juveniles unlikely to occur in Europe, though hybrids recorded Britain). Shows all-dark wings in flight. Much more retiring than Little Grebe, often staying among aquatic vegetation.
VOICE Call is a distinctive, far-carrying *kow kow kow kow kow*, likened to the bark of a primate (has been heard from vagrants).
HABITAT Shallow freshwater lakes and ponds with emergent vegetation, occasionally also on larger or brackish waters.
DISTRIBUTION Breeds from southern British Columbia to Nova Scotia and south across North and Central America, the Caribbean and all but southernmost South America. Northern birds migrate to winter chiefly in southern USA and Mexico.
EUROPEAN STATUS Very rare vagrant: 19 records, mainly in autumn and winter, though some individuals have remained for prolonged periods. Britain (15: has hybridised with Little Grebe); France (1: 17 Oct 1985); Iceland (1: 10 Oct 1976); Ireland (2: 24 May-21 June 1987; 23-24 Apr 1988).

BLACK-BROWED ALBATROSS

Diomedea melanophris L 83-93 cm (33-37 in)
DESCRIPTION Large seabird with obviously longer, narrower wings than Northern Gannet. Head, underparts and rump white; short, blunt-ended tail dark grey, appearing blackish. Mantle dark grey, merging into brownish-black back and upperwing; underwing shows black 'frame' with dark leading edge about as broad as white central stripe. Adult has dark eyebrow, giving 'frowning' expression, and yellowish bill which is often held pointing slightly down; juvenile has grey nape shawl and breast band, darker underwing, and pink bill with neat black tip which acquires adult coloration when four or so years old. Flight characteristic, with wings held at 90° from body and slightly bowed during wheeling arcs and glides; flaps more frequently in calmer conditions. Follows ships.
HABITAT Nests on remote islands. Ranges extensively over open oceans, often far from land, but will feed in inshore waters.
DISTRIBUTION Breeds on islands in southernmost oceans, ranging northwards to Tropic of Capricorn in the Pacific, Atlantic and Indian Oceans.
EUROPEAN STATUS Very rare vagrant: most records are of adults between spring and autumn, with occasional birds taking up residence in gannetries over many seasons (eg Britain from 1972 to 1994). Britain (18; also c 5 records at sea); Denmark (2: 19 July 1990; 23 Sept 1991); Faeroes (2: 1860-94; 10 May 1900); France (4: 21 Feb 1991; 4 Sept 1991; 20 Apr 1992; 6 Nov 1994); Germany (1: 5 Oct 1988); Iceland (2: 20 July 1966; 7 July 1990); Ireland (9 records, including one of two together in Sept 1976); Norway (7); Spain (1: 26 Dec 1987, dead; also one at sea, 3 July 1984); Sweden (1: 10 Apr 1990). Most other unidentified albatrosses reported in Europe probably belong to this species.

YELLOW-NOSED ALBATROSS

Diomedea chlororhynchos L 71-81 cm (28-32 in)
DESCRIPTION Slightly smaller than Black-browed Albatross, with longer bill, neck and tail. Adult has grey head with whiter nape, white underbody and rump, and dark grey tail. Blackish-grey mantle merges into blacker upperwings, which have white outer primary shafts; underwing looks white with very narrow black margins, broader on leading edge than on trailing edge. Bill of adult is black with orangey-yellow culmen; juvenile has all-blackish bill and whiter head, and may show broader dark leading edge to underwing. Flight as Black-browed. Follows ships.
HABITAT Nests on oceanic islands; otherwise at sea.
DISTRIBUTION Breeds in South Atlantic in Tristan da Cunha group and Gough Island, and also in southern Indian Ocean. Outside breeding season found throughout South Atlantic, vagrants sometimes reaching eastern USA, and through southern Indian Ocean east to Australasian waters.
EUROPEAN STATUS Extreme vagrant: one spring record. Norway (1 at sea: 13 Apr 1994). A specimen from Iceland dated c 1844 apparently refers to this species or Grey-headed Albatross *D chrysostoma*.

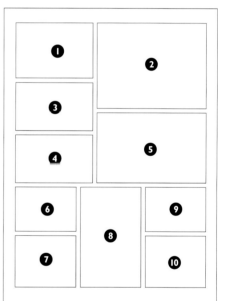

1 **White-billed Diver** (moulting adult, Jan 1986, Ardglass, Co Down, Ireland)
2 **White-billed Diver** (adult winter, Dec 1984, Scheveningen, Netherlands)
3 **White-billed Diver** (adult winter, Feb 1981, Hartlepool, Cleveland, Britain)
4 **Pied-billed Grebe** (adult summer, Apr 1992, Radley, Oxfordshire, Britain)
5 **Pied-billed Grebe** (adult summer, May 1993, Druridge Pool, Northumberland, Britain)
6 **Pied-billed Grebe** (winter plumage, Feb 1993, Argal Reservoir, Cornwall, Britain)
7 **Black-browed Albatross** (adult, June 1982, Unst, Shetland, Britain)
8 **Black-browed Albatross** (adult, June 1995*, Unst, Shetland, Britain)
9 **Yellow-nosed Albatross** (adult, Apr 1994, Sør-Trøndelag, Norway)
10 **Yellow-nosed Albatross** (adult, Apr 1994, Sør-Trøndelag, Norway)

WANDERING ALBATROSS

Diomedea exulans L 107-135 cm (43-54 in)

DESCRIPTION Huge albatross, significantly larger in body length and wingspan than Black-browed. Plumage of full adult males wholly white except for black outer wing, narrowing to black trailing edge on secondaries, and black outermost tail feathers; adult females often show darker mottling on crown, upperwing, breast and tail. Underwing white with black primaries and narrow black trailing edge at all ages. Full adult plumage can take more than 20 years to acquire, so many intermediate stages: juveniles are brown but for white face and adult-type underwing, with body, upperwing and tail progressively whitening with age. Massive bill is pink at all ages. Flight action similar to Black-browed Albatross. Follows ships.

HABITAT Marine species away from breeding islands, and in northern oceans likely to occur only well out to sea.

DISTRIBUTION Similar southerly circumpolar range to Black-browed Albatross, moving north outside breeding season to Tropic of Capricorn in Pacific, Atlantic and Indian Oceans.

EUROPEAN STATUS Extreme vagrant: five records. Belgium (2: Sept 1833, dead; 27 Apr 1887, dead); France (1: 1830); Italy (1: 4 Oct 1957); Portugal (1 at sea: 18 Oct 1963*).

FEA'S/ZINO'S PETRELS

Pterodroma feae/madeira L 32-36 cm (12.75-14.5 in)

DESCRIPTION Complex species pair probably inseparable in the field, and forming superspecies with Soft-plumaged Petrel *P mollis* of the southern oceans. Both show combination of grey head with dark eye mask and obvious white 'nose band', grey breast sides on otherwise white underbody (giving impression of broken breast band), slate-grey upperparts with dark outer wing and with dark carpal bars meeting across upper rump, largely blackish underwings, and pale grey uppertail-coverts and tail (which may appear whitish in certain angles/light). Zino's is smaller than Fea's (weighs one-third less), with slimmer bill and paler grey head; these differences, however, are currently regarded as impossible to assess in the field. Both have rapid, arcing zig-zag flight interspersed with short glides on boomerang-shaped wings.

HABITAT Both species breed in burrows on coastal clifftops above 500 m, coming ashore at night; otherwise reported in inshore waters and at sea.

DISTRIBUTION Fea's Petrel breeds on the Desertas, off Madeira, and the Cape Verde Islands (total population c 450 pairs), possibly also on the Azores; Zino's Petrel is restricted to the main island of Madeira (max. c 30 pairs). Distribution at other times poorly known, though birds occasionally seen at sea away from breeding areas, and also off western Africa and north-eastern United States.

EUROPEAN STATUS Very rare vagrant: at least 8 records, mainly August-October, and most/all believed to involve *feae/madeira* rather than *mollis*. Britain (2: 12, 13 and 14 Aug 1989; 6 Sept 1991, two); Ireland (4: 26 Aug 1990; 20 Aug 1991; 11 Aug 1993; 24 Aug 1994, two; also unidentified *Pterodroma* petrels, almost certainly *feae/madeira/mollis*, on 5 Sept 1974 and 14 Aug 1989); Netherlands (1: 24 Oct 1992); Portugal (1 at sea: 23 Aug 1992).

BULWER'S PETREL

Bulweria bulwerii L 26-27 cm (10.5-11 in)

DESCRIPTION Medium-sized petrel (close in size to Manx Shearwater) from mid-latitude warm waters of the world's oceans. Plumage is wholly sooty-black except for paler diagonal carpal bar across upperwing. Although often erroneously likened to an outsized, all-dark storm-petrel, Bulwer's is a very different seabird with long, almost shearwater-like wings and long, tapering tail (the latter's wedge shape is rarely apparent). Its flight may be low, fast and weaving – reminiscent of a small, dark skua – or, when feeding or flying in light winds, lazy and almost floppy. At such times its relaxed flight action, albeit on long wings, has quality of Black Tern or Little Gull.

HABITAT Mid-latitude pelagic species which approaches land only to breed. Nests in holes and crevices at ground level, usually on remote islands or inaccessible coasts. Nocturnal at breeding sites.

DISTRIBUTION In the Western Palearctic breeds on the Azores, Desertas (off Madeira), Salvage Islands, Canaries and Cape Verde Islands, moving south and west into the Atlantic in autumn. Also breeds in the Pacific and off China, with some birds dispersing as far west as the Indian Ocean.

EUROPEAN STATUS Very rare vagrant: 20 records. Britain (2: 8 May 1837, dead; 28 Feb 1908, dead); France (3: 12 May 1967, two; 17 June 1977; 15 Jan 1986; also 1 at sea between France and Italy, 3 June 1898); Ireland (1: 3 Aug 1975); Italy (1: 6 Feb 1994*; also 1 at sea, 3 June 1898, same as France); Portugal (10: possibly more regular than records suggest in offshore waters); Spain (2: 7 Feb 1982; 29 Apr 1984, at least 2 (possibly 14); also one record of a ship-assisted injured bird, 7 June 1983).

LITTLE SHEARWATER

Puffinus assimilis L 25-30 cm (10-12 in)

DESCRIPTION Very similar in appearance to larger Manx Shearwater, but appears more compact and shorter-winged with different flight jizz. Upperside entirely blackish except for pale grey panel towards outer secondaries and adjacent coverts, giving two-tone impression to upperwing. Underwing white with narrow dark borders. White on underparts extends onto 'face', becoming mottled with grey around eye but still giving a whiter-faced appearance than Manx; dark smudge on sides of breast is narrower than on that species. Typically flies in direct line close to water's surface, with stiff, fluttering wingbeats followed by short glides and tilts on slightly bowed wings, often jerking head. In strong winds, may bank and glide in more typical shearwater style.

HABITAT Breeds in crevices, holes and burrows up to 15 km inland, and apparently will often visit nest sites outside breeding season. Otherwise chiefly pelagic.

DISTRIBUTION Breeds in the North Atlantic in the Azores, Madeira group, Canaries and Cape Verde Islands; also in the southern Atlantic, Indian and Pacific Oceans.

EUROPEAN STATUS Rare on passage Gibraltar (scarce late summer) and Portugal (12), and possibly also Spain (3 accepted records, but presumed under-documented: 2 Nov 1981; 12 May 1986; 31 Aug 1991). Accidental elsewhere: Austria (2: 10 Sept 1978; 26 Aug 1988); Belgium (2: 19 Sept 1990; 25 Sept 1990); Britain (52); Channel Islands (1: 9 May 1994); Denmark (1: Sept 1912); France (34); Germany (2: 25 Apr 1962; 24 Sept 1988); Ireland (41, but early records currently under review); Italy (3: 10 Oct 1892; 5 Oct 1895; 23 May 1990).

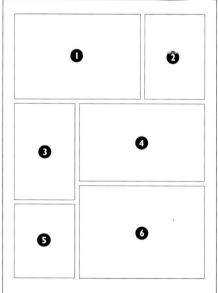

1 **Wandering Albatross** (*sub-adult, Dec, Antarctica*)
2 **Fea's/Zino's Petrel** (*Aug, Bugio, Desertas, Madeira*)
3 **Fea's/Zino's Petrel** (*Aug, Bugio, Desertas, Madeira*)
4 **Bulwer's Petrel** (*June, Canary Islands*)
5 **Bulwer's Petrel** (*July, at sea off Canary Islands*)
6 **Little Shearwater** (*adult, July 1981, Skomer, Britain*)

WILSON'S STORM-PETREL

Oceanites oceanicus L 15-19 cm (6-7.5 in)
DESCRIPTION Distinguished from European Storm-petrel by pale carpal bar on upperwing, all-dark underwing, square white rump extending onto vent, and long legs with diagnostic yellow-webbed feet (visible in very close views) projecting well beyond square-ended tail in flight. Wing has smoothly curved leading edge and straighter trailing edge, with no obvious kink at carpal joint; sometimes shows pale flush on underwing, but never as bold as white underwing-stripe of European Storm-petrel. Flight typically with fewer wingbeats and more frequent glides on outstretched wings; when feeding, wings characteristically held in V-shape high over back, with bird pattering and 'bouncing' along on surface of sea. Readily follows ships.
HABITAT Nests mainly on rocky islands. At other times found well out to sea; likely to be encountered inshore only after strong winds.
DISTRIBUTION Breeds on islands and rocky coasts in the South Atlantic and Antarctica, occurring in all oceans on passage. In North Atlantic most movement takes place in western sector, with much smaller numbers reaching waters bordering south-west Europe.
EUROPEAN STATUS Occurs in late summer along the continental shelf off Portugal (21), occasionally as far north as the Western Approaches off Britain (12 records: also at least 205 birds at sea) and Ireland (5: 1 Oct 1891, dead; 2 Oct 1891, dead; 18 Aug 1985; 24 Sept 1987; 15 Aug 1990; also 9 records involving a total of 89 birds at sea). Accidental elsewhere, and rarely seen from land: Denmark (1: Sept 1988); France (5); Germany (2: 7 Oct 1963; 5 Oct 1984); Iceland (1: 31 July 1988); Italy (2: before 1863; 20 July 1956); Norway (1 at sea: 25 Nov 1980); Spain (3: 6 Oct 1984; 28 Sept 1987; 5 June 1988; many others also reported at sea, where possibly regular).

WHITE-FACED STORM-PETREL

Pelagodroma marina L 20 cm (8 in)
DESCRIPTION Distinctively marked storm-petrel with unique combination of grey-brown upperparts and white underparts. Contrasting head pattern shows dark cap and patch around eye and ear-coverts, with white supercilium, lores, chin and throat; nape grey, extending onto neck sides. Mantle, back and upperwing-coverts mostly brownish-grey, contrasting with blacker flight feathers and narrow whitish bars on greater coverts; underwing white with dark trailing edge. Pale grey rump contrasts with blackish-brown tail. Very long legs with yellowish webs project even further beyond tail in flight than on Wilson's Storm-petrel. Travelling flight jerky and erratic on broad, rounded wings, and when feeding 'bounces' on surface of sea in similar manner to Wilson's. Rarely follows ships.
HABITAT Nests on rocky islands and coasts. At other times in pelagic waters, sometimes in small rafts.

DISTRIBUTION In north-east Atlantic breeds on the Salvages and Cape Verde Islands; has also bred Tenerife. Elsewhere, breeds in South Atlantic, Australia and New Zealand, dispersing into Indian and Pacific Oceans.
EUROPEAN STATUS Very rare vagrant: possibly more frequent than records suggest along the continental shelf off Portugal. Britain (1: 1 Jan 1897); France (1: Aug 1963); Netherlands (1: 23 Nov 1974, dead); Portugal (5: Aug 1962, several; 18 Aug 1988; 6 Aug 1989, three separate individuals).

SWINHOE'S STORM-PETREL

Oceanodroma monorhis L 19-21 cm (7.5-8.5 in)
DESCRIPTION The only dark-rumped storm-petrel proven to have occurred in European waters. In most respects very like Leach's Storm-petrel, with dark brown plumage showing contrasting pale grey carpal bar on upperwing, blackish-brown flight feathers and forked tail. Unlike Leach's, has solidly dark rump which is same colour as body (though note that some Leach's Storm-petrels from North Pacific population are also dark-rumped). Also shows white shafts to outer primaries, but this feature generally visible only in the hand. Structure, flight action and jizz much as Leach's, with which formerly considered conspecific.
HABITAT Nests on islands, but otherwise generally pelagic.
DISTRIBUTION Breeds on islands in the north-west Pacific Ocean off Japan, Korea and China, from where moves south into Indian Ocean and west to the Arabian Sea (has once strayed to Israel). Has also been trapped on the Salvage Islands in North Atlantic, suggesting possible tiny breeding population which could account for at least some European records.
EUROPEAN STATUS Extreme vagrant: six records, at least four of which trapped at night in late summer. Britain (3: 23 July 1989; 26 July 1989; 6/7 July 1990, and again on 30/31 July 1991, 29/30 July 1992, 21, 28 and 29 July 1993 and 11, 23 and 25 July 1994); France (1: 15 July 1989); Italy (1: 11 Aug 1991); Spain (1: 13 July 1994). Several other sight reports from British waters of storm-petrels with dark rumps may relate to this species.

MADEIRAN STORM-PETREL

Oceanodroma castro L 19-21 cm (7.5-8.5 in)
DESCRIPTION Closely resembles Leach's Storm-petrel, but plumage is slightly blacker-brown with a less obvious (but still distinct) pale brownish-grey carpal bar on the upperwing. Prominent white rump is not broken by grey central stripe and is squarer-shaped than on Leach's, also wrapping around slightly onto vent. In flight, wings show less pronounced kink at carpal joint and straighter trailing edge, also being held more horizontally than Leach's and producing faster, shallower wingbeats and more frequent glides; flight style less erratic, but will also soar at greater height above sea in manner of shearwater. Does not usually follow ships.

HABITAT Nests in burrows on rocky islands. Outside breeding season apparently highly pelagic.
DISTRIBUTION Breeding range includes Tenerife, Madeira, the Salvages and islets off Portugal, with other colonies in the South Atlantic and Pacific Oceans. On leaving colonies, birds in northern Atlantic possibly move north and west, but non-breeding distribution poorly known and species is rarely reported at sea, even in breeding areas.
EUROPEAN STATUS Breeds on the Berlengas and Farilhoes off Portugal (c 50 pairs). Accidental elsewhere: Britain (1: 19 Nov 1911, dead); Finland (1: 19 Jan 1993, found dying); France (3: 7 Oct 1984, dead; 15 Oct 1987; 16 Aug 1988); Ireland (1: 18 Oct 1931, specimen); Spain (5: early Nov 1951, two found dead; 15 Feb 1970; 3 Jan 1982; 3 July 1994; 30 July 1994).

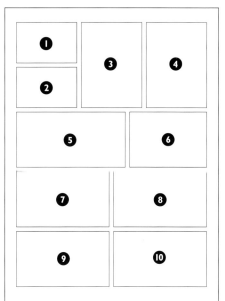

1 **Wilson's Petrel** (Aug 1993, at sea south-west of Bishop Rock, Cornwall, Britain)
2 **Wilson's Petrel** (Aug 1993, at sea south-west of Bishop Rock, Cornwall, Britain)
3 **Wilson's Petrel** (Aug 1993, at sea south-west of Bishop Rock, Cornwall, Britain)
4 **Wilson's Petrel** (Aug 1993, at sea south-west of Bishop Rock, Cornwall, Britain)
5 **White-faced Storm-Petrel** *(Mar, Cape Verde Islands)*
6 **Swinhoe's Storm-Petrel** (July 1994, Benidorm, Spain)
7 **Swinhoe's Storm-Petrel** (Aug 1991, Genoa, Italy)
8 **Swinhoe's Storm-Petrel** (July 1994, Benidorm, Spain)
9 **Swinhoe's Storm-Petrel** (July 1992, Tynemouth, Tyne and Wear, Britain)
10 **Madeiran Petrel** *(July, Canary Islands)*

RED-FOOTED BOOBY

Sula sula L 66-77 cm (26-31 in)
DESCRIPTION Obviously smaller than Northern Gannet, with variety of different colour morphs. Typical white phase adult has white head and body with variable golden tinge, and diagnostic white tail; upperwing white with blackish flight feathers, on underside also with isolated black patch on carpal. Brown morph is entirely brown or brownish with darker flight feathers and variable yellowish cast on head; intermediate morphs with white tail and/or white head also occur. Juvenile resembles brown morph but has blackish-brown bill and yellowish-grey legs; bill becomes bluer and legs redder with age, until adults show combination of blue-grey bill with pink at base and diagnostic bright red legs and feet. Highly gregarious; often attracted to ships.
HABITAT Nests colonially in trees on islands in the tropics, occurring far from land outside breeding season.
DISTRIBUTION Pantropical, breeding from Brazil and the Caribbean through the Pacific to South-East Asia, northern Australia and the Indian Ocean to Madagascar. Dispersal outside breeding season apparently mainly involves immature birds, but extent of wandering poorly known.
EUROPEAN STATUS Extreme vagrant: one record in summer. Norway (1: 29 June 1985).

MASKED BOOBY

Sula dactylatra L 81-92 cm (32-37 in)
DESCRIPTION Large, predominantly white booby, approaching Northern Gannet in size but separated by solidly black flight feathers and tail. Adult has white head with dark 'mask' around base of yellow bill enclosing eye; plumage otherwise white or whitish but for black primaries, secondaries, tips to longest scapulars and tail. Legs yellowish. Superficially similar adult white morph of smaller Red-footed Booby has diagnostic all-white tail, black carpal patch on underwing, and red legs and feet. Juvenile recalls smaller Brown Booby, with dark brown head, neck and upperside, but has narrow white collar and white underwing with dark covert bar and broad dark trailing edge; collar broadens and upperparts whiten with age. Plunge-dives in manner of Northern Gannet.
HABITAT Nests on offshore islands, often on cliffs; generally prefers deeper water to other boobies.
DISTRIBUTION Pantropical species, with widespread distribution in Atlantic, Pacific and Indian Oceans and the Caribbean. Mainly sedentary, but with some post-breeding dispersal in tropical and subtropical waters; occasionally occurs Gulf coast of Texas, and on eastern seaboard of USA has reached north to Carolina.
EUROPEAN STATUS Extreme vagrant: two records in autumn/winter. Spain (2: 10 Oct 1985; 14 Dec 1985).

BROWN BOOBY

Sula leucogaster L 64-74 cm (26-30 in)
DESCRIPTION Small, slim, brown and white sulid, likely to be mistaken only for juvenile of larger Masked Booby. Adult is dark chocolate-brown on head, neck and entire upperside, sharply demarcated across upper breast from white underparts. Underwing also dark brown, with broad white central area restricted to arm; dark leading edge narrower than trailing edge. Juvenile similar to adult, but with duller brown upperparts and diffuse brown mottling on white of underwing and underparts. Juvenile Northern Gannet is dark but far larger, typically spotted white above and without the clean-cut white underparts of adult Brown Booby. Low-level plunge-diver, often fishing in relatively shallow water.
HABITAT Breeds on cliffs, bare rock and beaches on islands, islets and reefs, and at other times typically also in inshore waters.
DISTRIBUTION Pantropical, occurring in Atlantic, Pacific and Indian Oceans and the Caribbean, and breeding as close to Europe as the Cape Verde Islands. Birds dispersing after breeding occasionally range up West African coast north to Canaries, and in Red Sea regularly to Eilat, Israel.
EUROPEAN STATUS Extreme vagrant: at least two records. Spain (2: 28 May 1983; 9 Sept 1986; others reported but records not yet submitted for consideration).

CAPE GANNET

Morus capensis L 85-90 cm (34-36 in)
DESCRIPTION Southern counterpart of Northern Gannet, which it mirrors in all plumage phases. Separated from adults of that species by all-black secondaries and tail, though some sub-adult Northern Gannets can apparently show near-identical amounts of black. Importantly, has diagnostic longer gular stripe, though this character will only be discernible on the closest of views (for example on birds following a boat or at a colony). In other respects adult plumages identical. Juvenile and immatures also very like respective ages of Northern Gannet and probably not separable until second or third year, when white on upperwing of Cape Gannet becomes restricted to coverts; in most sub-adult Northern Gannets, usually at least some white is also visible on secondaries, though a few near-adults may appear to show (variably) dark trailing edge. Adult Masked Booby also has black secondaries, but separable by other characters (eg white head, size and jizz). Flight, actions and behaviour as for Northern Gannet.
HABITAT Nests on offshore islands in large gannetries.
DISTRIBUTION Breeds in southern and south-western Africa, dispersing north along east coast as far as Mozambique and along west coast to at least Gulf of Guinea, where range may overlap with that of Northern Gannet. In recent years there have been uncorroborated

claims from further north off West Africa, including several from Morocco.
EUROPEAN STATUS Extreme vagrant: at least one record. Spain (1: 28 Jan 1985; others reported but records not yet submitted for consideration). Authenticity of a published report of a Cape Gannet specimen collected from gannetry in Britain (May 1831) deemed uncertain.

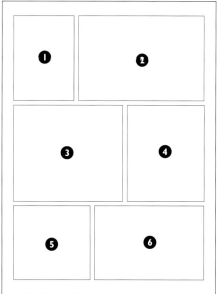

1 **Red-Footed Booby** (*immature, date unknown, Hawaii*)
2 **Red-footed Booby** (*adult brown morph, July, Galapagos*)
3 **Masked Booby** (*adult, date and location unknown*)
4 **Masked Booby** (*adult, July, Galapagos*)
5 **Brown Booby** (*adult, date and location unknown*)
6 **Cape Gannet** (*adult, Apr, South Africa*)

DOUBLE-CRESTED CORMORANT

Phalacrocorax auritus L 74-91 cm (30-36 in)
DESCRIPTION Slightly smaller than Cormorant, but very similar in all plumages. Chief distinction is brighter yellow-orange facial skin which extends clearly under chin, unlike Cormorant, which has prominent wedge of gular feathering (though this may be hard to see in the field); also has brighter pale orange upper lores. Adult in breeding plumage never shows white thigh patch and has all-dark head, lacking white 'mane' often shown by Cormorant; browner non-breeding adults also show little or no pale on throat or ear-coverts. First-winter very like Cormorant, but typically is darker and browner on belly and with largely yellow, not ivory-grey, lower mandible; adult plumage not acquired until third or fourth year, until which time sub-adult Double-crested best distinguished by characteristic whitish foreneck and breast and contrasting dark belly (sub-adult Cormorant of nominate European race is typically more evenly pale on neck and underside). In addition to smaller size, has more slender bill and fuller head, giving subtly distinct jizz.
HABITAT Nests on cliffs, islands and trees; occurs in both freshwater and maritime habitats.
DISTRIBUTION Breeds on east, west and Gulf coasts of North America, and inland mainly in southern Canada and northern USA. Winters south across North America to Mexico and the Caribbean.
EUROPEAN STATUS Extreme vagrant: one record. Britain (1: 11 Jan-21 Apr 1989).

MAGNIFICENT FRIGATEBIRD

Fregata magnificens L 89-114 cm (36-46 in)
DESCRIPTION Large, dark seabird with long forked tail and massive wingspan of up to 2.5 m (8 ft). Breeding male is all black, with head and upperparts glossed purplish and green; bright red gular pouch inflated only during display. Bill bluish-black; legs brown. Adult female similar, but with pale brown bar on upperwing-coverts, indistinct greyish collar and bold white patch on breast and upper flanks. Juvenile has pale covert bar on upperwing and white head, throat and breast, latter initially marked by broken dark breast band; loses this character to show wholly white underparts before gaining patchy brown-and-white breast markings of sub-adult plumage. Much variation in immature plumages, with gradual progression towards full adult. In all post-juvenile plumages (except adult male) best separated from other frigatebirds by pattern of axillaries, which are black with narrow white tips forming wavy bars on dark underwing. Highly aerial and very agile on long, narrow wings, only exceptionally alighting on sea (cannot swim); will parasitise other seabirds as well as snatch food from surface of sea, and readily attends fishing boats.
HABITAT Nests on bare ground, bushes or low trees; outside breeding season frequents inshore and oceanic waters.

DISTRIBUTION In east Atlantic nests only on Cape Verde Islands, otherwise breeding from southern Florida and Mexico south through Caribbean and Central America to Galapagos and Brazil.
EUROPEAN STATUS Extreme vagrant: five records. Britain (1: 10 July 1953, found dying); Denmark (1: Mar 1968); France (2: Oct 1852; Mar 1902); Spain (1: 29 Sept 1985). Other European records of unidentified frigatebirds (eg from Britain, Ireland, Norway and Spain) may also refer to this species.

AMERICAN BITTERN

Botaurus lentiginosus L 60-85 cm (24-34 in)
DESCRIPTION Closely resembles Bittern in general cryptic patterning and coloration, but is smaller, with browner and more uniformly coloured upperparts. Head pattern differs chiefly in dull rusty-brown forehead and crown (black in Bittern), dark eye-stripe, and elongated blackish moustachial stripe running down sides of unbarred neck, with longer bill which has obviously dark culmen. Also has distinctly plainer brown mantle, scapulars and coverts, showing only fine vermiculations at close range and lacking bold barring of Bittern. In flight, plainer coverts contrast noticeably with dark greyish flight feathers, which are unbarred (unlike Bittern, though in certain conditions this species may give impression of plain primaries) and tipped rufous-brown on secondaries and inner primaries; also has noticeably less rounded wings than Bittern. Juvenile very like adult, but lacks black neck stripes. Assumes same vertical posture as Bittern when alarmed and is equally terrestrial, but generally more prone to leave cover of reeds and feed in open.
HABITAT Frequents reedbeds and other marshy vegetation around margins of pools, shallow lakes and ditches; on migration occasionally also in saltmarshes.
DISTRIBUTION Summer visitor to much of North America except Alaska, northern Canada and south-eastern and south-western USA. Winters mainly from western and southern USA south to Mexico and Costa Rica.
EUROPEAN STATUS Rare vagrant: at least 74 records. Britain (38); Channel Islands; Denmark (1: Nov 1961); Faeroes (3: 1930; 12 Nov 1952; Sept 1967); Iceland (6); Ireland (22, all killed or found dying); Norway (1: 26 Aug 1956); Spain (2: 11 Jan 1961, dead; 17-30 Oct 1982).

LEAST BITTERN

Ixobrychus exilis L 28-36 cm (11.25-14.5 in)
DESCRIPTION New World counterpart of Little Bittern, and even smaller in size. Adult male has black-and-buff plumage pattern similar to that species, differing chiefly in rufous (not grey) ear-coverts and neck sides and white line on scapulars. Female has dark brown crown and mantle, unlike female Little Bittern, as well as white line on scapulars and dark streaking on throat and foreneck. In flight, both sexes reveal diagnostic deep rufous greater coverts (paler

on female) contrasting with buffish lesser and median coverts and black flight feathers, latter tipped deep rufous on inner primaries and outer secondaries; alula and greater primary coverts black, also tipped rufous. Juvenile resembles adult female, but has more rufous mantle and scapulars and is more heavily streaked below; first-winter plumage is adult-like, but with retained juvenile wing-coverts. Sidles up reed stems like Little Bittern, and can be equally secretive.
HABITAT Typically in reedbeds with scattered bushes and other vegetation; in south of range also in mangroves.
DISTRIBUTION Nominate race breeds in much of eastern and central North America north to southern Canada, and in California, Mexico and the Caribbean, wintering from Gulf coast south to Nicaragua. Other races breed mainly in Central America and northern, eastern and parts of western South America.
EUROPEAN STATUS Extreme vagrant: one autumn record. Iceland (1: 17 Sept 1970). A specimen from Britain (autumn 1852), originally labelled as Little Bittern, was reidentified as this species in 1984 but has never been formally considered for admission to the national list.

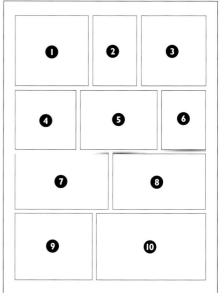

1 Double-crested Cormorant (first-year, Nov 1995*, Co Galway, Ireland)
2 Double-crested Cormorant (immature, Feb 1989, Billingham, Cleveland, Britain)
3 Double-crested Cormorant (immature, Feb 1989, Billingham, Cleveland, Britain)
4 Double-crested Cormorant (immature, Feb 1989, Billingham, Cleveland, Britain)
5 Magnificent Frigatebird (adult male, July, Galapagos)
6 Magnificent Frigatebird (juvenile, July, Galapagos)
7 American Bittern (Feb 1991, Marton Mere, Lancashire, Britain)
8 American Bittern (Nov 1981, Magor, Gwent, Britain)
9 Least Bittern (adult male, date and location unknown)
10 Least Bittern (adult male, Apr, Texas, USA)

GREEN HERON

Butorides virescens L 40-48 cm (16-19 in)
DESCRIPTION Smaller than Night Heron, with compact but sleeker and more attenuated form. Adult has blackish cap, white throat continuing as narrow streaks down foreneck, and deep vinous-chestnut on head sides, neck and breast merging into grey belly. Upperparts essentially bluish-grey, greener-toned on wings, with darker coverts showing distinct pale fringes. Long, dagger-like bill grey, with yellow lower mandible; bare lores and legs also yellow. At any range and in flight adult looks dark; sexes similar. Juvenile has browner upperparts, prominent pale triangular tips to coverts and paler, brown-streaked neck and breast; first-winter has more adult-like plumage but retains juvenile wing-coverts. Formerly known as Green-backed Heron and treated as conspecific with Striated Heron (latter occurring as close to Europe as Middle East).
HABITAT Favours ponds, freshwater and brackish marshes and streams with adjacent cover; typically feeds at water's edge from low perch or partly hidden in vegetation, and readily perches in trees.
DISTRIBUTION Summer visitor to much of eastern USA, south-easternmost Canada and west coast of USA south to Mexico, wintering in south of range and to northern South America.
EUROPEAN STATUS Very rare vagrant: five records, four in autumn and one in spring. Britain (3: 27 Oct 1889, shot; 27 Nov-6 Dec 1982; 25 Oct 1987, dead); Channel Islands (1: 17-21 Aug 1992 on Jersey, presumed same 13 Sept 1992 on Guernsey); France (1: 1 Apr 1994). Exact status of another individual, either this species or Striated Heron *B striatus*, from Norway (at sea on 27 Sept 1991) unclear.

SNOWY EGRET

Egretta thula L 56-66 cm (22-26 in)
DESCRIPTION Almost identical to Little Egret and separable only with great care. In adult plumage similarly snow-white, and identification reliant almost entirely on bare-part coloration: adult Snowy has rich yellow to deep red lores in breeding condition which remain rich yellow at other times, whereas adult Little's lores are variably pink-red to purple (occasionally rich orange-yellow, close to Snowy) at height of breeding, but usually blue-grey or greenish outside breeding season. Adult Snowy also shows variable amounts of yellow on sides and rear of black legs (often up to 'knee' joint, occasionally almost whole leg except front), while adult Little typically has all-black legs with yellow feet. Additional distinction between breeding adults is head feathering: Little usually has two or three long, individual plumes trailing from hindcrown and aigrettes on scapulars, whereas Snowy usually has only shorter nape feathers forming a distinctive, shaggy crest. Immatures harder to separate as bare-part coloration more variable; often same as non-breeding adults, but lores of young Snowy can

appear greyish, and young Little has been noted with more extensively yellow legs, so much caution required. Snowy differs subtly in structure from Little, appearing slightly shorter-necked and shorter-billed.
HABITAT Frequents ponds, marshes, lakes, coastal inlets and other wetlands.
DISTRIBUTION Breeds in North America chiefly on east and Gulf coasts and in western USA, and in West Indies, Central and South America. Northern birds winter south from southern USA and Mexico.
EUROPEAN STATUS Extreme vagrant: three records. Iceland (2: 6 Apr 1974; 6 June 1983; also 1 at sea, dead, in May or June 1985).

WESTERN REEF EGRET

Egretta gularis L 55-65 cm (22-26 in)
DESCRIPTION Occurs in two basic colour phases, with two separate races possibly reaching Europe. Dark morph is essentially charcoal-grey with white throat patch; apparently inseparable on plumage alone from rare claimed dark morph of Little Egret. White morph is entirely white and therefore very like Little Egret, but in all plumages has deeper-based, clearly longer bill with more curved culmen (on Little and Snowy Egrets, bill not so thick and more parallel-sided, tapering more sharply to point towards tip). Bill is dark brown on breeding birds of nominate West African race, paler brown on non-breeding birds, and yellow or yellow-brown throughout year on eastern *schistacea* birds. Lores dark olive or yellowish, lighter on white morph birds and more orangey during breeding season. Legs paler than Little Egret's, typically brownish with yellow or greenish-yellow feet, this colour extending onto legs on eastern birds. Immature of dark morph is paler brown-grey than adult; immature white morph has darker feathers in wing and occasional dusky mottling on body. Often appears more ungainly than Little Egret due to larger body but proportionately shorter, thicker legs; will 'umbrella-fish' by raising wings into canopy over feeding spot and looking into water.
HABITAT Primarily coastal species, fishing in tidal lagoons, creeks, estuaries and on open shorelines.
DISTRIBUTION Nominate western race breeds from Mauretania to Gulf of Guinea, eastern *schistacea* from Red Sea east to India.
EUROPEAN STATUS Rare vagrant: some records refer to individuals returning to same sites in successive years, and escapes also reported (eg in Germany). France (34); Greece (4: 18 Aug 1981; 20 Aug 1983; 2 May 1986; 13-19 May 1992); Italy (23); Spain (4: 16 June 1970; 7 June 1986; 15 June 1986; 16 Aug 1993; others reported); former Yugoslavia (1: Apr 1975).

BLACK-HEADED HERON

Ardea melanocephala L 92-96 cm (37-38 in)
DESCRIPTION About size of Grey Heron, but proportions rather slimmer. Adult usually has black head and hindneck, white chin, throat and

foreneck, and row of vertical white spots on lower neck; eye-ring and narrow supercilia white, latter meeting on forehead above bill, and lores greenish-yellow. Extent of white on foreneck may vary, but lacking on some and replaced by rufous on others. Plumage similarly rather variable; body often grey, but on some black of hindneck may extend over back and wings. Central underparts apparently always grey except in rare melanistic form, which also has wholly black chin. In breeding season, upperparts adorned with several lanceolate plumes. Juvenile similar, but with brownish-grey on neck and white underparts. In flight, white underwing-coverts characteristic. Bill bicoloured, with black upper and yellow lower mandibles; legs black.
HABITAT Breeds in small colonies, often with other herons, in trees or on ground; occurs in marshes, estuaries and other wetlands, but more often found away from water than most herons, in damp, open grasslands.
DISTRIBUTION Breeds throughout much of Africa south of the Sahara. Apparently migratory away from equatorial zone, moving to drier areas during rainy season; in West Africa moves north into Sahel during rains, and has wandered north to Algeria and Israel and east to Oman.
EUROPEAN STATUS Extreme vagrant: two records. France (2: c 1845; 29 Nov 1971).

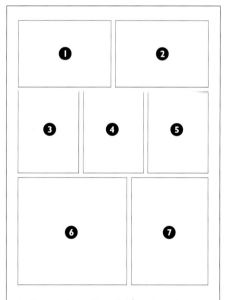

1 **Green Heron** (juvenile/first-winter, Sept 1992, St Martin, Guernsey, Channel Islands)
2 **Green Heron** (adult, Nov 1982, Stone Creek, Humberside, Britain)
3 **Snowy Egret** (adult, Sept, California, USA)
4 **Western Reef Egret** (breeding adult dark morph, May 1994, La Capellière, France)
5 **Western Reef Egret** (non-breeding adult dark morph, Sept 1994, La Capellière, France)
6 **Western Reef Egret** (breeding adult dark morph, May 1994, La Capellière, France)
7 **Black-headed Heron** (adult, Feb, Kenya)

NORTHERN BALD IBIS

Geronticus eremita L 70-80 cm (28-32 in)
DESCRIPTION Adult indisputably ugly, with bare pinkish-red head and bill, dark 'birthmark' on crown and dishevelled, elongated feathers on nape and neck; appearance somewhat redeemed by dark metallic bronze-green plumage with contrasting purplish median and lesser coverts. Juvenile duller, with bare head covered by greyish hairs, no 'shoulder' patch, little iridescence to plumage and greyer bare parts. Looks far less striking in flight, when differences from Glossy Ibis not so obvious; however, is larger, heavier, shorter-necked, has less rounded wings with distinct 'fingers' at tip, and shorter, dull red legs do not project beyond tail.
HABITAT Breeds on inland or sea cliffs, feeding on open hillsides, meadows, arable land and other dry, sparsely vegetated country.
DISTRIBUTION Declining and highly endangered species, with known range in the wild now confined to western Morocco (c 50 pairs), where present year-round. Extinct or nearly so in Algeria, and last Turkish colony also recently defunct; small feral population remains at same site in latter country. Still occasionally reported Yemen, Saudi Arabia and Israel, however, suggesting possible unknown breeding site in Middle East or continued presence of birds originally from Turkish colony. Has also wandered to the Canaries.
EUROPEAN STATUS Extreme vagrant: one record. Spain (1: 11 July 1958).

LESSER WHITE-FRONTED GOOSE

Anser erythropus L 53-66 cm (21-26 in)
DESCRIPTION Very like White-fronted Goose, but slightly smaller, shorter-necked and 'daintier'. Head is distinctly smaller, with higher forecrown and smaller, more conical bill. Adults have white blaze extending well up onto forecrown; when seen head-on, blaze forms point (usually rounded on White-front). Plumage otherwise generally similar to White-front, but darker grey-brown on head, neck and upperparts, with more pronounced white flank line. Black belly bars of adults said to be less extensive than on White-front, but huge variability in latter species makes this character unreliable in the field; juveniles, which have indistinctly barred upperparts and no white blaze on forehead, acquire belly bars from late winter. All plumages have bright yellow eye-ring, pink bill and orange or yellowish-orange legs. Feeding action when grazing is quicker than that of White-front – often a useful means of helping to detect presence of individuals of this species in mixed flocks.
HABITAT Nests on scrubby tundra, usually close to water. In winter chiefly on grazing marshes and arable land.
DISTRIBUTION Breeds from northern Scandinavia (sparsely) eastwards through Siberia, wintering in southern Caspian lowlands and south-east Europe, and in small numbers in central Europe and the Low Countries.
EUROPEAN STATUS Breeds Norway (30-50 pairs 1990), Sweden (1-5 pairs 1987; reintroduction scheme in operation) and Finland (only 1 pair found 1995; restocking scheme in operation); regular on passage Hungary (recent max. 450 in 1987; 100-200 annually), and scarce migrant in Estonia and Poland. Winters in Romania, Greece (max. 1,630 in Feb 1963) and the Netherlands (c 23 in Dec 1994); possibly also regular in former Yugoslavia and occasional (perhaps regular) Bulgaria. Accidental elsewhere, but escapes from captivity frequent: Austria (12); Belgium (c 65); Britain (127); Czech Republic (15+); Denmark (73); France (14); Germany; Ireland (1: 23-30 Mar 1969); Italy (c 30); Latvia; Lithuania; Luxembourg; Slovakia; Spain (3); Switzerland (1: Feb 1851).

SNOW GOOSE

Anser caerulescens L 65-80 cm (26-32 in)
DESCRIPTION Roughly size of Pink-footed Goose; occurs in two distinct colour phases. Adult white morph has entirely white plumage except for black primaries, which at rest are largely concealed by white tertials. Juvenile has pale greyish-brown upperparts, with white face, neck and underparts; some may also show contrastingly darker primaries. Adult blue morph, generally found only in smaller nominate western race, has white head and upper neck and largely dark blue-grey remainder of plumage, with contrasting paler grey coverts and blackish-brown flight feathers, edged white on inner secondaries, tertials and longer greater coverts and scapulars. Juvenile blue morph resembles adult but has dusky head and upper neck, and body is browner above and paler below. Legs and deep-based stoutish bill are pink in adult plumage and initially grey in juveniles, becoming pinker with age. Hybrids between morphs are relatively rare. In Europe, putative wild birds often occur among Greenland White-fronted or Pink-footed Geese.
HABITAT Nests on arctic tundra near water; in winter in wetlands and grasslands with suitable grazing.
DISTRIBUTION Breeds from western Greenland across arctic North America to Wrangel Island, off north-east Siberia. Winters on east coast of USA between Maryland and North Carolina, on Gulf coast and from California and neighbouring states south into Mexico.
EUROPEAN STATUS Frequent vagrant: occurs from late autumn to spring, chiefly in northern Europe in flocks of other geese and including proven (ringed) transatlantic vagrants, but escapes from captivity and feral birds (including breeding pairs) are responsible for many records. Countries of occurrence include the following: Austria; Belgium; Britain (many escapes and feral birds, but presumed wild individuals recorded most winters); Czech Republic (2: 24 Feb 1929; 7 Mar 1947); Estonia (13); Faeroes (1: 7-8 May 1982); Finland (c 86); France (category D1: 44); Germany (100+, treated as escapes); Iceland (126 individuals); Ireland (c 62 recorded to end 1992, but returning individuals likely to cause some duplication; records include a party of five in 1954); Italy (2: Dec 1978-Feb 1979; 9 Oct 1980); Luxembourg (fewer than 10); Norway (15+); Netherlands (many, a majority of which presumed feral, but including flock of 18 from 18-26 Apr 1980, one of which was ringed in Manitoba, Canada, in 1977); Poland (13); Spain (8 records of 13 individuals); Sweden (presumed escapes).

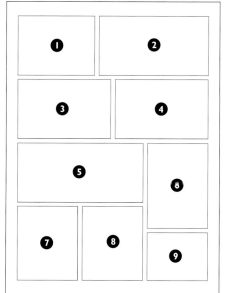

1 **Northern Bald Ibis** *(adult, Nov, Morocco)*
2 **Northern Bald Ibis** *(Jan, Morocco)*
3 **Lesser White-Fronted Goose** *(four adults, in front, with White-fronted and Barnacle Geese, Mar 1995, Anjum, Netherlands)*
4 **Lesser White-Fronted Goose** *(adult, Dec 1992, Den Bommel, Netherlands)*
5 **Lesser White-Fronted Goose** *(adult among White-fronted Geese, Jan 1995*, Slimbridge, Gloucestershire, Britain)*
6 **Snow Goose** *(adult white morph, Aug 1988, Turku, Finland)*
7 **Snow Goose** *(adult white morph, Nov 1991, Plex Moss, Lancashire, Britain)*
8 **Snow Goose** *(blue morph or possible hybrid, Nov 1992, Marshside, Lancashire, Britain)*
9 **Snow Goose** *(adults with White-fronted and Barnacle Geese, Jan 1991, Anjum, Netherlands)*

ROSS'S GOOSE

Anser rossii L 53-66 cm (21-26 in)
DESCRIPTION Obviously smaller and less bulky than Snow Goose, with size, smaller and more rounded head, shorter neck and tiny but deep-based bill imparting jizz more recalling Brent or Barnacle Goose. Plumage of white phase very like Snow Goose, being entirely white but for black primaries; has very rare blue morph which resembles blue morph of Snow, but with whiter belly and blue-grey coloration extending up hindneck to rear crown. Bill pink, with extensive bluish area at base; legs pink. Juvenile much whiter-looking than juvenile Snow, with pale brownish-grey wash confined largely to rear crown, nape and scapulars; bill and legs initially greenish-grey, becoming pinker during first winter. In Europe often associates with Barnacle Geese.
HABITAT Nests on lowland arctic tundra; on migration and in winter in stubble and rice fields and grasslands.
DISTRIBUTION Breeds almost exclusively in North-west Territories in arctic Canada, migrating mainly south-west to winter in California, New Mexico and Mexico. Smaller numbers probably move south along Mississippi to reach regular winter areas on Gulf coast; also wanders to eastern seaboard of USA.
EUROPEAN STATUS Extreme vagrant: three winter records. Netherlands (3 individuals: 30 Nov-1 Dec 1985; 20 Jan-Mar 1988, two, returning winter 1988/89; up to two, winter 1989/90, at least 1 returning to winter 1994/95). Other European records, including those from Belgium, Britain, Faeroes and Germany, relate to known escapes or birds of uncertain origin.

RED-BREASTED GOOSE

Branta ruficollis L 53-56 cm (21-22 in)
DESCRIPTION Unmistakable small, short-necked and distinctively marked goose, barely size of Brent Goose. In all plumages has black head with large white loral spot, white-bordered rich chestnut 'cheek' patch and neck, black breast and upperparts, and contrasting double white wing-bars, flanks and undertail-coverts. Juveniles less sharply marked than adults, with black areas slightly duller, greyer wing-bars and pale fringing to upperparts. Strikingly patterned plumage exaggerates odd shape for a *Branta* goose, with bill appearing disproportionately small on squarish head with bulging nape.
HABITAT Breeds on arctic tundra. In winter principally on grazing marshes and lowland coastal wetlands.
DISTRIBUTION In summer found in Siberia on the Taimyr, Gydan and Yamal Peninsulas, migrating in autumn to the Caspian Sea region and the western coast of the Black Sea. Declining in numbers.
EUROPEAN STATUS Winters mainly in Bulgaria (59,206 in winter 1992/93; 40,557 in 1994/95) and Romania (30,000 in Jan 1991; 14,650 in

winter 1992/93), with smaller numbers in Greece (max. *c* 2,000 in Mar 1985); annually also in Hungary (*c* 20 in 1994, increasing) and Netherlands (total of 387+). Accidental elsewhere, and occasional escapes from captivity also reported: Austria (annual); Belgium (*c* 40); Britain (43); Czech Republic (11); Denmark (23); Estonia (7); Finland (32 records of 38 individuals); France (24); Germany (100+); Italy (27); Latvia (2: Nov 1879; 15 Apr 1972); Lithuania (1: 19-27 July 1994); Luxembourg (fewer than 10); Norway (9); Poland (16); Slovakia (6); Spain (6 records of 7 birds; others reported but records not yet submitted for consideration); Sweden (84); former Yugoslavia.

RUDDY SHELDUCK

Tadorna ferruginea L 61-67 cm (24-27 in)
DESCRIPTION In all plumages has buff head, orange-brown body, black rump and tail, and striking wing pattern of black primaries, glossy greenish-black secondaries and white coverts. Adult male has deep buff hindneck and, in breeding season, narrow blackish collar; adult female has paler buff head with distinct white facial patch, but lacks collar. Juvenile like female, but has duller head and greyer tone to body; acquires adult-like plumage in first autumn. In Europe likely to be confused only with escaped female Cape and Paradise Shelducks, which have similar orange-brown body, wing pattern and pale areas on head; Cape Shelduck, however, has grey head with sharply demarcated white face, and Paradise Shelduck has all-white head, neither species showing Ruddy Shelduck's combination of pale buff with white.
HABITAT Breeds by rivers and lakes in open country, including uplands; winters in similar habitat in lowlands, generally avoiding coastal waters.
DISTRIBUTION Breeds in Morocco, where now largely resident (Moroccan birds formerly wintered in Spain), and Ethiopia, where also sedentary, but main range extends from south-east Europe and Turkey eastwards to northern China and Mongolia. Winters south to southern China, South-East Asia, parts of India, Afghanistan, Iran and Turkey, with perhaps a few in the Nile valley.
EUROPEAN STATUS Breeds Albania (0-10 pairs), Bulgaria (50-150 pairs, increasing), Greece (10-40 pairs, decreasing) and Romania (5-10 pairs, decreasing); winters irregularly Italy. Accidental elsewhere, but true pattern clouded by escapes and birds which wander from feral populations; periodic influxes of wild birds into Europe also occur (*eg* in 1892 and 1994). Recorded from much of Europe: Austria (vagrant, but recently only escapes and feral breeders from Germany recorded); Belgium; Britain (many, but excluding those regarded as part of 1994 influx, perhaps few or no wild birds since 1919); Czech Republic (11); Denmark; Estonia (4); Finland (*c* 60 records of 137 individuals); France (160+); Germany; Hungary (10, but at least 23 others

reported); Iceland (7 in July 1892); Ireland (19th century records include flocks of up to 20 in 1892; recorded in five years between 1945-93, with at least six individuals in latter year); Latvia (1: 10 July 1994); Lithuania (1: 19-27 July 1994, four); Netherlands (many); Norway (56); Poland; Portugal (1: 10 Aug 1990); Slovakia (4: 1874; undated; May 1976; 16 May 1994); Slovenia (1: 17 Mar 1984); Spain (28 records of 44 birds); Sweden (*c* 170, probably including some escapes).

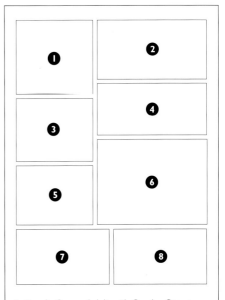

1 **Ross's Goose** (adult with Greylag Goose, Feb 1991, Lossiemouth, Grampian, Britain)
2 **Ross's Goose** (adult with Barnacle Geese, Feb 1995*, Stellendam, Netherlands)
3 **Red-breasted Goose** (adult, Nov 1993, Caerlaverock, Dumfries and Galloway, Britain)
4 **Red-breasted Goose** (adult with dark-bellied Brent Geese, Feb 1992, Zeeland, Netherlands)
5 **Red-breasted Goose** (juvenile, Oct 1994, Wells, Norfolk, Britain)
6 **Ruddy Shelduck** (non-breeding adult, Sept 1991, Voorus Meer, Netherlands)
7 **Ruddy Shelduck** (Oct 1994, Hayle, Cornwall, Britain)
8 **Ruddy Shelduck** (moulting adults, male in centre, Aug 1991, Dorpste, Netherlands)

AMERICAN WIGEON

Anas americana L 45-56 cm (18-22 in)
DESCRIPTION North American counterpart of Eurasian Wigeon, which it resembles closely in size, structure and habits. Plumage of breeding male distinctive, with whitish forehead and crown, 'freckled' grey head and neck, iridescent greenish-black band across eye to nape, pinkish-brown (Jay-coloured) body with fine dark grey vermiculations, white belly and ventral patch, and black rear end. Upperwing shows white covert patch, metallic green and black speculum and dark grey-brown primaries as male Eurasian Wigeon, but lesser coverts brownish (not grey) and underwing pale grey with white (not light greyish) central stripe. Eclipse male as female, but with darker upperparts, more rufous breast and flanks, and wing pattern as breeding male. Female and juvenile very like same plumages of Eurasian Wigeon, from which best distinguished by greyer head, rusty-toned breast and flanks, white axillaries and central underwing, and whiter greater coverts.
HABITAT Typically nests near lakes and marshes in open or lightly wooded country; in winter shows more marked preference for freshwater habitats than Eurasian Wigeon.
DISTRIBUTION Breeds in North America from Labrador and Hudson Bay westwards across much of Canada and Alaska, and south through western USA to northern Colorado. Winters chiefly down Atlantic coast from New England, Pacific coast from southern Alaska, across southern USA and south through West Indies and Central America to Colombia.
EUROPEAN STATUS Frequent vagrant: recorded mainly in autumn in western Europe, with some individuals returning in successive winters, but spring records more common in Scandinavia. Has occurred in small parties. Belgium (4: 1 May 1986; 14 Dec 1987; 30 Mar 1991; 10-11 Apr 1991); Britain (many, including a record of flock of 12+); Channel Islands (3: 9 Oct 1985-14 Mar 1986, returning 18 Jan-31 Mar 1987; 10 Oct 1987-19 Mar 1988; 2 Oct 1988-2 Mar 1989); Czech Republic (1: 10 Feb 1990); Denmark (2: 3-11 Apr 1992; 1-30 Dec 1994); Faeroes (1: 7 June 1984); Finland (16); France (15); Germany (c 5); Iceland (81); Ireland (min. estimated total of 49 birds to end 1993, including flock of 13 in Oct 1968 and numerous returning individuals); Luxembourg (1); Netherlands (20); Norway (5: 30 May and 1 June 1967; 25-26 May 1986; 13-20 Dec 1986; 26 Nov-c 15 Dec 1988 and 7 Jan-29 Apr 1989; 26 Feb 1989); Spain (2: 11-21 Oct 1971; 1-3 Apr 1988); Sweden (20).

FALCATED DUCK

Anas falcata L 48-54 cm (19-22 in)
DESCRIPTION Medium-sized, rather heavily-built dabbling duck. Breeding male recalls outsized male Common Teal in general coloration, with chestnut-bronze head (markedly peaked on forehead and with maned crest) extensively iridescent dark green across sides, white throat

with narrow black neck-collar, grey body with fine black scaling (most intense on breast), elongated curved tertials, buffish-white undertail-coverts with black surround, and black back, rump and tail. Upperwing-coverts pale grey with white greater-covert bar, primaries dark grey and speculum metallic greenish-black; underwing pale grey with whitish centre. Eclipse male resembles female, but is darker-headed and has pale grey upperwing-coverts. Drab female most recalls female Gadwall, but with darker, plainer head, upperparts also darker brown and flanks warmer, less buffish-brown; breast patch buffish, not white as on Gadwall and Eurasian Wigeon, and rear end also almost uniformly brown. Wing much as male's, but upperwing-coverts grey-brown with paler tips. Juvenile like buffer version of female, acquiring adult-like plumage by first winter. Long bill and legs dark grey or blackish in all plumages. Lone individuals in Europe often consort with flocks of Eurasian Wigeon; very shy.
HABITAT Frequents freshwater habitats, including lakes, rivers and water meadows; in winter also on floods, coastal lagoons and estuaries.
DISTRIBUTION Breeds in south-eastern Siberia, northern Mongolia, extreme northern China and northern Japan, wintering from southern Japan and Korea south through eastern China to Vietnam and west to north-eastern India.
EUROPEAN STATUS Probably very rare vagrant. Following records give incomplete picture, as many occurrences from other countries (eg Belgium, Britain, Finland, France and Germany) treated as referring to birds of captive or uncertain origin, and effect of escapes impossible to determine. Austria (1: 1839); Bulgaria (1: 23 Feb 1978); Netherlands (6); Poland (1: 18-20 Mar 1992); Spain (1: 12 Dec 1992-8 May 1993).

BAIKAL TEAL

Anas formosa L 39-43 cm (16-17 in)
DESCRIPTION Striking head pattern of black-and-white-bordered buff and green facial crescents, black area around eye and blackish-brown crown and nape renders breeding male instantly recognisable. Breast pinkish, with black speckling and vertical white stripe on greyer sides; flanks grey, centre of underparts and ventral patch white, and undertail-coverts black. Brownish upperparts have long trailing cream-and-black-edged scapulars, with black uppertail-coverts and brown tail. Upperwing pattern distinctive, with brownish coverts, blackish-brown primaries, and metallic greenish-black speculum bordered in front by rusty greater-covert bar and behind by white trailing edge; whitish underwing shows dusky leading edge and browner flight feathers. Eclipse male warmer-toned than female, with weaker facial pattern. Female recalls large female Common Teal but plumage is more rufous-brown, with head marked by well-defined white spot at bill base, often a dusky vertical line below eye, white chin and throat, more extensively dark crown, and supercilium

behind eye only; wing as male except upperwing-coverts dark greyish-brown. Juvenile like female, but with weaker facial pattern; adult-type plumage acquired from first winter.
HABITAT Nests in marshes and pools on tundra edge and in swampy taiga; winter habitats include freshwater lakes, flooded meadows and brackish marshes.
DISTRIBUTION Breeds in eastern Siberia south to Lake Baikal and east to Kamchatka, wintering mainly in southern Japan and southern and eastern China; has once reached Svalbard. Huge decline in numbers has taken place in last 25 years.
EUROPEAN STATUS Probably very rare vagrant; population decline is likely to have reduced the number of wild stragglers reaching Europe in recent times. Following records give incomplete picture, as recorded in other countries (eg Britain, Finland, Germany, Ireland, Sweden and Switzerland) where treated as of uncertain origin, and effect of escapes impossible to determine. Belgium (c 15: most recent on 31 Mar-1 Apr 1991); France (13); Italy (10); Netherlands (9); Poland (1: 27 May 1987); Spain (1: 19 Jan 1983).

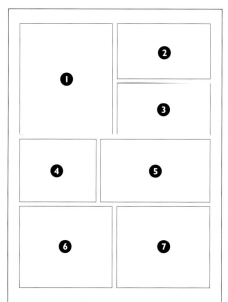

1 American Wigeon (male, apparently adult in eclipse, winter 1986, Hayle, Cornwall, Britain)
2 American Wigeon (juvenile female, Sept 1986, Fair Isle, Shetland, Britain)
3 American Wigeon (eclipse male, Sept 1990, Seaforth, Merseyside, Britain)
4 American Wigeon (adult male, Feb 1993, Martin Mere, Lancashire, Britain)
5 Falcated Duck (adult male, Dec 1987, Pitsford, Northamptonshire, Britain)
6 Falcated Duck (adult male with Gadwall and Tufted Duck, Jan 1992, Bloemendaal, Netherlands)
7 Baikal Teal (first-winter male, Dec 1994, Broekhuizen, Netherlands)

AMERICAN BLACK DUCK

Anas rubripes L 53-61 cm (21-24 in)
DESCRIPTION Close North American relative of Mallard. Male has head pattern recalling female Mallard, with blackish crown, hindneck and eye-stripe, pale brown face and neck and yellow bill; entire body contrastingly blackish-brown, with very narrow brown feather fringes visible at closer range. Upperwing uniform with body, except for bluish-purple speculum with black subterminal band and (usually) indistinct pale trailing edge; underwing strikingly white, with greyer flight feathers. Female very like male but usually less contrasting in appearance, with greyer head and neck, greener bill and bluer speculum. Juvenile somewhat browner, with greyish-olive bill, but adult-like plumage acquired by first winter. Confusion possible with very dark female Mallards, which should be separable by pale sides to tail, more patterned feathers on underparts and white basal bar to speculum; beware also frequent hybrid offspring with Mallard (successful mixed pairing recorded Britain), more difficult females of which best identified by white basal speculum bar. Habits much as Mallard's.
HABITAT Preferences generally as those of Mallard, though more tolerant of saltwater habitats and harsher weather.
DISTRIBUTION Breeds across eastern Canada and south through north-eastern USA to North Carolina. Northern birds migratory, wintering in eastern USA south to Florida, Gulf coast and eastern Texas.
EUROPEAN STATUS Rare vagrant: 52 records. Denmark (1: Oct 1988); Britain (14: has hybridised with Mallard); France (2: 30 Nov 1972; 10 Dec 1976); Iceland (26); Ireland (7); Norway (1: 12 Apr 1981); Spain (1: 11 Jan 1993-5 Feb 1994, and 17 Nov 1994); Sweden (1: Nov 1973).

BLUE-WINGED TEAL

Anas discors L 37-41 cm (15-16 in)
DESCRIPTION Breeding male readily identified by blue-grey head with prominent white vertical crescent between eye and bill, and black throat, forehead and crown. Body buff-brown, speckled darker on underparts and barred on upper border of flanks; has obvious white vent patch and black stern. In flight, blackish-brown upperwing shows bright pale blue coverts like Northern Shoveler, with white greater-covert bar above metallic green speculum; underwing white, with dusky leading edge and greyer flight feathers. Eclipse male much as female, but with darker crown and retained upperwing pattern. Female has buffish-brown face and neck, rest of plumage essentially dark brown with greyish-buff edges which form dark scallops on flanks; face pattern recalls elements of smaller females of both Common Teal and Garganey, having weak supercilium and subdued narrow eye-stripe of former but with latter's pale spot at base of bill. Duller upperwing has narrower white greater-covert bar which may not be visible in flight.

Juvenile resembles female. Black bill is longer than on both Common Teal and Garganey; legs and feet green (duller and greyer in young birds), unlike darker, gun-metal grey of Garganey. Beware also possible confusion of female and juvenile with same of Cinnamon Teal *A cyanoptera* (escape from collections and potential vagrant to Europe), which is typically warmer rufous-brown with plainer facial pattern.
HABITAT Favours marshes, pools and lakes in open country; in winter also in brackish coastal lagoons and more open waters.
DISTRIBUTION Breeds from south-east Alaska over much of southern Canada, interior of northern and central USA and along Atlantic seaboard from Newfoundland to North Carolina. Long-distance migrant, wintering from southern USA through West Indies and Central America south to northern Chile and Argentina.
EUROPEAN STATUS Frequent vagrant: most records in western Europe are during autumn, though spring occurrences more common in eastern Europe and Scandinavia. Austria (1: 8-9 Apr 1973); Belgium (5: 22 May 1966; 6 Apr-3 May 1986; 26-29 June 1986; 26 Apr-6 May 1989; 22 Apr 1990); Britain (c 154 individuals); Denmark (7: bred in 1986); Faeroes (3: 3 Nov 1972; 4 Nov 1980; 19 June-8 July 1991, two); Finland (7); France (28); Germany (5: 1952; 16-29 Apr 1988; 3-7 May 1989; 16 May 1993; 19 June 1993); Greece (1: 25-26 Apr 1986); Iceland (8); Ireland (38); Italy (4: 12 Nov 1948; 3 Feb 1952; 25 Oct 1960; 9 Nov 1975); Netherlands (19 individuals); Norway (2: 19 June-3 July 1991; 16 May 1994); Poland (1: 8 Apr 1984); Portugal (1: 21 and 28 Mar 1992); Spain (11+); Sweden (12 records of 13 birds); Switzerland (2: 5 Apr 1978; 24 Apr 1989).

MARBLED DUCK

Marmaronetta angustirostris L 39-42 cm (15-16 in)
DESCRIPTION Distinctive species related to pochards, but with clear affinities with dabbling ducks. Adult appears largely pale sandy-brown, with conspicuous blackish patch around and behind eye and short shaggy crest. Plumage shows fine brown barring on crown and darker brown barring on breast, belly and undertail-coverts, with whitish-buff spots on flanks; mantle, scapulars and rump somewhat darker brown with paler spots, but upperwing contrastingly plain light greyish-brown, palest on secondaries. Underwing appears whitish in flight. Bill blackish with grey subterminal band, but female's is usually duller and with green patch at base; legs greenish-yellow. Juvenile very like adult, but with duller and more diffuse body spotting and greyer underparts. In flight, long-necked appearance and pale brown plumage recall female Pintail, but smaller size, lack of speculum and dark eye patch distinctive. Feeds mainly by dabbling, though will also dive; flight typically low over water.
HABITAT Favours small freshwater lakes and ponds, and also brackish coastal lagoons.

DISTRIBUTION Breeding range includes Spain and Morocco in west, probably also Algeria and Tunisia, and from Turkey and Israel eastwards in isolated pockets through Iraq, Iran, southern Central Asia and adjacent countries. Western birds winter chiefly in Morocco, also Tunisia and occasionally south of Sahara; eastern birds move mainly to Iran, also Turkey and Egypt east to north-western India.
EUROPEAN STATUS Breeds Spain (50-230 pairs 1988-92, but only 34 pairs 1994; also winter visitor). Accidental elsewhere, but occasional escapes (eg in Britain) also reported: Albania; Bulgaria (4: 3 Dec 1973; June 1979; undated; 16 May 1991); Czech Republic (1: 25 July 1892, four); France (25+); Germany (c 5 vagrants/escapes); Greece (14 records 1857-1991, max. 20 on 11 Apr 1984; has bred); Hungary (3: 1893; Aug 1896; 3 Jan 1951); Italy (probably bred 19th century: 8 since 1900); Poland (1: 15 Mar 1989); Portugal (2: 10 Jan 1988; 17 Mar 1988); Romania; former Yugoslavia (formerly bred).

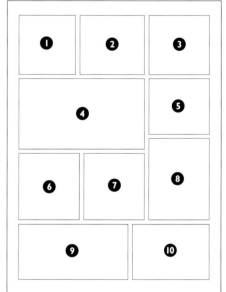

1 **American Black Duck** (adult male, Oct 1994, Tresco, Isles of Scilly, Britain)
2 **American Black Duck** (adult male, Oct 1994, Tresco, Isles of Scilly, Britain)
3 **American Black Duck** (adult male, Oct 1994, Tresco, Isles of Scilly, Britain)
4 **Blue-winged Teal** (adult female, Aug 1989, Upton Warren, Worcestershire, Britain)
5 **Blue-winged Teal** (adult male, Dec 1991, Lokeren, Belgium)
6 **Blue-winged Teal** (juvenile male, Oct 1995*, Reykjavík, Iceland)
7 **Blue-winged Teal** (female/immature male, Oct 1986, Cape Clear, Co Cork, Ireland)
8 **Marbled Duck** (adult, July 1990*, Kingsbury Water Park, Warwickshire, Britain)
9 **Marbled Duck** (Apr 1985, Coto Doñana, Spain)
10 **Marbled Duck** (Jan, Morocco)

CANVASBACK

Aythya valisineria L 48-61 cm (19-24 in)
DESCRIPTION In all plumages closely recalls Pochard, but is larger and has distinctive, sleeker head-and-bill profile. Adult male in breeding plumage has pale grey body (showing no contrast in coloration between flanks and mantle), black breast and stern, and chestnut neck and head which, unlike male Pochard's, shade towards blackish on throat and front of head. In eclipse, male's plumage becomes duller, with brown tips to feathers. Female recalls female Pochard, but has obviously paler and greyer body contrasting with browner breast, and similar buff-white 'spectacles' around and behind eye. Juvenile resembles female, but has darker upperparts and browner underparts. In all plumages, bill is excellent distinction from Pochard (and from Redhead *A americana*, one 1996 European record pending): on Canvasback, bill is wholly blackish with no paler subterminal band, long and deep-based, and merges smoothly into long sloping forehead to produce unique, 'ski-slope' profile to front of head (congeners have shorter, patterned bill and – especially Redhead – steeper forehead). Longer neck of Canvasback also apparent in alert posture and in flight, when more uniform appearance of upperwing, lacking Pochard's contrast between darker grey forewing and pale grey flight feathers, is also striking. Gregarious and sociable.
HABITAT Nests in waterside vegetation in prairie marshes; in winter occurs on larger, more open lakes and coastal waters.
DISTRIBUTION Breeds from central Alaska through western and central Canada to western USA as far south as northern California. Winters in southern British Columbia, western, southern and eastern USA and northern Mexico.
EUROPEAN STATUS Extreme vagrant: one spring record. Iceland (1: 11 Apr 1977).

RING-NECKED DUCK

Aythya collaris L 37-46 cm (15-18 in)
DESCRIPTION New World counterpart of Tufted Duck, from which it differs structurally in having 'bump' on rear crown rather than crest, longer bill, squarer body, and longer tail which is often held cocked. Breeding male appears black with pale grey flanks, which fade sharply to white at breast sides; at close range, rusty neck-collar and purplish head gloss may be visible. In flight, upperwing shows black coverts, dusky primaries and pale grey secondaries. Eclipse male browner, especially on flanks, and with whitish loral patch. Female has dark grey-brown upperparts, warm brown breast and flanks and whitish belly; crown blackish-brown, with mottled greyish sides of head, pale area around base of bill, and conspicuous whitish eye-ring and line running back from eye. Upperwing as male's, but coverts browner. Juvenile very like female, but head and neck browner; adult plumage acquired during first winter. Bill of adult slate-grey, with narrow white band around base, broader white subterminal band and extensively black tip; juvenile lacks white bill markings. Beware Tufted-type hybrids, which can resemble Ring-necked but usually have small crest (not bump) on hindcrown, little or no white around bill base and some white in wing.
HABITAT Nests by freshwater lakes and ponds, moving in winter to larger waters, including coastal lagoons.
DISTRIBUTION Breeds chiefly across central and southern Canada and northern USA. Winters in coastal zone from British Columbia south to Mexico, and from New England south through south-eastern USA to Guatemala and the West Indies. Range expanding in eastern North America.
EUROPEAN STATUS Frequent vagrant: recorded chiefly from autumn through to spring, with some returning to traditional sites each winter. Austria (1: 19 Nov 1989, two); Belgium (9); Britain (c 273 to end 1993); Denmark (5); Faeroes (1: 20-27 Sept 1984); Finland (1: 28 Apr-3 May 1989); France (46); Germany (13); Iceland (29); Ireland (c 59 individuals); Netherlands (16); Norway (22); Spain (5+ individuals); Switzerland (12); Sweden (16 individuals).

LESSER SCAUP

Aythya affinis L 38-46 cm (15-18 in)
DESCRIPTION Very similar to Greater Scaup but slightly smaller, with less bulky body, shorter neck, smaller bill and distinct squared-off 'bump' on hindcrown. Breeding male differs chiefly in usually purplish, not green, sheen to head (very difficult to see in the field), broader and darker vermiculations on pale grey upperparts, and wing-bar which is white on secondaries but grey on inner primaries (on Greater Scaup white extends onto inner primaries). Eclipse male slightly browner than eclipse male Greater Scaup, but best separated by size and shape. Female and juvenile almost identical to corresponding plumages of Greater Scaup, but usually with less extensive white around base of bill, reduced pale cheek patches, and wing-bar pattern as adult male; latter plumage fully acquired by young males in second winter. Bill pale blue-grey with fine black nail in adult male, duller grey with grey-black nail in female, darker grey in juvenile. Hybrid Pochard x Tufted Duck can closely resemble Lesser Scaup, but has more extensively black nail, darker and more finely vermiculated grey mantle, darker eye and often browner tone to head. Vagrants in Europe often found in company with Tufted Duck.
HABITAT Nests by lakes and pools in open country, moving to larger waters in winter but continuing to favour freshwater habitats more than Greater Scaup.
DISTRIBUTION Breeds central and southern Alaska, across western and central Canada and in north-central USA, with isolated outposts further south and east. Winters from British Columbia south to California, across southern USA north to New Jersey and almost to Great Lakes, and throughout West Indies and Central America to northernmost South America.
EUROPEAN STATUS Very rare vagrant: at least 15 records. Britain (8); Denmark (1: 5-7 May 1985); France (2: 9 Feb 1992; 20 Nov 1993); Ireland (1: 13 Feb-14 Apr 1988, returning each subsequent winter up to 1992/93 at least); Netherlands (1: 21 Nov 1994-15 Jan 1995); Spain (1: 12 Jan-23 Mar 1991); Sweden (1: 17 May 1994). Records from Switzerland (winters 1992/93 and 1993-94) considered to relate to bird of uncertain origin and placed in category D.

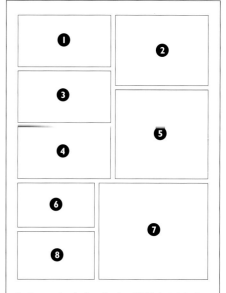

1 **Canvasback** (female, Apr 1977, Arfadalsvik, Iceland)
2 **Ring-necked Duck** (adult male, Dec 1992, Kendal, Cumbria, Britain)
3 **Canvasback** *(adult male, date unknown, USA)*
4 **Ring-necked Duck** (female, right, with male Pochard, Dec 1991, Telemark, Norway)
5 **Ring-necked Duck** (adult male, winter 1993, Strumpshaw, Norfolk, Britain)
6 **Lesser Scaup** (first-winter male, Dec 1994, Pine Lake, Cumbria, Britain)
7 **Lesser Scaup** (adult male, Feb 1994, Vevex, Switzerland)
8 **Lesser Scaup** (adult male, Nov 1994, Lechlade, Oxfordshire, Britain)

KING EIDER

Somateria spectabilis L 47-63 cm (19-25 in)
DESCRIPTION Smaller than Common Eider, with different head-and-bill profile. Adult male in breeding plumage unmistakable, with large head swollen in front by black-edged orange frontal shield above red bill and behind by bulging lavender-blue rear crown and nape. Green sides of head below eye bordered behind by narrow black and white lines. Neck, upper breast, mantle and ventral patch white, often pinkish on breast, but body otherwise black; inner scapulars raised into small pointed 'sails'. Appears smaller and stockier than Common Eider in flight, and on upperwing shows white only on median and greater coverts. Eclipse male sooty-brown with reduced pinkish-orange bill shield, but retains white coverts and often some whitish on breast and mantle. Female very like female Common Eider, but more rusty-toned than most of latter and with darker crescentic flank barring: differences include more concave bill-and-forehead profile, with bump of forecrown in front of (rather than above) eye, and obvious gape line through pale feathering at bill base which gives 'smiling' expression. Juvenile like female but greyer; young males start to acquire white in plumage during first winter, reaching adult plumage in third winter. Gregarious and sociable; vagrants often found among flocks of Common Eider.
HABITAT High-arctic tundra breeder, both along coasts and inland; in winter frequents ice-free coastal waters and open sea.
DISTRIBUTION Found in summer along arctic coasts and islands from westernmost Russia eastwards to Siberia, Canada and northern Greenland. Winters northern Scandinavia, Iceland, from southern Greenland south to Newfoundland, and in the Bering Sea.
EUROPEAN STATUS Winters Norway (c 10,000) and Iceland (537 recorded 1979-94: some present all year); also Faeroes, Finland and Sweden (c 1,365). Accidental elsewhere: Austria; Belgium (2: 13 Dec 1984-30 Jan 1985; 11 Jan 1986); Britain (131); Denmark (98 to end 1992); Estonia (12); France (6); Germany (c 14); Hungary (4: 1875; 1957; 7-18 Jan 1973; 3-6 Apr 1986); Ireland (9); Italy (7); Latvia (1: 24 Oct 1990); Lithuania (2: 25 Mar 1979; 30 Mar 1990); Netherlands (6); Poland (31); Spain (1: 21 June 1987); Switzerland.

SPECTACLED EIDER

Somateria fischeri L 52-57 cm (21-23 in)
DESCRIPTION Recalls slightly larger Common Eider in head-and-bill shape and general proportions, but in all plumages has distinctive pale eye patches and feathered bill shield. Adult male in breeding plumage has green head, becoming more yellowish-green towards crown, with large black-rimmed white circular patches around eyes; feathering of forehead extends over base of orange bill (with paler nail), where edged white. Chin, throat, neck, upper breast, mantle and scapulars white, rest

of body from back and lower breast to tail black, with white patch at sides of vent. In flight, male shows black primaries, secondaries and greater coverts, with rest of upperwing white; underwing dusky, with whitish coverts and axillaries. In eclipse, wholly greyish plumage relieved only by paler eye patches and white wing-coverts. Female is warm rufous-brown, barred darker; head and neck paler brown, with darker bill shield, crown and nape and contrasting large pale creamy-brown circular eye patches. Upperwing dark brownish; underwing greyish-brown, with paler shading and axillaries. Juvenile has less barred underparts and weaker eye patches than female; both appear paler than respective plumages of other eiders. Young males start to acquire whiter markings in first winter, reaching maturity in third winter. Flight action lighter and faster than that of other eiders, but otherwise habits similar.
HABITAT Nests by small tundra pools, mainly near coasts; winters in offshore waters.
DISTRIBUTION Breeds from coastal north-eastern Siberia east to western Alaska. Winter distribution formerly unknown, but over half of world population recently discovered wintering in tiny ice-free area 300km inside Bering Sea pack-ice.
EUROPEAN STATUS Extreme vagrant: three records. Norway (3: 12 Dec 1933; 1 May 1970; 23-24 Feb 1988).

STELLER'S EIDER

Polysticta stelleri L 43-47 cm (17-19 in)
DESCRIPTION Small size and 'conventional' head-and-bill shape readily distinguish all plumages of Steller's from other eiders. Adult male in breeding plumage unmistakable, with black eye patch, chin, throat and neck-collar on white head which has pale green spot on lores and 'bump' on hindcrown. Pale orange breast and flanks bordered by white above and with prominent black spot on breast sides, with black central upperparts and stern, white sides of mantle and back, and white-edged elongated black scapulars. In flight, when lack of black belly immediately eliminates all other male eiders, upperwing shows white coverts, white trailing edge to purplish-blue speculum and black outer wing; underwing white, with greyer flight feathers. In eclipse, male retains white upperwing-coverts but is otherwise very like female, which is uniformly dark reddish-brown except for pale buff eye-ring, duller blue speculum bordered above and below by white, and dark-mottled leading edge to underwing. Juvenile like adult female, but less warmly coloured and appears slightly barred; speculum duller still and may lack white borders. Young males reach adult-like plumage by second winter. Gregarious, flocks often diving simultaneously; lone birds may associate with other eiders.
HABITAT Nests near pools and rivers on arctic tundra, often well inland; at other times in inshore coastal waters.
DISTRIBUTION Breeds mainly from arctic coasts

of eastern Siberia eastwards to Alaska, wintering in northernmost Scandinavia, the Baltic and the Bering Sea.
EUROPEAN STATUS Winters Norway (8,000-15,000), and since about 1969 in the Baltic in increasing numbers in Estonia (1,500-5,000), Finland (100-500), Latvia (4 records of up to 22 birds since 1989), Lithuania (800 in 1990) and Poland (c 80); also increasing in Denmark (60+) and Sweden (c 3,040 records). Accidental elsewhere: Britain (13); Faeroes (1: 13 Apr-9 May 1994); France (1: Feb 1855); Germany (c 27); Iceland (7); Netherlands (3: 5 July 1980, returning summers 1981 and 1982; 13 Apr 1986; 28 Feb 1987).

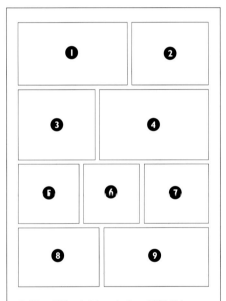

1 **King Eider** (adult male, June 1987, Ythan Estuary, Grampian, Britain)
2 **King Eider** (adult male, Feb 1991, Hoek, Netherlands)
3 **King Eider** (juvenile female moulting to first-winter plumage, Oct 1994, Scheveningen, Netherlands)
4 **King Eider** (juvenile female moulting to first-winter plumage, Oct 1994, Scheveningen, Netherlands)
5 **Spectacled Eider** (adult female, June, Siberia)
6 **Spectacled Eider** (adult male, June, Siberia)
7 **Steller's Eider** (adult male, Aug 1984, South Uist, Western Isles, Britain)
8 **Steller's Eider** (adult male, Jan 1987, Lelystad, Netherlands)
9 **Steller's Eider** (two adult males, two adult females, six second-calendar-year males and one second-calendar-year male/female, May 1992, Virolahti, Finland)

HARLEQUIN DUCK

Histrionicus histrionicus L 38-45 cm (15-18 in)
DESCRIPTION Adult male shows diagnostic combination of blue-grey head, breast and upperparts, chestnut flanks and black stern, patterned by white facial crescent extending up sides of black forehead and crown and continuing as chestnut line towards nape, white spots on ear-coverts and vent, white stripes on neck and breast sides and white scapulars and tertials; most white markings are bordered by black. In flight, upperwing reveals odd white spots on coverts and blue-glossed speculum. At range, males look all dark. Those from Siberia and western North America said to be duller, with less chestnut in supercilium, and sometimes described as race *pacificus* (though this form not generally recognised). In eclipse, duller and browner male approaches plumage of female, which is wholly sooty-brown but for white patch at front of face (on some, broken by dark loral stripe), white spot on ear-coverts, mottled whitish underparts and blue gloss on secondaries. Juvenile much as female, though marginally browner above and without blue gloss to secondaries; male acquires adult plumage from first winter. Bill and legs greyish in all plumages. Often found in pairs or small parties, usually apart from other seaducks; frequently loafs on rocks and feeds close inshore.
HABITAT Nests by turbulent mountain rivers and streams; in winter in rugged inshore coastal areas.
DISTRIBUTION Breeds in the Atlantic in Iceland, southern Greenland and north-east Canada, wintering south to New England. In the Pacific, breeds north-west USA, western Canada, Alaska and in Siberia from Lake Baikal eastwards, wintering along adjacent coasts and in Asia south to northern China.
EUROPEAN STATUS Resident Iceland (2,000-3,000 breeding pairs 1975-89). Accidental elsewhere, with at least two *pacificus*-type birds (Sweden 1893) possibly originating from North America: Austria (2: Mar 1924; 2 Jan 1988); Britain (12); Faeroes (6); Germany (6, of which recent records considered to relate to escapes); Italy (4: 2 Mar 1902; 27 Nov 1945; 30 Nov 1945; 3 Dec 1945); Netherlands (1: Dec 1982-May 1983); Norway (7, but 4 oldest records poorly documented); Poland (3: 8 Mar 1875, five; June 1887; 29 Mar 1987); Slovakia (2: date unknown; 28 Feb 1867); Sweden (2: 21 Apr 1862; 4 Apr 1893, pair). In addition, four records from France placed in category D.

SURF SCOTER

Melanitta perspicillata L 45-56 cm (18-22 in)
DESCRIPTION Closer in size to Common than to Velvet Scoter, and in all plumages shares wholly dark wings with former species. Adult male entirely black but for conspicuous white forehead blaze and nape patch (latter usually obscured during summer and autumn). Deep-based bill of male diagnostic, appearing extensively red and yellow on whitish

background, with prominent black patch at sides of base, and combined with sloping forehead gives head profile recalling Common Eider. Female dark brown above and slightly paler brown below; head shows grey bill (less swollen than on male) and darker crown above brown face with two whitish circular patches, which compared to female Velvet appear as more vertically aligned spot/bar at bill base and rounder spot on ear coverts, and also has variably whitish patch on nape. Juvenile paler and browner than female, with whitish belly, less well-defined face patches and no nape patch; adult characters acquired from first winter. Vagrants in Europe often found among Common and Velvet Scoters, when diving action ('flip-dives' with almost no forward lunge and with wings partially open like Velvet) and wing-flapping habits (keeps head level and neck rigid, unlike Common) may be further clues to identification.
HABITAT Nests by lakes, ponds and other waters within or north of tree limit; winters in shallow bays and inshore coastal waters.
DISTRIBUTION Breeds in much of Alaska, and across north-western, central and eastern Canada to Labrador, wintering chiefly on the east coast of North America south to North Carolina, in the Great Lakes region and on the west coast south to California.
EUROPEAN STATUS Frequent vagrant: some individuals in Britain and Ireland now semi-resident or returning each year, making accurate analysis of totals almost impossible. Britain (c 275); Czech Republic (1: 20 July 1967); Denmark (11); Estonia (1: 7 June 1971, pair); Faeroes (4: 23 Nov 1847; 23 Sept 1896; May 1979; July-15 Sept 1987); Finland (31 records of 32 individuals); France (28); Germany (1: 9 Oct 1851); Iceland (26); Ireland (90 individuals); Netherlands (7); Norway (35); Poland (1: 7 Jan 1988); Spain (at least 6 records of 7 individuals); Sweden (43 individuals).

BUFFLEHEAD

Bucephala albeola L 32-39 cm (13-16 in)
DESCRIPTION Adult male in breeding plumage unmistakable, with diagnostic tall, rounded blackish head showing striking white triangular 'rear quarter' behind eye. At close range, head reveals iridescent bronze, green and purple glosses. Plumage otherwise recalls Common Goldeneye, with white body and black upperparts, chief distinction being wholly black scapulars; also resembles that species in flight, especially in upperwing pattern, but white head patch obvious even at great range and underwing dusky with white secondaries, not dark grey. In eclipse, male resembles adult female but retains wing pattern of breeding plumage and has more extensive white on side of head. Adult female greyish-brown, darker on mantle and greyer on rump, and with white on blackish-brown upperwing restricted to secondaries and some greater coverts; brown head is smaller than male's, and marked with elongated white flash on rear cheeks. Juvenile similar to female, but with smaller white face

patch. Bill of male blue-grey, duskier at base and nail; dark grey on female and juvenile. Very active and restless species, frequently diving and flying short distances; less sociable than the goldeneyes.
HABITAT Nests in tree holes around wooded lakes and rivers; in winter on larger inland waters, estuaries and inshore coastal waters.
DISTRIBUTION Breeds in North America from Great Lakes region west to Alaska, western Canada and north-west USA, wintering on west coast from Alaska south to northern Mexico and across southern USA as far north in east as New England.
EUROPEAN STATUS Very rare vagrant: exact number of wild occurrences questionable, and records from some countries (eg Belgium, Finland, France and Netherlands) regarded as likely escapes or of uncertain origin. Britain (9); Channel Islands (1: 8 Nov 1967); France (2: 14-22 Mar 1980; 17 Jan-15 Feb 1987); Iceland (2: Nov 1956; 15 May 1988, returning annually until 8 Mar 1993); Portugal (1: 24 Jan-7 Feb 1993, origin unknown); Spain (1: 25 Dec 1992-9 Jan 1993); Sweden.

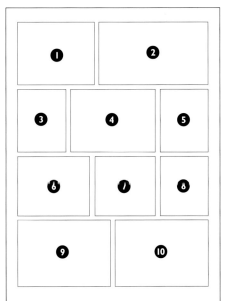

1 **Harlequin Duck** (female, Mar 1991, Wick, Highland, Britain)
2 **Harlequin Duck** (adult males, June, year unknown, River Laxá, Iceland)
3 **Harlequin Duck** (adult female, Dec 1982, Noordholland, Netherlands)
4 **Harlequin Duck** (first-summer females, Apr 1996*, Girvan, Strathclyde, Britain)
5 **Surf Scoter** (first-winter male, Apr 1989, Grafham Water, Cambridgeshire, Britain)
6 **Surf Scoter** (juvenile, Oct 1994, Bryher, Isles of Scilly, Britain)
7 **Bufflehead** (adult male, Mar 1994, Colwick, Nottinghamshire, Britain)
8 **Bufflehead** (adult male, Mar 1994, Colwick, Nottinghamshire, Britain)
9 **Bufflehead** (first-summer male, June 1994, Coatham, Teesside, Britain)
10 **Bufflehead** (adult male, Mar 1994, Colwick, Nottinghamshire, Britain)

BARROW'S GOLDENEYE

Bucephala islandica L 42-53 cm (17-21 in)
DESCRIPTION In all plumages very similar to
Common Goldeneye, but slightly larger and
with obviously bulging forehead. Adult male in
breeding plumage separated by longer white
crescent (not spot) between eye and bill,
purple rather than green gloss to head, and
blacker upperparts which lack Common
Goldeneye's more extensive white on scapulars
and which reach onto breast sides. In flight,
further distinguished by black line dividing
white on arm of upperwing (on Common
Goldeneye, entire arm behind dark leading
edge appears white). Eclipse male resembles
female, but with all-dark bill and with
upperwing as breeding male's. Female and
juvenile very like respective plumages of
Common Goldeneye, from which best
separated by darker brown head and structural
differences. In flight, adult female Barrow's lacks
white on median coverts shown by adult female
Common, but note that juvenile Common also
lacks this feature; juvenile Barrow's has blacker
upperparts than adult female. Bill stouter than
Common Goldeneye's, black on male and
fleshy-yellow with blackish base on female
(wholly yellow on western birds). Habits much
as those of Common Goldeneye, with which it
occasionally associates in winter, but Barrow's
is generally less sociable.
HABITAT Nests in old woodpecker holes,
nestboxes or on ground along lakeshores and
rivers; in winter moves to ice-free waters and
coasts.
DISTRIBUTION Breeds Iceland (where resident),
irregularly south-west Greenland and in
eastern Canada, and more extensively in
western North America from Alaska south to
northern California. In America, eastern birds
winter south to New England and western
birds along coasts adjacent to breeding range.
EUROPEAN STATUS Resident Iceland (400-800
breeding pairs 1975-89). Accidental elsewhere,
though escapes also recorded: Britain (1: 4
Nov-28 Dec 1982); Czech Republic (1: 21 Nov
1887, origin uncertain); Estonia (1: 13 May
1978); Faeroes (4: May 1944; 27 Jan 1945; Apr
1949; 24 Nov-31 Dec 1982); France (5: 1829;
1834; 14 Jan 1972; 8 Feb 1983; 2 Dec 1989);
Germany (5: 23 Feb 1955; 6 Mar 1955; 26 Feb
1956; 7 Apr 1956; 3-5 Mar 1957); Norway (3:
1848; 7 Sept 1851; 22 Dec 1986, returning in
subsequent winters to 1993/94); Spain (1: 22
Dec 1871).

HOODED MERGANSER

Mergus cucullatus L 42-50 cm (17-20 in)
DESCRIPTION In all plumages shows distinctive
large, bushy crest which can be raised into a fan
to produce outsized 'rectangular' head. Adult
male in breeding plumage unmistakable, with
black head showing broad white patch flaring
outwards from behind yellow eye, white breast
with double black vertical bars at sides, rufous
flanks vermiculated grey, and brownish-black
upperparts with black-and-white striped

tertials. In flight, shows blackish-brown
upperwing with contrasting paler brown
median coverts, white greater-covert bar and
white outer webs to inner secondaries;
underwing appears dusky with white coverts.
Eclipse male separated from female by male-
type median coverts and bare-part colours.
Female generally grey-brown, brownest on
head, darker grey on upperparts, with shorter
tertials than male, and whitish throat, foreneck
and breast; gingery-brown crest shorter than
on male, and eye dark. Wing as on male, but
lacks contrasting paler median coverts. Juvenile
like female, but has shorter crest, paler brown
upperparts and plainer tertials; in flight, lacks
white on greater coverts. Slender bill is black
on male; on female and juvenile largely blackish,
but yellow on lower mandible and at base. Tail
often held cocked like a stiff-tail's. Less sociable
than most diving ducks.
HABITAT In breeding season found around
wooded lake margins and along rivers, where
nests in tree holes and nestboxes; winters in
similar habitat and on more open lagoons and
estuaries.
DISTRIBUTION In summer breeds from south-
central and south-eastern Canada south
through inland eastern USA, and from southern
Alaska south through western Canada to
north-west USA. Eastern birds winter in
Atlantic and Gulf states south to northern
Mexico, western birds south to California.
EUROPEAN STATUS Rare vagrant: true pattern
clouded by frequent escapes, and some more
recent records (eg from Austria, Belgium,
Britain, Finland, Germany and Sweden)
considered particularly suspect. Britain (1:
winter 1830/31); Iceland (1: 21 May-30 Sept
1994); Ireland (3: Dec 1878, pair; Jan 1881; 21
Dec 1957); Norway (3: late Sept 1985; 20-29
Dec 1989; 13 Jan-20 Apr 1991).

WHITE-HEADED DUCK

Oxyura leucocephala L 43-48 cm (17-19 in)
DESCRIPTION Distinctive diving duck, likely to
be confused only with introduced Ruddy Duck.
Differs from that species in larger size, heavier
head and conspicuously swollen bill base.
Breeding adult male has diagnostic white head
with bright pale blue bill and prominent dark
eye below blackish central crown; upper neck
blackish, but body and wings otherwise
chestnut-brown, brightest on breast, greyer on
upperparts and lacking the white undertail-
coverts of Ruddy Duck. In eclipse, body toned
greyer and head has more dusky patches. Adult
female recalls female Ruddy Duck, but has
blacker crown, broader blackish band across
cheek and more rufous-brown body; in winter
body is duller brown and sides of face whiter,
with dark bands even more contrasting.
Juveniles resemble winter females, but have
even more striking face pattern and slightly
shorter, spikier tail; by first spring, young males
have head mottled darker, very rarely
appearing entirely black-headed. Like all stiff-
tails, typically holds tail cocked when swimming;
rarely seen in flight.

HABITAT Favours fairly shallow, reed-fringed
freshwater lakes in open country; also on more
saline waters.
DISTRIBUTION Breeds locally in Spain, Tunisia,
perhaps Algeria, and Turkey, and more
extensively in Central Asia (especially
Kazakhstan) east to extreme north-west China.
In winter some dispersal occurs in North
Africa; Central Asian birds winter chiefly from
western Turkey east to Pakistan.
EUROPEAN STATUS Resident Spain (50-100
pairs: 786 counted in Jan 1992, 579 in Aug
1994); in winter regular Bulgaria (183 counted
in early 1993), Greece (max. 850-900 on 12
Dec 1994) and Romania (fewer than 100;
probably no longer breeds). Accidental
elsewhere, though some birds regarded as of
uncertain origin (eg in Belgium and Britain):
Albania (7+); Austria (regular in 19th century,
but only 3 records since 1900); Czech Republic
(12); France (bred Corsica until 1965; 19 other
records); Germany (17); Hungary (formerly
bred: some recent records possibly attributable
to failed reintroduction scheme); Italy (last bred
in 1977); Netherlands (10); Poland (11);
Portugal (most recent on 17-20 Oct 1994);
Slovakia (2: prior to 1857; 22 Feb 1974);
Switzerland (10).

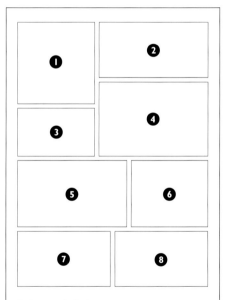

1 **Barrow's Goldeneye** (adult male, June
1988, Reykjavík, Iceland)
2 **Barrow's Goldeneye** (female with
ducklings, July 1995, Laxárdalur, Iceland)
3 **Barrow's Goldeneye** (adult male, Nov
1982, Irvine, Strathclyde, Britain)
4 **Hooded Merganser** (adult male, Nov 1989,
Scarborough, Yorkshire, Britain)
5 **Hooded Merganser** (adult male, Nov 1989,
Scarborough, Yorkshire, Britain)
6 **White-headed Duck** (female/immature,
Feb 1987, Utrecht, Netherlands)
7 **White-headed Duck** (female/immature,
Dec 1991*, Bruges, Belgium)
8 **White-headed Duck** (second-calendar-
year male, Feb 1995*, Abberton, Essex, Britain)

BLACK-WINGED KITE

Elanus caeruleus L 31-35 cm (12.5-14 in)
DESCRIPTION Small, pale and compact raptor, with broad head, stocky body and short tail combining to produce a somewhat owl-like silhouette. Adult has pale bluish-grey upperparts and white underparts with contrasting prominent black 'shoulder' patch. White face has distinctive expression, with black eyebrows and deep red irides which give an intense, 'concentrating' look. In flight, appears very pale except for black covert patch on upperwing, black tips to primary coverts forming small dark crescent (visible only at close range) and black undersides to primaries, this last character recalling underwing of Hen and Pallid Harriers. Short, barely notched bluish-grey tail shows white outer feathers. Bill black, with yellow cere; legs yellow. Juvenile differs in dark eye, duller cere, white-streaked brown crown, brownish upperparts, less well-defined blackish shoulder patch, and chestnut wash on breast and neck sides; adult-like plumage acquired from first spring. In flight, wings pressed forward and held in a V when gliding, and frequently hovers; often perches on telegraph wires.
HABITAT Favours open country with scattered trees, plains and steppes, but also woodland fringe and cultivated land, often near water.
DISTRIBUTION Chiefly resident in Iberia, North Africa from Morocco to Tunisia and in the Nile valley, and occurs more widely in southern, East and West Africa (where partially migratory), the Indian subcontinent and South-East Asia.
EUROPEAN STATUS Breeds in Spain (c 1,000 pairs) and Portugal (100-1,000 pairs 1989), and possibly colonising France (31: 1-2 breeding pairs 1990 94). Accidental elsewhere: Austria (1: 24 May 1986); Belgium (1: 27-28 Apr 1992); Bulgaria (2: 12 Apr 1979; 24 Apr 1980); Czech Republic (1: 31 Mar 1938); Gibraltar (4: 14 May 1977; 6 Apr 1986; 8 May 1988; 4 May 1991); Germany (6); Greece (2: mid-19th century; 14 Dec 1987); Italy (3: 20 Oct 1938; 1969; 22 Nov 1974); Netherlands (1: 31 May 1971); Poland (1: May 1984); Romania; Switzerland (2: 29 Apr 1990; 30 Oct 1994).

LAMMERGEIER

Gypaetus barbatus L 100-115 cm (40-46 in)
DESCRIPTION Massive wingspan, diamond-shaped tail and buff-and-black plumage of adult eliminate possibility of confusion with any other raptor. Head creamy-white or yellowish with black eye mask and drooping moustaches at base of bill; underparts more orangey-buff from breast, which may show incomplete band of darker spots, to undertail-coverts. Upperwing, mantle, rump and tail rather uniform charcoal-grey, appearing black at a distance; underwing shows more contrast between blackish coverts and dark grey flight feathers. Juvenile readily separated on size and structure from all other raptors, but plumage less distinctive than adult; has blackish-brown upperparts with darker

flight feathers and tail, paler rump and uppertail-coverts, dirty-buff body, and blackish head with paler patches above and below eye. Bill and legs usually grey-black. Long, rather pointed wings and tail shape distinctive even at great distance; usually seen singly or in pairs. Has characteristic habit of dropping bones from great height to extract marrow.
HABITAT Usually found in remote mountainous terrain, but will also forage over lower valleys and even around upland settlements.
DISTRIBUTION Resident in the Pyrenees, Corsica and the Balkans, also Atlas Mountains of north-west Africa and in eastern and southern Africa, and from Turkey and northern Middle East eastwards across Central Asia and northern India to southern Siberia and north-west China.
EUROPEAN STATUS Breeds Albania (0-5 pairs 1968, declining), France (25 pairs 1990; reintroduction programme also in operation), Greece (12-18 pairs 1990) and Spain (50 pairs and 11 other territories 1994), and until 19th century in Germany; reintroduction programme also well advanced in Austria and Switzerland. Accidental elsewhere: Bulgaria (2 since 1980); Slovenia (1: 20 Nov 1994).

PALLID HARRIER

Circus macrourus L 40-48 cm (16-19 in)
DESCRIPTION Adult male is paler plain blue-grey than Hen and Montagu's Harriers, almost whitish on underside, with contrasting narrow black wedges on primaries emphasising pointed wing shape. Female has darker, more uniform secondaries on upperwing than Montagu's, with underwing showing darker 'smudgy' greater coverts and secondaries, pale tips to inner primaries, often a diagnostic pale, unbarred crescent at base of primaries and dark, unpatterned axillaries (barred on Montagu's); distinct white neck-collar also usually characteristic. Juvenile best separated from juvenile Montagu's by head pattern, with wide, pale and unstreaked collar bordered by uniformly dark brown neck sides and upper breast virtually diagnostic; also shows pale tips to inner primaries, like adult female. Actions much as Montagu's.
HABITAT Favours rough, dry grassland and arid open country, often without trees; also in agricultural areas.
DISTRIBUTION Breeds from extreme south-east Europe eastwards to Central Asia. Winters chiefly in India and sub-Saharan Africa, and in smaller numbers in south-east Europe, the Middle East and North Africa. Migration into Africa in autumn chiefly through Middle East, but return passage more westerly, with some moving through Tunisia into southern Europe.
EUROPEAN STATUS Breeds Romania (fewer than 10 pairs), exceptionally elsewhere (eg Sweden in 1952 and with Montagu's Harrier in Finland in 1993). Regular on migration in Greece, Italy (especially spring), probably Bulgaria (has bred; may also winter) and Hungary (2-4 annually), and possibly Albania and former Yugoslavia (no data). Accidental

elsewhere: Austria (c 15); Belgium (18); Britain (7); Czech Republic; Denmark (65 to end 1993); Estonia (9 records of at least 13 birds); Finland (114); France (36); Germany (has bred at least 6 times); Gibraltar (1: 23 Mar 1992); Latvia (none since 1900); Lithuania (10+); Luxembourg (4: 10 Apr 1983; 9 June 1983; 16 Apr 1984; 20 Oct 1994); Netherlands (8 individuals); Norway (27); Poland (30 since 1950); Slovakia; Spain (8+); Sweden (198 individuals); Switzerland (12).

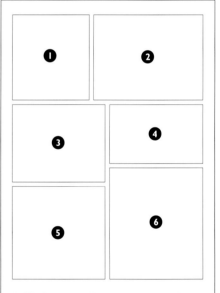

1 **Black-winged Kite** (*adult of race* vociferus, *Jan, India*)
2 **Lammergeier** (*adult male of race* meridionalis, *Aug, South Africa*)
3 **Pallid Harrier** (*juvenile, Sept 1994, Lista, Vest-Agder, Norway*)
4 **Pallid Harrier** (*adult male, Apr 1995*, Bremen, Germany*)
5 **Pallid Harrier** (*second-summer male, June 1995*, Birsay, Orkney, Britain*)
6 **Pallid Harrier** (*second-summer male, June 1993, Worpsnede, Germany*)

SWAINSON'S HAWK

Buteo swainsoni L 43-55 cm (17-22 in)
DESCRIPTION Slightly smaller than Common Buzzard, with proportionately longer and more pointed wings; occurs in two colour phases. Pale birds recall pale morph of same-sized Booted Eagle, with whitish or pale buff body and underwing-coverts and darker, barred flight feathers, but brown upperside lacks pale hindneck, carpal bars, 'blotchy' mantle and whitish spots at leading edge of wing-join, and bases of outer primaries and primary coverts paler than rest of hand. Additionally, Swainson's has brown head and breast band isolating white throat, variable darker markings on underside of body, pale U-shaped band across uppertail-coverts, and grey tail with narrow dark bars, dark subterminal band and white tip. Dark morph may similarly recall dark Booted Eagle, differences from which include wing shape, darker hindneck and upperside, no whitish spots at wing-join, lack of paler wedge on underside of inner primaries, and tail pattern as pale morph. Intermediate birds also occur, often showing dark and variably barred body but paler rufous underwing-coverts. Juvenile typically pale, with more streaked head, pale supercilium, dark moustache, variably streaked or spotted underparts and pale edges to brown upperside; adult-type plumage acquired over two years. Small blackish bill has yellow cere; legs yellow. Soars with wings held in deep V-shape.
HABITAT Found in plains, prairie and desert habitats.
DISTRIBUTION Breeds in southern and western Canada and across much of western USA south to northern Mexico, wintering South America.
EUROPEAN STATUS Extreme vagrant: one spring record, Norway (1: 6 May 1986).

LONG-LEGGED BUZZARD

Buteo rufinus L 50-65 cm (20-26 in)
DESCRIPTION Large, long-winged and heavily built buzzard, closer in structure and flight action to Rough-legged than to Common, but plumage often very like eastern *vulpinus* race of latter (known as Steppe Buzzard). Occurs in pale, intermediate, rufous and blackish morphs, but much individual variation. Well-marked adult typically has rather plain, pale creamy head and breast, contrasting dark reddish-brown unbarred lower breast, belly and 'trousers', uniformly buffish to reddish-brown underwing-coverts with solidly blackish carpal patches, and more or less unbarred pale flight feathers with broad black trailing edge; mantle and upper forewing typically rufous or sandy, with blackish-brown greater coverts and flight feathers, conspicuous pale bases on leading primaries, and lower back often darker than mantle. Tail appears pale orange on upperside, whiter from below and often paler at base, typically unbarred or with hint of terminal barring or band. Juvenile most easily aged by lack of well-defined black trailing edge to underwing. Birds of smaller North African race *cirtensis* usually paler or more rusty; blackish morph occurs mainly in Asia. Flight action heavier than Steppe Buzzard's, and holds wings in deeper V when soaring.
HABITAT Wooded hilly areas and mountains, gorges, steppe and semi-deserts; nests on crags.
DISTRIBUTION Breeds from North Africa, south-east Europe, the Middle East and Turkey eastwards across Central Asia. Northern populations (including most European birds) migratory, wintering sub-Saharan Africa (especially in east), Middle East, south-west Arabia and Turkey eastwards to northern India.
EUROPEAN STATUS Breeds Albania (0-10 pairs), Bulgaria (150-250 pairs 1980-90), Greece (c 150 pairs), Romania and former Yugoslavia (20 pairs); also annual visitor to Hungary (260+: bred 1992 and 1994). Accidental elsewhere: Austria (c 35); Czech Republic (25+); Denmark (5); Finland (1: 28 Sept 1987); France (5: 2 Sept 1878; 3 Oct 1902; 29 Apr 1972; 27 July 1979; 4 Oct 1994); Germany (15: only recent record on 18 Sept 1993); Italy (formerly rare vagrant; recent increase in records); Netherlands (1: 12 Dec 1905); Norway (1: 6 Sept 1986); Poland (22); Slovakia; Slovenia (2: 23 Jan 1982; 9 Jan 1983); Spain (5+); Sweden (6); Switzerland (10).

SPOTTED EAGLE

Aquila clanga L 65-72 cm (26-29 in)
DESCRIPTION Bulky medium-sized eagle but rather compact in proportions, with broad wings and relatively short tail. Adult almost uniformly dark brown, with underwing-coverts only slightly darker than flight feathers; upperwing shows indistinct whitish bases to primaries, appearing as bolder crescent on underside. Juvenile blackish-brown with pale spots on scapulars and upperwing-coverts, pale trailing edge to wing, dark underwing-coverts contrasting with paler flight feathers, more 'bulging' secondaries, narrow U-shaped white band on uppertail-coverts and pale-tipped tail. Paler *fulvescens* variant has much paler brown head, body and wing-coverts in all plumages. Smaller but very similar adult Lesser Spotted Eagle separated from typical adult Spotted by narrower wings, slightly paler brown head, body and wing-coverts, more prominent white upperwing flash and double white carpal crescents; underwing of juvenile Lesser Spotted more uniformly dark brown than on juvenile Spotted. Full adult plumage acquired after four or five years. When soaring or gliding, holds wings almost level (Lesser Spotted typically holds wings angled downwards).
HABITAT Favours forested hillsides or lowlands for breeding, particularly in areas near water; on passage and in winter in more open country, including marshes.
DISTRIBUTION In summer, range extends from eastern Europe across Russia and central Siberia to northern China. Largely migratory, wintering discontinuously from south-east Europe (in tiny numbers further west), Middle East and north-east Africa to India, South-East Asia and China.

EUROPEAN STATUS Breeds in very small numbers in Finland (0-2 pairs 1993; c 218 records), Latvia (at least 1 pair), Poland (10-15 pairs) and possibly Lithuania (up to 2 pairs); scarce or very scarce in winter in Bulgaria, France (117), Greece (max. 37 in Jan 1989), Italy and Romania. Accidental elsewhere: Austria (c 60); Belgium (10); Britain (12, but none since 1915); Czech Republic; Denmark (37); Estonia (9, but possibly regular); Germany; Gibraltar (1: Mar 1987); Hungary (70*: has bred); Ireland (1: Jan 1845, two); Luxembourg; Netherlands (15); Norway (5: Aug 1973; June 1984; 17-19 May 1989; 22 July 1991; 23 Apr 1994); Slovakia; Slovenia (4: 30 Jan 1985; 10 Jan 1991; 27 Sept 1991; 30 Jan 1992); Spain (10+); Sweden (219+ individuals: has bred); Switzerland (28); former Yugoslavia (has bred).

1 **Swainson's Hawk** (second-year pale morph, May 1986, Røst, Nordland, Norway)
2 **Swainson's Hawk** (second-year pale morph, May 1986, Røst, Nordland, Norway)
3 **Long-legged Buzzard** (*adult of race cirtensis, Jan, Morocco*)
4 **Long-legged Buzzard** (*adult of race cirtensis, Nov, Morocco*)
5 **Spotted Eagle** (juvenile, Feb 1988, Kontich, Belgium)
6 **Spotted Eagle** (juvenile, Dec 1994, Hortobágy, Hungary)
7 **Spotted Eagle** (juvenile, Dec 1994, Hortobágy, Hungary)

STEPPE EAGLE

Aquila nipalensis L 65-80 cm (26-32 in)
DESCRIPTION Larger, more powerfully built and with longer and broader wings than Spotted Eagle, but adult plumages very similar. Adult Steppe is generally dark brown, often with paler nape and patch on back, and with white bases to primaries forming obvious flash on hand, longer 'fingered' wing tips and slightly paler and barred tail and flight feathers, latter with dark trailing edge; coverts on underwing range from light to dark brown, variably contrasting with flight feathers, but on upperwing typically paler than remiges. Juvenile paler brown with blackish-brown barred flight feathers and tail, both broadly tipped white, narrow white tips to greater coverts on upperwing and white U-shaped band on uppertail-coverts; all greater coverts on underwing white, forming distinctive pale stripe which reduces with age until adult plumage reached after five years, by which time underwing-stripe very narrow or absent. When soaring, arm held level and hand slightly depressed, with wing often angled slightly backwards at carpal.
HABITAT Occurs mainly in open hilly and steppe country and semi-desert.
DISTRIBUTION Breeds from Caucasus east across Central Asia to Mongolia. Western race *orientalis* migrates through Middle East to winter through much of sub-Saharan Africa to South Africa; nominate eastern *nipalensis* winters largely in Indian subcontinent and western South-East Asia.
EUROPEAN STATUS Rare vagrant: most have occurred in spring and autumn, with occasional records in winter. Bulgaria; Czech Republic (5: July 1974; June 1932; 28 Aug 1943; 15 May 1967; 27 Jan 1985); Denmark (14 to end 1993); Estonia (1: 15-16 May 1993); Finland (20); France (1: 4 May 1960); Germany (1: 26-27 Oct 1967); Greece (16-18, including 5 on 22 Feb 1963); Hungary (c 8-10); Italy (9); Luxembourg (2: 23 Dec 1958-21 Jan 1959; 8 Feb 1963); Netherlands (2: 8 May 1967; 10 Jan-7 Feb 1984); Norway (4: 8 Aug 1973; 2 July 1983; 17-19 May 1989; 22 July 1991); Poland (8); Romania (annual); Slovakia (4 records given as *Aquila rapax* (Tawny Eagle) or *nipalensis* presumed to be this species); Sweden (27); former Yugoslavia.

AMERICAN KESTREL

Falco sparverius L 22-27 cm (8.75-10.75 in)
DESCRIPTION Clearly smaller and slightly shorter-tailed than Eurasian Kestrel; all plumages have distinctive head pattern. Head of male beautifully marked, with chestnut centre to blue-grey crown, buff nape with black central spot, and white face with black moustachial stripe and vertical bar on ear-coverts. Upperparts chestnut, with blue-grey coverts and tertials, all coarsely barred black, and blackish flight feathers with distinctive white subterminal spots; rump and tail warm chestnut, latter barred white at edges and with broad black subterminal band behind narrow white tip. Underparts warm buff, washed with rufous, spotted black on lower breast and fading to white on undertail-coverts; underwing whitish, with fine black spotting, dark-tipped primaries with characteristic row of white subterminal spots, and white trailing edge to secondaries. Female uniform duller brown above with denser and more regular black barring, lacking blue-grey of male except in more subdued head pattern; underparts whiter with rufous streaking, and tail with narrower subterminal band. Juvenile male similar to adult male, but with less well-defined head pattern, more heavily barred mantle and streaked upper breast; juvenile female as adult female. Bill horn-blue, cere and legs yellow. Habits and flight action much as Eurasian Kestrel's; pumps tail on alighting and when excited.
HABITAT Inhabits similar wide range of habitats to Eurasian Kestrel, including built-up areas.
DISTRIBUTION Breeds across North, Central and South America except far north. Northern birds migratory, vacating much of Canada and interior northern USA in winter for southern states and Central America.
EUROPEAN STATUS Extreme vagrant: three records. Britain (2: 25-27 May 1976; 13-28 June 1976); Denmark (1: late 1901). In addition, a specimen from Britain (dated May 1882) has never been formally considered for admission to the national list.

ELEONORA'S FALCON

Falco eleonorae L 36-40 cm (14.5-16 in)
DESCRIPTION Medium-sized, sleek and long-tailed falcon with two distinct plumage phases. Commoner pale phase recalls smaller Hobby in coloration, but streaked pale underparts are washed rufous, lacking that species' contrast between red 'trousers' and white belly; from underneath, separated by contrast between blackish underwing-coverts, paler greyish bases to flight feathers and pale rufous body with white throat. Dark phase almost uniform sooty-black, distinguished from adult male Red-footed Falcon by larger size, longer tail, evenly dark upperwing, dark underwing with contrasting paler bases to flight feathers, lack of red 'trousers', and yellow (not red) bare parts; also has characteristic wing action with a deep, rather loose stroke which is very easily recognised and unlike Red-footed. Potential confusion with smaller Sooty Falcon (has occurred Malta) eliminated by latter's greyer-toned plumage with contrasting darker wing tips and tail tip and protruding central tail feathers. All juvenile Eleonora's Falcons resemble pale phase adults but are browner, with pale fringing to upperparts, paler underside and barred underwing-coverts. Flight masterly and graceful. Gregarious in home range, often in loose parties hunting flying insects; breeds in autumn, when feeds mainly on migrating passerines.
HABITAT Nests around sea cliffs, but ranges over wide area, often far inland, to feed.
DISTRIBUTION Breeds only on islands and coasts in Mediterranean and north-western Morocco. Migrates through Middle East, north-east Africa and the Rift Valley to reach wintering grounds on Madagascar.
EUROPEAN STATUS Breeds Greece (2,500-3,000 pairs), Italy (400-500 pairs 1987), Spain (600+ pairs) and former Yugoslavia (100-150 pairs); scarce or very scarce on passage Gibraltar and Portugal (autumn). Accidental elsewhere: Albania; Britain (3: 8-9 Aug 1977; late Oct 1981, dead; 14 June 1985); Bulgaria (at least 8 reports up to 1988; apparently more frequent subsequently); Denmark (3: 21 Oct 1987; 4 Oct 1988; 25 May 1989); France (218+); Hungary (2: 12 Aug 1968*; 9 May 1993); Poland (4: 12 Sept 1982; 29 Sept 1984; 20 Sept 1990; 12 Aug 1992); Slovenia (2: 21 Aug 1987; 21 Aug 1993); Sweden (5).

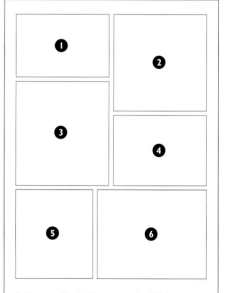

1 **Steppe Eagle** (immature, Jan 1984, Someren, Netherlands)
2 **Steppe Eagle** (second-calendar-year, July 1990, Turku, Finland)
3 **Steppe Eagle** (second-calendar-year, June 1992, Inkoo, Finland)
4 **American Kestrel** *(adult male, date unknown, Florida, USA)*
5 **Eleonora's Falcon** (dark morph, date unknown, Sardinia, Italy)
6 **Eleonora's Falcon** (dark morph, date unknown, Sardinia, Italy)

LANNER FALCON

Falco biarmicus L 34-50 cm (13.5-20 in)
DESCRIPTION Size of Peregrine, but less
pointed wings, longer tail and general pattern
and coloration of plumage all closer to larger
Saker Falcon. Adult of European race *feldeggii*
typically has more patterned head than latter,
with blackish forehead, eye-stripe and
moustache, rufous crown and white cheeks;
underparts from throat to undertail-coverts
creamy-white, marked below by dark barring
on flanks and 'trousers'. Upperparts blue-
brown, becoming darker on flight feathers and
paler on rump and tail, which is barred darker.
Underwing pale, barred and darkening on flight
feathers and lacking contrast with darker
coverts often shown by adult Saker. Juvenile
typically plain dark brown above and evenly
streaked below, with unbarred central tail
feathers recalling Saker; paler birds with
relatively unmarked head may closely resemble
juvenile of latter, which usually has paler crown
and upperparts and contrasting darker flight
feathers on upperwing. North African race
erlangeri is smaller, paler and almost unmarked
below; Middle Eastern race *tanypterus is*
intermediate in characters. Wings often held
slightly upturned when soaring; flight lighter
than Saker's.
HABITAT Typically found in dry upland, steppe
or desert terrain, but frequently hunts over
more cultivated areas.
DISTRIBUTION Mainly resident in south-east
Europe, Turkey, the Middle East, locally in
Arabian peninsula and in North Africa; more
widespread in sub-Saharan, East and southern
Africa.
EUROPEAN STATUS Breeds Albania, Greece
(20-40 pairs), Italy (150-200 pairs) and former
Yugoslavia (10-20 pairs). Accidental elsewhere:
Czech Republic (1: Sept 1906); Gibraltar (c 15);
Spain (10+: bred in 19th century). Possibly also
recorded Romania.

SAKER FALCON

Falco cherrug L 45-55 cm (18-22 in)
DESCRIPTION Heavily-built and powerful
raptor, among European falcons second only to
Gyr in size and bulk. Adult has pale creamy-
white head with indistinct crown streaking,
eye-stripe and moustache, and pale underparts
variably marked with coarse brown streaking
which is densest on lower flanks, belly and
'trousers'. Mantle and upperwing grey-brown
with paler rufous edges, becoming darker on
primaries and paler brown on tail, which has
unmarked centre and rows of pale spots,
rather than bars, on outer feathers. Underwing
usually shows marked contrast between darker
coverts and paler flight feathers. Juvenile
typically has more heavily streaked crown,
stronger eye-stripe and moustache, heavier
streaking on underbody and more heavily
marked underwing-coverts. Eastern
populations, with greyer upperparts and tail
barring, more closely resemble Lanner Falcon
in plumage. In fast and powerful flight, wings
appear broad-based, long and slightly rounded
at tip, with heavy body and long tail; soars on
level wings with tail held closed.
HABITAT Occurs in steppe and upland plateaux,
also in more wooded areas.
DISTRIBUTION In summer, range extends from
central Europe eastwards through southern
Russia and Central Asia to western Siberia;
vacates latter areas to winter chiefly in
southern Asia. European populations partially
migratory, wintering north-east Africa, the
Middle East, very locally in southern Europe,
and possibly North Africa.
EUROPEAN STATUS Breeds Austria, Bulgaria
(20-40 pairs), Czech Republic and Slovakia
(combined total 8-12 pairs 1985-89), Hungary
(120-140 pairs, increasing), Romania (c 20 pairs
1977) and former Yugoslavia (10-15 pairs);
regular in winter in Greece, and on passage
there and in Italy (very scarce). Accidental
elsewhere: Albania; Denmark (1: 7 May 1991);
Finland (1: 29 Apr 1992); France (9); Germany
(26); Poland (41); Slovenia (4: 1970; 1 May
1982; 20 May 1991; 30 Apr 1993); Sweden
(1: Nov 1900).

GYR FALCON

Falco rusticolus L 55-60 cm (22-24 in)
DESCRIPTION The largest and most powerful
falcon, occurring in white and grey morphs in
Europe (and also in dark morph in North
America) but with much individual variation.
Adult white morph birds often patterned only
by scattered black spots on body and wings and
darker tips to outer primaries; juvenile has
browner streaking on crown and upperparts,
less so on underparts. Individuals of grey
morph vary from pale grey to darker brownish-
grey, with whitish forehead, darker crown, eye
patch and moustache (narrower and weaker
than in Peregrine, and grey, not black), barred
upperparts, heavily-marked paler underparts
and barred tail; juvenile has less barred
upperparts and greater contrast between
darker (spotted/barred) underwing-coverts and
plainer and paler flight feathers. Paler juveniles
may resemble juvenile Saker Falcon, from
which separated by more heavily-marked head,
more uniform upperparts, more evenly
streaked underparts and darker-barred tail;
confusion also possible with escaped large
hybrid falcons. In flight, looks deep-chested
with long, broad-based wings (wingspan can
match that of Common Buzzard); at rest, wing
tips reach two-thirds of way down to tail tip,
whereas in Peregrine wing tips almost touch tip
of tail. Powerful flier.
HABITAT Breeds mainly on crags in river valleys
in tundra locations, either open or forested,
and in uplands; also on coastal cliffs and islands.
In winter ranges over wide variety of open
habitats, including coastal marshes and
moorland.
DISTRIBUTION Circumpolar in distribution,
breeding from Iceland and Scandinavia
eastwards through arctic Russia and Siberia,
Alaska, northern Canada and Greenland. White
morph birds originate from Greenland and
coastal Labrador; individuals from high arctic
populations migratory, wintering to south of
breeding range; low arctic and subarctic
populations (mainly grey morphs) generally less
dispersive.
EUROPEAN STATUS Breeds Iceland (300-400
pairs), Finland (very rare), Norway (c 30 pairs
1976) and Sweden (c 100 pairs); populations
declining. Accidental elsewhere: Austria (8);
Belgium (2: before 1873; 15 Apr 1900); Britain
(c 244+); Czech Republic (1: 1926); Denmark
(83); Faeroes (rare: only 4 since 1960); France
(15); Germany (30+); Ireland (c 101); Lithuania;
Luxembourg; Netherlands (5: 16 Oct 1849,
specimen; 3 Dec 1864, specimen; 8 Dec 1900,
specimen; 7 Dec 1909, specimen; 14 Jan-27
Mar 1987); Poland (16); Portugal (1: 15-22 Mar
1991); Switzerland (2: 28 Dec 1962-20 Jan
1963; 26 Dec 1984).

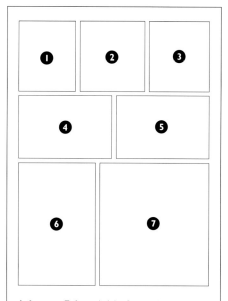

1 **Lanner Falcon** (adult of race erlangeri, Jan,
Morocco)
2 **Lanner Falcon** (adult of race erlangeri, Jan,
Morocco)
3 **Saker** (juvenile, Aug 1994, Cserepes,
Hungary)
4 **Gyr Falcon** (juvenile, Feb 1987, Eemshaven,
Netherlands)
5 **Gyr Falcon** (adult white morph, Apr 1986,
Berry Head, Devon, Britain)
6 **Gyr Falcon** (third-calendar-year white
morph, Apr 1986, Co Wexford, Ireland)
7 **Gyr Falcon** (adult white morph, Apr 1986,
Berry Head, Devon, Britain)

SORA

Porzana carolina L 20-25 cm (8-10 in)
DESCRIPTION Size of Spotted Crake and very similar in general appearance, but somewhat bulkier, with slightly longer neck and tail which is often held cocked like Water Rail's. Adult has diagnostic black mask at front of face which extends onto throat, and blackish central stripe on chestnut-brown crown, with rest of face, neck and upper breast rather plain bluish-grey but for small white spot behind eye. Lower underparts heavily patterned with white barring; undertail-coverts white, variably tipped buffish. Upperparts chestnut-brown from crown to tail, blacker feather centres more obvious on mantle and wings, and overall less densely marked with white than any Spotted Crake. Heavier and deep-based yellowish bill, lacking orange or red base of Spotted's, is further useful character; legs yellowish. Buffish juvenile has paler throat and only hint of adult's black mask; diagnostic black crown-stripe, less heavily spotted body and whitish, not buff, undertail-coverts distinguish it from same plumage of Spotted Crake. Juvenile plumage moulted before or after autumn migration, after which like adult but with less black on face (mottled grey in young female), paler grey on sides of neck and often with slight olive tinge on breast; vagrants readily distinguished from first-winter Spotted Crake by black on face and absence of copious spotting on sides of head and neck.
HABITAT Favours reedy or well-vegetated margins in freshwater and brackish marshes.
DISTRIBUTION Breeds across much of Canada except north and far west, and throughout northern USA, in west south to California. Long-distance migrant, wintering from southern USA through Caribbean and Central America into South America as far south as northern Peru.
EUROPEAN STATUS Very rare vagrant: 20 records. Britain (11); France (1: 3 Jan 1963); Ireland (1: 11 Apr 1920; also 1 at sea some months previously); Spain (3: 30 Dec 1975; 10 Apr 1988; 25 Apr 1990); Sweden (3: June 1966; 25 May-25 June 1987; 22 June-9 July 1987).

ALLEN'S GALLINULE

Porphyrula alleni L 22-24 cm (8.75-9.5 in)
DESCRIPTION Reminiscent of small, slim and brightly marked Moorhen. Plumage of adult iridescent bluish-black on head, shading to blue on neck and underparts and darkening again on belly, with contrasting white lateral undertail-coverts. Upperparts olive-green on hindneck, mantle and scapulars; upperwing shows green-tinged blue coverts and contrasting blackish-blue flight feathers. Bill red, with dark blue frontal shield (duller on non-breeding birds); legs and feet red. Juvenile has sandy-brown head and neck, with paler face, white throat and belly and otherwise buffish underparts; upperparts warm brown with paler edges, giving rather scaly appearance, and has green-blue wash on upperwing and rump. Actions

much as those of Moorhen.
HABITAT Favours dense marshy vegetation, where often rather skulking.
DISTRIBUTION Occurs across much of sub-Saharan Africa, where mostly migratory north and south of equator.
EUROPEAN STATUS Very rare vagrant: at least 22 records. Britain (1: 1 Jan 1902); Denmark (1: Dec 1929); Finland (1: 10 May 1979); France (3: Oct 1895; 29 Dec 1951; 18 Jan 1991); Germany (2: Feb 1936; 14 Dec 1986); Italy (6); Portugal (1: 31 Mar 1973; also unsubmitted record on 27 Apr 1990); Spain (7).

AMERICAN PURPLE GALLINULE

Porphyrula martinica L 30-36 cm (12-14.5 in)
DESCRIPTION Approximately size of Moorhen. Adult most closely resembles adult Allen's Gallinule in plumage, chief distinctions being browner back, greener upperwing-coverts, and all-white vent and undertail-coverts with no darker central divide (unique character among rails and crakes recorded in Europe); bare-part coloration also differs from Allen's, with deeper-based red bill tipped yellow, and yellow (not red) legs. Juvenile differs from juvenile Allen's in plainer brown upperparts which lack 'scaly' feather edges, pale buffish (not pure white) throat and dull yellow legs; wholly white rear underparts give bird a pale appearance when viewed from behind. In first-winter plumage (acquired by moult after autumn migration), separated from first-winter Moorhen by at least some green iridescence on back and blue iridescence on breast, no white flank stripe, yellower legs and lack of dark division on white undertail coverts. Actions recall Moorhen, with which it sometimes associates in home range; less skulking than Purple Swamp-hen (Gallinule) of Europe.
HABITAT Freshwater ponds, lakes, marshes and slow-moving rivers with emergent and floating vegetation; can climb up stalks and, like Moorhen, perch among branches of waterside trees.
DISTRIBUTION Breeds in south-eastern USA north to South Carolina (occasionally further north) and west to Texas, and south through West Indies and Central America to northern Argentina. Some northern birds winter within breeding range but many move south; far-flung wanderers have reached Greenland and South Africa.
EUROPEAN STATUS Very rare vagrant: seven records. Britain (1: 7 Nov 1958); Iceland (2: 5-12 Sept 1976; 26 June 1983); Italy (2: before 1883; 9 May 1890); Norway (1: autumn 1883); Switzerland (1: 1 Dec 1967).

AMERICAN COOT

Fulica americana L 31-37 cm (12.5-14.75 in)
DESCRIPTION Slightly smaller than both native European coots. Plumage similarly blackish (darkest on head and breast), but shows diagnostic white sides to undertail-coverts, like Moorhen. Head pattern also distinctive: less extensive white frontal shield is variably dull

reddish-brown above, and white bill has dark chestnut subterminal band (appears blackish in the field). In flight or when wing-stretching, reveals white tips to secondaries forming more obvious white trailing edge to wing than on Eurasian Coot. Juvenile very similar to juvenile of latter, but readily separated by white on undertail-coverts; adult-like plumage acquired from first autumn. Habits and behaviour as those of Eurasian Coot.
HABITAT Frequents lakes, ponds, rivers and marshes, but in winter more likely than Eurasian Coot to occur in saltwater habitats.
DISTRIBUTION Breeds from southern Canada south across much of USA (except parts of north-east), West Indies, Central America and into South America south to central Andes. Northernmost birds migratory, wintering south of breeding range, including eastern USA.
EUROPEAN STATUS Extreme vagrant: five records. Faeroes (1: 1 Nov 1985); Iceland (2: 7 Nov 1969; 10 Mar 1981); Ireland (1: 7 Feb-3 Apr 1981); Portugal (1: 17 Sept 1972).

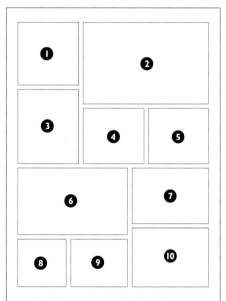

1 **Sora** (adult plumage, Oct 1985, Pagham, West Sussex, Britain)
2 **Sora** (first-winter, Oct 1991, St Mary's, Isles of Scilly, Britain)
3 **Sora** (adult plumage, Oct 1985, Pagham, West Sussex, Britain)
4 **Allen's Gallinule** (juvenile, Jan 1991, Vendée, France)
5 **Allen's Gallinule** (juvenile, Jan 1991, Vendée, France)
6 **American Purple Gallinule** (*adult, Sept, Florida, USA*)
7 **American Coot** (probably first-summer, Apr 1996*, Stodmarsh, Kent, Britain)
8 **American Coot** (probably first-summer, Apr 1996*, Stodmarsh, Kent, Britain)
9 **American Coot** (probably first-winter male, Feb 1981, Ballycotton, Co Cork, Ireland)
10 **American Coot** (probably first-summer, Apr 1996*, Stodmarsh, Kent, Britain)

SANDHILL CRANE

Grus canadensis L 88-95 cm (35-38 in)

DESCRIPTION Adult readily separable from both European cranes by lack of black markings on head and neck. Red forehead, crown and upper face distinctive; appearance otherwise unremarkable, with whitish face and foreneck and rest of plumage pale grey, variably marked with copper-brown on scapulars, wing-coverts and breast (iron staining from feeding activities may also colour parts of head and neck). In flight, upperwing shows less contrastingly dark flight feathers than Common Crane. Juvenile lacks red on head and thus confusable with juvenile of latter species, best distinctions from which include browner upperparts, contrast between upperwing-coverts and flight feathers, voice and structure. Size approaches that of Common Crane, but build somewhat slimmer and tail shorter, with smaller head and slimmer grey (not yellow) bill.

VOICE Call given as a trumpeting, rolling and far-carrying *gurruk-gok-gok*, lower in pitch than Common Crane's.

HABITAT Found in wide range of open habitats, including tundra, wet prairie, marshes, lakes and rivers; on passage and in winter also in fields.

DISTRIBUTION Breeds in USA in north, north-west and south-east, also in Cuba, and from northern Canada west through much of Alaska to north-east Siberia. Winters from California and southern USA to Central America.

EUROPEAN STATUS Extreme vagrant: five records involving four birds. Britain (2: 26-27 Apr 1981; 17-27 Sept 1991, same as Netherlands); Faeroes (1: 14 Oct 1980); Ireland (1: 12-14 Sept 1905); Netherlands (1: 28-30 Sept 1991, same as Britain).

DEMOISELLE CRANE

Anthropoides virgo L 90-100 cm (36-40 in)

DESCRIPTION On ground, appears slimmer and more elegant than Common Crane, with less prominent 'bustle' at rear end. Adult paler and more uniformly grey, with conspicuous white tufts behind eye, and black on sides of head and neck extending lower down foreneck. Juvenile has duller plumage and head pattern, with shorter white ear tufts. Smaller size of little use in separation from Common Crane in flight, when shorter-necked appearance, lighter flight action and voice are most helpful characters.

VOICE Call is higher-pitched than Common Crane's, a useful distinction with migrating birds.

HABITAT Breeds in steppe country and mountain plateaux near water; in winter also around lakes and rivers.

DISTRIBUTION Probably still breeds in tiny numbers in Morocco and possibly Algeria, but principal range extends from eastern Turkey and northern Black Sea region eastwards across Central Asia. Regular on passage in Cyprus en route to wintering grounds in

western Ethiopia, Sudan and Chad; eastern populations winter mainly in Pakistan and India, also parts of South-East Asia.

EUROPEAN STATUS Rare vagrant: some records from Europe (eg Austria in 1989, Britain in 1993, and others from Germany, Netherlands and Norway) considered likely to relate to birds of captive origin. Bulgaria; Denmark (6); Finland (7); Germany (1: May 1837); Greece (3: 5 Apr 1859; 2 May 1956; c 1986); Hungary (4 accepted records, but reported almost annually); Italy (6); Netherlands (1: 30 Apr 1993); Norway (1: 20-27 May 1966); Poland (3: 18th century; 11 Aug 1911; Apr 1912); Romania (formerly bred); Slovakia (3 records of 14 birds: Dec 1871; 28 Mar 1953; 4 Dec 1984); Spain (status unclear: no recent records); Sweden (10); former Yugoslavia.

HOUBARA BUSTARD

Chlamydotis undulata L 55-65 cm (22-26 in)

DESCRIPTION Intermediate in size between Great and Little Bustards, but proportionately less bulky than former, with longer and more slender neck. Adult generally pale in appearance except for contrasting black stripe down sides of neck and breast, where bordered above by white. Otherwise head, neck and breast pale sandy-grey, fading to whitish on face and foreneck, with white tuft on crown and white lower underparts. Upperparts slightly browner in tone, appearing loosely spotted with black and barred darker on relatively long tail. In flight, wing shows lesser and median coverts as mantle, but greater coverts are white and flight feathers black, with bold white patches on primary coverts and leading edge of hand. Female and juvenile much as adult male but with black neck 'frills' less developed. If disturbed, may run at speed or take to air on long, narrow wings with shallow beats.

HABITAT Occurs in *Artemisia* steppe, semi-desert and arid stony plains, often with sparse vegetation.

DISTRIBUTION Formerly more widespread resident in North Africa from Canary Islands and Mauretania discontinuously east to Jordan, but numbers much reduced through excessive hunting and now probably local or absent in significant percentage of this range. Migratory populations from Central Asia, wintering from north-west India west to Iraq and northern Arabia, similarly overhunted.

EUROPEAN STATUS Rare vagrant: most records probably relate to migratory Central Asian and Middle Eastern race *macqueenii* (recently mooted as possible distinct species), but rarely recorded in recent times. Belgium (3: Nov 1842; Dec 1844; 13 Dec 1845); Czech Republic (1: 6 Sept 1889); Britain (5: 7 Oct 1847; 5 Oct 1892; 17 Oct 1896; 24 Oct 1898; 21 Nov-29 Dec 1962); Denmark (1: Oct 1892); Finland (1: 19 Sept 1861); France (3: Dec 1807; Feb 1833; 1910); Germany (8); Greece (1: June 1841); Italy (13); Latvia (1: Sept 1880); Luxembourg (1); Netherlands

(1: 10 Dec 1850); Poland (5: 1800; 1811; Nov 1848; Dec 1862; 12 Dec 1977); Romania; Slovenia (1: 12 Nov 1970); Spain (2: both prior to 1871); Sweden (3: Feb 1847; Oct 1933; Oct 1974); Switzerland (4: 20 May 1839; 18 Nov 1840; 1864; 18 Nov 1916); former Yugoslavia (2: Nov 1934; Nov 1970).

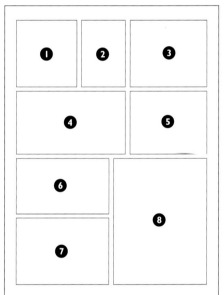

1 Sandhill Crane (first-summer moulting to second-winter, Sept 1991, Exnaboe, Shetland, Britain)
2 Sandhill Crane (first-summer moulting to second-winter, Sept 1991, Paesens-Moddersgat, Netherlands)
3 Sandhill Crane (first-summer moulting to second-winter, Sept 1991, Exnaboe, Shetland, Britain)
4 Demoiselle Crane (with Common Cranes, July 1993, Hortobágy, Hungary)
5 Demoiselle Crane (adult, Sept 1993*, Spurn, Humberside, Britain)
6 Demoiselle Crane (first-summer, May 1994, Maaninka Kinnulanlahti, Finland)
7 Houbara Bustard (probably Asian form *macqueenii*, Nov 1962, Walberswick, Suffolk, Britain)
8 Houbara Bustard (probably Asian form *macqueenii*, Nov 1962, Walberswick, Suffolk, Britain)

CREAM-COLOURED COURSER

Cursorius cursor L 22-24 cm (8.75-9.5 in)
DESCRIPTION Unmistakable. Adult has bluish-grey hindcrown shading to blackish triangular patch at rear, above white supercilia and black rear eye-stripes which meet in double V-shape on nape. Plumage otherwise unmarked sandy-buff, becoming slightly paler on underparts; at distance appears uniformly pale. In relaxed but fast flight, long, pointed wings reveal black primaries and primary coverts on upperside, contrastingly all-dark underside and narrow white trailing edge on secondaries; also has narrow black subterminal band on white-tipped tail. Quickly moulted juvenile plumage is similar to adult's, but with weaker, paler head pattern and more scaly upperparts. Longish dark bill is noticeably decurved; legs creamy or off-white. Stop-start feeding action recalls a plover; often runs away at speed if disturbed. Usually solitary, but occasionally in loose parties.
VOICE Call is a sharp, whistled *quit* or, in flight, *praak-praak*.
HABITAT Typically inhabits arid, open semi-desert and desert fringe with little or no vegetation; European vagrants have been found in various open habitats including sandy estuaries and ploughed fields.
DISTRIBUTION Breeds from Cape Verde and Canary Islands through North Africa, parts of Middle East and northern Arabia to south-west Central Asia. Northern birds at least partially migratory, wintering south to Gambia in west and India in east. Additional population in north-east Africa latterly treated as conspecific with Burchell's Courser *C rufus* of southern Africa.
EUROPEAN STATUS Frequent vagrant. Austria (2: 10 Oct 1899; 25 Sept 1991); Belgium (1: 27 Aug 1881); Britain (32); Channel Islands (1: 19 Oct 1896); Czech Republic (3: 2 May 1891; 29 Aug 1893; 6 Aug 1929); Denmark (4: Nov 1881; Nov 1888; Oct 1953; Dec 1955); Finland (2: 20 Oct 1893; 25 Sept 1989); France (23); Germany (26); Greece (4: 3 Apr 1963; 6 Apr 1977; 23 Apr 1990; 31 Mar-4 Apr 1993); Ireland (1: Dec 1952 or Jan 1953); Italy; Netherlands (2: 18 Oct 1933; Oct 1986); Norway (1: 16 Oct 1915); Portugal (2: 6 May 1987; 19 Mar 1993); Slovenia (1: 3 Oct 1976); Spain (10+); Sweden (3: 26 Oct 1905; 16 Oct 1933; 4-5 Sept 1942); Switzerland (5); former Yugoslavia (5).

ORIENTAL PRATINCOLE

Glareola maldivarum L 23-24 cm (9.25-9.5 in)
DESCRIPTION Very like Collared and Black-winged Pratincoles, in adult plumage with plain darkish brown head, neck, upper breast, flanks and upperparts, neat black-and-white-edged creamy 'bib' on cheeks and throat which extends back to below eye, white belly and rump, and white-edged blackish tail. Shares some characters of both European pratincoles, with chestnut-red underwing-coverts of Collared but more uniformly darker grey-brown upperwing with dark trailing edge of

Black-winged (Collared has contrastingly darker primaries and white-tipped secondaries). Additionally, has much shorter tail-streamers than both species, producing shorter and more shallowly forked tail; at rest, tip of tail falls well short of primary tips (at rest both Collared and Black-winged Pratincoles have tip of tail as long as, or longer than, primary tips, though beware of effects of wear). Unlike other two species, Oriental usually has orangey-buff wash on lower breast. On close views, black line below eye separating buff throat from brown sides of head is clearly thicker than the fine line shown by Collared and Black-winged. Quickly-moulted juvenile plumage very like that of congeners, but shares with Black-winged narrower and buffy-white tips to secondaries (broader and whiter on Collared), some of which retained into first winter. Habits and actions as for those species.
VOICE Range of tern-like calls, including sharp *kyik* or *chik*, apparently similar to those of Collared Pratincole.
HABITAT Similar to other pratincoles, breeding on open flat areas with sparse vegetation, often dried-mud margins of wetlands, and on migration also in marshes and cultivated areas.
DISTRIBUTION Breeds from northern India east through South-East Asia to eastern China. Some Indian and most east Asian birds are migratory, wintering southern India, Indonesia, New Guinea and north-west Australia. In addition to European vagrancy, has wandered west to Cyprus, where once recorded in mixed flock with both European pratincoles.
EUROPEAN STATUS Extreme vagrant: five records. Britain (5: 22 June-8 July and c 6 Aug-11 Oct 1981; 21 or 22 June-3 Oct 1988; 14 May-21 June and 13 July-17 Aug 1993; 29-30 Aug 1993; 4 and 19 Sept 1993).

BLACK-WINGED PRATINCOLE

Glareola nordmanni L 23-26 cm (9.25-10.5 in)
DESCRIPTION Plumages much as for Oriental Pratincole (see above), but shows diagnostic combination of black underwing-coverts and, in adult, lack of white trailing edge to secondaries which separates it from both that species and Collared Pratincole. Tail obviously longer than in Oriental, with length of streamers much as for Collared; at rest wing tips clearly project beyond tail tip. Like Oriental, Black-winged usually shows less red at base of bill than Collared, but differs from both in black of lores often intermixing into crown and forehead, creating in some a darker-faced impression. Also differs subtly in slightly larger size, broader wings and longer legs. All characters on these three species, however, often very difficult to ascertain in the field. Has hybridised with Collared Pratincole in Europe.
VOICE Calls resemble those of Collared, but are lower in pitch and distinguishable with care.
HABITAT Similar to Collared, among colonies of which pairs have bred in Europe, but often in steppe areas near water with slightly taller vegetation.
DISTRIBUTION Breeds from south-easternmost

Europe (where declining) eastwards to Central Asia. Migrates through Middle East to reach wintering grounds in west-central and southern Africa.
EUROPEAN STATUS Breeds in very small numbers in Romania (up to 10 pairs). Accidental elsewhere: Austria (4: 14-27 Sept 1967; 5 Sept 1971; 30 July 1982; 29 May 1994); Belgium (1: 30 Aug 1949); Britain (27); Bulgaria (has bred); Czech Republic (2: 15 Sept 1951; 12 Nov 1970); Denmark (4: May 1930; Sept 1934; June 1980; June 1987); Finland (14); France (13); Germany (15: bred in 1966); Greece (fewer than 20); Hungary (has bred at least four times); Iceland (3: 7-8 Oct 1979; 8 Oct 1983; 11 June 1987); Ireland (2: 22 Aug 1953; 5 Aug 1974); Italy (6); Netherlands (21); Norway (2: 3 Aug 1884; 3-7 June 1974); Poland (9); Slovakia (2: 28 May 1983; 10 Oct 1990); Spain (1: 25 Apr 1992); Sweden (12); Switzerland (1: 17 June 1974); former Yugoslavia (1: 31 May 1990).

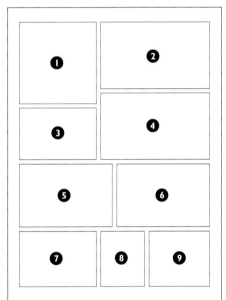

1 **Cream-coloured Courser** (adult, Sept 1989, Kullaa, Finland)
2 **Cream-coloured Courser** (first-winter, Oct 1984, Hadleigh, Essex, Britain)
3 **Cream-coloured Courser** (first-winter, Oct 1986, Noordholland, Netherlands)
4 **Oriental Pratincole** (May 1993, Gimingham, Norfolk, Britain)
5 **Oriental Pratincole** (June 1981, Old Hall Marshes, Essex, Britain)
6 **Oriental Pratincole** (May 1993, Gimingham, Norfolk, Britain)
7 **Black-winged Pratincole** (first-winter, Oct 1992, Davidstow, Cornwall, Britain)
8 **Black-winged Pratincole** (probably first-winter, Sept 1993, Great Livermere, Suffolk, Britain)
9 **Black-winged Pratincole** (juvenile, Aug 1983, Maasvlakte, Netherlands)

SEMIPALMATED PLOVER

Charadrius semipalmatus L 17-19 cm
(6.75-7.5 in)
DESCRIPTION Nearctic counterpart of Ringed
Plover, from which extremely difficult to
separate in all plumages. Diagnostic character
of partial webbing between all three fore-toes
(Ringed is webbed only between outer and
middle toe) is usually difficult to assess in the
field. On juveniles, best feature is dark loral
stripe which narrows at front to meet bill
above gape, leaving white 'wedge' between
dark lores and gape, whereas on juvenile
Ringed broader dark loral stripe meets bill at
gape; this distinction is less consistent with
adult Semipalmateds, however, which are
often more extensively black on lores (like
Ringed). Other differences, often hard to
determine, include shorter white wing-bar
extending less onto outer primaries (though
juveniles of both species may have more
extensively white wing-bars), shorter and less
prominent whitish supercilium, indistinct and
narrow yellowish orbital ring (usually lacking in
Ringed), subtly narrower white collar between
crown and mantle, in breeding adult browner
rear ear-coverts and narrower black breast
band, duller-coloured legs, and marginally
smaller, more compact and rounder-headed
appearance, with slightly shorter and stubbier
bill. Beware misinterpretation of these
characters, however, and overlap in at least
some of them with Ringed Plover, particularly
of smaller, darker *tundrae* race, which has
previously been taken for Semipalmated Plover
in Europe. Ageing sequence and actions as for
Ringed Plover.
VOICE Call quite unlike that of Ringed Plover,
a distinctive, almost monosyllabic, rising *shu-
wick* reminiscent of a quiet Spotted Redshank.
HABITAT As European congener, favours
sandy and muddy margins of wetlands, coastal
marshes, estuaries and beaches.
DISTRIBUTION Breeds in North America from
Nova Scotia west across northern Canada to
Alaska. Long-distance migrant, wintering from
South Carolina and California southwards
throughout Caribbean, Central America and
much of coastal South America to Patagonia.
EUROPEAN STATUS Extreme vagrant: three
records. Britain (1: 9 Oct-9 Nov 1978); Spain
(2: 17 July 1988; 13 May-15 Aug 1990).

KILLDEER

Charadrius vociferus L 23-26 cm (9.25-10.5 in)
DESCRIPTION Large, long-tailed Nearctic
plover showing diagnostic double breast band
at all ages. Adult male in breeding plumage has
black mask with white forehead extending
under eye, white rear supercilium, orange eye-
ring, brown crown, nape and upperparts
(latter often with rufous fringes), and white
collar and underparts with double black breast
band and browner intervening area at sides. In
flight, displays white wing-bars across blackish
greater coverts and flight feathers and has
striking chestnut-orange back, rump and

uppertail-coverts above long, graduated,
white-edged blackish tail. Breeding female as
male, but often with browner mask and breast
bands and duller eye-ring. In winter,
upperparts fringed paler and black areas often
browner. Juvenile like non-breeding adult, but
with buffer fringing on upperparts and
indistinct dark subterminal markings; much as
adult by first winter. Relatively long bill is
black; legs greyish. Noisy and conspicuous
species, but usually solitary.
VOICE Call is a characteristic, penetrating *kill-
dee* or similar, often repeated.
HABITAT Inhabits wide variety of open
agricultural land, uplands, meadows and
wetlands.
DISTRIBUTION Breeds from south-east Alaska
and southern Canada south to Mexico,
wintering from New York and southern
British Columbia south to northern South
America. Also resident in West Indies, Peru
and northern Chile.
EUROPEAN STATUS Rare vagrant: unlike many
Nearctic waders, occurrences in western
Europe are often in winter. Britain (38*);
Channel Islands (2: 1 Jan 1971; Sept 1973);
Faeroes (1: Sept 1939); France (6); Hungary
(2: 1 Nov-30 Dec 1986; 8 Aug 1992); Iceland
(3: 19 Mar 1939; 15 Dec 1970; 17-18 Oct
1980); Ireland (12); Norway (1: 10 Apr 1974);
Romania (1: Sept 1985); Spain (1: 8-18 Sept
1988); Switzerland (2: 4-8 May 1974; 5-26 Dec
1977).

LESSER SAND PLOVER

Charadrius mongolus L 19-21 cm (7.5-8.5 in)
DESCRIPTION Adult male in breeding plumage
has black face mask and forehead (latter
variably whiter in eastern races) and sandy-
brown crown above chestnut collar and breast
band which isolate neatly demarcated black-
edged white throat from white underparts.
Upperparts plain sandy-brown, tail finely edged
white; flight feathers blackish-brown with
white bar. Female has black areas of male
toned browner. In non-breeding plumage,
adult recalls larger, longer-legged and longer-
billed non-breeding Ringed Plover, with brown
head, patches on breast sides and pale-fringed
upperparts, and white forehead, throat and
underparts, but lacks white collar. Juvenile like
non-breeding adult, but with extensive sandy-
buff fringing above and buffy breast patches;
difficult to separate after first autumn. Bill
black; legs usually grey. For differences from
Greater Sand Plover, with which Lesser Sand
Plover often associates (ranges overlap
considerably), see that species.
VOICE Typical call is variously given as a short
and sharp *chitik*, or *kiripp*, recalling call of
drake Pintail.
HABITAT Nests mainly on upland plateaux; at
other times chiefly around tidal mudflats and
sandy beaches.
DISTRIBUTION Breeds in Central Asia, parts of
eastern Siberia and Kamchatka. Long-distance
migrant, wintering mainly around Pacific and
Indian Ocean coasts and islands from South

China Sea, Indonesia and eastern Australia
west to Persian Gulf and eastern and southern
Africa.
EUROPEAN STATUS Very rare vagrant: eight
records. Austria (1: 17 Sept 1964); Denmark
(1: 2-3 July 1988); Norway (1: 22 July 1973);
Poland (1: 17 June 1977); Spain (1: 21 June
1981); Sweden (2: 29-30 June 1988; 5-13 Aug
1993); former Yugoslavia (1: 24 Apr 1987*,
photographed).

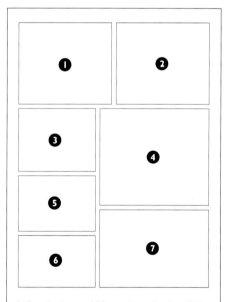

1 **Semipalmated Plover** (juvenile, Oct 1978,
St Agnes, Isles of Scilly, Britain)
2 **Killdeer** (probably juvenile, Oct 1982, St
Martin's, Isles of Scilly, Britain)
3 **Killdeer** (age uncertain, Dec 1993*, Anglesey,
Britain)
4 **Killdeer** (probably first-winter, Nov 1989, St
Mary's, Isles of Scilly, Britain)
5 **Lesser Sand Plover** (adult, Aug 1993,
Öland, Sweden)
6 **Lesser Sand Plover** (adult summer, Apr
1987, Petrovac, former Yugoslavia)
7 **Lesser Sand Plover** (adult, Aug 1993,
Öland, Sweden)

GREATER SAND PLOVER

Charadrius leschenaultii L 22-25 cm (8.75-10 in)
DESCRIPTION Generally larger, heavier-billed and longer-legged than Lesser Sand Plover, but very similar in all plumages and smallest individuals of shorter-billed western race *columbinus* not always separable. Chief differences include bulkier build, with longer bill and larger head (often with flatter forehead) creating front-heavy impression, more horizontal stance, wing-bar which broadens on primaries (more even in width on Lesser), paler legs which project beyond tail tip in flight, and more white at sides and tip of tail. In breeding plumage, Greater typically has narrower breast band, more often some chestnut on mantle and, on some, cinnamon-tinged underparts. Feeding action also cited as useful distinction: Greater runs longer distances and pauses for longer than Lesser when searching for prey items.
VOICE Calls are similar to Lesser Sand Plover, but usually softer, longer and deeper; commonest flight call is a soft trilling *prrrirt*, recalling Turnstone.
HABITAT Nests on dry, open terrain near water; coastal at other times, favouring sandy beaches, mudflats and estuaries.
DISTRIBUTION Breeds locally in central Turkey and Middle East, and eastwards across Central Asia to Lake Baikal and Mongolia. Winter range much as Lesser Sand Plover's, but regular in Middle East and on passage west to Cyprus.
EUROPEAN STATUS Rare vagrant: most records fall between May and August. Austria (1: 13 June 1979); Belgium (5: 21-23 July 1954; 27 Sept 1975; 21-25 and 29 July 1972; 23 July 1986; 14-15 July 1993); Britain (11); Bulgaria (1: June 1984); Denmark (1: 4-5 May 1994); Finland (3: 9 June 1964; 19-22 June 1971; 6-7 May 1994); France (4: 21 June 1969; 6 May 1970; 17 May 1980; 17 July 1994); Germany (2: 15 Sept 1931; 2-3 July 1988); Greece (11-15); Hungary (1: 7-14 July 1992); Italy (1: 22-23 July 1994); Netherlands (5: 20 July 1977; Aug 1984; Aug 1985; 10 Aug 1993; 4 Sept 1994); Norway (2: 5-7 Aug 1984; 25 June 1985); Poland (4: 20 Sept 1961; 4-12 Sept 1978; 16-21 Oct 1983; 5-8 Apr 1984); Spain (1: 25-29 Aug 1993); Sweden (5: 26-27 June 1938; 9 Aug 1954; 17-21 May 1961; 4-12 July 1981; 26 July 1990).

CASPIAN PLOVER

Charadrius asiaticus L 18-20 cm (7.25-8 in)
DESCRIPTION In size and general appearance recalls Lesser and Greater Sand Plovers, but has elegant, slimline structure and more attenuated rear end. Adult male in breeding plumage has diagnostic combination of mainly white face and broad chestnut breast band which is sharply demarcated from white underparts by narrow blackish border. Crown, nape and broad rear eye-stripe brown, forming surround to conspicuous white supercilium; upperparts also brown from mantle to tail, which is edged whiter and darkens towards tip.

In flight, shows short narrow wing-bar centred on inner primaries and darker brown flight feathers. Breeding female has browner breast band and yellowish tint to face; non-breeding adults drabber still, with paler breast band and weaker head pattern. Juvenile similar to non-breeding adult, but upperpart feathers have darker centres and rufous-buff or buff fringes, and breast band is mottled grey-brown; much as adult from first autumn. Bill black; longish legs dull yellowish-grey.
VOICE Commonest call is a loud *tyup*; in flight, utters a sharp *kwitt*.
HABITAT Frequents dry, open country, breeding on steppes and wintering on short grasslands, fields or dried margins of lakeshores; occasionally in wetter habitats outside breeding season.
DISTRIBUTION Breeds from eastern Black Sea region eastwards to Central Asia as far as Lake Balkhash, wintering extensively in eastern and southern Africa.
EUROPEAN STATUS Very rare vagrant: 15 records. Britain (3: 22 May 1890, two, one of which shot; 21 May 1988; 12-13 July 1988); Bulgaria (1: 1879); France (3: 20 Aug 1980; Apr 1985; 6 Aug 1988); Germany (2: 16 Nov 1850; 19 May 1859); Greece (1: 23 July 1988); Italy (3: 12 Nov 1887; 20 Nov 1898; 30 Mar 1978); Norway (1: 9-15 June 1978); Romania (1: May 1979).

AMERICAN GOLDEN PLOVER

Pluvialis dominicus L 24-28 cm (9.5-11.25 in)
DESCRIPTION Smaller New World counterpart of Eurasian Golden Plover, and formerly treated as conspecific with Pacific Golden Plover as Lesser Golden Plover. Pattern of breeding adult generally recalls Eurasian Golden, but black on underparts usually extends over flanks and ventral region and white border terminates in prominent lobe-shaped patch at sides of breast. Upperparts rather darker and less patterned with gold, and has dusky grey, not mainly white, underwing (see also Pacific Golden Plover below). Non-breeding adult appears more grey-brown than either of congeners, with more prominent whitish supercilium. Juvenile similarly plumaged, but with darker grey mantle (with less spotting on upperparts than juvenile Pacific Golden), bolder and whiter supercilium and more mottled underparts; first-summers have little or no black below. In size and build intermediate between Eurasian and Pacific Golden, but distinctly longer wings than both those species give American Golden a more attenuated appearance. Dark grey legs do not project beyond tail in flight.
VOICE Call is a short *kweep*; in flight, utters a clear, variable and whistling *kluilip* or *kuee-eep*.
HABITAT Nests on tundra beyond tree limit; on migration and in winter in fields and short grasslands, less often in coastal wetland areas.
DISTRIBUTION Breeds across arctic North America from Baffin Island to Alaska, where range overlaps with that of Pacific Golden Plover. Long-distance migrant, wintering in

central South America mainly from Bolivia and southern Brazil to central Argentina.
EUROPEAN STATUS Frequent vagrant: total number of records given for this and for Pacific Golden Plover omit significant number of individuals not specifically identified (including all birds of both species in some countries, eg 5 *dominicus/fulva* in Poland). Britain (c 147); Channel Islands (1: 2-5 June 1989); Czech Republic (1: 18 Sept-4 Oct 1981); France (14); Germany (2: 20 Dec 1847; 7-8 May 1992); Iceland (8); Ireland (40); Netherlands (6); Norway (2: 19 June 1985; 23-29 June 1986); Portugal (1: 7 Oct 1989); Spain (8); Sweden (8).

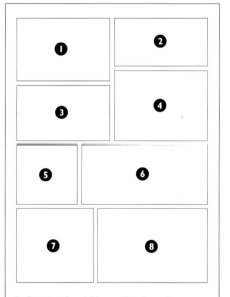

1 **Greater Sand Plover** (female or first-summer, Aug 1992, Cley, Norfolk, Britain)
2 **Greater Sand Plover** (adult, Aug 1991, River Don, Aberdeen, Britain [this individual often considered to be Lesser Sand Plover])
3 **Greater Sand Plover** (female or first-summer, July 1988, Walney, Cumbria, Britain)
4 **Caspian Plover** (female, June 1996*, Skellbery, Shetland, Britain)
5 **Caspian Plover** (adult male, May 1988, St Agnes, Isles of Scilly, Britain)
6 **American Golden Plover** (juvenile, left, with juvenile Eurasian Golden Plover, Oct 1993, St Mary's, Isles of Scilly, Britain)
7 **American Golden Plover** (moulting adult, Oct 1994, Texel, Netherlands)
8 **American Golden Plover** (juvenile, Oct 1991, St Mary's, Isles of Scilly, Britain)

PACIFIC GOLDEN PLOVER

Pluvialis fulva L 23-26 cm (9.25-10.5 in)
DESCRIPTION Very like American Golden Plover but marginally smaller, slimmer and shorter-winged, with longer legs and bill. Differs in breeding plumage in having less white at sides of breast which continues through broken black markings on flanks (rarely all-black on some males) to undertail, recalling Eurasian Golden Plover; also has narrower black band above bill. Additionally, upperparts more heavily spangled with gold than on American Golden, again recalling Eurasian Golden, but readily distinguished from latter in all plumages by smaller and more slender build and, in flight, by dusky underwing and legs projecting beyond tail tip. Non-breeding adult appears generally yellowish-buff with white belly and undertail, less grey-brown than American Golden, and with weaker supercilium. Juvenile like non-breeding adult, but buff-suffused breast mottled brownish-yellow and grey-brown; difficult to age from first autumn, but young birds often become darker-mantled with wear.
VOICE Call sharper than American Golden Plover's, a distinctive *chu-wit* like Spotted Redshank's.
HABITAT Nests on arctic tundra beyond tree limit; at other times more often in coastal and wetland habitats than American Golden, but also occurs on open grasslands and fields.
DISTRIBUTION Breeds in arctic Siberia from Yamal Peninsula east to western Alaska, where nests alongside American Golden Plover. Powerful long-distance migrant, wintering mainly on Pacific and Indian Ocean coasts and islands south to New Zealand and west to eastern Arabia and East Africa, with smaller numbers reaching east to California.
EUROPEAN STATUS Frequent vagrant: fewer records than American Golden Plover, but more frequently recorded than that species in much of continental Europe. Individuals identified only as *fulva/dominicus* are not included in the following totals. Belgium (1: 16 Sept 1992); Britain (24); Denmark (3: Aug 1982; July 1989; 28 July 1992); Finland (25); France (1: 17 July 1994); Germany (9); Greece (3: 15 Feb 1963; 12 Apr 1985; Apr 1989); Ireland (6); Italy (10); Netherlands (15 individuals); Poland (4); Spain (2: 1877; 1982); Sweden (20 individuals).

SPUR-WINGED LAPWING

Hoplopterus spinosus L 25-27 cm (10-10.75 in)
DESCRIPTION Unmistakable. Adult has black cap from forehead to nape, white collar and sides of face below eye, and narrow black throat stripe linking cap and bill to wholly black breast, flanks and upper belly; lower belly and ventral region white. Upperparts pale brown from mantle to upper rump and on upperwing-coverts, latter separated from blackish-brown primaries and tips to outer secondaries by narrow white band; appears even more pied from underside in flight, when reveals all-white

underwing-coverts and black flight feathers. Lower rump white, tail black. Juvenile similar to adult, but with pale fringes on upperparts and black areas of head and underparts tinged brownish and flecked with white; ageing difficult from first autumn. Rather hunched, neckless appearance and long black legs create distinctive jizz.
VOICE Commonest call on breeding grounds is a loud, repeated *kik*.
HABITAT Freshwater and brackish wetlands with sparsely vegetated sandy or muddy fringes; also feeds on irrigated farmland.
DISTRIBUTION Summer visitor to Greece and Turkey, and resident in the Middle East, the Nile valley and across sub-Saharan Africa discontinuously from Ethiopia to Senegal and south to Zaire. Migrants regular in Crete and Cyprus; winter quarters presumed within range in Africa.
EUROPEAN STATUS Breeds Greece (first bred in 1959; 32-45 pairs 1993). Accidental elsewhere, though escapes occasionally also recorded (eg in Belgium, Britain and Germany): Bulgaria (1: 1962); Czech Republic (1: 21 Sept 1989); Hungary (1: 17-24 Oct 1993); Italy (1: 9 Sept 1989); Romania (2: 1964; Aug 1977); Spain (1: May 1956, three); Sweden (2 records of 3 birds: 28 May-Aug 1989; 23 May 1989); former Yugoslavia (5).

SOCIABLE LAPWING

Vanellus gregaria L 27-30 cm (10.75-12 in)
DESCRIPTION Breeding adult readily identified by plain grey-brown plumage with black crown and eye-stripe, broad white supercilium and forehead, warm buffy cheeks, black-and-chestnut belly and white ventral region. In flight, black outer wing, white triangle on secondaries and grey-brown coverts recall upperwing pattern of Sabine's Gull; lower back, rump and tail white, latter with narrow black subterminal band. In winter, somewhat drabber, with weaker head pattern and pale belly. Juvenile resembles non-breeding adult, but pale fringes and dark subterminal marks on upperparts and streaks on sides of underparts give more patterned appearance; much as adult by first winter, but first-summers lack dark belly patch. Bill and relatively long legs black. Vagrants to Europe often associate with Northern Lapwing flocks.
VOICE Utters harsh, rasping *etch-etch-etch* when breeding, but generally silent at other times.
HABITAT Steppe breeder in zone between grassland and sagebrush, often in vicinity of water; in winter often on ploughed fields and stubble.
DISTRIBUTION Summer visitor to central Russia and Kazakhstan south towards Caspian and Aral Seas and Lake Balkhash. Eastern birds winter in western India, Pakistan and Baluchistan, western birds in Iraq, Israel, locally in Arabia and more widely in north-east Africa.
EUROPEAN STATUS Frequent vagrant. Austria (3: 2 Apr 1982; 20 Mar 1990; 24 Oct 1994); Belgium (5: 8-13 Apr 1962; 7-8 June 1962; 5 Apr 1966; 25 May 1970; 18 Apr 1993); Britain

(34); Czech Republic (5: 2 Oct 1971; 28 Mar 1981; 2 Apr 1985; 12 Apr 1985; 27 Sept-10 Oct 1986); Denmark (2: 1857; June 1930); Finland (5: 28 Apr-8 May 1951; 4 Aug 1988; 6 May-13 June 1990; 9 June 1992; 8 May 1994); France (34); Germany (26); Greece (2: 3 Jan 1868; 29 Apr 1986); Hungary (3: 29 Sept 1900; 24-26 Apr 1992; 9 Oct 1992); Ireland (3: 1 Aug 1899; c 25 Dec 1909; Nov-Dec 1985); Italy (records include flock of 12 on 16 Sept 1990); Netherlands (27); Poland (6); Romania; Slovakia (2: 1-14 May 1963; 2-12 Apr 1971); Slovenia (2: 25 Mar 1967; 3 Apr 1983); Spain (8); Switzerland (6); former Yugoslavia (2: Mar 1967; Apr 1983).

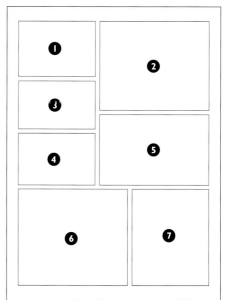

1 **Pacific Golden Plover** (adult, Aug 1990, Cley, Norfolk, Britain)
2 **Pacific Golden Plover** (juvenile, Sept 1990, Korsnas, Finland)
3 **Pacific Golden Plover** (adult, June 1993, Naerlandstranden, Norway)
4 **Spur-winged Lapwing** (*adult, Nov, Yemen*)
5 **Sociable Lapwing** (adult summer, Apr 1993, Holkham, Norfolk, Britain)
6 **Sociable Lapwing** (first-summer or adult moulting from summer into winter plumage, Aug 1982, Schiermonnikoog, Netherlands)
7 **Sociable Lapwing** (adult summer, Apr 1990, Benschop, Netherlands)

WHITE-TAILED LAPWING

Vanellus leucura L 26-29 cm (10.5-11.5 in)
DESCRIPTION Slightly smaller than Sociable Plover, and readily distinguished in all plumages by plainer head with longer black bill and by strikingly long yellow legs which project well beyond tip of tail in flight. Plumage of adult generally pale brown, toned lilac or grey above and becoming creamier on sides and front of face; buffer neck shades to grey on lower breast, above pinkish belly and white undertail-coverts. In flight, reveals similar upperwing pattern to Sociable Plover's, but white on secondaries extends onto primary coverts and is separated from brown secondary coverts by narrow black bar; rump and tail white. Juvenile has crown mottled darker, 'blotchy' dark-centred upperpart feathers, indistinct tail band, and paler underparts mottled grey-brown; from first autumn much as adult. Unusually for a lapwing, often wades in water and will submerge head to feed.
VOICE When breeding utters various calls reminiscent of Northern Lapwing, but otherwise largely silent.
HABITAT Generally in or near shallow margins of lakes, marshes and slow-moving watercourses; in breeding areas often loosely associates with Black-winged Stilts and Collared Pratincoles.
DISTRIBUTION Breeds from Caspian Sea east to Lake Balkhash, locally in northern Iran, and in Iraq; probably also breeds regularly in small numbers in Syria, and has bred south-east Turkey. Northern birds migratory, wintering chiefly in north-western India, Pakistan and Baluchistan, and in north-east Africa.
EUROPEAN STATUS Very rare vagrant: 22 records, nine of which relate to one influx in 1975. Austria (2: 7-8 Aug 1960, 29 Mar-30 Apr 1975); Britain (4: 12-18 July 1975; 3 July 1979; 21 May 1984; 24-25 May 1984); Finland (2: 11-16 May 1975; 15 May 1990); France (1: 25 Nov 1840); Germany (2: 16 July 1987; 25 May 1989); Greece (4: 14 Apr 1958; Aug 1966; 24 Apr 1986; 6 Apr 1994); Hungary (1: 23 May 1975); Italy (1: 19 Apr 1975); Netherlands (3: 9-12 July 1975; June 1984; July 1984); Poland (1: 30 Apr 1975); Romania (1: May 1977); Sweden (1: 10 May 1975).

GREAT KNOT

Calidris tenuirostris L 26-28 cm (10.5-11.25 in)
DESCRIPTION The largest calidrid; appreciably bigger and bulkier than Knot. Breeding adult easily distinguished by lack of red on head and underparts, which have white ground colour overlaid by dense black streaks on crown, face and neck, spots on breast and chevrons on flanks. Upperparts blackish or grey with whitish fringing, except for at least a few diagnostic bright chestnut scapulars, tipped black in fresh plumage. In flight, shows narrower white wing-bar than Knot, with white (not barred) rump and uppertail-coverts and dark grey (not pale grey) tail. Grey-and-white non-breeding adult similar to Knot, but separated by more streaked appearance of crown, mantle and breast, paler lores, less distinct supercilium and heavier bill. Juvenile differs from non-breeding adult in darker crown and pale-fringed upperparts and in streaked and spotted buff-washed breast. Black bill is longer, deeper-based and more tapering than Knot's; legs darker greenish-grey. Gregarious; often among Knots and other shore waders in home range.
VOICE Typically silent, but has Knot-like *nyut-nyut* flight call.
HABITAT Nests on open uplands with sparse vegetation; on migration and in winter mainly on tidal mudflats, estuaries and coasts.
DISTRIBUTION Breeds north-east Siberia. Long-distance migrant, wintering Pakistan (a few west to Oman and United Arab Emirates), Bay of Bengal, South-East Asia, southern China, Indonesia, New Guinea and much of coastal Australia.
EUROPEAN STATUS Very rare vagrant: seven records in autumn and one in spring. Britain (1: 15 Sept 1989); Denmark (2: 7 Oct 1987; 2-3 Sept 1993); Germany (1: 1 Aug 1987); Netherlands (1: 19 Sept-6 Oct 1991); Norway (1: 12 Sept 1987); Spain (1: 7 Apr 1979).

SEMIPALMATED SANDPIPER

Calidris pusilla L 13-15 cm (5.25-6 in)
DESCRIPTION Very similar in size and in non-breeding plumages to Little and Red-necked Stints and Western Sandpiper. Breeding adult is dullest of this black-legged group, lacking rufous head and breast markings of first two and rusty-chestnut field marks of latter species; upperparts show no obvious pale 'tramlines', and underparts are largely white with band of fine brown streaking mainly restricted to breast. Adult in grey-and-white non-breeding plumage very difficult to separate from corresponding plumages of Little Stint and other congeners except by call and, in case of most Western Sandpipers, by bill length and size. Juvenile differs from confusion species in colder plumage tones and absence of obvious white tramlines on mantle, with usually little or no rufous fringing above; typical pattern is of scaly upperparts with characteristic blackish 'anchor' markings on white-tipped pale grey lower scapulars and white-edged, pale-centred tertials and coverts. Juvenile often appears 'capped', with dark-streaked crown, whitish supercilium and dark ear-coverts. Black bill is blunt-tipped and usually shortish, but can overlap in length with Western Sandpiper's; legs and feet also black, but palmations (shared only with Western) are diagnostic difference from Little and Red-necked. With care, usual approachability of this and other stint species may enable observer to detect presence of palmations on feet; this may be made easier by much more plover-like stop-start gait of Semipalmated compared to close congeners, when it often pauses and holds one foot slightly off ground. Structurally, appears slightly chunkier than Little Stint, with marginally heavier bill and shorter primary projection.
VOICE Commonest call given as a loud, low-pitched *chrup* or *kyet*.
HABITAT Nests on wet tundra; mainly coastal outside breeding season, when found at estuaries and mudflats.
DISTRIBUTION Breeds across northern North America from Labrador to Alaska, wintering from Pacific coast of Guatemala and southern West Indies southwards to main winter range in South America (south to Peru and Uruguay).
EUROPEAN STATUS Rare vagrant. Britain (40); Denmark (1: 18 Sept 1987); France (6); Germany (1: 9-10 Oct 1970); Iceland (3: 1 Oct 1989; 8 July 1990; 5 Oct 1991); Ireland (33); Netherlands (1: 11-13 June 1989); Norway (2: 10-12 Aug 1987; 30 June-2 July 1991); Portugal (1: 18 Oct 1992); Spain (2: 5 Oct 1991; 7-10 Oct 1991).

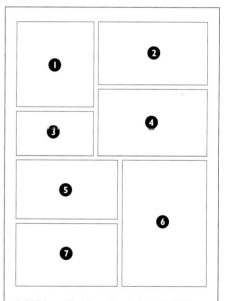

1 **White-tailed Lapwing** (adult, July 1975, Packington, Warwickshire, Britain)
2 **Great Knot** (juvenile, Oct 1991, Camperduin, Netherlands)
3 **Great Knot** (adult summer, Sept 1989, Virkie, Shetland, Britain)
4 **Great Knot** (juvenile, Oct 1991, Camperduin, Netherlands)
5 **Semipalmated Sandpiper** (juvenile, Sept 1980, North Bull, Dublin, Ireland)
6 **Semipalmated Sandpiper** (juvenile, Oct 1986, St Mary's, Isles of Scilly, Britain)
7 **Semipalmated Sandpiper** (adult in worn summer plumage, Aug 1993, Tresco, Isles of Scilly, Britain)

WESTERN SANDPIPER

Calidris mauri L 14-17 cm (5.5-6.75 in)

DESCRIPTION Averages larger and longer-billed than Semipalmated Sandpiper, but overlap means some individuals are very difficult to separate. Breeding adult distinctive, differing especially in chestnut on crown sides, nape, ear-coverts and scapulars, and denser black 'arrowhead' streaking on breast and flanks. Non-breeding adult rather colder grey than Semipalmated but otherwise almost identical; best separated by bill length and fine dark breast streaking, which usually forms band across breast (typically broken on Semipalmated). Juvenile usually brighter and less uniform above than juvenile Semipalmated, from which most easily separated by bright rufous on upper scapulars and centre of mantle contrasting with greyish lower scapulars; tertials also typically edged in similar bright rufous. Also has much less contrasting head pattern with greyer crown, less striking supercilium, and more prominent eye due to plainer eye-stripe and ear-coverts. Typically longish, fine-tipped and slightly drooping black bill recalls Dunlin's; legs and feet black, but partial webbing between toes difficult to see in the field. Jizz of typical longer-billed birds recalls Dunlin, and wades more readily than other stints; often rather approachable.
VOICE Commonest calls are thin, high-pitched and drawn-out, variously transcribed as *chiet*, *jeet* or *krreep* and similar variations.
HABITAT Tundra breeder; on migration uses inland wetlands, but in winter favours coastal inlets and beaches, less often on larger expanses of mud.
DISTRIBUTION Breeds northern and western Alaska and extreme north-east Siberia. Winters west, south and east coasts of USA, and throughout Central America and Caribbean to Peru and Surinam.
EUROPEAN STATUS Very rare vagrant: 10 records, typically between August-September, and only one in spring. Britain (6); France (1: Sept 1973); Ireland (1: 3-6 Sept 1992); Spain (1: 8 Sept 1979); Sweden (1: Aug 1988).

RED-NECKED STINT

Calidris ruficollis L 13-16 cm (5.25-6.5 in)

DESCRIPTION Adult in breeding plumage very like Little Stint, but face, throat and upper breast typically brick-red (duller rufous on Little, which also has white throat) and neatly demarcated from white lower breast; streaked breast sides also whitish (rufous-toned on Little). Additionally, has at best indistinct pale 'tramlines' on mantle, and lower scapulars, wing-coverts and tertials are mainly pale grey, lacking blackish centres and rufous fringes of Little. Non-breeding adult even less distinct than same plumage of Little, and best identified by call and structure. Juvenile (recorded only once in Europe) also extremely similar to Little; chief differences are greyer greater coverts and tertials lacking extensive rufous fringing, indistinct pale tramlines on mantle, more

diffusely streaked breast sides, and plainer head with darker lores (latter also good distinction from juvenile Semipalmated Sandpiper, which has darker crown and ear-coverts). Differs subtly in structure from slightly smaller Little, with proportionately shorter and blunter-tipped black bill, heavier build, shorter black legs and, especially, longer wings and tail forming more attenuated rear end.
VOICE Typical monosyllabic calls intermediate in pitch between those of Semipalmated and Western Sandpipers, and quite different from Little Stint's; variously transcribed as *kreep*, *kreet* or *treet*.
HABITAT Nests on low-level tundra; mainly on coastal marshes and estuaries at other times.
DISTRIBUTION Breeds in northern and north-eastern Siberia from the Taimyr Peninsula eastwards. Long-distance migrant, wintering Bay of Bengal, South-East Asia, Indonesia, New Guinea and Australasia.
EUROPEAN STATUS Very rare vagrant: 21 records, almost half of which in Sweden and all bar one of which (in Britain) relating to adults. Austria (2: July 1975; Aug 1984); Belgium (1: 16 Aug 1988); Britain (3: 22-29 July 1986; 2-3 Aug 1992; 1 Sept 1994, dead); Denmark (1: Aug 1986); Finland (1: 1 June 1991); France (1: 15 July 1994); Germany (1: July 1979); Italy (1: 17 July 1994); Netherlands (1: 29 May 1987); Sweden (9).

LONG-TOED STINT

Calidris subminuta L 13-15 cm (5.25-6 in)

DESCRIPTION Readily separated from all other stints except Temminck's and Least Sandpiper by yellowy-green legs. Breeding adult has streaked chestnut crown reaching bill base, rufous ear-coverts, dusky lores, whitish supercilium, and blackish-brown upperparts tipped white and broadly fringed rufous; white underparts washed grey-buff on breast, with darker streaking, especially at sides. Thin white wing-bar barely reaches onto primaries; white rump divided by dark brown centre extending onto greyish tail. Non-breeding adult essentially grey-brown above, with darker feather centres giving scaly appearance, dark cap, and whitish underparts with dense streaking across breast. Juvenile differs from breeding adult in brighter rufous cap, whitish lateral crown-stripes, paler hindneck, white 'tramlines' on mantle, greyer inner wing-coverts and fresher plumage. Short blackish bill often tinged orange or greenish-yellow at base. Always more strongly marked than rather plain, greyish and shorter-legged Temminck's Stint, but closely similar to Least Sandpiper (which see for plumage differences). Has long-necked, more elongated appearance, longer legs and often more upright posture than latter; long toes difficult to see in the field. Often solitary or in small groups.
VOICE Most frequently uttered call is a soft, rolling *chrrup* or similar.
HABITAT Nests in variety of tundra and taiga habitats; at other times mainly favours freshwater or brackish marshes, often creeping around muddy margins or vegetation at water's

edge, but also on mudflats and other intertidal areas.
DISTRIBUTION Breeds from River Ob region in central Siberia eastwards to Kamchatka and north-east Siberia. Winters from southern India eastwards through South-East Asia to south China, and south through Philippines and Indonesia to western and southern Australia.
EUROPEAN STATUS Extreme vagrant: four records. Britain (2: 7-8 June 1970; 28 Aug-1 Sept 1982); Greece (1: 28 Mar 1991); Sweden (1: 4 Oct-5 Nov 1977).

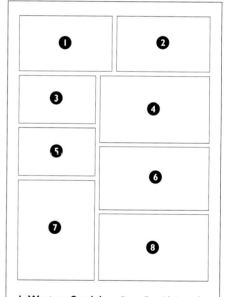

1 **Western Sandpiper** (juvenile with juvenile Ringed Plover, Sept 1992, Co Wexford, Ireland)
2 **Western Sandpiper** (adult with Ringed Plover, Aug 1988, Rönnen, Skåne, Sweden)
3 **Red-necked Stint** (adult summer, May 1987, Lauwersmeer, Netherlands)
4 **Red-necked Stint** (adult summer, Aug 1995*, River Wansbeck, Northumberland, Britain)
5 **Red-necked Stint** (adult summer, July 1986, Blacktoft, Humberside, Britain)
6 **Long-toed Stint** (juvenile, Sept 1982, Saltholme, Teesside, Britain)
7 **Long-toed Stint** (juvenile, Sept 1982, Saltholme, Teesside, Britain)
8 **Long-toed Stint** (adult summer, June 1970, Marazion, Cornwall, Britain)

LEAST SANDPIPER

Calidris minutilla L 13-15 cm (5.25-6 in)
DESCRIPTION In all plumages very like Long-toed Stint. Breeding adult differs mainly in darker upperparts with less extensive rufous fringing, less distinct whitish supercilia which join pale forehead between chestnut crown and black bill, darker lores, and coarser streaking which extends across centre of breast. Non-breeding adult has narrower black centres to feathers on upperparts, giving less scaly appearance. Juveniles very similar, but Least has weaker-patterned head than Long-toed, as in adult plumage, and shows at best faint whitish lateral crown-stripes; 'tramlines' on mantle also weaker or absent, inner wing-coverts have rufous fringes and are not contrastingly grey against scapulars, and breast is more heavily streaked. Consistently, Least shows whiter, bolder wing-bar, shorter legs and very slightly decurved, fine all-black bill which lacks yellowish-ochre base to lower mandible shown by Long-toed. Often has more horizontal gait and busier feeding action than Long-toed, but can adopt equally upright posture. Often crouches when alarmed, but may be very tame.
VOICE Commonest call is a high-pitched, ringing, drawn-out *kreep*; also a lower *prrrt*.
HABITAT Nests on wet tundra, damp open areas within spruce forests and also flat sandy islands; away from breeding areas habitat similar to that of Long-toed Stint, but often more coastal.
DISTRIBUTION Breeds from Nova Scotia and Newfoundland westwards across northern Canada to Alaska. Winters in southern USA, Central America, Caribbean and northern South America.
EUROPEAN STATUS Very rare vagrant: 50 records. Austria (1: 15 June 1976, two); Britain (28); Finland (1: 5 June 1847); France (7); Germany (1: 20-21 Sept 1985); Iceland (3: most recent on 23 Sept 1990); Ireland (7); Italy (1: 12 Feb 1994); Spain (1: 11 Oct 1987).

WHITE-RUMPED SANDPIPER

Calidris fuscicollis L 15-18 cm (6-7.25 in)
DESCRIPTION Slightly smaller than Dunlin, with diagnostic combination of slightly decurved medium-length bill (often appearing straight in the field) and white uppertail-coverts. Breeding adult has dark-streaked crown, pale supercilium, and dense streaking on whitish breast and flanks. Mainly dark-centred upperparts fringed rufous, grey and buff, with grey-brown coverts fringed whitish. Flight feathers dark brown with narrow white wing-bar; uppertail-coverts white, tail dark greyish. During moult into drabber grey-and-white non-breeding plumage, shows characteristic isolated black feathers in otherwise plain grey upperparts; whitish supercilium more prominent than on non-breeding Baird's Sandpiper. Juvenile has chestnut-streaked crown and ear-coverts, pale nape, and mainly dark-centred upperparts with rufous edges of varying intensity to scapulars and tertials

(coverts generally duller); on brightest individuals, whitish edges to scapulars can form narrow tramline against mantle and between groups of upper and lower scapulars. Underparts white, washed buffish-grey on neck, breast and flanks and lightly streaked darker. Bill black, with paler base to lower mandible; legs black. Like Baird's, has long wings which project beyond tail tip and give more elongated appearance to body than in other calidrids.
VOICE Commonest call is a characteristic squeaky, high-pitched *jeet* or *tzreet*.
HABITAT Nests on arctic tundra; frequents wide range of inland and coastal wetlands at other times.
DISTRIBUTION Breeds from southern Baffin Island and northernmost Canada and adjacent arctic islands west to northern Alaska. Long-distance migrant, wintering from northern Chile and Paraguay through southern South America to Tierra del Fuego.
EUROPEAN STATUS Frequent vagrant. Austria (4: 17 May 1959; 11 Oct 1959; 18-22 Oct 1986; 18 Oct 1987); Belgium (1: 28 Sept 1991); Britain (246); Denmark (9); Finland (4: 9 Aug 1980; 13-17 May 1982; 23-25 May 1994; 20-21 July 1994); France (7); Germany (7); Iceland (46); Ireland (118); Netherlands (2: Oct 1977; 19-21 Aug 1994); Norway (10); Spain (8); Sweden (11); Switzerland (4: 12 Oct 1860; 24 Oct 1964; 24-28 May 1971; 1 Nov 1981).

BAIRD'S SANDPIPER

Calidris bairdii L 14-17 cm (5.5-6.75 in)
DESCRIPTION Resembles White-rumped Sandpiper in size and long-winged appearance, but somewhat buffer in all plumages, with dark-centred uppertail. Breeding adult differs mainly in buffish tone to head which shows indistinct pale supercilium, lack of rufous on head and upperparts, buff-washed breast more heavily streaked at sides, and unmarked flanks. Non-breeding adult only slightly duller than in breeding plumage, and buffer-toned above and below than White-rumped with less distinct breast streaking. Juvenile is rather uniform buffish on head and breast with indistinct darker streaking, and has weak supercilium and white chin; feathers on upperparts appear strikingly scaly, with grey-brown centres darkening towards tip and fringed white or buff. All-black bill straight; legs black.
VOICE Flight call variously given as a soft, low-pitched and rolling *krrru* or *kyrrt*.
HABITAT Nests in upland tundra; at other seasons favours drier and vegetated margins of inland wetlands and damp grasslands, less often in coastal habitats.
DISTRIBUTION Breeds from western Greenland, Baffin Island and northernmost Canada and arctic islands west to northern and western Alaska and extreme north-east tip of Siberia. Long-distance migrant, wintering in South America from Peru and Uruguay south to Tierra del Fuego.
EUROPEAN STATUS Frequent vagrant. Austria (1: 11-16 Oct 1988); Britain (120); Czech Republic (1: 2 Sept 1981); Finland (3: 20 Sept

1962; 29 Aug-1 Sept 1971; 1 Sept 1973); France (11); Germany (4: most recent on 2-6 Aug 1994); Greece (1: 21 Apr 1986); Iceland (1: 3 Sept 1994); Ireland (54); Netherlands (3: 21-28 Sept 1980; 23-28 Aug 1981; 31 July-1 Aug 1993); Norway (1: 27 May 1975, two); Poland (2: 21 Aug 1978; 19-26 Oct 1993); Spain (1: 20-21 Aug 1988); Sweden (3: Aug 1982; Oct 1983; Sept-Nov 1989).

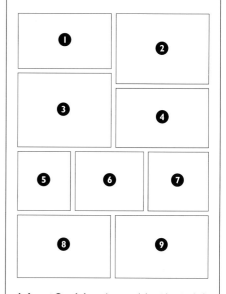

1 **Least Sandpiper** (worn adult with crippled feet, Aug 1984, Dungeness, Kent, Britain)
2 **Least Sandpiper** (juvenile, Sept 1993, Hayle, Cornwall, Britain)
3 **Least Sandpiper** (first-summer, Apr 1986, Porscatho, Cornwall, Britain)
4 **White-rumped Sandpiper** (first-summer or adult moulting into winter plumage, Aug 1990, Sidlesham Ferry, West Sussex, Britain)
5 **White-rumped Sandpiper** (juvenile (feeding bird), commencing moult to first-winter plumage, with Baird's Sandpiper, Oct 1989, Stithians, Cornwall, Britain)
6 **White-rumped Sandpiper** (first-summer or adult moulting into winter plumage, Aug 1994, Lista, Vest-Agder, Norway)
7 **Baird's Sandpiper** (juvenile, Aug 1981, Noordholland, Netherlands)
8 **Baird's Sandpiper** (juvenile commencing moult to first-winter plumage, Sept 1994, Eyebrook, Leicestershire, Britain)
9 **Baird's Sandpiper** (juvenile, Sept 1991, Fair Isle, Shetland, Britain)

PECTORAL SANDPIPER F

Calidris melanotos L 19-23 cm (7.5-9.25 in)
DESCRIPTION Rather robust, deep-chested calidrid with broadly similar patterning in all plumages. Breeding adult has dark-streaked crown, indistinct pale supercilium, and pale buffish head and breast with dense streaking which forms neat pectoral band (often darker on male) above clean white underparts. Upperparts blackish-brown, fringed chestnut, pale brown or buff; wing-coverts grey-brown, fringed paler. In flight, shows very thin white wing-bar and fairly broad dark centre to white rump and grey uppertail. In non-breeding adult, upperparts plainer with darker feather centres. Juvenile has whiter supercilium and bolder white, chestnut and buff fringing to upperparts, often forming white V-pattern on mantle and scapulars, and buff-fringed wing-coverts; buff breast heavily streaked with brown. Medium-length, slightly decurved bill brownish-black with yellowish or greenish basal third; legs dull yellowish-green.
VOICE Characteristic flight call is a distinctive, far-carrying single *prrrrp* note, often repeated and sounding as if made through pursed lips.
HABITAT Nests near tundra wetlands; on passage and in winter found mainly at freshwater marshes and on damp grassland, but also uses coastal wetlands.
DISTRIBUTION Breeds from Hudson Bay westwards across northernmost Canada, Alaska and Siberia as far west as the Taimyr Peninsula. Winters chiefly in southern South America from Bolivia to southern Argentina, with smaller numbers in south-east Australia and New Zealand.
EUROPEAN STATUS Frequent vagrant/visitor: most (but not all) arrivals are from the west in autumn, occasionally involving small parties. Austria (19); Belgium (25); Britain (many, eg 31-88 annually (total 421) between 1986-93); Channel Islands (24+); Czech Republic (5: 12 Sept 1973; 25 Sept 1976; 28 Sept 1980; 17-27 Sept 1989; 28 Aug 1993); Denmark (20); Faeroes (2: 25 May 1984; 23-24 Oct 1987); Finland (33); France (196); Germany (90); Hungary (6); Iceland (26); Ireland (423); Italy (7); Netherlands (64+); Norway (50); Poland (16); Portugal (5: 27-28 Sept 1990; 26 Sept 1992; 11 July 1993; 20 Aug 1993; 30 Sept 1993); Slovakia (2: 8 Sept 1973; 16 Sept 1987); Spain (51+ individuals); Sweden (87); Switzerland (13).

SHARP-TAILED SANDPIPER

Calidris acuminata L 17-21 cm (6.75-8.5 in)
DESCRIPTION Recalls Pectoral Sandpiper, but variably streaked underparts lack latter's clear demarcation above white belly. Breeding adult has black-streaked rufous crown and ear-coverts; rest of head, neck and upper breast whitish-buff, with dense brown streaking becoming bolder chevrons on whiter lower breast, flanks and belly. Upperparts mainly blackish-brown, wing-coverts greyer, all fringed dull chestnut or whitish-buff; flight feathers

dark brown with narrow white wing-bar, rump and uppertail with broad dark centre, and tail brownish. Non-breeding adult has dark cap, brighter supercilium, browner upperparts with paler fringing, and less heavily-marked underparts. Juvenile has bright rufous cap, conspicuous pale supercilium and eye-ring (latter much less conspicuous than in Pectoral), dark reddish lores and ear-coverts, pale hindneck, broad chestnut fringes to dark-centred feathers on mantle, scapulars and tertials, and paler edges to duller wing-coverts; breast washed buff, with narrow collar of streaking below throat and on breast sides. Bill black with yellow-brown base, slightly decurved but usually noticeably shorter than Pectoral Sandpiper's; legs greenish-grey, with clearly longer toes than Pectoral (which may be obvious during feeding).
VOICE Flight call a soft, clear *wheep* or similar, and a Swallow-like *tree-trit*.
HABITAT Tundra nester; on migration and in winter on damp grasslands, wetland margins and coastal lagoons and mudflats.
DISTRIBUTION Breeding range restricted to north-east Siberia between Yana river and Kolyma. Long-distance migrant, wintering in south-west Pacific from New Guinea and Tonga to New Caledonia, Australia and New Zealand.
EUROPEAN STATUS Very rare vagrant: 37 records of 36 individuals. Austria (1: 6-8 Aug 1983); Belgium (1: 3-5 Sept 1989, same as in Netherlands); Britain (21); Denmark (2: 16 Aug 1989; 25 Aug 1989); Finland (1: 23-24 Aug 1984); France (1: 18 Sept 1972); Ireland (1: 6-21 Aug 1994); Netherlands (1: 14-21 Sept 1989, same as in Belgium); Norway (4: 4 Aug 1984; 24 May 1986; 24 June 1986; 27-28 May 1989); Sweden (4: 23-25 July 1975; 24 Sept 1976; 24-25 Aug 1977; 26 July 1985).

STILT SANDPIPER

Micropalama himantopus L 18-23 cm (7.25-9.25 in)
DESCRIPTION Large, distinctive sandpiper with long, slightly decurved black bill recalling Curlew Sandpiper's and long, greenish legs. Breeding plumage unmistakable, with whitish supercilium, rusty-tinted crown, lores and ear-coverts, and rest of head and underparts whitish, heavily patterned with brown streaks on face, neck and upper breast and bars on lower breast and underbody. Mantle, scapulars and tertials blackish or brown, edged chestnut and white, with contrasting plainer grey wing-coverts. Lacks distinct wing-bar on brownish flight feathers, and white rump and uppertail-coverts partly obscured by darker bars in breeding plumage; toes project well beyond grey tail in flight. Non-breeding adult has dark grey cap and lores, whitish supercilium, plainer grey-brown upperparts, and diffuse grey streaking on white underparts. Juvenile dark brown above, fringed rufous or whitish-buff, with dark brown crown, less distinct supercilium, faintly streaked buff-washed breast and white belly. Often wades in deeper water

among larger shorebirds; usually solitary or in small groups. Actions may suggest a dowitcher more than any other species.
VOICE Migrants often silent, but calls include a soft, rattling *grrrt.*
HABITAT Usually breeds on areas of drier, open tundra; at other times frequents shallow pools, lake margins, flooded marshes and coastal lagoons.
DISTRIBUTION Breeding range extends from west Hudson Bay and Victoria Island through north-western Canada to northern Alaska. Winters in small numbers in parts of southern USA, but chiefly in central South America from southern Brazil to northern Argentina and Uruguay.
EUROPEAN STATUS Very rare vagrant: 37 records. Austria (1: 9 Aug 1969); Britain (18); Finland (1: 20-22 June 1983); France (4: 23 July 1989; 5 Aug 1991; 17 Sept 1991; 25 Sept 1991); Iceland (1: 17 June 1985); Ireland (8); Norway (2: 16-17 June 1987; 27-30 May 1993); Spain (1: 6-7 May 1983); Sweden (1: July 1963).

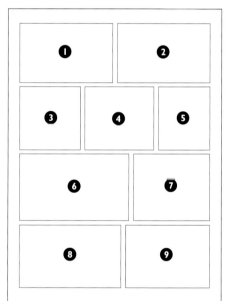

1 **Pectoral Sandpiper** (adult, Aug 1992, Bell's Pond, Northumberland, Britain)
2 **Pectoral Sandpiper** (juvenile, Oct 1995*, Oudenberg, Belgium)
3 **Pectoral Sandpiper** (juvenile, Sept 1982, St Sampson, Guernsey, Channel Islands)
4 **Sharp-tailed Sandpiper** (adult summer, left, May 1989, Vardø, Finnmark, Norway)
5 **Sharp-tailed Sandpiper** (adult, Sept 1993, Scatness, Shetland, Britain)
6 **Sharp-tailed Sandpiper** (adult summer, Aug 1994, Tacumshin, Co Wexford, Ireland)
7 **Stilt Sandpiper** (adult with Ringed Plover, May 1993, Rogaland, Norway)
8 **Stilt Sandpiper** (first-summer, Apr 1984, Frodsham, Cheshire, Britain)
9 **Stilt Sandpiper** (adult, Aug 1990, Trimley Marshes, Suffolk, Britain)

BUFF-BREASTED SANDPIPER

Tryngites subruficollis L 18-20 cm (7.25-8 in)
DESCRIPTION Resembles a small, compact juvenile Ruff with a shorter, straight bill. Adult is pale buff on head and underparts, streaked dark brown on crown, hindneck and breast sides, and with a prominent dark eye on otherwise plain face. Upperparts appear scaly, with dark-centred feathers having buffish-brown edges; in flight, upperwing shows darker and plainer flight feathers with no wing-bar, unlike Ruff, and Buff-breasted lacks latter's white sides to rump and uppertail. Juvenile like adult, but aged by pattern of upperpart feathering, which shows dark subterminal markings and whiter fringes; much as adult by first spring. Bill dark brown, tinged yellow at extreme base; legs bright yellow. Gregarious and often tame.
VOICE Rarely heard away from breeding territory, but may utter a low *pr-r-r-reet* flight call.
HABITAT Nests on arctic tundra; on migration and in winter favours dry grasslands of various kinds.
DISTRIBUTION Breeds in far north of Canada and Alaska. Long-haul migrant, wintering mainly in central Argentina and Paraguay.
EUROPEAN STATUS Frequent vagrant/visitor: parties of up to 15 recorded. Austria (4: 15-22 Sept 1968; 10 Sept 1970; 11 Sept 1980; 3-21 Oct 1986); Belgium (4: 27 Aug-11 Sept 1984; 4 July 1986; 12 June 1988; 9-11 Sept 1993); Britain (c 418 to end 1993); Bulgaria; Channel Islands (11); Czech Republic (1: 15 Oct 1983); Denmark (10); Faeroes (1: Apr 1977); Finland (10); France (99); Germany (c 15); Hungary (1: 10-22 Oct 1993); Iceland (8); Ireland (177, including several flocks; also 2 at sea); Italy (11); Netherlands (9); Norway (16); Poland (10); Portugal; Spain (10+); Sweden (18); Switzerland (5: 31 Aug-2 Sept 1973; 3 Oct 1973; 14-22 Nov 1981; 25-28 Aug 1982; 2-3 Sept 1994).

SHORT-BILLED DOWITCHER

Limnodromus griseus L 25-29 cm (10-11.5 in)
DESCRIPTION Breeding adult essentially pale chestnut-red on neck and breast, paler around head, with dark brown crown and lores and white supercilium; belly and undertail whitish or pale chestnut-red. Underparts finely spotted from foreneck to centre of vent, and variably barred on flanks and undertail. Upperparts have black-centred feathers with rusty-buff or pale cinnamon fringes, and rusty-barred tertials; wing-coverts grey-brown with whiter fringes. Narrow whitish trailing edge to secondaries, and white upper rump extending as narrow triangle up back, characteristic in flight; rest of rump and tail white with dark brown barring. Non-breeding adult has grey-brown upperparts fringed paler, white supercilium, dark lores, and pale grey wash over neck and breast with finer speckling, especially at join with white belly. Juvenile has dark brown upperparts broadly fringed chestnut-buff, less so on coverts, and diagnostic 'tiger-striped' brown-and-buff tertials

and inner greater coverts; underparts mainly buffish-white, finely streaked and spotted on breast, flanks and undertail. Longish straight bill blackish-brown, tinged greenish on basal half; proportionately rather short legs greyish-green, yellower on juveniles. Feeding action rather snipe-like; will also swim readily. For differences from Long-billed Dowitcher, see that species.
VOICE Typical call is a low, fairly rapid, trisyllabic *tu-tu-tu*, given in flight and reminiscent of Turnstone.
HABITAT Nests in bogs and open marshes; on migration occurs in wide range of wetlands, but in winter primarily coastal, favouring intertidal mudflats, sandy shorelines and adjacent saltmarsh.
DISTRIBUTION Has more southerly range than Long-billed Dowitcher, breeding chiefly in Quebec and Labrador, much of central Canada and southern Alaska. Winters from south-eastern USA and California along Caribbean and Central American coasts south to Peru and northern Brazil.
EUROPEAN STATUS Extreme vagrant: five accepted autumn records, though some of the many records of unidentified dowitchers in Europe may possibly relate to this species. Germany (1: 9-16 Oct 1981); Ireland (1: 30 Sept-2 Oct 1985); Norway (2: 6 July 1971; 17 Aug 1976); Portugal (1: 15 Oct 1983).

LONG-BILLED DOWITCHER

Limnodromus scolopaceus L 27-30 cm (10.75-12 in)
DESCRIPTION In all plumages very like Short-billed Dowitcher, and many dowitchers reaching Europe are never specifically identified. However, attention to very different calls can be relied upon for identification at all times. Breeding adult has darker all-reddish underparts (often whiter on belly and undertail on Short-billed) with more heavily marked foreneck, breast and flanks; in non-breeding plumage lack of speckling on breast, which is more clearly demarcated from white underparts, discernible only at very close range, and more patterned vent and undertail difficult to judge on lone bird. Separation less problematic with juvenile, which has darker, much plainer tertials lacking diagnostic striping of Short-billed. Other differences at all ages include tail barring (white bars never wider than black ones on Long-billed, usually the reverse on Short-billed) and voice (see below); also averages slightly larger than Short-billed, with longer bill and legs, but beware wide overlap in measurements.
VOICE High, sharp and emphatic *keek* note, alternatively rendered as *peep* or *pip* and sometimes repeated, is easily distinguished from calls of Short-billed Dowitcher.
HABITAT Nests in tundra swamps and marshes; favours fresh or brackish pools over intertidal preference of Short-billed, but both species may occur together in same habitat.
DISTRIBUTION Breeds in extreme north-west Canada, northern and western Alaska and

north-eastern Siberia. Winters from southernmost British Columbia to Mexico and across southern USA.
EUROPEAN STATUS Frequent vagrant: most occurrences in autumn, but overwintering regularly recorded. There are many other records of dowitchers not specifically identified. Britain (131); Channel Islands (2: 20-24 Sept 1975; 28 Mar-1 Apr 1982); Denmark (5); Finland (6); France (21); Germany (6); Greece (1: 7 May 1962); Hungary (1: 25 Sept 1993); Iceland (3: 23 Aug 1980; 19 Oct 1980; 30 July 1983); Ireland (52; records include one of a party of 5); Italy (2: 26 Sept 1985; 2 May 1989); Netherlands (9); Norway (6); Portugal (1: 17 Feb 1992); Spain (4: 14 May 1985; 18 Sept 1987; 20 Sept 1987; 29 Sept 1987); Sweden (10).

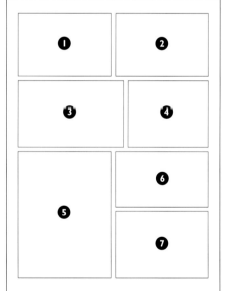

1 **Buff-breasted Sandpiper** (juvenile, Sept 1991, Joensuu, Finland)
2 **Buff-breasted Sandpiper** (juvenile, Sept 1994, Draycote Water, Warwickshire, Britain)
3 **Buff-breasted Sandpiper** (juvenile, Sept 1987, Anglers Country Park, West Yorkshire, Britain)
4 **Short-billed Dowitcher** (adult winter, Oct, New York, USA)
5 **Long-billed Dowitcher** (adult summer, Aug 1993, Strand Lough, Co Down, Ireland)
6 **Long-billed Dowitcher** (adult summer, May 1989, Lauwersmeer, Netherlands)
7 **Long-billed Dowitcher** (juvenile, Oct 1990, Lynn Point, Norfolk, Britain)

69

HUDSONIAN GODWIT

Limosa haemastica L 37-41 cm (14.75-16.5 in)
DESCRIPTION Adult in breeding plumage readily identified by 'reversed' colour pattern of Black-tailed Godwit, with paler head and neck merging on upper breast into variably vinous-chestnut dark-barred underparts (darker on male) and whitish undertail. Mantle, scapulars and tertials blackish-brown, notched pale chestnut and buffish; wing-coverts plainer grey-brown. In flight, upperside very like Black-tailed Godwit's, but wing-bars are shorter and concentrated on outer secondaries and inner primaries, and white band above black tail is narrower. In non-breeding plumage more easily taken for Black-tailed, when underwing pattern of black (not white) coverts and axillaries and white bases to secondaries and inner primaries (diagnostic in all ages and plumages) is best character; typically also darker grey-brown on forecrown and upperparts, and underparts evenly washed grey-brown except for white belly and vent. Juvenile differs in browner upperparts with pale buff fringing and 'smoky' brownish-buff wash on underparts. In all plumages shows conspicuous white supercilium. Long, slightly upcurved bill is dark brown with basal third pinkish-brown (more extensively so in summer); long legs blue-grey or dark grey.
VOICE Migrants not very vocal, but has range of calls based on high-pitched *toe-wit* or *wit* notes.
HABITAT Nests in lowland marshes near water; also favours flooded meadows, coastal marshes and estuaries.
DISTRIBUTION Breeds in Canada in south-west Hudson Bay area and extreme north-west, and in southern and western Alaska. Long-distance migrant, wintering in south-eastern South America.
EUROPEAN STATUS Extreme vagrant: three records. Britain (2: 10 Sept-3 Oct 1981, presumed same 22 Nov 1981-14 Jan 1982 and 26 Apr-6 May 1983; 26 Sept 1988); Denmark (1: Sept 1986).

LITTLE CURLEW

Numenius minutus L 29-32 cm (11.5-12.75 in)
DESCRIPTION Diminutive curlew with body size only that of Eurasian Golden Plover. Adult has buffish face with dark lateral crown-stripes and rear eye-stripe, buff median crown-stripe and streaked ear-coverts, recalling Whimbrel (hence former common name of Little Whimbrel). Upperparts brown, fringed and spotted buff; in flight, entire upperside appears brownish except for paler median coverts. Neck and underparts largely buff, streaked browner on neck and particularly on breast, much less marked on flanks and becoming white towards undertail; underwing buff, barred with brown. Juvenile similar, but darker above, with neat spots and pale buff fringes on scapulars, and buffer below, with less densely streaked breast and barely marked flanks; much as adult from first autumn. Medium-

length, decurved bill blackish-brown has pinker base; legs yellowish or blue-grey. Readily identifiable by small size and bill shape; only similar species is near-extinct American counterpart Eskimo Curlew *N borealis* (six 19th century European records, all from Britain), which is slightly larger and longer-winged, with rustier underwing.
VOICE Has *te-te-te* flight call reminiscent of Whimbrel's, but is shorter and higher-pitched.
HABITAT Nests in clearings in open taiga; at other seasons favours wet and dry grassland habitats.
DISTRIBUTION Breeds central and north-east Siberia, passing through eastern Asia to winter mainly in New Guinea and on plains of northern and eastern Australia.
EUROPEAN STATUS Extreme vagrant: three autumn records. Britain (2: 30 Aug-6 Sept 1982; 24 Aug-3 Sept 1985); Norway (1: 14 July 1969).

SLENDER-BILLED CURLEW

Numenius tenuirostris L 36-41 cm (14.5-16.5 in)
DESCRIPTION Resembles smaller, slightly paler version of Eurasian Curlew, with shorter, more evenly decurved bill (longer on female). Plumage recalls that species, but ground colour of face, neck and breast whitish or very pale brown; well-defined dark brown streaking on breast becomes rounded or heart-shaped spots on flanks (on adults). Other differences include slightly darker cap and loral stripe accentuating pale supercilium, very dark outer wing, largely all-whitish underwing, and whiter rump and tail, latter less heavily barred. Vagrants often associate with Eurasian Curlew.
VOICE Calls include a *cour-lee* note like Eurasian Curlew's, but shorter and higher-pitched in tone.
HABITAT Apparently nests in marshy taiga; at other times frequents wetland habitats, including estuaries, fresh or brackish lagoons and adjacent dry or damp meadows.
DISTRIBUTION Formerly widespread, and described from parts of European migration range in 19th century as abundant; has since undergone dramatic decline, and now highly endangered. Presumed to breed in Siberia, but exact location and range unknown; now rarely recorded on passage, and in winter, apart from recent records in southern Italy, last reported regularly only from Morocco, where tiny population now apparently extinct. Occasionally reported also from Arabia.
EUROPEAN STATUS Widely recorded in 19th century, but very few records since (though occasionally reported in small parties). Possibly still regular Hungary (almost annual: 5 accepted records since 1988, including flock of 6 on 1-2 Dec 1990) and Italy (many old records; very rare but almost regular winter visitor in recent years). Other national totals are followed by records since 1900 where known: Albania (2: 2); Austria (11); Belgium (7: 0); Bulgaria (7); Czech Republic (4: Mar 1885; Sept 1899; autumn 1934; 7 Apr 1974); France (9); Germany (2: Sept 1878; 23 Sept 1980);

Greece (87); Hungary (85); Latvia (1: 1929); Netherlands (7: 4); Poland (5: 4); Romania (16 since 1900); Slovakia (4, including 3 in 1895-96); Spain (no accepted records, but at least 6 published reports of 30+ individuals); Switzerland (1: 27 Aug 1973); former Yugoslavia (44 since 1900).

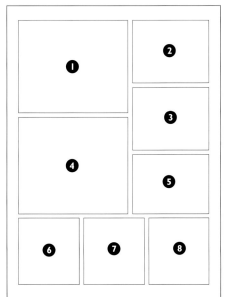

1 **Hudsonian Godwit** (adult, left, with adult Black-tailed Godwit, Oct 1981, Countess Wear, Devon, Britain)
2 **Hudsonian Godwit** (adult, Oct 1981, Countess Wear, Devon, Britain)
3 **Hudsonian Godwit** (adult, Oct 1981, Countess Wear, Devon, Britain)
4 **Little Curlew** (adult, Aug 1985, Cley, Norfolk, Britain)
5 **Little Curlew** (adult, Sept 1982, Sker Point, Mid Glamorgan, Britain)
6 **Little Curlew** (adult, Sept 1982, Sker Point, Mid Glamorgan, Britain)
7 **Slender-billed Curlew** (Feb 1968, La Rochelle, France)
8 **Slender-billed Curlew** (*Jan, Morocco*)

UPLAND SANDPIPER

Bartramia longicauda L 28-32 cm (11.25-12.75 in)
DESCRIPTION Has characteristic gawky appearance, with combination of large eye, small head, slender neck and deep-chested, elongated body unmatched by any other wader. Adult is buffish, with dark brown crown and indistinct buff median crown-stripe, richer brown pale-fringed scapulars, dark-barred wing-coverts and tertials, and blackish-brown back, rump, uppertail-coverts and central tail feathers; sides of rump white, outer tail paler than centre and barred darker. Underparts washed buff from throat to upper belly and streaked brown, streaks continuing as dark chevrons on flanks; belly and ventral region white. Upperwing shows darker flight feathers; underwing barred whitish and brown on coverts, more heavily still on axillaries. Juvenile differs chiefly in darker, more uniform scapulars and upperwing-coverts which show dark submarginal lines with buff fringes; as adult from late autumn. Relatively short, thin and slightly decurved bill brown, with yellowish sides to base; legs yellow. In alarm bobs rear end; exceptionally can be extremely tame and confiding. Usually solitary.
VOICE Often silent outside breeding areas, but usual flight call given as a piping *quip-ip-ip-ip*.
HABITAT Nests on prairies and dry grassy areas, where often perches on posts and telegraph poles; broadly similar habitat at other times includes airfields, pasture, golf courses and even saltings.
DISTRIBUTION Breeds in southern, central and western Canada, eastern Alaska, and northern USA south to Colorado; declining in east of range. Long-distance migrant, wintering in south-eastern South America.
EUROPEAN STATUS Rare vagrant: 65 records, mostly in September-November. Britain (35); Channel Islands (1: 1-2 Oct 1988); Denmark (1: Nov 1920); France (5: 18 Sept 1965; 26 Sept 1969; 5 Sept 1985; 21 Sept 1987; 6 Jan 1992); Germany (1: early 19th century); Iceland (3); Ireland (10); Italy (8); Norway (1: 22 Oct-9 Nov 1994).

MARSH SANDPIPER

Tringa stagnatilis L 22-25 cm (8.75-10 in)
DESCRIPTION Elegant, long-legged wader with slender body, long, needle-like bill and graceful poise. Breeding adult has buffish-brown head and hindneck streaked dark brown, and dark brown feathers on upperparts marked with buffish-grey and tipped white in fresh plumage; underparts whitish, streaked and spotted brown on lower neck and breast and with dark chevrons on flanks. In flight resembles slim, diminutive Greenshank, with dark brownish-grey wings and white of rump extending as triangular patch up back, but long legs clearly project further beyond shorter dark-barred white tail. In non-breeding plumage distinctly plainer, paler and greyer above, with whiter head and dark 'shoulder' patch. Juvenile differs from non-breeding adult in browner upperparts

which are fringed and spotted with white or buff, and strikingly white underparts, with streaking confined to sides of breast; can also appear very dark-capped. By first winter more like non-breeding adult, but grey upperpart feathers have narrow dark subterminal bars and whitish or buffish fringes. Legs usually greenish; long, straight bill brownish-black, with greenish-grey base.
VOICE Flight call is a whistled *plew* or *kiew*; also utters a repeated *yip* or *kiup* note when flushed.
HABITAT Nests in lowland wetlands and river valleys; outside breeding season favours inland pools, marshes and lake margins, also brackish coastal lagoons.
DISTRIBUTION Breeds from the Baltic and easternmost Europe (where range apparently expanding westwards) eastwards across Russia and Siberia as far as Lake Baikal region. Winters from Mediterranean (Tunisia, Middle East and southern Europe) and much of sub-Saharan Africa to Persian Gulf and India, with smaller numbers in South-East Asia, Indonesia and parts of Australia.
EUROPEAN STATUS Breeds sporadically in Finland (0-5 pairs, last in 1993) and Latvia (10 pairs), and regular on passage in Austria (bred 1914), Bulgaria, Czech Republic (20+), France, Germany, Hungary (formerly bred), Italy (also winters in small numbers), Romania (may breed regularly), Spain (also occasional in winter) and Switzerland (especially spring). Accidental elsewhere, but records increasing: Albania; Belgium (120+); Britain (82); Denmark (23); Estonia (6); Ireland (3: 7-13 Aug 1982; 4-5 Aug 1984; 17-21 Aug 1994, with two birds on first date); Lithuania (1: 15 July 1994); Luxembourg (2: 7-8 May 1963; 31 Aug 1971, two); Netherlands (155+); Norway (8); Poland (c 130 to 1990: breeds irregularly); Portugal (2*); Slovakia; Slovenia (20+), Sweden (159), former Yugoslavia.

GREATER YELLOWLEGS

Tringa melanoleuca L 29-33 cm (11.5-13.25 in)
DESCRIPTION Recalls slim Greenshank in size and structure, but browner in all plumages, with square white rump patch and bright yellow legs. Breeding adult has dark grey-brown upperparts heavily streaked, spotted or notched with white or cream; underparts white, heavily streaked darker on breast and marked with chevrons and bars on lower breast and flanks (unlike Lesser Yellowlegs). Long wings, patterned on coverts and secondaries much as mantle but with darker, plainer primaries and primary coverts, project noticeably beyond dark-barred white tail at rest. In non-breeding plumage, upperparts more uniform grey-brown with finer white spotting, notching and fringing; underparts also lack stronger markings. Juvenile similar, but with darker, browner upperparts more strongly spotted and notched bright buff, and dark streaking on breast often forming band; first-winter plumage very like adult, but some juvenile coverts and tertials usually retained, and full adult plumage not acquired in first

summer, unlike Lesser Yellowlegs. Most Greaters are separable without difficulty from latter species, but on tricky individuals one of safest distinctions is bill-to-tibia ratio: in Greater bill is obviously longer than tibia (upper leg), in Lesser bill is usually same length as or slightly shorter than tibia.
VOICE Commonest call is a ringing, Greenshank-like *tew-tew-tew*.
HABITAT Nests in open marshy areas with scattered trees; on migration and in winter inhabits wide range of fresh and brackish wetlands, also muddy coasts and estuaries.
DISTRIBUTION Breeds from Newfoundland and Labrador in broad band across central Canada to south-east Alaska. Winters from east and west coasts of USA south through West Indies and Central America and throughout South America.
EUROPEAN STATUS Very rare vagrant: 44 records. Belgium (1: 27 Nov-2 Dec 1994); Britain (19); Czech Republic (1: 26 Aug 1964); Denmark (1: Aug 1988); France (4: 26 Aug 1987; 18 Nov 1989; 26 Apr 1990; 22 Sept 1990); Iceland (2); Ireland (11); Norway (1: 8-9 May 1993); Poland (2: 23-27 Aug 1986; 25 Sept 1987); Spain (1: 21 Aug-2 Sept 1983); Sweden (1: Aug 1976).

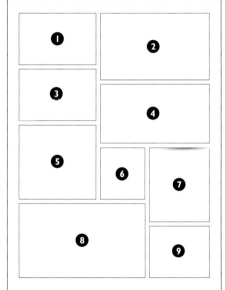

1 **Upland Sandpiper** (juvenile, Oct 1983, St Mary's, Isles of Scilly, Britain)
2 **Upland Sandpiper** (juvenile, Oct 1993, St Mary's, Isles of Scilly, Britain)
3 **Upland Sandpiper** (juvenile, Oct 1982, St Agnes, Isles of Scilly, Britain)
4 **Marsh Sandpiper** (juvenile, Aug 1994, De Lier, Netherlands)
5 **Marsh Sandpiper** (first-summer or adult, May 1992, Bardney, Lincs, Britain)
6 **Marsh Sandpiper** (adult summer, Mar 1995*, Longarini, Sicily, Italy)
7 **Marsh Sandpiper** (adult summer, May 1993, Auleben, Germany)
8 **Greater Yellowlegs** (first-winter, Oct 1994, Rockliffe, Cumbria, Britain)
9 **Greater Yellowlegs** (first-summer, Apr 1995*, De Braakman, Netherlands)

LESSER YELLOWLEGS

Tringa flavipes L 23-25 cm (9.25-10 in)
DESCRIPTION Distinctly smaller and more
delicate in form than Greater Yellowlegs,
though differences not always obvious with lone
birds; best separated on structure by bill-to-tibia
ratio (see under Greater Yellowlegs). Main
plumage distinctions from that species include
less heavily-marked breast and flanks (breeding
adult), brown-washed breast with darker
streaking (juvenile) and plainer, unnotched flight
feathers (all plumages). Bill is a constant and
useful distinction: Greater has long, very slightly
uptilted blackish bill with at least basal third
paler; Lesser has shorter, straighter black bill
which is pale only at extreme base.
VOICE Call is a whistled *chu* or *chu chu* recalling
Redshank.
HABITAT Nests in lightly-wooded boggy terrain;
at other times in wide range of inland and
coastal wetlands.
DISTRIBUTION Breeds in North America from
James Bay westwards across much of Canada
and Alaska. Winters from south-eastern USA
and California southwards through West Indies,
Central America and South America.
EUROPEAN STATUS Frequent vagrant. Austria
(2: 24-31 Aug 1975; 25 Oct 1978); Belgium (3:
22 Aug-2 Sept 1983; 12-13 May 1986; 25 July
1993); Britain (168); Denmark (2: 1912; July
1982); Finland (1: 14 Oct 1978); France (22);
Germany (2: 10 May 1980; Nov 1990-1 Jan
1991); Greece (1: 9 Aug 1986); Hungary (2: 12
Sept 1959, dead; 26 June 1990); Iceland (9);
Ireland (62); Italy (5: 17 Oct 1978; 16 May 1962;
6 Apr 1985; 22 Mar 1989; July 1994);
Netherlands (2: 18-19 Nov 1979; 11 Oct 1991);
Norway (8); Poland (1: 26 Sept 1990); Portugal
(4: 7 Jan 1990; 12 Nov-7 Dec 1993; 31 Dec
1993; 8 Dec 1994); Spain (12); Sweden (5: 3-4
Oct 1969; 20 Oct 1969; 8-16 Nov 1985; 1 June
1990; 9-14 June 1992).

SOLITARY SANDPIPER

Tringa solitaria L 18-21 cm (7.25-8.5 in)
DESCRIPTION Plumages most closely recall
Green Sandpiper, with dark, finely spotted
greenish-grey upperparts, white eye-ring, pale
fore-supercilium, dark lores, dark breast, and
rest of underparts contrasting white. Chief
distinctions are dark (not white) rump and dark
central feathers to black-barred white tail,
enabling easy separation in flight (when also
reveals less uniformly dark underwing); at rest,
dark tail-bars reach edge of tail (outer feathers
usually white on Green). Slightly smaller but
longer-legged and more elegant than Green
Sandpiper, with longer, narrower wings which
extend beyond tail tip at rest.
VOICE Typical *tweet-wheet-wheet* call recalls
Common Sandpiper's in quality, and is often
quieter than Green Sandpiper's.
HABITAT Nests in trees in northern forests; at
other times at freshwater habitats such as
muddy pools, ponds, marshes and ditches.
DISTRIBUTION Breeds across much of Canada
from Labrador to Yukon and west into Alaska.

Winters from Mexico and Caribbean south to
central Argentina.
EUROPEAN STATUS Very rare vagrant; 37
records. Britain (26); France (4: 28 Aug 1961;
24 Aug 1969; 14 Jan 1979; 14 Sept 1986);
Iceland (2: 2 Aug 1940; 24 Aug 1969); Ireland
(3: 21-22 Sept 1968; 5-7 Sept 1971; 15-17 Sept
1974); Portugal (1: 26 June 1989); Sweden (1:
May 1987).

TEREK SANDPIPER

Xenus cinereus L 22-25 cm (8.75-10 in)
DESCRIPTION Curious combination of long
upcurved bill and relatively short yellow legs
diagnostic. Has rather featureless grey-brown
head (lores variably darker), breast patches and
upperparts, and white underparts. Shows long
blackish lines over scapulars and black carpal
area, and in flight broad white trailing edge and
darker outer wing; rump and tail grey-brown,
latter edged white. Non-breeding adult slightly
paler grey-brown, usually lacking dark scapular
lines; juvenile darker above, with indistinct dark
subterminal bars and paler fringes. Has fast
feeding action; rocks body like Common
Sandpiper.
VOICE Range of calls includes a sharp, fluty *wit-
wit-wit* and a soft, Redshank-like *chu-du-du*.
HABITAT Nests along rivers and lakeshores;
outside breeding season favours estuaries,
mudflats and brackish marshes.
DISTRIBUTION Breeds from the Baltic eastwards
across Russia and interior Siberia to beyond the
Kolyma river; breeding range expanding
westwards. Winters on Pacific and Indian
Ocean and Arabian coasts and islands from
eastern Australia west to south-west Africa.
EUROPEAN STATUS Breeds regularly in Finland
(max. 20-30 pairs) and Latvia (7 pairs); regular
on passage in Greece and possibly Romania
(annual). Accidental elsewhere: Austria (8);
Belgium (8); Britain (40); Bulgaria (1: Aug 1980);
Czech Republic (5: 3 June 1962; 19 May 1979;
5-10 Sept 1981; 24 June 1983; 29 July 1989);
Denmark (22); Estonia (5: undated 19th century
record; 1 June 1900; summer 1903; 12 Aug
1954; 26 Aug 1992); France (56); Germany (39);
Hungary (8 accepted records, others reported);
Italy (c 40, mainly in autumn); Lithuania (2: 16-17
May 1988, two; 20 May 1994); Luxembourg (1);
Netherlands (11); Norway (5: 24 July 1967;
11 and 15 May 1975; 19 June 1976; 17-19 Nov
1983; 20 May 1986); Poland (42); Slovakia (7
records of 9 birds); Spain (11+); Sweden (85
individuals); Switzerland (6).

SPOTTED SANDPIPER

Actitis macularia L 18-20 cm (7.25-8 in)
DESCRIPTION In breeding plumage unmistakable,
with heavily black-spotted white underparts,
pink legs and black-tipped pink bill. Non-
breeding adult and juvenile very like Common
Sandpiper, from which best separated by greyer
upperparts, less distinct white wing-bar, shorter
tail with slightly less white in outer feathers,
more prominent eye-ring, shorter bill and
proportionately longer yellow legs; juvenile also

has more heavily barred coverts and plainer
tertials than juvenile Common.
VOICE Utters repeated, rising *peet* notes in
flight, slightly sharper than calls of Common
Sandpiper.
HABITAT Uses similar wide range of waterside
habitats to Common Sandpiper.
DISTRIBUTION Breeds across North America
except far northern Canada and southernmost
USA, wintering mainly from east and west
coasts of USA south to northern Chile and
northern Argentina.
EUROPEAN STATUS Frequent vagrant. Austria
(1: 20-21 Oct 1990); Belgium (2: 1883/84; 1887);
Britain (99: bred 1975); Channel Islands (1: 25
May 1988); Finland (2: 3 June 1982; 14-22 May
1989); France (7); Germany (12); Greece (1: 11
May 1992); Iceland (4: undated; 28 July 1984; 15
Sept 1990; 2-6 Nov 1991); Ireland (10); Italy (1:
19 Apr 1986); Netherlands (2: 18 July 1975; Aug
1980); Spain (4: 20-23 Aug 1979; 14 May 1982;
29 Sept-9 Oct 1983; 4 Oct 1986-1 May 1987);
Switzerland (2: June 1891; 23 May 1970).

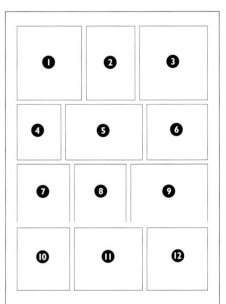

1 **Lesser Yellowlegs** (juvenile, Sept 1989,
Drift Reservoir, Cornwall, Britain)
2 **Lesser Yellowlegs** (adult summer, May
1994, Cley, Norfolk, Britain)
3 **Lesser Yellowlegs** (juvenile moulting into
first-winter plumage, Nov 1995*, Knighton
Reservoir, Shropshire, Britain)
4 **Solitary Sandpiper** (adult, Aug 1995*,
Laugárdalur, Reykjavík, Iceland)
5 **Solitary Sandpiper** (juvenile, Oct 1983,
Tresco, Isles of Scilly, Britain)
6 **Solitary Sandpiper** (juvenile, Sept 1992,
Fair Isle, Shetland, Britain)
7 **Terek Sandpiper** (adult, June 1985, Huizen,
Netherlands)
8 **Terek Sandpiper** (adult, Apr 1993, Orroir,
Belgium)
9 **Terek Sandpiper** (first-winter, Nov 1989,
Blyth Estuary, Northumberland, Britain)
10 **Spotted Sandpiper** (juvenile, Oct 1990,
Lake Constance, Vorarlberg, Austria)
11 **Spotted Sandpiper** (adult, Sept 1991,
Lerwick, Shetland, Britain)
12 **Spotted Sandpiper** (juvenile, Oct 1994,
Welney, Norfolk, Britain)

GREY-TAILED TATTLER

Heteroscelus brevipes L 24-27 cm (9.5-10.75 in)
DESCRIPTION Recalls Redshank in general size and build, but shorter legs and long wings and tail impart distinctive jizz. Breeding adult essentially plain slate-grey across entire upperparts, relieved only by darker outer primaries and primary coverts, white tips to outer greater coverts and inner primary coverts, and faintly white-barred uppertail-coverts; underwing also grey, with white-tipped coverts slightly darker than flight feathers. Head marked by prominent white supercilia meeting above bill, dark lores and whitish eye-ring. Underparts whitish, lightly streaked and barred grey on neck, breast and upper flanks. Non-breeding adult has whiter foreneck, and streaking and barring on underparts replaced by grey wash on breast sides. Juvenile similar, but wing-coverts, scapulars and tertials patterned with neat whitish spots and outer tail notched whitish; spotted coverts replaced by middle of first winter. Straight, rather thick bill is blackish with dull yellowish base; legs yellow. Teeters in manner of Common Sandpiper when feeding.
VOICE Flight call is usually a disyllabic, whistled *tu-whip* or *tuee-dee.*
HABITAT Nests along mountain rivers; at other times typically on coastal mudflats, tidal mangroves, estuaries and rocky and sandy beaches.
DISTRIBUTION Breeding range poorly known, but principally in eastern Siberia east of the Lena river and around the upper Yenisey. Long-distance migrant, wintering southern South-East Asia, Indonesia, New Guinea and Australasia.
EUROPEAN STATUS Extreme vagrant: two late autumn/winter records. Britain (2: 13 Oct-17 Nov 1981; 27 Nov-27 Dec 1994).

WILLET

Catoptrophorus semipalmatus L 33-41 cm (13.25-16.5 in)
DESCRIPTION Rather large, heavily built shank-like wader with diagnostic black-and-white wing pattern. Breeding adult grey-brown above, streaked and barred darker, with white rump and grey-washed tail; whitish below, streaked brown on neck and breast and barred on flanks. Head shows white fore-supercilium and eye-ring and darker lores. Pattern of open wing striking, with grey coverts, black outer wing and outer secondaries, and broad white dividing wing-bar from inner secondaries to outer primaries, recalling Black-tailed Godwit; underwing even more boldly marked, with white lesser coverts, rest of coverts black, and white flight feathers with black tips to primaries. Non-breeding adult nondescript greyish above, narrowly fringed white, and white below with pale grey wash on breast and flanks. Juvenile similar, but slightly darker on upperparts, with feathers showing dark subterminal lines and broad pale fringes, and with pale notches on tertials and rear

scapulars; much as adult by mid-winter. Rather heavy blue-grey legs and straight blackish-grey bill with paler base distinctive.
VOICE Very vocal, with range of calls including a musical *pill-will-willet,* from which name is derived, a harsh *wee-wee-wee* in flight, and hard *kip* and *krep* notes, often repeated in alarm.
HABITAT In east of range breeds in short saltmarsh vegetation, in west around lakes and ponds on prairies; both populations coastal in winter, frequenting saltmarshes, estuaries, beaches and mudflats.
DISTRIBUTION Breeds eastern North America from Nova Scotia to the Gulf of Mexico and West Indies, wintering south to northern South America, and in interior southern Canada and north-west USA, wintering on the Pacific coast from California to Peru and the Galapagos.
EUROPEAN STATUS Extreme vagrant: three records. Finland (1: 21 Sept 1983); France (1: undated 19th century record); Norway (1: 14 and 19 Oct 1992-23 Mar 1993).

WILSON'S PHALAROPE

Phalaropus tricolor L 22-24 cm (8.75-9.5 in)
DESCRIPTION Largest of the three phalaropes, with distinctly longer neck and bill, pot-bellied shape and diagnostic white rump. Summer adult female beautifully marked, with pearly-grey forehead and crown, whiter hindneck, broad black band from base of bill through eye which becomes deep chestnut on neck sides, short white supercilium, and white chin and throat above orange flush on sides of foreneck and breast. Neck striping extends onto upperparts, which are patterned with broad chestnut and grey bands, but upperwing and tail are plain grey. Bill and legs black. Breeding male has variably subdued, browner version of female plumage. Non-breeding adult has very pale grey upperparts, white face with dark eye smudge, white underparts and yellow legs; appears remarkably plain in flight, with virtually no wing-bar, plain grey back, white rump and uppertail coverts, and grey tail. Juvenile dark brown above, fringed paler, and with buffish wash to breast and pinkish-yellow legs; first-winter very like adult winter, but first-summer often lacks full breeding plumage. Often tame and approachable; more terrestrial than other phalaropes, seldom swimming and preferring to feed with fast, mincing gait.
VOICE Usually silent away from breeding sites; in flight, may utter a soft *aangh.*
HABITAT Nests in shallow prairie marshes; at other times usually around marshy ponds, lagoons and other inland wetlands, and rarely off coasts or at sea like Red-necked and Grey Phalaropes.
DISTRIBUTION Breeds in North America from interior of western Canada south to California and Utah, and locally in Great Lakes region. Long-distance migrant, wintering from Peru and Bolivia south to Argentina and Chile.
EUROPEAN STATUS Frequent vagrant. Belgium (12); Britain (188); Channel Islands (2: 9-19 Sept 1970; 25-28 Sept 1981); Denmark (5);

Estonia (1: 6 Oct 1989); Finland (4: 15-21 May 1973; 14 May 1974; 12 June 1985; 14-17 Sept 1989); France (56); Germany (8); Iceland (2: Sept 1979; 20 Sept 1992); Ireland (67); Italy (2: 30 Mar 1978; 14 May 1981); Netherlands (15); Norway (4: 20 and 22 May 1980; 11 May 1984; 13-16 June 1993; 20 Sept 1994); Portugal (2: 9 Apr 1988; 23 Sept 1989); Spain (7); Sweden (7).

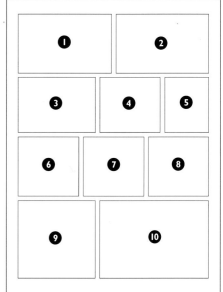

1 Grey-tailed Tattler (juvenile, Dec 1994, Burghead, Grampian, Britain)
2 Grey-tailed Tattler (juvenile, Dec 1994, Burghead, Grampian, Britain)
3 Grey-tailed Tattler (juvenile, Dec 1994, Burghead, Grampian, Britain)
4 Willet (first-winter, Oct 1992, Mølen, Vestfold, Norway)
5 Willet (first-winter, Oct 1992, Mølen, Vestfold, Norway)
6 Willet (first-winter, Oct 1992, Mølen, Vestfold, Norway)
7 Willet (first-winter, Oct 1992, Mølen, Vestfold, Norway)
8 Wilson's Phalarope (first-winter, Oct 1995*, Gardur, Iceland)
9 Wilson's Phalarope (adult female, June 1995*, Porlock Marsh, Somerset, Britain)
10 Wilson's Phalarope (juvenile moulting to first-winter plumage, Sept 1994, Steart Point, Somerset, Britain)

GREAT BLACK-HEADED GULL

Larus ichthyaetus L 57-61 cm (23-24 in)
DESCRIPTION Large, long-winged and powerfully-built gull with long, sloping forehead, deep chest and attenuated rear end giving distinctive shape. Adult summer has full black hood with white eye-crescents; long bill is orangey-yellow with black subterminal band and reddish tip. Upperparts pale grey, with white wing tip showing black subterminal markings on outermost primaries. Legs yellow. In winter, hood replaced by dark smudge from eye to nape/hindcrown. First-winter has similar head pattern and (unusually for a large gull) largely pale grey mantle and scapulars and white underparts, but brownish coverts and dark outer primaries, secondary bar and tail band. May acquire hood in first summer; by second winter more extensively grey above, with blackish outer wing and narrow black tail band, and usually with fuller hood in second summer. Third-winter has blacker outer primaries and remnants of tail band, fading through third summer to reach adult plumage in following winter.
HABITAT Breeds on lakes and rivers in steppe terrain; winters chiefly in coastal areas and estuaries.
DISTRIBUTION Occurs sparsely from the Black Sea eastwards through southern Central Asia to westernmost China; winters Israel, Egypt, Red Sea and the Persian Gulf east to Thailand.
EUROPEAN STATUS Almost annual in recent years in Romania. Accidental elsewhere: Austria (1: 30 Sept and 2 Oct 1992); Belgium (1: 4 and 22-23 June 1936); Britain (1: May or June 1859); Bulgaria (1: 9-12 Jan 1993, three); Czech Republic (1: 27 Sept 1992); Denmark (2: 11 Oct 1987; 10 Oct 1993); Germany (3: 17 Feb 1991; 12 Jan and 29 Feb 25 Mar 1992; 26 Feb-6 Mar 1994); Greece (10-12); Hungary (8 records of possibly 6 individuals, all since 1992); Italy (4: 2 Mar 1901, two; 6 May 1906; Jan-Mar 1993; 5 Mar 1994); Latvia (1: 28 May 1974, two); Lithuania (2: 20 June 1988; 9 July 1994); Netherlands (2: 16 June 1946; 22 June-23 Sept 1974, returning 9-30 Aug 1975 and 15 July-15 Aug 1976); Norway (2: 8 Mar 1986; 29 Apr 1987); Poland (9); Sweden (2: 12 Sept 1956; 2 June 1958).

LAUGHING GULL

Larus atricilla L 36-41 cm (14.5-16.5 in)
DESCRIPTION Almost size of Common Gull, but has darker grey upperparts and distinctive rakish appearance, with long wings and relatively long, drooping bill. Adult in summer plumage has full black hood with white eye-crescents, dull red bill with black band near tip, and dull red legs; upperwing dark grey, with black outer primaries (tipped white) and broad white trailing edge. In winter, shows greyish patch on ear-coverts often extending onto crown, and blackish bill and legs. First-winter is grey on hindneck, breast and flanks, with brown inner wing-coverts, blackish primaries and secondary bar and black band on grey tail.

By first summer shows less grey on head and neck, and paler brown wing-coverts; by second winter wings more uniformly grey with black tips, but usually has remnants of dark secondary bar and tail band, and grey wash to neck, breast and flanks. In second summer has partial or full hood, reaching adult-like plumage in third winter. Long wings extend well beyond tail when perched; confusion likely only with Franklin's Gull, which see below for diagnostic differences.
HABITAT Nests in colonies on islets and in coastal marshes; mainly coastal in winter, but ranges inland and will follow plough or come to bread.
DISTRIBUTION Breeds from north-east USA south along east coast to Caribbean, Central America and northernmost South America. Winters from southern part of breeding range south to northern Chile.
EUROPEAN STATUS Frequent vagrant: records scattered throughout year. Austria (1: 11 Aug 1972); Belgium (1: 28-29 Oct 1994); Britain (56); Denmark (3: June 1985; July 1985; July 1988); France (19); Gibraltar (2: 15 and 27 Nov 1988; 14 Mar 1994); Greece (1: 15 Aug 1984); Iceland (7); Ireland (9); Spain (14); Sweden (3 records of 4 birds: Jan 1964; Oct 1987; Sept 1989).

FRANKLIN'S GULL

Larus pipixcan L 32-36 cm (12.75-14.5 in)
DESCRIPTION Slightly smaller, shorter-winged and more compact-looking than Laughing Gull, which it otherwise resembles in plumage. Chief differences shown by adult summer Franklin's Gull include less black in wing tip, with more extensive white tips to primaries and broad band of white towards base of primaries separating grey inner wing from black on outer wing; also has pink flush to underparts, unique grey-centred tail (all white on Laughing) and, in adult winter, diagnostic blackish 'half-hood'. First-winter differs from first-winter Laughing in also having well-defined half-hood with thick white eye-crescents (often joined at rear), largely white underparts, mainly grey inner primaries, white tips to most primaries and more restricted tail band. Plumage differences less obvious in first-summer and second-winter plumages, but include head, wing tip and tail patterns; Franklin's Gull reaches adult plumage by second summer, a year earlier than Laughing. Structural differences also useful: Franklin's has shorter bill lacking drooping profile, shorter legs and shorter, more rounded wings.
HABITAT Nests exclusively in freshwater marshes; occurs inland and in coastal areas in winter.
DISTRIBUTION Breeds in central North America west of the Great Lakes. Long-distance migrant, wintering chiefly from Guatemala along the Pacific coast south to Chile.
EUROPEAN STATUS Rare vagrant: records scattered throughout year. Belgium (1: 8, 11 and 13 June-11 July 1987); Britain (29); Faeroes

(1: 20 May 1976); France (7); Germany (2: 20-24 Sept 1986; 8-13 Nov 1993); Hungary (1: 19-22 Sept 1992); Iceland (2: 21-26 Sept 1984; 29 Sept 1992); Ireland (1: 7-11 May 1993); Netherlands (2: 10 June-July 1987; June 1988); Norway (5: 16-17 June 1979, two; 24 Dec 1979; 16 Nov 1980; 9 Oct 1985; 12 Nov 1985); Spain (4: 3 May 1978; Oct 1983; 1-4 May 1989; 26 Dec 1990-15 Jan 1991); Sweden (7).

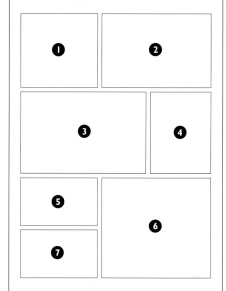

1 Great Black-headed Gull (*adult moulting into summer plumage, Dec, Israel*)
2 Laughing Gull (adult summer, May 1990, Penzance, Cornwall, Britain)
3 Laughing Gull (second-summer with Common and Black-headed Gulls, Sept 1989, Lerwick, Shetland, Britain)
4 Laughing Gull (first-winter, Dec 1991, Walcott, Norfolk, Britain)
5 Franklin's Gull (first-summer, left, with Black-headed Gulls, June 1987, Noordbrabant, Netherlands)
6 Franklin's Gull (second-winter, Mar 1987, Helston, Cornwall, Britain)
7 Franklin's Gull (first-winter, Jan 1982, Plymouth, Devon, Britain)

SABINE'S GULL

Larus sabini L 27-32 cm (10.75-12.75 in)
DESCRIPTION Distinctive and elegant gull, in all plumages showing unique combination of grey (or grey-brown) mantle and inner wing-coverts, black outer primaries and white 'triangle' on rear wing. Adult summer has yellow-tipped black bill and dark grey hood, retained well into autumn; in winter plumage, head white with blackish patch or half-collar on hindcrown and nape. Juvenile darker grey-brown above, with pale fringes giving scaly impression and mantle colour extending onto nape, head and breast sides; shallowly-forked tail has black band. Does not moult into adult-like first-winter plumage until migration completed. In first summer acquires partial hood, but other traces of immaturity barely visible and usually completely lost by second winter. Has buoyant, graceful flight.
HABITAT Nests on marshy coastal tundra; outside breeding season almost entirely pelagic, on migration usually occurring off headlands and coasts mainly during strong onshore winds.
DISTRIBUTION Circumpolar range in high arctic, breeding Siberia, Alaska, Canada and Greenland. Siberian and Alaskan birds winter off Pacific coast of South America, those from Canada and Greenland in southern Atlantic off southern Africa.
EUROPEAN STATUS Regular on passage along Atlantic coasts of Britain (eg 114+ in 1993), Ireland (total 764 individuals) and France (occasionally very numerous, eg 2,000+ in 1993), but less frequent off Spain (c 43 accepted records, but reported regularly at sea off north coast). Fewer enter North Sea and move through English Channel, where recorded Belgium (160), Channel Islands (1: 24 Oct 1982), Denmark (regular), Germany (c 160), Netherlands (regular), Norway (55) and Sweden (107 individuals). Accidental elsewhere: Austria (1: 19th century); Bulgaria (1: May 1988); Czech Republic (2: 8 Dec 1985; 16 Feb 1990); Estonia (1: 31 July 1964); Faeroes (4: undated; 1915; 1918; 23 Aug 1988); Finland (3: 13 Oct 1929; 29 May 1982; 15-28 Sept 1991); Gibraltar (7); Hungary (1: 17 Dec 1941); Iceland (27); Italy (2: 13 Sept 1959; 2 Oct 1971); Latvia (3: 28 July 1919; 1924; 21 Oct 1938); Poland (12); Portugal (13); Romania; Switzerland (13).

BONAPARTE'S GULL

Larus philadelphia L 28-30 cm (11.25-12 in)
DESCRIPTION Resembles small, petite Black-headed Gull. Adult has slightly darker grey upperparts, with similar upperwing pattern of white outer wedge and black trailing edge to primaries, but diagnostic underwing pattern showing translucent white (not dusky) inner primaries with narrow black border. In summer has pink flush to underparts and blackish hood with white eye-crescents; hood replaced by dark ear-covert spot in winter, when also develops pale grey 'shawl' on hindneck and orangey-red legs become paler (often pink). First-winter has blackish-brown (not warm brown as on Black-headed) diagonal carpal bar on grey upperwing, with black outer and grey inner primary coverts, less white on outer primaries and narrower black trailing edge. Bill black, occasionally dark red at base on first-year birds and in winter. Second-year birds as adults, though some retain darker greater primary coverts and (rarely) tail band. Flight more tern-like than that of Black-headed Gull; picks food items off water's surface like Little Gull.
HABITAT The only tree-nesting gull, breeding in coniferous stands near water in the tundra zone; at other times frequents lakes, rivers, marshes and coasts.
DISTRIBUTION Breeds in North America from Alaska east to central Canada, wintering on the Great Lakes and all coasts south to Mexico and the West Indies.
EUROPEAN STATUS Frequent vagrant: most records are in August-March. Britain (69); Czech Republic (1: 24 Apr 1988); Denmark (1: Aug 1988); France (4: 24 Mar 1910; 22 Oct 1987; 20 Feb 1990; 14 Mar 1992); Iceland (7); Ireland (14); Netherlands (4: 4 Aug 1985; 16 June 1988-28 Jan 1989; 11-19 Feb 1990; 6 Apr 1994); Norway (1: 8 and 10-11 Aug 1972); Portugal (5: 28 Feb-8 Apr 1990; 3 Feb-3 Mar 1991; 12 Feb-23 Mar 1991; 11 Jan-11 Mar 1992; 16 Jan-8 Feb 1993); Spain (6); Sweden (1: 1 Feb 1990).

GREY-HEADED GULL

Larus cirrocephalus L 39-42 cm (15.5-16.75 in)
DESCRIPTION Larger and broader-winged than Black-headed Gull, with darker grey upperparts and diagnostic wing pattern of extensive white across hand and black outermost primaries with obvious white 'mirrors'. Underwing appears dusky at all ages. Relatively long neck and bill reminiscent of Slender-billed Gull. In summer, hood of adult is more extensive than on Black-headed Gull and is grey, varying in shade from dove-grey to whitish around base of dark red bill; eyelids white. Legs bright red. Winter adult has paler and less well-defined hood and paler legs. First-winter has indistinct dark ear spot, more black on outer primaries than white, broad blackish trailing edge to entire wing, and diffuse brown diagonal carpal bar and dark tail band. Most second-winter Grey-headed Gulls show more extensive black on primaries than adults, as in first-year, but have less obvious dark trailing edge and little or no dark carpal bar than latter plumage. Full hood usually acquired by second summer. On ground, posture typically more upright than Black-headed Gull's; in flight, wings held straighter, and tends to glide more frequently.
HABITAT Frequents inland freshwater lakes and wetlands; also nests on offshore islands and along coasts.
DISTRIBUTION Breeds in East Africa, Madagascar, isolated parts of southern and West Africa north to Mauretania, and also in eastern and western South America. Dispersive. Has also occurred Israel.
EUROPEAN STATUS Extreme vagrant: two records. Gibraltar (1: 17 Aug 1992); Spain (1: 30 June-15 Aug 1971).

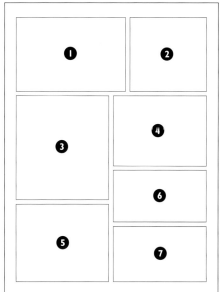

1 **Sabine's Gull** (juvenile, Oct 1991, Flevoland, Netherlands)
2 **Sabine's Gull** (first-summer, Sept 1988, Heysham, Lancashire, Britain)
3 **Sabine's Gull** (adult summer, Aug 1987, at sea off Cornwall, Britain)
4 **Bonaparte's Gull** (adult moulting from summer into winter plumage, Aug 1988, Skagen, Denmark)
5 **Bonaparte's Gull** (first-summer, June 1988, Ijmuiden, Netherlands)
6 **Bonaparte's Gull** (adult moulting into summer plumage, Apr 1990, Seaforth, Merseyside, Britain)
7 **Grey-headed Gull** (second-summer, Mar, Israel)

RING-BILLED GULL

Larus delawarensis L 43-47 cm (17-19 in)
DESCRIPTION In many respects resembles an outsize Common Gull. Summer adult has paler grey mantle and wings, smaller white mirrors in black wing tip (recalling Herring Gull), and yellow bill with well-defined broad black subterminal band. First-winter lacks Common's 'dark-saddled' look but is more strongly patterned above, with blacker outer primaries contrasting with greyer inners, blackish secondary bar, darker brown carpal bar, 'messier' tail band with scattered barring often also present on tail base, tail and rump washed grey (white in Common), and more distinct spots on nape and breast sides, becoming crescentic bars on flanks (more diffusely mottled on Common). In first summer acquires whiter head and body, more faded wing pattern and clearer bill band, and by second winter has grey upperparts with minimal traces of secondary bar and tail band. Adult-type plumage acquired after moult in second summer. Larger form, slightly longer legs, heavier bill, flatter forehead and, from second year, pale (not black) iris give a bulky, fiercer jizz recalling larger gulls.
HABITAT Nests in freshwater locations and in wide variety of coastal situations; winters inland and on coast.
DISTRIBUTION Breeds across central North America from south-east Canada through Great Lakes region to west coast, wintering south to Central America and the Caribbean.
EUROPEAN STATUS Frequent vagrant/visitor: increasingly numerous, with some individuals returning to winter in successive years. Albania (1: 7 Apr-2 June 1993); Austria (2: 8 Apr-9 May and 19-22 May 1993, returning 26 Mar-19 May 1994; Dec 1994); Belgium (3: 12 May 1988; 18-19 Apr 1992; 20-21 Apr 1994); Britain (many, eg 81+ in 1993); Bulgaria (2: 28 Feb 1992; 2 Aug 1993); Channel Islands (10); Czech Republic (1: 16 July 1994); Faeroes (2: 21 Jan 1981; 4 July 1991); France (114); Germany (2: 1 May 1982; 24-26 Feb 1991); Gibraltar (2: Dec 1983; 21 June 1992); Hungary (1: 21 Dec 1990); Iceland (43); Ireland (many, eg c 81 in 1994); Netherlands (3: July 1986; 18-19 Apr 1992; 6 Dec 1992); Norway (17, one of which ringed and recovered Canada); Poland (4: 5 Apr 1984; 25 Feb 1985; 19 Jan 1987; 17 Dec 1988); Portugal (20+); Spain (at least 83 individuals); Sweden (8).

ROSS'S GULL

Rhodostethia rosea L 29-31 cm (11.5-12.5 in)
DESCRIPTION Slightly larger than Little Gull, with proportionately longer, more pointed wings and almost diamond-shaped tail. Pale grey upperwing has broad white trailing edge on secondaries and innermost primaries, unlike narrower but complete white wing border of Little Gull; underwing is uniformly mid-grey, paler than on Little Gull. Summer adult has distinctive fine black neck ring and pink flush to underparts; in winter, neck ring replaced by

pale grey 'shawl' on nape and dark smudge behind ear-coverts. First-winters have noticeably pale grey mantle and scapulars, with a broad black W across upperside which is retained into first summer; separated from first-winter Little Gull by pure white secondaries and inner primaries, indistinct grey (not black) cap, greyer underwing and centrally-elongated black-tipped tail (rather than black tail band). Juveniles (not yet seen Europe) have blackish cap and hindneck and extensive blackish-brown on mantle and scapulars, extending to sides of breast. Flight graceful and tern-like.
HABITAT Breeds on tundra lakes, nesting in small colonies on islands and promontories with permafrost under the soil. Mainly pelagic outside the breeding season.
DISTRIBUTION Breeds in north-east Siberia, and more recently in isolated areas of the Canadian arctic, Manitoba, Greenland and Spitsbergen. In winter usually in arctic and subarctic waters.
EUROPEAN STATUS Frequent vagrant: most in mid-winter, but occasionally also in spring and summer. Britain (58); Denmark (6); Estonia (1: 23-24 May 1988); Faeroes (5: 1 Feb 1863; 1922; 1927; 24 Dec 1942; 9 Mar 1959); Finland (4: 15 June 1973; 10-11 July 1982; 14 Feb 1988; 6-9 Jan 1993); France (1: 22 Dec 1913); Germany (6); Iceland (27); Ireland (10); Italy (1: Jan 1906); Lithuania (1: 6 Nov 1992); Netherlands (7); Norway (5: 6 May 1909; 28 May 1938; 19 Jan 1949; 28 June 1975; 21 May 1981); Poland (1: 15 Jan 1994); Spain (1: 6-11 Apr 1994*); Sweden (11).

IVORY GULL

Pagophila eburnea L 40-43 cm (16-17 in)
DESCRIPTION Slightly larger than Common Gull, but proportionately shorter-winged and more stocky; readily identifiable in all plumages. Adult (rare in Europe) is entirely ivory-white throughout the year, with black eye and legs and yellow-tipped greyish bill; face may be stained darker from feeding. First-winter is white with blackish forehead, lores and chin, and prominent white eye-ring in front of eye; plumage is marked with variable amount of delicate black spotting on mantle and scapulars, rarely also on breast, and wings have black subterminal spots on coverts and tertials and black crescentic tips to primaries, broadest on outermost feathers (on some birds also extending onto secondaries). Tail shows black subterminal marks forming broken band, sometimes also with black spots on uppertail-coverts. Bill duller than adult's. Dusky face and extent of spotting reduced in first-summer plumage, after which appearance is much as adult. Often scavenges on carrion; vagrants are frequently tame.
HABITAT Breeds on bare ground or cliffs by sea, feeding around areas of ice; in winter usually remains within drift ice and close to edge of pack ice.
DISTRIBUTION Breeds Spitsbergen, Franz Josef Land, Novaya Zemlya, Severnaya Zemlya, Canadian arctic and northern Greenland.

Winters largely in arctic waters.
EUROPEAN STATUS Possibly occasional winter visitor to Iceland (147 individuals recorded). Accidental elsewhere: Britain (102); Channel Islands (1: 3 Jan 1993, dead); Denmark (6); Faeroes (8); Finland (c 22 records of c 24 individuals); France (3: 1830 or 1834; 7 Dec 1895; 29 Dec 1984); Germany (4: 20 Jan 1850; 5 Nov 1880; 3-4 Oct 1963; 20 Apr 1980); Ireland (13); Italy (2: 13 Feb 1958; 18 Aug 1972); Netherlands (2: Feb 1987; 9-19 Feb 1990); Norway (57); Poland (1: 25 Sept 1989); Sweden (20); Switzerland (1: 10 Mar 1817).

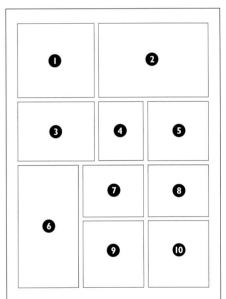

1 **Ring-billed Gull** (first-winter with first-winter and adult winter Common Gulls, Jan 1993, Bergen, Hordaland, Norway)
2 **Ring-billed Gull** (adult summer, Mar 1994, Rhyl, Clwyd, Britain)
3 **Ring-billed Gull** (adult winter with Black-headed Gulls, Feb 1991, Uxbridge, Middlesex, Britain)
4 **Ross's Gull** (adult summer, May 1992, Flói, Iceland)
5 **Ross's Gull** (second-winter with remnants of first-summer plumage, Nov 1992, IJmuiden, Netherlands)
6 **Ross's Gull** (adult winter, Jan 1993, Fraserburgh, Grampian, Britain)
7 **Ross's Gull** (adult summer in worn plumage, June 1958, Friesland, Netherlands)
8 **Ivory Gull** (first-winter, Feb 1990, Stellendam, Netherlands)
9 **Ivory Gull** (first-winter, Feb 1986, Saltburn, Cleveland, Britain)
10 **Ivory Gull** (adult summer, July 1995*, Inverness, Highland, Britain)

ROYAL TERN

Sterna maxima L 45-50 cm (18-20 in)
DESCRIPTION Large tern, roughly size (but not quite bulk) of Caspian Tern. Breeding adult has black cap with shaggy crest; rest of body, including rump and forked tail, white. Upperwing appears very pale grey, with outer primaries appearing duskier grey and darkening towards tip; primaries white on underside, with black trailing edge on outer feathers. Compared to Caspian, has less stout, more orange bill – not blood-red with black behind tip – and lacks dark undersides to primaries. In non-breeding plumage, Royal's forehead is white (streaked dark grey in Caspian). Juvenile plumage, with brown-tinged upperparts, gull-like dark lesser and greater wing-covert and secondary bars and dark tail band, gives way in late autumn to greyer first-winter plumage, in which wing-covert bars are less prominent. First-summer like adult winter, though secondary bar retained into second winter.
HABITAT Coastal species, breeding on sandy islands in lagoon systems; in winter also along estuaries and rivers and in harbours.
DISTRIBUTION Breeds in equatorial West Africa, range extending in winter north to Morocco and south to Angola, and in many areas of southern coastal USA and West Indies, wintering south to Ecuador and Argentina.
EUROPEAN STATUS Very rare vagrant: possibly irregular passage migrant southern Iberia. Britain (4: 28-29 July 1965; 2 Sept 1971; 24 Nov 1979; 21 Dec 1987); Gibraltar (9); Ireland (1: 24 Mar 1954, dead); Norway (1: 26 June 1976); Portugal (1: 10 Oct 1991); Spain (5 records of 6 individuals, including an Oct recovery of a North American-ringed bird).

LESSER CRESTED TERN

Sterna bengalensis L 40 cm (16 in)
DESCRIPTION Size of Sandwich Tern. Breeding adult has black cap with shorter shaggy crest than Royal Tern, grey rump and forked tail (concolorous with back and wings), and rest of body white. Cap whitens on forehead during summer, acquiring black band from eye to nape from early autumn. Upperwing pale grey, a shade darker than on Sandwich, with outer primaries contrastingly silvery-grey with darker trailing edge; underwing white. Relatively long, slightly drooping bill is bright orangey-yellow, yellower in winter; legs black. Juvenile resembles juvenile Royal; rump paler grey than adult's. Upperparts greyer during first winter, when legs may be yellow. In first-summer plumage, some retain dark wing-covert bars but others are more like adult winter; dark secondary bar retained into second winter. Has hybridised with Sandwich Tern in Europe, producing offspring showing characters of both parents.
HABITAT Coastal, breeding on sandy beaches, islands and coral reefs.
DISTRIBUTION Breeds Libya, Red Sea and Gulf of Kuwait, moving west out of Mediterranean to northern West Africa and south and east widely along Indian Ocean coasts; also breeds northern Australia, dispersing to Indonesian and South-East Asian waters.
EUROPEAN STATUS Rare vagrant, occasionally breeding: possibly regular but very scarce on passage in southern Iberia, and some records involve birds returning annually to Sandwich Tern colonies. Austria (2: 4-5 Aug 1980, two; 31 July 1983); Britain (4: 13 July 1982; 9 Aug-17 Sept 1983, presumed same bird returning each subsequent year to 1994 and after; 17-20 July 1985; 13 May 1986); France (14); Gibraltar (12); Greece (3: 11-13 June 1987; 4 July 1990; July 1993); Italy (1-2 pairs annually; others recorded); Slovenia (1: 5 June 1993*); Spain (1-2 pairs annually); Switzerland (2: 3 Sept 1946; 19-20 Aug 1977).

ELEGANT TERN

Sterna elegans L 39-43 cm (16-17 in)
DESCRIPTION Slightly larger than Lesser Crested Tern but otherwise very similar in appearance. Breeding adult has black cap with longer, drooping shaggy crest, grey-tinged white rump and forked tail (paler than back and wings), and rest of body white; some may have diagnostic pink tinge to underparts. Black 'hind-mask' of winter plumage broader than on Royal and Lesser Crested Terns. Upperwing paler grey than on Lesser Crested, with darker trailing edge. Slender, slightly drooping bill is longer than Lesser Crested's and yellowish-orange to red, becoming yellower in winter; legs black, occasionally red-brown. Juvenile has variegated upperparts and greyish-yellow bill; darker primaries, wing-covert and secondary bars and tail band retained into first-winter plumage, when upperparts greyer. First-summers retain winter-plumage head, dark secondary bar and dark primaries, becoming more like adult by second winter.
HABITAT Coastal, often nesting alongside Royal Terns in restricted Nearctic range.
DISTRIBUTION Range confined to coastal California and Pacific coast of Mexico in summer; winters chiefly in western Central America and north-western South America.
EUROPEAN STATUS Extreme vagrant: four records. France (2: first in June 1974, returning several subsequent years and paired to Sandwich Tern; second in 1984, one bird returning until at least 1991); Ireland (1: 22 June-3 July 1982, then 1 Aug 1982); Spain (1: 24-30 Apr 1993*). Additional record from Belgium in 1988 not accepted, as possibility of hybrid not ruled out.

ALEUTIAN TERN

Sterna aleutica L 32-34 cm (12.75-13.5 in)
DESCRIPTION Similar to Common Tern in structure, but with longer and broader wings. Adult summer has neat black cap with white forehead, bordered below by narrow black line through eye. Area immediately below cap white, as are rump and tail, but plumage otherwise smoky mid-grey, darker above than below. In flight, white-edged grey upperwing shows contrast between whiter inner primaries (translucent against light) and darker grey outer primaries; on underwing, outer primaries show dark trailing edge and secondaries a distinct greyer bar. In winter plumage, acquires whiter forehead and white lores to give head pattern recalling winter Arctic Tern; underparts also white. Bill and legs black. Browner juvenile plumage moulted into progressively greyer sub-adult plumages which resemble adult winter but are paler above, with darker 'shoulder'.
VOICE Has distinctive whistling, wader-like call.
HABITAT Inhabits subarctic islands and coasts, nesting among vegetation on rocky or sandy ground, often in loose association with Arctic Terns and Kittiwakes.
DISTRIBUTION Breeds north-west Canada, Alaska, Aleutian Islands, Bering Sea and eastern Siberia. Migration routes and winter range poorly known, with no records from Canada or USA south of Gulf of Alaska; small numbers recently discovered wintering near Philippines, but only other reports from Asia concern c 10 records from Japan (where breeding suspected in 1980) and first records in Hong Kong (190+ in autumn 1992).
EUROPEAN STATUS Extreme vagrant: one spring record. Britain (1: 28-29 May 1979).

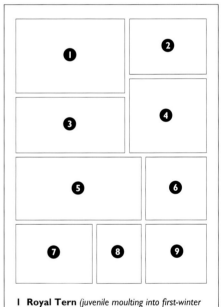

1 **Royal Tern** (*juvenile moulting into first-winter plumage, date unknown, New Jersey, USA*)
2 **Royal Tern** (*sub-adult, date unknown, Florida, USA*)
3 **Lesser Crested Tern** (adult summer, June 1994, Farne Islands, Northumberland, Britain)
4 **Lesser Crested Tern** (adult winter, Aug 1993, Cagliari, Sardinia, Italy)
5 **Lesser Crested Tern** (adult summer among Sandwich Terns, Mediterranean and Black-headed Gulls, Apr 1995*, Llobregat Delta, Spain)
6 **Elegant Tern** (adult summer, June 1982, Greencastle, Co Down, Ireland)
7 **Elegant Tern** (possibly hybrid, July 1988*, Zeebrugge, Belgium)
8 **Elegant Tern** (possibly hybrid, July 1988*, Zeebrugge, Belgium)
9 **Aleutian Tern** (adult summer, May 1979, Farne Islands, Northumberland, Britain)

FORSTER'S TERN

Sterna forsteri L 33-36 cm (13.25-14.5 in)
DESCRIPTION Very like Common Tern in summer plumage, but slightly larger, with heavier bill and impression of somewhat broader and longer wing hand and more relaxed flight. Breeding adult has black cap enclosing eye, pure white body with long tail-streamers, and pale grey upperparts; rump white, contrasting with greyer tail. Compared to Common and Arctic Terns, front of black cap is separated from red bill by a broader area of white along side of forehead – producing a different facial expression, obvious even at range. Silver-grey primaries are palest part of upperwing (a quick means of distinguishing Forster's from Common and Arctic Terns); outer primaries show dark grey tips on underside. In winter plumage has distinctive black oval-shaped 'mask' over eye and ear-coverts; black-tipped orangey-red bill then becomes all black. Juvenile has similar head pattern, brown-tinged upperparts and red legs and bill base, soon acquiring black bill, pale grey mantle and contrastingly darker wing of first-winter plumage; in flight, darker secondary bar especially apparent. First-summer like adult winter, but with darker primaries and secondary bar; subsequent immature plumages as adult. Plunge-dives, but also picks prey items from water's surface.
HABITAT Frequents coastal but particularly inland waters in natural range, breeding on marshes, islands and tidal creeks; vagrants in Europe typically coastal.
DISTRIBUTION Has fragmented range in North America, from Canada south to the Gulf of Mexico and on both coasts. Winters from California and south-east USA south to Central America.
EUROPEAN STATUS Very rare vagrant: overwintering occasionally recorded. Britain (12); Gibraltar (1: Oct 1987); Iceland (1: 22 Oct 1959); Ireland (9+); Netherlands (1: Nov 1986); Portugal (1: 31 Dec 1993); Sweden (1: 26 Apr 1993).

BRIDLED TERN

Sterna anaethetus L 30-32 cm (12-13 in)
DESCRIPTION Strikingly distinctive tern, likely to be confused only with Sooty Tern. Breeding adult has head pattern recalling Little Tern, with isolated black cap broken at front by white patch extending short distance up forehead and coming to point at sides just behind eye. Grey-brown mantle colour extends across upperwing (flight feathers slightly darker) and from rump to tail, which is somewhat greyer with white outer feathers. Underwing predominantly white, with contrasting dark band on trailing edge; outermost three primaries paler, forming whitish tip to hand. Underparts white, becoming greyer especially on belly. Legs black. Adult winter paler, with whiter forecrown and white flecking on mantle. Juvenile variable, often recalling young Common Tern with greyer upperparts, but some are all dark on head and

upperparts. First-winter like adult winter, but with juvenile wing and tail; first-summer lacks white in tail. Flight buoyant and graceful, with slow, 'elastic' wingbeats.
HABITAT Breeds primarily on oceanic islands, nesting on ground under bushes or in cave or hollow on cliff face; at other times remains offshore.
DISTRIBUTION Closest breeding sites to Europe are in southern Morocco, Mauretania, Red Sea and Persian Gulf; otherwise widely distributed in Caribbean, Indian Ocean, South-East Asia, Indonesia and Australia.
EUROPEAN STATUS Very rare vagrant: most records fall in July-August. Belgium (1: 9-22 July 1989); Britain (19); Denmark (1: July 1987); France (6); Greece (1: 6 June 1987); Ireland (1: 29 Nov 1953, dead); Netherlands (1: present intermittently 4 July-1 Aug 1989, two).

SOOTY TERN

Sterna fuscata L 33-36 cm (13-14.5 in)
DESCRIPTION Larger, longer-winged and more black-and-white than Bridled Tern, but differences less obvious at range. Breeding adult has similar head pattern, but white forehead patch appears rounder (not triangular) and at sides ends in front of (not behind) eye. Black cap joined to black-brown upperparts which are uniformly dark across wings, rump and tail; latter has long streamers with white outer feathers. Underwing is bicoloured, with white coverts and extensively blackish-grey flight feathers. Underparts appear clean white. Bill and legs black. Juvenile striking, with white tips on black mantle and wings forming rows of spots, sooty-brown head, throat and breast, and dingy pale belly; underwing similar to adult's but with greyer coverts. Forehead, nape and underparts become paler in first winter, with more traces of adult plumage by first summer; thereafter very like adult, but with some dark spotting on white areas. Powerful flier, spending much of life on the wing; surface-feeder.
HABITAT Breeds on tropical islands among grass or on exposed sand and rock, often in large colonies. Highly pelagic outside breeding season.
DISTRIBUTION Widely distributed on breeding islands in South Atlantic, Caribbean, Indian and Pacific Oceans, dispersing to winter at sea.
EUROPEAN STATUS Rare vagrant: most records fall in June-August. Britain (25); Denmark (1: June 1989); France (11); Germany (3: 5 Aug 1843; 22 Sept 1929; 12-21 July 1957); Iceland (1: 12 June 1969); Italy (4: 28 Oct 1862; 19 Sept 1907; 11 Aug 1909; 11 Mar 1926); Norway (1: 15 May 1976, two); Spain (5+); Sweden (2: 6 July 1977; 26 July 1977).

BROWN NODDY

Anous stolidus L 38-40 cm (15-16 in)
DESCRIPTION Tropical species with uniquely dark year-round plumage. Adult is entirely blackish-brown except for pale greyish or greyish-white forehead, crown and eye-crescents. Upperwing shows slight contrast, with blacker flight feathers, and in worn

plumage median coverts may appear fractionally paler, forming hint of carpal bar. Long, shallowly forked streamerless tail is wider in centre than at base or tip, forming blunt wedge shape; appears pointed when closed. Long, powerful bill is black and droops slightly at tip; legs dark red-brown. Very little seasonal variation, with usually limited dark flecking on crown in winter. Juvenile like adult, but with duller blackish-brown plumage and less pale grey on crown; coverts and upperparts have pale fringing visible at close range. Subsequent immature plumages very like adult. Direct flight is strong and purposeful, but frequently alights on flotsam, post or beach; surface-feeder.
HABITAT Breeds on marine islands and reefs, usually on ground or cliffs but occasionally in tree-top or bush.
DISTRIBUTION Widely distributed in tropical and subtropical oceans, including South Atlantic, Caribbean, Indian Ocean and the Pacific. Dispersive in parts of range, apparently wintering at sea.
EUROPEAN STATUS Extreme vagrant: two records. Germany (1: Oct 1912); Norway (1: 3 Aug 1974).

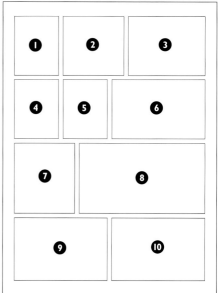

1 Forster's Tern (adult winter, Nov 1986, Penmon, Anglesey, Britain)
2 Forster's Tern (adult winter, Nov 1986, Zeeland, Netherlands)
3 Forster's Tern (adult winter, left, with Sandwich Tern, Oct 1986, Abergele, Clwyd, Britain)
4 Forster's Tern (adult winter, Nov 1986, Zeeland, Netherlands)
5 Bridled Tern (adult, July 1989, Ijmuiden, Netherlands)
6 Bridled Tern (adult with Arctic Terns, July 1988, Cemlyn Bay, Anglesey, Britain)
7 Bridled Tern (adult, July 1989, Ijmuiden, Netherlands)
8 Bridled Tern (adult, June 1994, Foulney Island, Cumbria, Britain)
9 Sooty Tern (first-summer showing characters of nominate race, May 1980, Ditchford Gravel Pits, Northants, Britain)
10 Brown Noddy *(adult, Jan, Seychelles)*

BRÜNNICH'S GUILLEMOT

Uria lomvia L 39-43 cm (16-17 in)
DESCRIPTION In all plumages very like Guillemot. Breeding adult is darker brownish-black above, almost approaching blackness of Razorbill; white of underparts ends in point on foreneck, not 'rounded off' as on Guillemot. Unlike that species, retains breeding plumage well into autumn and non-breeding plumage into spring, when easier to separate with black extending further below eye and around neck sides than on Guillemot, which instead shows characteristic narrow black line running behind eye onto white rear cheeks. At close range, shorter, stouter bill with evenly decurved culmen and white along sides of gape, forming clear stripe, is also good distinction; white stripe reduced and may be lacking in winter. First-winter like adult, but with smaller bill and usually some dusky mottling on throat. Has subtly different structure from Guillemot, with stockier build and shorter nape; in flight appears more compact and hunch-backed, and, unlike Guillemot, has extensive white at rump sides and no streaking on flanks.
HABITAT Nests in large colonies on northern sea cliffs; pelagic outside breeding season.
DISTRIBUTION Breeds on coasts and islands in northernmost Europe, Siberia, Canada and Greenland. Winters at sea.
EUROPEAN STATUS Breeds in Iceland (600,000-800,000 pairs) and Norway (c 3,000 pairs); visitor to Faeroes. Accidental elsewhere: Austria (1: 20 June 1882); Belgium (3: 4 Jan 1981; 18 Jan 1981; 7 Dec 1981); Britain (30); Denmark (8); Finland (c 63, of which 58 in 1902); France (2: 21 Apr 1978; 21 Jan 1981); Germany (3: 1 Nov 1959; 8 Mar 1966; undated); Ireland (1: 24 Dec 1986); Netherlands (8); Poland (10: Apr 1964), Spain, Sweden (23).

ANCIENT MURRELET

Synthliboramphus antiquus L 24-27 cm (9.5-11 in)
DESCRIPTION Small, stocky alcid unlikely to be misidentified in European waters. Adult summer has black head and throat, white rear supercilium extending onto nape, small, pointed horn-coloured bill, and white neck sides above black half-collar. Upperparts otherwise mid-grey, in flight revealing contrasting black flight feathers and tail and largely white underwing with blackish 'frame'; underparts white. Non-breeding adult similar, but lacks white supercilium and well-defined black throat. First-winter has whiter face and smaller, duskier bill. Clearly smaller than Puffin, but even at range when size harder to assess may be separated from all other European auks by dark head and contrasting grey upperparts.
HABITAT Nests in burrows under tree roots in closed-canopy coniferous forest; largely pelagic outside breeding season.
DISTRIBUTION Breeds in North Pacific, from Commander Islands and Kamchatka south to Korea, and from the Aleutians and Alaska south to Queen Charlotte group, British Columbia. Most winter at sea away from colonies, in North America south to waters off California; occasionally 'wrecked' inland.
EUROPEAN STATUS Extreme vagrant: one record of returning individual. Britain (1: 27 May-26 June 1990, returning 14 Apr-20 June 1991 and 30 Mar-29 Apr 1992).

TUFTED PUFFIN

Lunda cirrhata L 36-41 cm (14-16 in)
DESCRIPTION Unmistakable. Breeding adult has extensively white face sides from bill base to rear ear-coverts, with diagnostic long, straw-coloured plumes trailing back from behind eye and down nape. Plumage otherwise entirely glossy black, extending up back of head between 'tufts' and onto crown and upper forehead, almost reaching massive red bill which has yellowish-green base to upper mandible. Outside breeding season sheds sheath of bill, which becomes dusky grey with extensively red tip; extent of white on face reduces to large dirty-white oval patch around pale eye, and has brownish plumes, blackish-grey upperparts and brownish-grey underparts. Immature has smaller, dull horn-yellow bill, short ear tufts, paler chin and brownish-grey underparts (often tipped white on belly). Easily separated from smaller Atlantic Puffin by lack of white underparts.
HABITAT Nests in colonies on rocky coasts and islands, often foraging far out to sea. Pelagic outside breeding season.
DISTRIBUTION Breeds in North Pacific from north-east Siberia south to northern Japan, through the Bering Sea to the Aleutians, Alaska and south to northern California. Winters at sea. Has straggled to Atlantic coast of USA.
EUROPEAN STATUS Extreme vagrant: one summer record. Sweden (1: 1 and 8 June 1994).

PALLAS'S SANDGROUSE

Syrrhaptes paradoxus L 30-41 cm (12-16 in)
DESCRIPTION Male has extensively orange face, pale grey hindcrown, ear-covert line, neck and breast, black-barred sandy-brown upperparts, largely plain sandy-brown wing-coverts, and black belly patch and breast bar divided by buff-white. Tail long and pointed. Elongated longest primary gives wing distinctive pointed shape at close range. Female similar, but with dark speckling (not barring) on upperparts extending onto nape, ear-coverts, sides of neck and wing-coverts; also has thin black neck-collar and no dark breast band. Juvenile has browner breast, no orange on head and plainer upperparts.
VOICE Flight calls include characteristic *kep* and low-pitched *cu-ruu cu-ruu cu-ouruu*.
HABITAT Favours arid plains, steppe, semi-desert and uplands, which occasionally forced to vacate in large numbers during inclement weather in breeding season.
DISTRIBUTION Breeds from Caspian Sea eastwards in broad belt through Central Asia to China. Partial migrant, leaving northern parts of range to winter further south.
EUROPEAN STATUS Very rare vagrant outside infrequent irruption years: many records relate to influxes in late 19th and early 20th centuries (eg in 1863, 1888 and 1908), after which breeding widely recorded, but very few recent occurrences. Austria; Belgium (125+, has bred: most recent record on 29 May-9 June 1961); Britain (many: 7 since 1958, most recent on 19 May-4 and 22 June 1990); Bulgaria; Channel Islands (records include flock of c 12 on 15 May 1888); Czech Republic (prior to 1935); Denmark (most recent record in Jan 1972: has bred); Estonia (4: most recent on 22 June 1908); Faeroes (recorded 1863 and 1888); Finland (7 records of 14 birds); France (3); Germany (recorded 1863, 1888 and 1908; also on 9 Nov 1937 and 31 July 1983); Greece (1: spring 1888); Hungary (recorded in 15 years during 1859-1944: breeding attempted 1864); Ireland (127+); Italy (4 pre-1958 records under review); Latvia; Lithuania (5: all in 19th century); Luxembourg; Netherlands (bred 1863 and 1888: 8 individuals since 1900); Norway (14: most recent 20 July-11 Nov 1990); Poland (most recent on 29 Apr 1990, seven, and 25 Apr 1992, four); Romania; Spain (1: 9 June 1888); Slovakia (prior to 1950); Sweden (58: many pre-1900, most recent on 23-25 June 1969); Switzerland (4: Aug 1863; Aug 1863; Nov 1863; Dec 1863); former Yugoslavia.

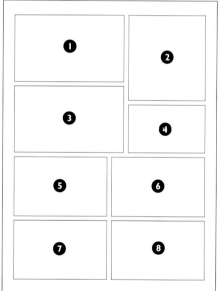

1 **Brünnich's Guillemot** (winter, Jan 1995*, Shetland, Britain)
2 **Brünnich's Guillemot** (summer, July 1994, Hujfilbjarg, Iceland)
3 **Ancient Murrelet** (with Guillemots, June 1990, Lundy, Devon, Britain)
4 **Ancient Murrelet** (June 1990, Lundy, Devon, Britain)
5 **Tufted Puffin** (adult summer, Aug, Alaska, USA)
6 **Pallas's Sandgrouse** (adult male, May 1990, Quendale, Shetland, Britain)
7 **Pallas's Sandgrouse** (adult male, May 1990, Quendale, Shetland, Britain)
8 **Pallas's Sandgrouse** (adult male, May 1990, Quendale, Shetland, Britain)

ORIENTAL TURTLE DOVE

Streptopelia orientalis L 33-35 cm (13.25-14 in)
DESCRIPTION Very like Turtle Dove but larger and heavier, with shorter 'triangular' primary projection and tail. Eastern race *orientalis* has more extensively black centres to rufous-fringed scapulars and tertials, paler diffuse fringes to wing-coverts (creating impression of wing panel), browner breast and belly, pale grey undertail-coverts, and more black in white undertail. Head shows contrast between grey crown and brownish nape; eye has round (not oval) orbital ring, and looks more centrally placed on face. Neck patch appears bluish with up to six narrow black bars (fewer, thicker bars on white background on Turtle Dove). Smaller western race *meena* less distinctive, with whiter belly and wing-covert pattern similar to Turtle Dove. In flight, species shows more contrasting pattern on shorter wings, with blacker secondaries and outer wing and at least two pale wing-bars. Juveniles browner, with less contrasting plumage and no neck patch.
VOICE Very different from purring of Turtle Dove: a repeated, hoarse *woo-woo-kak-coor*, recalling Wood Pigeon.
HABITAT Nests in variety of forested and wooded terrain, but vagrants show no particular habitat preference.
DISTRIBUTION Breeds from Urals across Asia to Pacific coast and south to India and Burma; northern populations winter in south of range.
EUROPEAN STATUS Very rare vagrant: 46 records between autumn and spring, with occasional overwintering. Britain (5: 23 Oct 1889, shot; 29 Jan 1946, shot; 2-6 May 1960; 31 Oct-1 Nov 1974; 8 Nov 1975); Denmark (9); Finland (7, including 3 *meena* and 2 *orientalis*); France (2: 12 Oct 1981; 16 Oct 1988); Germany (1: 25 Oct 1943); Greece (5: 18 Sept 1948; 22 Apr 1963; 21 Aug 1965; Sept 1966; 27 Apr 1986); Hungary (1: 18 Dec 1985); Italy (1: 25 Sept 1901); Norway (4: 13 Nov 1903; 20 Nov 1907; 21 Feb-20 Mar 1978; 25 Jan-12 and 16-17 Feb 1992); Spain (1: 3 Feb 1994*); Sweden (10, including one bird returning each winter 1985-94).

LAUGHING DOVE

Streptopelia senegalensis L 25-27 cm (10-10.75 in)
DESCRIPTION Recalls smaller, more warmly coloured Turtle Dove, but structure and tail like Collared Dove. Head, neck, breast and underparts to belly pinkish-buff, with black-flecked copper-coloured gorget on upper breast; belly and undertail white. Upperparts richer, uniform chestnut-brown with no darker patterning, but contrasting bright grey-blue panel across median and greater coverts; flight feathers dusky, giving pattern on open wing recalling Turtle Dove. Rump grey-blue, becoming duskier through centre of tail, which has black outer feathers broadly tipped white. Juvenile duller than adult, and lacks gorget. Flight rather weak and fluttering. Often tame.
VOICE Generally rather silent, but song transcribed as *pooo poo puoo-poou hoo*.

HABITAT In natural range as often around human habitation as Feral Rock Dove, favouring city centres, parks and gardens, often with trees, and villages and settlements among cultivations.
DISTRIBUTION Breeds from Algeria east to the Middle East as far north as Turkey, throughout much of West, East and southern Africa, southern Arabia and from Iran east to Central Asia and India. Some apparently local movements recorded, but otherwise resident.
EUROPEAN STATUS Very rare vagrant: 12 records, though kept in captivity and some occurrences in Europe (eg in Finland, France, Germany and Sweden) presumed to relate to escapes. Greece (7); Italy (5: 30 Aug 1974; 17 Nov 1985; Apr 1987; 29 Mar 1994; 1 Sept 1994).

AMERICAN MOURNING DOVE

Zenaida macroura L 31 cm (12.5 in)
DESCRIPTION Smaller and slimmer than Collared and Turtle Doves, with much longer, rapier-shaped tail and faster flight. Head and body rather grey-buff, with black eye, white eye-ring, black crescent on side of neck and marked pinkish wash to breast. Upperparts browner, with sparse black flecking on back and scapulars; lesser and median coverts paler brown, contrasting with duskier black-tipped flight feathers on open wing. Long, 'rhomboid' tail is wide at base but tapers to a point; concolorous with upperparts except for outermost feathers, which have broad white tips and black subterminal band producing characteristic pattern when bird takes flight. Juvenile more heavily spotted than adult, with dense black flecking on throat, breast and wing-coverts; head duskier. Often very tame.
VOICE Commonest call is a plaintive *oowoo woo woo woo*.
HABITAT Abundant species, occurring in wide variety of habitats from cities, town parks and suburbs to meadows, cultivated fields, open woodland and desert.
DISTRIBUTION Breeds across North America from western Canada east through Great Lakes region to Atlantic coast, and south across almost entire USA to Central America. Northern birds are migratory, moving south in winter.
EUROPEAN STATUS Extreme vagrant: one autumn record. Britain (1: 31 Oct 1989, found dead 1 Nov 1989).

BLACK-BILLED CUCKOO

Coccyzus erythrophthalmus L 27-31 cm (10.75-12.5 in)
DESCRIPTION Clearly smaller than Common Cuckoo, with shorter wings but longer, more parallel-sided tail; two-tone plumage likely to cause confusion only with Yellow-billed Cuckoo, also from Nearctic. Head, upperparts and tail grey-brown with bronze lustre, greyest on face, rump and tail, which on underside is grey with indistinct white feather tips contrasting with black subterminal bars

(reduced or lacking in first-winter). Underparts off-white from throat to undertail-coverts. Eye-ring red in adult, buff in juvenile, which also has greyer bill base, narrow pale tips to upperpart feathers, slightly more rufous tone to primaries (though never as marked as on Yellow-billed Cuckoo) and buffish tail spots with no subterminal bar. Rather shy and usually moves within vegetation, unlike Common Cuckoo.
VOICE Song is a repeated *cu cu cu*; vagrants likely to be silent.
HABITAT Breeds in forest edge and woodlands, often in upland areas, as well as more open thickets, orchards and cultivated land with trees; often near wet ground.
DISTRIBUTION In summer found in large area of central North America from Rockies to Atlantic coast, chiefly in southern and south-eastern Canada, the Mid-West and north-east USA south to South Carolina and Tennessee. Migrates south-west to winter in north-western South America.
EUROPEAN STATUS Very rare vagrant: 18 records. Britain (12); Denmark (1: Oct 1970); Germany (1: 8 Oct 1952); Iceland (2: end 1935; 21-25 Oct 1982); Ireland (1: 25 Sept 1871); Italy (1: 1858). Also one category D record from France (20 July 1886).

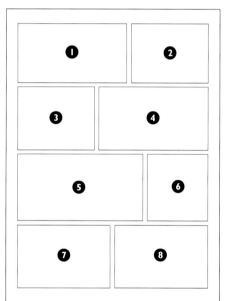

1 **Oriental Turtle Dove** (adult, Mar 1985, Helsinki, Finland)
2 **Oriental Turtle Dove** (first-winter, Nov 1975, Spurn, Humberside, Britain)
3 **Oriental Turtle Dove** (first-winter showing characters of race *meena*, Mar 1995*, Uumaja Holmsund, Finland)
4 **Laughing Dove** (adult, Apr, Israel)
5 **American Mourning Dove** (first-winter, probably male, Oct 1989, Calf of Man, Isle of Man, Britain)
6 **American Mourning Dove** (first-winter, probably male, Oct 1989, Calf of Man, Isle of Man, Britain)
7 **Black-billed Cuckoo** (first-winter, Oct 1985, St Mary's, Isles of Scilly, Britain)
8 **Black-billed Cuckoo** (first-winter, Oct 1985, St Mary's, Isles of Scilly, Britain)

YELLOW-BILLED CUCKOO

Coccyzus americanus L 28-32 cm (11.25-12.75 in)
DESCRIPTION Slightly larger than Black-billed Cuckoo. Plumage similarly olive-brownish above, becoming mid-grey on face and rump, but warmer brown on wings; extensively rusty primaries form distinctive panel on wing, obvious in flight. Underparts whitish, often with buff-grey tinge on throat and breast. Long tail has black underside with diagnostic pattern of two parallel rows of large white spots. Slightly decurved bill is obviously yellow on lower mandible and base of upper mandible, with darker tip and duskier culmen; eye-ring also yellow. Juvenile similar to adult, but has more extensive rusty hue to wing and less distinct tail pattern. Newly-arrived vagrants of either Nearctic species in Europe often sit in tired, 'hunched' posture with wings slightly drooped, frequently within cover.
VOICE In breeding range utters hollow, rapid *kuk kuk kuk* song, becoming slower and descending in pitch towards end; vagrants to Europe likely to be silent.
HABITAT Favours broad-leaved woodland, orchards, streamside thickets and groves.
DISTRIBUTION Breeds in North America across much of USA east of the Rockies and in south-easternmost Canada, from Great Lakes in the north to central Mexico and Caribbean in the south. Migrates on broad front to winter in South America east of the Andes south to central Argentina, with small numbers as far north as Panama.
EUROPEAN STATUS Rare vagrant: 76 records. Belgium (1: 22 Oct 1874); Britain (50); Denmark (1: Oct 1936); France (2: 6 Nov 1924; 31 Oct 1957); Iceland (3: 3 Jan 1954; 5 Oct 1954; 13 Oct 1987); Ireland (9); Italy (7); Norway (1: 7 Oct 1970, also 1 at sea, late Feb 1902); Spain (1: 28 Oct 1994).

EGYPTIAN NIGHTJAR

Caprimulgus aegyptius L 24-26 cm (9.5-10.5 in)
DESCRIPTION Very pale, 'washed-out'-looking nightjar lacking in obvious field marks. Appears largely sandy-grey-buff, plumage finely patterned on upperparts with black and buff feather tips. Face has pinkish tone, marked below by narrow white patches on sides of throat. Only significant contrast of entire plumage is brownish outer secondaries, primaries and greater primary coverts, all of which are barred blacker; white spots near base of primaries indistinct in the field. Underside of wings, tail and most of body noticeably pale with grey barring, making bird seem wholly pale from below. Sexes similar. Juvenile paler still, and even more lacking in contrast. Plumage of North African race *saharae* slightly more sandy, with upperparts having obvious rufous tone. Roosts by day under shelter of bush or ridge, taking to wing at dusk to hawk insects.
VOICE Song of male given as series of rapid *korr* sounds, becoming progressively slower; vagrants likely to be silent.
HABITAT Breeds in flat, hot low-lying deserts and semi-deserts, and sand dunes with scattered trees or bushes, often not far from water.
DISTRIBUTION Exact breeding range poorly known, but found from Morocco to Tunisia south of coastal belt, Egypt, Iraq and Iran, and Central Asia east of the Caspian Sea; formerly bred Israel. Some remain Egypt year-round, but otherwise migratory, wintering in sub-Saharan West Africa and Sudan.
EUROPEAN STATUS Very rare vagrant: 13 records, those in northern Europe all falling in May-June. Britain (2: 23 June 1883; 10 June 1984); Denmark (1: May-June 1983); Germany (1: 22 June, probably 1875); Italy (8); Sweden (1: May 1972).

COMMON NIGHTHAWK

Chordeiles minor L 23-25 cm (9.25-10 in)
DESCRIPTION Smaller and shorter-tailed than European Nightjar, but long pointed wings disguise visible difference in size. Similar intricately-marked black, brown, buff and white plumage is colder-toned and more evenly patterned than European Nightjar's; most obvious distinctions are large, pure white throat of male (smaller and more buff on female), dark-barred whiter belly and undertail-coverts, dark-tipped tail (with white V-shaped subterminal band on underside on male), and unbarred black flight feathers with bold white 'oval' patch near base of primaries on both surfaces of wing, almost reaching trailing edge (larger and closer to carpal than on European Nightjar). Tail slightly forked. Juvenile has paler, greyer upperparts and whitish fringes to flight feathers. Less crepuscular than European Nightjar, often feeding in daytime (especially late afternoon); flight stronger, and may hawk insects at some height in rapid bursts of speed.
VOICE Utters distinctive harsh *peent* or *peeik* flight call, but vagrants apparently silent.
HABITAT Widespread in range of habitats, including towns, suburbs, meadows, fields and open woodlands; roosts on flat roofs and posts as well as in trees and on the ground.
DISTRIBUTION Widespread in summer across much of North America except Alaska and the tundra zone of northern Canada east to Newfoundland, as well as in Central America south to Panama; more numerous in west of range. Winters in South America from Colombia to Argentina.
EUROPEAN STATUS Very rare vagrant: 15 autumn records, all mid-September to early November. Britain (13); Faeroes (1: 1 Oct 1955); Iceland (1: 23 Oct 1955).

CHIMNEY SWIFT

Chaetura pelagica L 12-14 cm (4.75-5.5 in)
DESCRIPTION Much smaller than Common Swift – almost size of Sand Martin – with blunter wing tips and noticeably short tail which combine to produce a characteristic stubby shape. Appears almost uniform dark grey-brown except for pale grey throat patch; black area around eye above paler throat may give impression of dark 'cap' in the field. Only other obvious plumage contrast is on underwing, with primaries, secondaries and greater coverts slightly paler brown than median and lesser coverts. Tail has row of short spine-like feathers projecting beyond tip. All plumages very alike in the field, but juvenile has narrow white tips to inner primaries, secondaries and tertials.
VOICE Utters series of accelerating and decelerating chipping noises.
HABITAT Nests chiefly in chimneys and other man-made structures, but uses wide variety of habitats for feeding; frequently roosts in large numbers in chimneys and other structures.
DISTRIBUTION Breeds across North America east of the Rockies, from central Canada eastwards to the Atlantic seaboard, and south to Florida and the Gulf coast. Migrates south across the Gulf of Mexico and through Central America to winter largely in Peru.
EUROPEAN STATUS Extreme vagrant: five autumn records. Britain (5: 21-27 Oct 1982, joined by second bird 23-25 Oct; 4-9 Nov 1986; 18 Oct 1987; 8-10 Nov 1991).

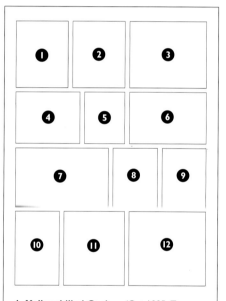

1 **Yellow-billed Cuckoo** (Oct 1985, Tresco, Isles of Scilly, Britain)
2 **Yellow-billed Cuckoo** (Oct 1989, Landguard, Suffolk, Britain)
3 **Yellow-billed Cuckoo** (Oct 1985, Tresco, Isles of Scilly, Britain)
4 **Egyptian Nightjar** (May/June 1983, Christansø, Denmark)
5 **Egyptian Nightjar** (May/June 1983, Christansø, Denmark)
6 **Egyptian Nightjar** (May/June 1983, Christansø, Denmark)
7 **Common Nighthawk** (juvenile, Sept 1989, Tresco, Isles of Scilly, Britain)
8 **Common Nighthawk** (juvenile, Sept 1989, Tresco, Isles of Scilly, Britain)
9 **Common Nighthawk** (juvenile, Sept 1989, Tresco, Isles of Scilly, Britain)
10 **Chimney Swift** (Oct 1982, Porthgwarra, Cornwall, Britain)
11 **Chimney Swift** (Nov 1986, St Mary's, Isles of Scilly, Britain)
12 **Chimney Swift** (Nov 1991, St Andrews, Fife, Britain)

WHITE-THROATED NEEDLETAIL

Hirundapus caudacutus L 19-20 cm (7.5-8 in)
DESCRIPTION Large, aerodynamic and strikingly patterned swift. Adult has dark brown body with black eye patch and white on throat, across lores, on forehead, and on lower flanks and undertail-coverts, latter markings forming characteristic 'horseshoe'. Upperparts dark brown, with conspicuous pale 'saddle' on lower mantle and back. Upperwing uniformly blackish-brown; on underwing, flight feathers appear slightly paler than largely blackish coverts. Blue and green gloss on head and upperwing may be visible on adults in fresh plumage. Juvenile has grey-brown forehead and lores, less striking pale saddle, black flecking on white horseshoe, and less gloss in plumage. Cigar-shaped body and relatively long, broad wings give distinctive, powerful structure. Family name derives from row of spines projecting beyond tail tip. Flight very fast and dynamic.
VOICE Call is quieter than those of other swifts, a rapid, insect-like chattering.
HABITAT Often occurs over wooded terrain, grasslands and river valleys at variety of altitudes in natural range, but European vagrants may appear anywhere.
DISTRIBUTION Two distinct populations. Northern birds breed central Siberia, north-east China, Korea and Japan, wintering chiefly in Indonesia and eastern Australia; southern birds found in the Himalayas, where probably resident.
EUROPEAN STATUS Very rare vagrant: 15 records, mainly in late spring. Britain (9); Finland (3: 21 May 1933; 21 Apr 1990; 5 May 1991); Ireland (1: 20 June 1964); Norway (1: 17 May 1968); Spain (1: 4 Oct 1990); Sweden (1: 22-27 May 1994).

PACIFIC SWIFT

Apus pacificus L 17-18 cm (6.75-7.25 in)
DESCRIPTION Slightly larger than Common Swift, with proportionately longer and narrower wings. Plumage similarly blackish-brown, but with more extensive and whiter throat patch, broad white fringing on dark underbody giving distinctly scaly impression, and very slight pale fringing on dark 'saddle' (difficult to see in the field). Narrow white band across rump edges onto flanks and slightly forwards, giving subtle impression of U-shape from some angles; beware partially albino Common Swifts, which can show white rump patch (but separable by other features, for example less distinct throat patch and uniformly dark underparts). Structural differences from Common Swift slight, but include larger, more protruding head and broader-based, more deeply forked tail, which appears narrow and parallel-sided when held closed. Juvenile very like adult and difficult to separate in the field. General appearance can recall an oversized, more powerfully-built White-rumped Swift.
VOICE Recalls the scream of Common Swift, but softer and less wheezy.

HABITAT Occurs in wide range of habitats and altitudes from arctic to tropical climes; like Common Swift, often near human habitation.
DISTRIBUTION Breeds from central and northern Siberia eastwards to Kamchatka and Japan, south through China to South-East Asia and in parts of the Himalayas. Northern birds migrate to winter in southern India, South-East Asia and Australia.
EUROPEAN STATUS Extreme vagrant: two records in late spring. Britain (1: 30 May 1994; also 1 at sea, 19 June 1981).

WHITE-RUMPED SWIFT

Apus caffer L 14 cm (5.5 in)
DESCRIPTION Small, sleek swift with slim body and relatively long, pointed wings and tail. Plumage appears uniformly black on body, upperwing and tail, contrasting with paler grey-brown underwing, which is darkest on leading edge of coverts. Tips of secondaries and inner primaries white, forming fine trailing edge, but difficult to see in the field. White on face confined to throat patch, forehead just above bill and fore-supercilium. White on rump looks slightly U-shaped and is relatively narrow in depth compared with Little Swift, emphasising long appearance of rear end. Attenuated shape enhanced further by long, forked tail, which appears as a 'spike' when held closed. Flight action graceful; highly gregarious, often mixing with other swifts.
VOICE Often silent, but has a twittering trill which is deeper than that of Little Swift.
HABITAT Frequently takes over old Little Swift or swallow nests, though in southern Europe avoids urban areas; feeds over wide range of terrain, in breeding season usually not far from colony or nest site.
DISTRIBUTION Summer visitor to southern Iberia, where range expanding, and Morocco, but otherwise found south of Sahara in Senegal and from Ivory Coast eastwards to Ethiopia, throughout East Africa south to the Cape, and in coastal Angola and Namibia.
EUROPEAN STATUS Breeds regularly only in Spain (10+ pairs, increasing); has also bred recently in Portugal, where very few previous records. Accidental elsewhere: Finland (1: 18 Nov 1968, dead); Gibraltar (1: 9 July 1988); Norway (2: 18 May 1984; 15 June 1986, two).

LITTLE SWIFT

Apus affinis L 12 cm (4.75 in)
DESCRIPTION Similar to slightly larger White-rumped Swift, but looks more compact, with bold white rump patch and distinctive square-ended tail (appears rounded when spread). Plumage generally brownish-black, not so uniformly dark as White-rumped, with blackest tones on 'saddle', upperwing-coverts and underparts, and contrastingly paler on underside of primaries and secondaries and on tail. Face extensively pale, with whitish markings extending up forehead and across throat in large rounded patch. Square white rump clearly more extensive than on White-

rumped, and 'wraps around' onto sides of lower flanks. Structure distinctive: body looks chunky, with more compact rear end than White-rumped. Often feeds among other swifts, though away from breeding areas may be less visible as frequently flies at high levels.
VOICE Most frequently uttered call is a harsh, rapid trilling.
HABITAT Breeds commonly on houses and at other man-made sites, also on cliffs and crags; during feeding sorties and on migration, seen over wide range of open country.
DISTRIBUTION Breeds in Morocco, Algeria and Tunisia, across much of sub-Saharan Africa except south-west and south-central regions, locally in the Middle East (south-east Turkey, Jordan and Israel), south-west Arabia and from Iran eastwards to India and Sri Lanka. Mainly resident, but in north and southern Africa and the Middle East probably at least partially migratory.
EUROPEAN STATUS Very rare vagrant: 26 records, mostly in late spring and late autumn. Britain (9); Greece (1: 27 May 1988); Ireland (1: 12 June 1967); Italy (2: 14 May 1890; 6 July 1890); Portugal (1: 1951); Spain (9 records of 16 birds); Sweden (4: June 1979; Nov 1982; Aug 1985; Sept 1988).

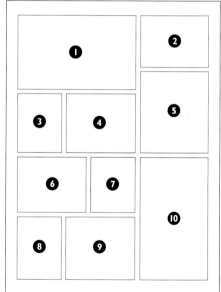

1 **White-throated Needletail** (May 1991, Wierton Hill, Kent, Britain)
2 **White-throated Needletail** (June 1988, Hoy, Orkney, Britain)
3 **White-throated Needletail** (May 1984, Quendale, Shetland, Britain)
4 **White-throated Needletail** (June 1988, Hoy, Orkney, Britain)
5 **Pacific Swift** (May 1993, Cley, Norfolk, Britain)
6 **Pacific Swift** (May 1993, Cley, Norfolk, Britain)
7 **Pacific Swift** (May 1993, Cley, Norfolk, Britain)
8 **White-rumped Swift** (June 1979, Spain)
9 **Little Swift** (May 1981, Skewjack, Cornwall, Britain)
10 **Little Swift** (May 1981, Skewjack, Cornwall, Britain)

WHITE-BREASTED KINGFISHER

Halcyon smyrnensis L 27-28 cm (10.75-11.25 in)
DESCRIPTION Unmistakable. Adult has chestnut head and body, white throat and breast, and bright blue mantle, rump, tail and dark-tipped wings, the latter with contrasting blackish-chestnut lesser and median coverts forming dark 'shoulder' patch. Wing pattern more striking in flight, when black primaries reveal bold white bases forming conspicuous panel on outer wing. Massive bill is salmon-pink, with lower mandible uptilted towards tip. Sexes generally similar, though female averages paler brown than male; juvenile resembles adults but duller, with dark scalloping on breast and browner bill. Often conspicuous, frequently perching on roadside posts and trees.
VOICE Very vocal: utters loud, cackling call, typically on flying from perch, and sings from top of tree.
HABITAT At home in wide range of dry terrain, including palm plantations, woodland edge and large gardens; also wetter areas, including creeks, canals, mangroves and beaches.
DISTRIBUTION Breeds in southern Turkey, Levant and north-east Egypt, and from Euphrates marshes eastwards across Indian subcontinent and South-East Asia. Partial migrant, but movements largely confined to within breeding range.
EUROPEAN STATUS Extreme vagrant: four records. Greece (4: 30 Apr 1941; 1960-65; 11 Aug 1988; 9 Aug 1989).

PIED KINGFISHER

Ceryle rudis L 25 cm (10 in)
DESCRIPTION Large, long-billed kingfisher with entire plumage strikingly patterned black and white. Male has black forehead, crown, crest, ear-coverts and hindneck contrasting with long white supercilium and black-and-white-striped neck sides. Upperparts black with broad white fringing, creating chequered impression; extensively white inner secondaries and coverts form broken white patch on closed wing. Underparts white except for narrow double black breast band and black flank streaking. Bill and legs black. Adult female differs in having one, broader, black breast band, broken in middle. Juvenile very like adult female, but with brownish tinge to face and greyer breast band. In flight, black outer wing flashes bold white patches on base of primaries. Gregarious; hunts from perches, but frequently also by hovering and plunge-diving.
VOICE Loud, high-pitched chattering *kwik* call frequently uttered. In flight, also has *kittle-te-ker* call, uttered constantly after leaving perch.
HABITAT Common in marshes, lakes, paddyfields, rivers, sheltered estuaries and coasts.
DISTRIBUTION Breeds across sub-Saharan Africa except far south-west, with range extending north along Nile valley to the delta. Other populations breed in the Middle East (including Israel, Syria and Turkey) and from Afghanistan and India eastwards through South-East Asia to

southern China and Hong Kong. Mainly sedentary.
EUROPEAN STATUS Very rare vagrant: seven records. France (1: 29 Dec 1990-7 Jan 1991); Greece (5: 2 undated 19th-century records; 1850; 14 Feb 1882; 3 Apr 1992); Poland (1: Aug 1859).

BELTED KINGFISHER

Ceryle alcyon L 28-35 cm (11.25-14 in)
DESCRIPTION Very large, thickset kingfisher with prominent shaggy crest and long, dagger-like bill. Adult male is blue-grey on head, mantle, most of wings, tail and breast band, and has white neck-collar, underparts and obvious white spot on black loral area; primaries blackish above, greyer below. Bill steely grey-black, paler at base. Adult female very like male, but has rufous flanks and narrow second breast band. Juveniles differ chiefly in pattern of breast bands: young males have faint rufous band flecked with grey, young females also with broken, paler version of adult female's rufous secondary band. Catches aquatic prey like other kingfishers, but often perches on telegraph wires and posts, and roosts high up in trees at night.
VOICE Commonest call is a loud, far-carrying rattle recalling Mistle Thrush; usually given in flight, and often first clue to bird's presence.
HABITAT Aquatic species, frequenting lakes, ponds, rivers, streams and creeks, as well as mangroves and coastal waters; occasionally fishes short distances offshore.
DISTRIBUTION Breeds widely across North America, from Alaska east to Labrador and Newfoundland, and south to California, Texas and the Gulf of Mexico. Common on Atlantic seaboard during migration en route to the Caribbean, central America and northernmost South America.
EUROPEAN STATUS Very rare vagrant: seven records. Britain (2: Nov 1908, shot; 21 Nov 1979-June 1980, and again 23-29 Aug 1980); Iceland (1: late Sept 1901); Ireland (3: mid-Dec 1978-3 Feb 1979, when shot; 12 Oct 1980, shot; 28 Oct 1984-8 Mar 1985); Netherlands (1: 17 Dec 1899).

BLUE-CHEEKED BEE-EATER

Merops persicus L 24-26 cm (9.5-10.5 in)
DESCRIPTION Strikingly beautiful bee-eater with long tail-streamers and predominantly green plumage at all ages. Adult appears almost wholly apple-green except for subtly contrasting face pattern of white-bordered black mask, pale blue forehead and cheeks, yellow chin and deep rufous throat patch. In flight, reveals narrow dusky trailing edge to wings, conspicuous copper-coloured underwings and dark underside to tail. Long, gently decurved bill is black. Sexes alike. Juvenile has duller green body patterned with pale scalloping, lacks blue and white on face, has much fainter rufous patch on throat and shows pale rufous tone to nape; iris dark, red in adult. Actions as European Bee-eater's, but long wings and tail render flight even more graceful and swooping; very

gregarious, and often mixes with European.
VOICE Call very like European Bee-eater's, but subtly harsher, shorter and clearly disyllabic.
HABITAT In its breeding range frequents steppe, deserts and semi-deserts with scattered trees, telephone wires and other perches from which to hunt; on migration in all kinds of open country, including farmland and river valleys.
DISTRIBUTION Breeds in West Africa, Morocco and Algeria, parts of Middle East including Egypt, north Israel, Syria, south-eastern Turkey, Iran, Iraq and Oman, and extensively across steppes from Caspian Sea to India. Winters in savanna country of West Africa, throughout much of East Africa from Sudan to Mozambique, and in Angola.
EUROPEAN STATUS Rare vagrant: June-July is the peak period for occurrences in western Europe. Britain (7); Bulgaria (2: 18 Sept 1993, three; 26 June 1994); Denmark (2: 21-22 June 1989; 29 June 1993); Finland (1: 7-9 July 1991); France (5: 11 May 1832; May 1875; 1914; 25 Apr 1927; Oct 1993); Germany (1: 19 June 1993); Gibraltar (1: 9 Sept 1973); Greece (12-15); Italy (7); Netherlands (1: 30 Sept 1961); Spain (1: 15 June 1989); Sweden (3: Aug 1961; July 1968; May 1985); former Yugoslavia (1: May 1953).

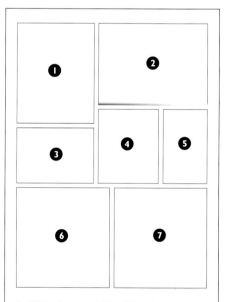

1 **White-breasted Kingfisher** *(Jan, India)*
2 **Pied Kingfisher** *(male, Feb, Israel)*
3 **Belted Kingfisher** (first-winter female, Nov 1984, Ballyvaughan, Co Clare, Ireland)
4 **Belted Kingfisher** (second-calendar-year male, Aug 1980, Boscathnoe Reservoir, Cornwall, Britain)
5 **Blue-cheeked Bee-eater** (June 1989, Christansø, Denmark)
6 **Blue-cheeked Bee-eater** (July 1989, Cowden, Humberside, Britain)
7 **Blue-cheeked Bee-eater** (July 1989, Cowden, Humberside, Britain)

NORTHERN FLICKER

Colaptes auratus L 32 cm (12.75 in)
DESCRIPTION Large, distinctive woodpecker with unmistakable plumage combination. Adult male has pinkish-brown (Jay-coloured) face with black moustachial stripe flaring onto cheek, grey crown and nape separated by conspicuous red band, pale brown upperparts patterned with narrow black barring, narrow black gorget on upper breast, white underparts with dense black spotting, white rump, mottled uppertail-coverts and black tail. Adult female similar but lacks moustachial stripe; juvenile like adult male but with fewer black markings and grey-brown (not reddish-brown) iris. Eastern form ('Yellow-shafted' Flicker), most likely to occur in Europe, has yellowish underwing. Jizz similar to Green Woodpecker rather than 'pied' woodpeckers. Active species; often feeds on ground.
VOICE Noisy, with range of calls including loud, rapid *wek-wek-wek-wek-wek* and a single, loud *kleeer*.
HABITAT In natural range, common in open woodland, suburban areas, parks and large gardens.
DISTRIBUTION Widespread across much of North America, from tree limit in northern Canada south to Gulf coast and California, and also in Central America and Cuba. Almost all Canadian birds migrate to winter south from south-eastern USA.
EUROPEAN STATUS Extreme vagrant: two records. Denmark (1: 18 May 1972, presumed ship-assisted or escape); Ireland (1: 13 Oct 1962, ship-assisted). Also one category D record from Britain (July 1981), of corpse, presumed to have died on ship at sea.

YELLOW-BELLIED SAPSUCKER

Sphyrapicus varius L 19-20 cm (7.5-8 in)
DESCRIPTION Relatively small, short-billed woodpecker. Adult male unmistakable, with bright red forehead and crown, black-and-white-striped face, and red throat patch edged in black and bordered below by black gorget. Breast pale yellowish, becoming whiter on belly, with dusky chevrons on flanks. Black mantle and back mottled white, with bold white panel across median and greater coverts appearing as T-shape on forewing in flight; black flight feathers also barred white. White on rump extends down centre of tail. Adult female of northern and eastern race *varius* (most likely to occur in Europe) has white throat. Juvenile is browner, especially on face and breast, but still with traces of red on head and black-and-white-mottled upperparts; adult-type plumage not acquired until following spring. Rather shy.
VOICE Commonest call is downward-inflected *cheerrr*.
HABITAT Favours deciduous forests and woodland, occasionally also in mixed and even pure coniferous stands; also orchards and other wooded areas, often near water.
DISTRIBUTION Breeds from southern Canada eastwards through Great Lakes region and

north-east USA. Migratory, wintering in central and southern USA, Central America south to Panama and the Greater Antilles.
EUROPEAN STATUS Extreme vagrant: three records. Britain (1: 26 Sept-6 Oct 1975); Iceland (1: 5 June 1961, dead); Ireland (1: 16-19 Oct 1988).

EASTERN PHOEBE

Sayornis phoebe L 17-18 cm (6.75-7.25 in)
DESCRIPTION Large, rather distinctive Nearctic flycatcher. Upperparts plain brownish-grey, becoming darker on hindneck and head. Wings also darker brownish-grey, with at best indistinct paler wing-bars. Underparts whitish, with dull olive wash on breast and upper flanks; autumn birds have dull yellowish cast to breast and belly. Relatively long tail also dark brownish-grey, lacking contrasting paler markings. First-winter very like adult, but usually retains some buff-tipped greater coverts and tertials from juvenile plumage. All-black bill and lack of eye-ring distinguish species from other similar North American flycatchers. Active species, often pumping and spreading tail on prominent perch between frequent fly-catching sallies.
VOICE Song is a distinctive harsh *fee-bee*, with emphasis on first syllable.
HABITAT Found in open woodland, farmland and suburbs, often near water, and frequently around buildings and other man-made structures with eaves and ledges.
DISTRIBUTION Breeds across much of western, central and south-easternmost Canada, and south extensively through eastern USA except Gulf coast region and Florida. Mainly migratory, wintering from south of breeding range, south-east USA, Gulf coast and Mexico southwards.
EUROPEAN STATUS Extreme vagrant: one spring record. Britain (1: 24-25 Apr 1987).

ACADIAN FLYCATCHER

Empidonax virescens L 12 cm (4.75 in)
DESCRIPTION Unlikely to be confused with any European species, but very similar to several other North American *Empidonax* flycatchers which could conceivably reach Europe: probably only safely separable by voice and, in the hand, wing formula. Slightly smaller than Spotted Flycatcher, with brownish-olive head, nape, mantle, back and rump; wings darker dusky-olive, with pale yellow tips to median and greater coverts forming bold double wing-bars, and pale edges to tertials and inner secondaries forming panel on closed wing. Underparts dull white, faintly mottled grey on throat, with breast rather olive-toned, becoming yellower on flanks, vent and undertail-coverts; central belly often white, on some (especially non-breeding adult) all yellowish. Tail plain dusky-olive. Long, broad bill is horn-brown on upper mandible, yellowish-flesh on lower; legs dark grey. First-winter is browner above, with buff-toned wing-bars and wing panel; underparts whitish, still with olive on breast, but whiter, not yellow, on belly. In jizz most recalls a

Ficedula flycatcher; wags (but does not cock) tail.
VOICE Vocalisations are safest distinction from other species in genus: song is a characteristic, loud *peet-see*, with call given either as first note of song, *peet*, or as emphatic *weece*.
HABITAT Favours mature deciduous forest and thickets, often in vicinity of water, and swamps.
DISTRIBUTION Widespread in eastern North America from Gulf coast to southern Great Lakes, though absent from southern Florida. Migrates south to winter in Central and South America from Nicaragua to Ecuador and Venezuela.
EUROPEAN STATUS Extreme vagrant: one autumn record. Iceland (1: 4 Nov 1967).

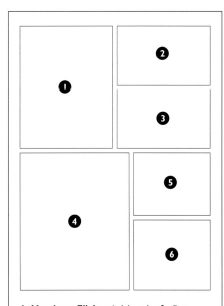

1 **Northern Flicker** (*adult male of yellow-shafted form, date unknown, New York, USA*)
2 **Yellow-bellied Sapsucker** (*immature female, Oct 1988, Cape Clear Island, Co Cork, Ireland*)
3 **Yellow-bellied Sapsucker** (*immature female, Oct 1988, Cape Clear Island, Co Cork, Ireland*)
4 **Eastern Phoebe** (*first-winter, Sept, Cape May, USA*)
5 **Acadian Flycatcher** (*May, Ontario, Canada*)
6 **Acadian Flycatcher** (*Apr, Texas, USA*)

BAR-TAILED DESERT LARK

Ammomanes cincturus L 15 cm (6 in)
DESCRIPTION Small, compact lark, likely to be confused only with larger, stockier and heavier-billed Desert Lark *A deserti* (not recorded Europe). Rather uniformly pale and unpatterned in appearance, with upperparts unstreaked sandy-buff and underparts paler, with very diffuse or no streaking on breast. Has indistinct pale supercilium and, unlike Desert Lark, whitish neck sides which form pale crescent below ear-coverts. Flight feathers tinged rufous (notably on tertials at rest), with blackish tips to primaries. Tail also pale rufous, with blackish feather tips forming distinct dark terminal band. Rounded head and small, rather stubby pink bill can give almost finch-like impression; Desert has stouter, yellow bill with dusky culmen and tip. Very active on ground, running in short fast bursts.
VOICE A characteristic and simple trisyllabic fluty song, likened to sound of a squeaky gate.
HABITAT Frequents sand or gravel deserts, semi-deserts and plains with almost no vegetation.
DISTRIBUTION Breeds from Morocco and northernmost West Africa eastwards discontinuously through North Africa and the Middle East to Iran and Pakistan. In North Africa chiefly resident, but with some dispersive movements.
EUROPEAN STATUS Extreme vagrant: three records. Italy (2: 8 Jan 1972; 28 Mar 1975); Spain (1: 24-26 Mar 1994*).

BIMACULATED LARK

Melanocorypha bimaculata L 17 cm (6.75 in)
DESCRIPTION Very similar to Calandra Lark, but slightly smaller, with proportionately longer wings and shorter tail. Typically sandier brown above than that species, with dark streaking on back appearing more contrasting. Creamy-white below, with narrower crescent-shaped black patches on sides of neck extending to centre of throat, sometimes joining. Bill and head more distinctly marked than on Calandra, with darker culmen, whiter supercilium and eye-ring, more obvious dark eye-stripe and surround to rufous ear-coverts, and darker lores. In flight, wings appear more pointed than Calandra's, with browner flight feathers contrasting less with brown coverts, and no obvious white trailing edge; underwing less solidly blackish than on Calandra. Tail has buff outer feathers, with white restricted to tip.
VOICE Very like Calandra Lark's. Song is a rich and varied mixture of short phrases, often including mimicry, and given in flight or from a perch. Calls include a Skylark-like *churrup*.
HABITAT Typically inhabits steppe, semi-desert and other barren areas, often occurring at higher elevations than Calandra Lark. On migration also on cultivated land, sometimes with other larks.
DISTRIBUTION Breeds from Turkey, Lebanon and north Israel eastwards to Iran, Afghanistan and Central Asia. Winter range extends to Arabia and north-west India, and occurs on passage in Egypt, southern Israel and regularly in small numbers in Cyprus.
EUROPEAN STATUS Very rare vagrant: nine records. Britain (3: 7-11 May 1962; 24-27 Oct 1975; 8 June 1976); Finland (1: 17-23 Jan 1960); Greece (1: 1 May 1988); Italy (2: 5 Jan 1919; 4 Oct 1978); Sweden (2: May 1982; Dec 1983).

WHITE-WINGED LARK

Melanocorypha leucoptera L 18 cm (7.25 in)
DESCRIPTION Large lark with conspicuous white wing panels visible both in flight and at rest. Essentially pale grey-brown above and whiter below, with chestnut on crown and in wing-coverts and darker streaking on mantle and breast sides. Male is more boldly chestnut on crown, ear-coverts and lesser and primary coverts; female is also streaked on crown, and more heavily so on underparts than male. First-winter is more heavily streaked and less chestnut than adults. In flight, appears long-winged with diagnostic wing pattern: leading edge chestnut, mid-wing black and trailing edge white, latter in broad band on secondaries and inner primaries, recalling pattern shown by Redshank. Beware aberrant individuals of other larks (for example partially albinistic Skylark), which may show white in wing.
VOICE Song said to resemble a slow, less monotonous version of Skylark's. Calls given as *tscher-ee* and a thin *sit-sit-sit*.
HABITAT Found chiefly on dry grassy steppes; on migration sometimes also on arable land.
DISTRIBUTION Breeds from Kazakhstan east across Asia to Mongolia. Short-distance migrant, wintering mainly to the south and west of breeding range in the former Soviet Union, Iran and regularly as far west as the Black Sea region.
EUROPEAN STATUS Possibly regular in winter in Romania. Accidental elsewhere, mainly from March to November. Austria (1: 20 Apr 1910); Britain (2: 22 Nov 1869; 22 and 24 Oct 1981); Finland (1: 9 June 1971); Germany (2: 2 Aug 1881; 2 July 1886); Greece (3: 4 May 1959; 24 Feb 1963; June 1966); Italy (8); Norway (2: 12 Oct 1961; 29 Oct 1972); Poland (5: 22 Mar 1932; 21 Oct 1975; 4 Aug 1978; 30 Mar 1988; 12 May 1993, two); Spain (1: Oct-Nov 1974); Switzerland (1: 11 Nov 1924); former Yugoslavia.

BLACK LARK

Melanocorypha yeltoniensis L 19-20 cm (7.5-8 in)
DESCRIPTION The largest lark of the region. Male is unmistakable in all-black plumage with pale yellow or horn-coloured bill; in winter, extent of black reduced by pale fringing to head and body feathers. Slightly smaller female is brown, with variably darker (on some almost blotchy) streaking on head, upperparts and breast, and with blacker flight feathers and tail; more evenly-marked females may resemble Calandra Lark, but have diagnostic black legs, black underwing-coverts contrasting with duskier flight feathers (on Calandra, whole underwing is uniformly dark), and no white in wings or tail.
VOICE Song variously compared with those of White-winged and Calandra Larks, but deeper and slower than the former and in shorter bursts than the latter; sometimes given in flight, but typically from low perch or on ground. Calls apparently Skylark-like, but poorly known.
HABITAT Steppes and semi-deserts with short grass, preferably near water. In winter also on cultivated steppe.
DISTRIBUTION Breeds principally in Kazakhstan and southern Russia, but declining in numbers and range contracting. Partial migrant, some wintering south and west of breeding range in northern Black Sea region; large numbers occasionally wander from regular areas.
EUROPEAN STATUS Very rare vagrant: at least 18 records. Austria (1: second half of 19th century); Czech Republic (1: 28 Nov 1981); Finland (2: 24 Mar 1989; 8 Apr 1989); Germany (4: 27 Apr 1874; 27 July 1882; 10 July 1909; 20 Jan 1962); Greece (4: spring 1930; 20 Apr 1958; 20 Feb 1963; 8 Feb 1964); Italy (2: autumn 1803; 3 May 1961); Poland (1: 17 Jan 1988); Romania (2: Mar 1897; Mar 1900); Sweden (1: 6-7 May 1993). Possibly also recorded Bulgaria.

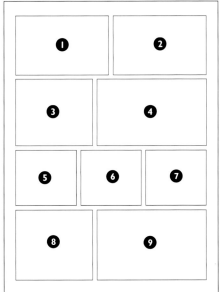

1 **Bar-tailed Desert Lark** (Mar 1994, Cabo de Salinas, Mallorca, Spain)
2 **Bar-tailed Desert Lark** (Mar 1994, Cabo de Salinas, Mallorca, Spain)
3 **Bar-tailed Desert Lark** (Mar 1994, Cabo de Salinas, Mallorca, Spain)
4 **Bimaculated Lark** *(Apr, Cyprus)*
5 **Bimaculated Lark** *(Apr, Israel)*
6 **White-winged Lark** *(male, June, Kazakhstan)*
7 **White-winged Lark** *(male, June, Kazakhstan)*
8 **Black Lark** (adult male, May 1993, Karlstad, Sweden)
9 **Black Lark** (adult male, May 1993, Karlstad, Sweden)

TREE SWALLOW

Tachycineta bicolor L 13 cm (5.25 in)
DESCRIPTION Recalls largish House Martin in general plumage pattern and shape, but lacks white rump and has all of upperparts toned more intensely blue apart from black flight feathers, which form contrast not found on House Martin. Adults are wholly white below, the white extending slightly onto rump sides (at all ages), producing a pattern distinct from other hirundines. Juvenile is greyish-brown above and white below, recalling Sand Martin, but greyish wash on breast does not form solid breast band; juvenile plumage is moulted August-October, males then acquiring adult-like coloration but females taking up to two years to develop bluish upperparts.
VOICE Song comprises three descending notes followed by a musical warble, usually repeated several times; has been heard singing in Europe.
HABITAT Open or wooded country, preferably near water and where dead trees provide suitable nesting holes; also nests in man-made structures.
DISTRIBUTION Widespread breeding species in North America, range extending from Alaska and the northern tree limit south to Tennessee in the east and California in the west; winters in southern USA, Central America and the West Indies.
EUROPEAN STATUS Extreme vagrant: one record. Britain (1: 6-10 June 1990).

AMERICAN CLIFF SWALLOW

Hirundo pyrrhonota L 13 cm (5.25 in)
DESCRIPTION Reminiscent of a dingy, short-tailed Red-rumped Swallow, with dark blue upperside (streaked paler on mantle) and ginger rump and collar, but has dark face, pale forehead and thick, square-ended tail – a unique distinction from the forked tail or streamers of other hirundines. Face and chin rufous, bordered by dark patch on throat and upper breast (lacking on duller and greyer young birds). Underside pale grey-brown to whitish, with undertail-coverts appearing dark-streaked. Soars more than other swallows when feeding. All vagrants hitherto recorded in Europe have been juveniles.
VOICE Limited range of vocalisations includes a squeaky twittering song and a single *purr* alarm call.
HABITAT Frequents a wide range of habitats including farmland, open country and built-up areas.
DISTRIBUTION A Nearctic hirundine, breeding across much of North America south to Mexico except northernmost Alaska and Canada and the south-eastern corner of the USA. Migrates to winter in South America chiefly from Brazil south to central Argentina, with small numbers remaining as far north as Panama.
EUROPEAN STATUS Extreme vagrant: three records in October. Britain (2: 10-27 Oct 1983; 23 Oct 1988); Iceland (1: 12 Oct 1992).

RICHARD'S PIPIT

Anthus richardi L 18 cm (7.25 in)
DESCRIPTION Large, robust pipit, separated from Tawny Pipit at all ages by paler lores, larger size, and longer legs, hindclaw and tail. Upperparts brown, with darker streaking on crown and mantle; underparts pale buffish, with warm apricot hue to flanks and fine dark streaking on breast. Has prominent pale supercilium, pale lores with eye-stripe more prominent behind eye than in front, and relatively long, powerful bill. Often adopts bold, upright stance, and uses longer legs to good effect in strong, active gait through grass tussocks; frequently hovers like Skylark before landing. For differences from very similar Blyth's Pipit, see that species.
VOICE Song is a series of monotonous chirruping phrases, usually delivered in flight. Typical flight call a distinctive *schrreep*; also a variety of other calls, including *chup*, sometimes repeated, and a House Sparrow-like *chirp*.
HABITAT Favours grassy areas, often damp; on migration often in coastal meadows.
DISTRIBUTION Widespread species in Siberia, Mongolia and China, moving south in winter to the Indian subcontinent and southern China. Other closely-related forms, sometimes regarded as subspecies of Richard's, occur in Africa, Asia and Australasia.
EUROPEAN STATUS Frequent vagrant/visitor: recorded chiefly in autumn (sometimes in relatively large numbers), but some in spring, and a few in winter. Austria (c 30); Belgium (160+, including 62+ in Flanders in autumn 1994); Britain (many, eg 76+ in 1993); Bulgaria; Channel Islands (rare autumn migrant); Czech Republic (4: Sept 1852; Sept 1856 or 1868; 20 Sept 1925; 17 July 1963); Denmark (250+); Finland (253+ to end 1993); France (126); Germany (many, eg 157 on Heligoland during 1987-94); Greece (fewer than 30); Hungary (1: 21 Sept 1994); Ireland (61); Italy; Latvia (1: 8 Sept 1990); Luxembourg (1: 11 Apr 1991); Netherlands (many); Norway; Poland (31); Portugal (several); Spain (19+ individuals); Sweden (c 305); Switzerland (4: 1901; 13 Sept 1913; 13 Sept 1959; 9 Nov 1979); former Yugoslavia (1: Mar 1907).

BLYTH'S PIPIT

Anthus godlewskii L 17 cm (6.75 in)
DESCRIPTION Very like Richard's Pipit, and often inseparable under normal field conditions except by call. With good views, appears slightly smaller and more compact, with proportionately shorter tail, legs and hindclaw; actions may recall those of smaller pipits. Some individuals are slightly greyer and more heavily streaked above than Richard's, with more uniformly buffish underparts, neater breast streaking and often more contrastingly rufous-tinged ear-coverts. Best plumage character on adults and first-winters is pattern of central median (and often also greater) coverts, which have squarer, more clear-cut dark centres and slightly paler edges, accentuating strength of

wing-bar; on juveniles and on first-winter birds retaining juvenile median coverts, however, pattern of unmoulted feathers is same as on young Richard's and of no use in separation.
VOICE Has two different calls, both quite distinct from those of Richard's Pipit: a softer, higher-pitched version of latter's, often given when flushed, and an abrupt, harsh *chep* recalling Tawny Pipit. Song said to resemble Corn Bunting's.
HABITAT Open country and grassland, apparently preferring drier areas to Richard's Pipit.
DISTRIBUTION Breeding range centred on Mongolia and adjacent areas of China and Siberia. Winters chiefly in India and Sri Lanka.
EUROPEAN STATUS Very rare vagrant: at least 13 records, all in northern Europe and chiefly in late autumn. Belgium (1: 16 Nov 1986); Britain (2: 23 Oct 1882; 4-10 Nov 1994; several other well-documented records pending); Finland (9); Netherlands (1: 13 Nov 1983).

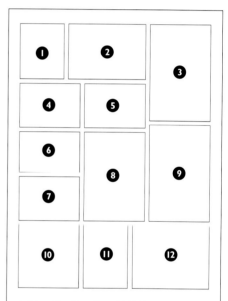

1 **Tree Swallow** (June 1990, St Mary's, Isles of Scilly, Britain)
2 **Tree Swallow** (June 1990, St Mary's, Isles of Scilly, Britain)
3 **Tree Swallow** (June 1990, St Mary's, Isles of Scilly, Britain)
4 **American Cliff Swallow** (juvenile, Oct 1983, St Mary's, Isles of Scilly, Britain)
5 **American Cliff Swallow** (juvenile, Oct 1995*, Spurn, Humberside, Britain)
6 **Richard's Pipit** (first-winter, Oct 1987, Maasvlakte, Netherlands)
7 **Richard's Pipit** (first-winter, Oct 1994, St Mary's, Isles of Scilly, Britain)
8 **Richard's Pipit** (Sept 1981, Valkeakoski, Finland)
9 **Blyth's Pipit** (first-winter, Nov 1994, Landguard, Suffolk, Britain)
10 **Blyth's Pipit** (first-winter, Oct 1990*, Skewjack, Cornwall, Britain)
11 **Blyth's Pipit** (first-winter, Oct 1993*, St Mary's, Isles of Scilly, Britain)
12 **Blyth's Pipit** (first-winter, Sept 1995*, Mustasaari, Finland)

OLIVE-BACKED PIPIT

Anthus hodgsoni L 14.5 cm (5.75 in)
DESCRIPTION Rather like Tree Pipit, but typically olive-green above, only the most worn birds approaching that species' browner plumage tones, and mantle only faintly streaked. Head shows subtle blackish streaking on crown and blackish crown sides forming a dark brow, with long, bold bicoloured supercilium (buffish in front of eye, creamy-white behind) and usually distinctive pale and dark spots on rear ear-coverts. White underparts are buff-washed on heavily streaked/spotted breast, with streaking extending more finely down flanks. Dark bill is pinkish on lower mandible; legs flesh-coloured. In behaviour very like Tree Pipit, often pumping tail and frequently flying up to a perch when flushed.
VOICE Song apparently faster and higher-pitched than Tree Pipit's. Typical call a thin *tseep*, very like Tree Pipit's but clearer and less buzzing in tone.
HABITAT In summer inhabits northern taiga, often at forest edge and clearings. Outside the breeding season sometimes in more open country.
DISTRIBUTION Breeds from north-east Russia eastwards across Siberia to China and Japan, wintering in India and south-east Asia.
EUROPEAN STATUS Frequent vagrant: great majority of records fall in autumn, but few also in spring and winter, and exceptionally in summer. Britain (185); Denmark (4: Oct 1982; Nov 1987; Apr-May 1989; 30 Sept-10 Oct 1990); Estonia (1: 24 Apr 1992); Faeroes (1: 4 Oct 1984); Finland (18); France (5: 31 Oct 1987; 22 Oct 1988; 22 Nov 1990; 20 Oct 1991; 5 Nov 1994); Germany (15); Ireland (7); Netherlands (7); Norway (??); Poland (9); Portugal (1: 16 Nov 1994); Spain (1: 10-11 Oct 1990); Sweden (6).

PECHORA PIPIT

Anthus gustavi L 14 cm (5.5 in)
DESCRIPTION Closely resembles non-breeding Red-throated Pipit, but shows subtle differences in structure with distinct projection of primaries beyond tertials (unique among pipits), shorter tail and longer, heavier bill. Plumage more contrasting than non-breeding Red-throated, with more rufous-toned head and upperparts, bolder white braces on darker-streaked mantle, whiter underparts contrasting with buffish breast, and more prominent double white wing-bar; like that species, has heavily streaked rump. Streaks on breast converge to form conspicuous dark spots on sides of neck. Bill has pinkish (not yellowish) on lower mandible; legs pink. Typically skulks in ground vegetation and difficult to observe; flushes reluctantly.
VOICE On breeding grounds utters a distinctive buzzing and varied song, very different from those of other pipits. Flight call is a diagnostic and abrupt *tsep*, but vocalisations of any kind are rarely given by

vagrants, even when flushed.
HABITAT Breeds in damp short-grass areas, and occupies similar habitat on migration. In winter apparently also in forest clearings.
DISTRIBUTION In summer occurs across northern Russia and Siberia from the Ural Mountains east to Kamchatka. Migrates partly through Korea and eastern China, but winter range poorly known.
EUROPEAN STATUS Rare vagrant: September is the peak month. Britain (53); Finland (2: 9 Sept 1972; 19 May 1973); France (1: 16 Sept 1990); Iceland (1); Lithuania (1: 4 Nov 1994); Norway (4: 29 Sept 1976; 21 Sept 1991; 1 Oct 1992; 10 Oct 1994); Poland (2: 30 Sept 1983; 14 Apr 1985); Spain (1: 29 Apr 1969; at least one other report not yet submitted); Sweden (1: 5-20 Sept 1991).

BUFF-BELLIED PIPIT

Anthus rubescens L 14.5 cm (5.75 in)
DESCRIPTION North American counterpart of Water Pipit, with which formerly treated as conspecific. Differs structurally in being slightly smaller, slimmer and more delicate, with thinner bill. Unlike Water Pipit, underparts are buff outside breeding season, with variable gorget of streaking on upper breast enclosing conspicuous unmarked buff throat; flanks show only limited streaking. Diagnostically, lores are almost unpatterned, unlike Water Pipit which has dark loral stripe breaking eye-ring. Adult summer has greyer upperparts and more orange-toned (not pink) underparts with more distinct streaking on breast and flanks than that species. In autumn and winter, upperparts are brown with diffuse darker streaking, and pale regions of head are a similar pale buff to underparts, with submoustachial stripe especially prominent; malar stripe poorly developed, though it merges into patch of heavy streaking on side of neck which highlights pale submoustache. Small size and general appearance may recall Meadow Pipit, from which distinguished by, among other characters, less streaking on crown and darker grey-brown upperparts. When walking, frequently wags tail in manner of wagtail, unlike other pipits. Most records in Europe relate to nominate North American race described above, but Asiatic subspecies *japonicus*, with whiter belly, bolder streaking below and paler legs, has also been recorded.
VOICE Song said to recall Rock Pipit's. Double-noted and thin *sip-sip* call is quite similar to Meadow Pipit's.
HABITAT Breeds on tundra and in mountains. In winter found in wider range of wet and dry habitats, from beaches and marshes to dry fields and rough grassland.
DISTRIBUTION In summer nominate race found in Greenland, across northern Canada and south along Rockies; winters mainly in southern USA and Central America. Race *japonicus* breeds north-east Siberia and winters chiefly in Japan and China, with some regularly as far west as Israel.
EUROPEAN STATUS Very rare vagrant: 15

records, mainly in autumn but with two spring records. Britain (3: 30 Sept 1910; 17 Sept 1953; 9-19 Oct 1988); Germany (3: 6 Nov 1851; 17 May 1858; 26 Sept 1899); Iceland (5: 16 Oct 1977; 14 Nov 1977; 5 Oct 1983; 21 Oct 1989; 24 Apr 1993); Ireland (2: 8-16 Oct 1953; 19 Oct 1967); Italy (2: 13 Nov 1951; 26 Oct 1960).

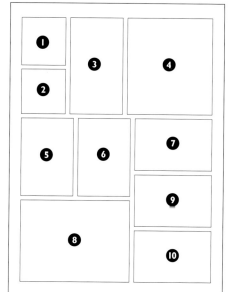

1 **Olive-backed Pipit** (Oct 1992, Utsira, Rogaland, Norway)
2 **Olive-backed Pipit** (Feb 1991, Noordwÿk, Netherlands)
3 **Olive-backed Pipit** (Oct 1993, Holkham, Norfolk, Britain)
4 **Olive-backed Pipit** (Oct 1993, Holkham, Norfolk, Britain)
5 **Pechora Pipit** (first-winter, Oct 1994, Filey, North Yorkshire, Britain)
6 **Pechora Pipit** (first-winter, Oct 1994, Filey, North Yorkshire, Britain)
7 **Pechora Pipit** (Oct 1989, Fair Isle, Shetland, Britain)
8 **Buff-bellied Pipit** (winter plumage, nominate North American race, Oct 1988, St Mary's, Isles of Scilly, Britain)
9 **Buff-bellied Pipit** (winter plumage, nominate North American race, Oct 1988, St Mary's, Isles of Scilly, Britain)
10 **Buff-bellied Pipit** (winter plumage, nominate North American race, Oct 1988, St Mary's, Isles of Scilly, Britain)

CITRINE WAGTAIL

Motacilla citreola L 17 cm (6.75 in)
DESCRIPTION Adult male distinguished by bright yellow head and underparts, black collar, grey back and two pure white wing-bars. Female less colourful, with greyish or olive-tinged crown, nape and ear-coverts (often with dark border) and grey flanks. Adults of both sexes duller in winter. First-winters are grey and white, resembling some first-winter Yellow Wagtails, but with broad whitish supercilium, distinct ear-covert surround, contrasting pale brown forehead, palish lores, and broader, whiter wing-bars and edges to tertials. First-summer males sometimes retain darker feathers on yellow crown, ear-coverts and breast. Undertail-coverts white, not washed yellowish as on Yellow Wagtail. More like Pied than Yellow in structure.
VOICE Call a distinctive, needling *tsreep*, harsher than typical Yellow Wagtail call; beware some eastern forms of Yellow Wagtail, which may sound similar.
HABITAT Lake margins, marshes, water meadows and damp pastures.
DISTRIBUTION Breeds from western Russia eastwards to western Siberia and Central Asia; range expanding, now probably breeding regularly in eastern Turkey and recently in the Baltic. Winters in India and South-East Asia, a few in Middle East (Israel), and on passage occurs regularly west to Cyprus.
EUROPEAN STATUS Frequent vagrant/visitor: colonising eastern Europe. Austria (10); Belgium (1: 9 May 1993); Britain (73); Bulgaria (2: second on 31 Mar 1993); Czech Republic (6: bred 1977); Denmark (8); Estonia (3: 21 July 1990; 16 May-17 June 1991, bred; 19 July 1993); Finland (81 records of 87 birds: up to 3 breeding pairs); France (4: 6 Apr 1987; 23 Apr 1989; 2 Sept 1990; 11 May 1991); Germany (25); Greece (7); Hungary (5: 6 May 1989; 6 May 1992; 14 May 1992; 22 Apr 1993; 7 May 1993); Iceland (3: 29 Oct 1982; 20 Oct 1990; 11 Sept 1994); Ireland (3: 15-17 Oct 1968; 6-12 Sept 1980; 4 Oct 1993); Italy (6); Latvia (11: 3 pairs bred 1994); Lithuania (10-12 pairs in 1994); Luxembourg; Netherlands (4: Aug-Sept 1984; 29 Apr 1991; 4-5 May 1993; 5 Sept 1994); Norway (32); Poland (56 up to 1993: 4 pairs bred 1994, increasing); Romania (possibly annual); Slovakia (5: date unknown; 9 Sept 1982; 19 Apr 1986; 29 Apr 1987; 12 May 1991); Slovenia (1: 26 Apr 1987); Spain (6); Sweden (90 individuals: bred 1994); Switzerland (3: 30 Apr 1980; 21 Apr 1994; 1-2 May 1994); former Yugoslavia (1: Apr 1987).

CEDAR WAXWING

Bombycilla cedrorum L 18 cm (7.25 in)
DESCRIPTION Smaller, browner and plainer version of Bohemian Waxwing. Although Cedar shares waxy red tips to secondaries with that species, adults readily distinguished by wholly plain wing except for narrow white line formed by white inner edges to tertials. Furthermore, black throat patch is small and less demarcated, lower belly is washed yellow and, diagnostically at all ages, undertail-coverts are white (always fox-red on Bohemian). Head is also more reddish-brown, with black eye-mask bordered by narrow white line both above and below (on Bohemian, only below). Juveniles may migrate in streaky plumage; first-winter like adult, but lacks waxy tips to secondaries and has much less distinct yellow tone to belly. Highly gregarious.
VOICE Call is a softer, higher-pitched and less trilling version of Bohemian Waxwing's.
HABITAT Found in most habitats with trees and shrubs offering plentiful supply of berries, including open woodland, parks and gardens.
DISTRIBUTION Breeds across central and southern Canada, and in the USA in far west and through much of north-east. In winter vacates northernmost breeding areas and winters south to Central America.
EUROPEAN STATUS Extreme vagrant: one record. Iceland (1: mid Apr-late July 1989). An additional individual in Britain on 25-26 June 1985 considered of uncertain origin and currently placed in category D.

NORTHERN MOCKINGBIRD

Mimus polyglottos L 25 cm (10 in)
DESCRIPTION Blackbird-sized Nearctic vagrant unlikely to be mistaken for any other species occurring in Europe. Mid-grey above and paler below, with darker grey wings showing white greater primary coverts and narrow double white wing-bars; long tail is dark grey with white outer feathers. Iris conspicuously pale; bill dark and slender, with downcurved upper mandible. Sexes similar. In flight, pattern of plumage recalls washed-out Great Grey Shrike; on ground, actions are thrush-like. Conspicuous and noisy species.
VOICE Song is a mixture of original phrases and imitations of other species; also mimics other sounds such as barking dogs, pianos *etc.* Male sings for prolonged periods in spring; both sexes sing in autumn to declare feeding territories.
HABITAT Woodland edges, scrub, parks, gardens and built-up areas.
DISTRIBUTION Breeds across much of North America south of Great Lakes, northernmost birds moving south in winter. Range expanding northwards.
EUROPEAN STATUS Extreme vagrant: three records. Britain (2: 30 Aug 1982; 17-23 May 1988; also a third record currently placed in category D, perhaps relating to an escape or ship-assisted individual, from 24 July-11 Aug 1978); Netherlands (1: 16-23 Oct 1988).

BROWN THRASHER

Toxostoma rufum L 29 cm (11.5 in)
DESCRIPTION Large, long-tailed, babbler-like vagrant from North America. Head, mantle, wings and tail entirely uniform reddish-brown except for prominent double wing-bar formed by pale, black-bordered tips to median and greater coverts. Underparts pale buffish with heavy black spotting. Conspicuously long tail contrasts with short wings to give an oddly proportioned shape. Dark bill is heavy, long and slightly decurved; legs brownish. Iris yellowish in adults, browner or greyer in first-years. Sexes similar. Ground-loving and generally skulking, though not shy; will readily fly to higher perch if disturbed.
VOICE Song, given from open perch (usually in tree), said to recall repetition of varied phrasing of Song Thrush, but rarely mimics other species. Call of British vagrant given as harsh *chip*, like Magpie.
HABITAT Found in woodland edges, thickets, hedgerows and brush, often near human habitation.
DISTRIBUTION Resident in south-eastern USA, in summer also north-west to southern Canada. Migratory northern birds winter in southern USA, within and slightly west of range of resident population.
EUROPEAN STATUS Extreme vagrant: two records, one of an overwintering individual. Britain (1: 18 Nov 1966-5 Feb 1967); Germany (1: Oct 1837).

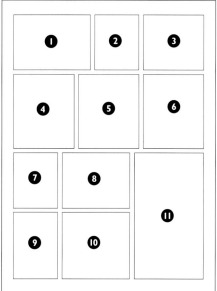

1 **Citrine Wagtail** (first-summer male, May 1993, Fleet, Hampshire, Britain)
2 **Citrine Wagtail** (first-winter, Aug 1991, Lista, Vest-Agder, Norway)
3 **Citrine Wagtail** (first-winter, Aug 1995*, Tresco, Isles of Scilly, Britain)
4 **Citrine Wagtail** (male, June 1990, Oulu, Finland)
5 **Cedar Waxwing** (probably first-winter, Mar 1996*, Nottingham, Britain)
6 **Cedar Waxwing** (probably first-winter, Mar 1996*, Nottingham, Britain)
7 **Cedar Waxwing** (May 1989, Gerdar, Iceland)
8 **Northern Mockingbird** (May 1988, Horsey Island, Essex, Britain)
9 **Northern Mockingbird** (Oct 1988, Schiermonnikoog, Netherlands)
10 **Brown Thrasher** (date unknown, New York, USA)
11 **Brown Thrasher** (Nov 1966, Durlston Head, Dorset, Britain)

GREY CATBIRD

Dumetella carolinensis L 18.5 cm (7.5 in)
DESCRIPTION Dark, long-tailed passerine approaching size of a small thrush. Plumage appears uniformly dark grey but for black cap high on crown and extending from forehead back above eye to nape. Undertail-coverts are bright rufous; tail is blackish, and rounded at the tip. Apart from the restricted black cap, head is uniformly grey with the dark eye prominent. Sexes generally similar, though females usually duller, with slightly paler throat and belly, and some grey in undertail-coverts. First-winter has slightly browner flight feathers and duller, not deep red-brown, iris, though eye always appears dark in the field. Rather skulking in behaviour, often remaining concealed in vegetation, but responds readily to 'pishing'.
VOICE Song is varied and melodious, occasionally including mimicry. Typical call is a cat-like nasal mewing.
HABITAT Found in woodlands, thickets, dense parkland and shrubbery, often in vicinity of damp areas or water.
DISTRIBUTION Breeds from southern Canada south across much of USA except the south-west, Gulf coast and Florida. Winters in small numbers in eastern USA, but chiefly from Gulf coast south through Central America and in parts of the West Indies.
EUROPEAN STATUS Extreme vagrant: four records. Channel Islands (1: mid-Oct to early Dec 1975); Germany (2: 28 Oct 1840; 2 May 1908); Ireland (1: 4 Nov 1986).

SIBERIAN ACCENTOR

Prunella montanella L 14.5 cm (5.75 in)
DESCRIPTION Brightly patterned accentor, longer-tailed than Dunnock and with different shape. In summer, shows black crown with greyer central stripe, blackish ear-coverts, broad yellow-ochre supercilium, throat, breast and rufous-streaked flanks (becoming buffer in worn plumage), cream-coloured belly, grey neck sides, essentially chestnut upperparts with indistinct buff or olive streaking, and grey-brown rump. White tips to median and greater coverts form two narrow bars on largely rufous wing. First-winter generally less rufous above, with duller face pattern than adult. Similar but larger Radde's Accentor *P ocularis* (occurs from Turkey eastwards, not recorded in Europe) has less rufous upperparts and whitish supercilium and throat. Perches much more than ground-loving Dunnock.
VOICE Song, given from tree-top, is very like Dunnock's, but more emphatic. Contact call is a trisyllabic *tee-see-see*.
HABITAT In summer, frequents scrub and open woodland in river valleys and on mountainsides up to treeline. Prefers riverside vegetation in winter.
DISTRIBUTION Breeds from northernmost Urals eastwards to Pacific coast, with isolated populations in central Siberian mountains. Winters in Korea and eastern China.

EUROPEAN STATUS Very rare vagrant: most occur in October-November. Austria (one in early 19th century); Czech Republic (1: 29 Dec 1943); Denmark (1: 5 Oct 1992); Finland (4: 7 Oct 1975; 7 Oct 1976; 10-17 Oct 1986; 22-23 Oct 1988); Italy (3: 8 Nov 1884; 4 Nov 1901; 5 Nov 1907); Poland (1: 26-27 Mar 1988); Slovakia (1: Dec 1994); Sweden (7). In addition, one record of Siberian/Black-throated Accentor from Norway (5 Oct 1992), where the two are treated as conspecific.

BLACK-THROATED ACCENTOR

Prunella atrogularis L 15 cm (6 in)
DESCRIPTION Resembles Siberian Accentor, but has black throat patch, usually a diffusely streaked central crown, narrower creamy (not yellow) supercilium and malar stripe, browner rump, and duller earth-brown tone to black-streaked upperparts. Breast is rich buff and appears unstreaked except in worn plumage, when may show indistinct spotting; flanks diffusely streaked blackish. Belly and vent cream or whitish, noticeably paler than breast. On some birds in winter plumage, much of the black bib is masked by paler fringing; these individuals also have more patchily-marked black lores and ear-coverts. In first-winter plumage upperparts duller than adult's, with less contrasting face pattern and heavier streaking below.
VOICE Call and song both resemble Siberian Accentor's.
HABITAT Frequents tangled thickets and juniper scrub, stunted spruces, and coniferous and broad-leaved woodland. On passage also in riverine vegetation, but generally avoids open areas.
DISTRIBUTION Breeds in the Urals and in Central Asia, with northern population moving south to winter also in Central Asia and south to Afghanistan and Pakistan.
EUROPEAN STATUS Extreme vagrant: three records. Finland (2: 19 Oct 1987; 23-24 Oct 1993); Sweden (1: 14-16 June 1988). Additionally, one in Germany (13-16 Feb 1994) considered of doubtful origin; see also Norway under Siberian Accentor.

SIBERIAN RUBYTHROAT

Luscinia calliope L 14 cm (5.5 in)
DESCRIPTION Male unmistakable, with dazzling ruby-red throat patch contrasting with white supercilium and submoustachial stripe, black lores, greyish tone to sides of neck and breast, brown upperparts and whitish belly. Female rather featureless, with brownish upperparts, buffer underparts, pale supercilium and usually whitish throat, though some may show traces of pink. First-winter male resembles adult but is browner, with duller throat patch. Rather like Bluethroat in habits, skulking in or near dense ground cover; often cocks tail.
VOICE Song is a rich, varied and sustained warbling, including some mimicry. Call is a characteristic two-note whistle, *eee-oo*; also *chak*.

HABITAT In summer inhabits lowland copses, thickets and woodland edges, occasionally also at higher altitudes, but avoids dense coniferous belts. In winter often in ditches, tangles and scrub near water.
DISTRIBUTION Breeds across much of Siberia west to the Urals, and in northern China and Japan, wintering chiefly in South-East Asia, Philippines and Bangladesh.
EUROPEAN STATUS Very rare vagrant: most records fall between late September and early November. Britain (1: 9-11 Oct 1975); Denmark (1: Oct 1985; another in Nov 1990 considered to be an escape); Estonia (1: 25 May 1975); Finland (1: 15 Oct 1991); Iceland (1: 8 Nov 1943); Italy (6). Also four category D records from France (all in 19th century).

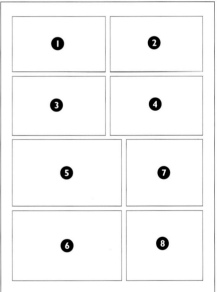

1 Grey Catbird (Oct 1975, Jersey, Channel Islands)
2 Siberian Accentor (Oct 1991, Landsort, Sweden)
3 Black-throated Accentor (first-year, Oct 1987, Helsinki, Finland)
4 Black-throated Accentor (first-year, Oct 1987, Helsinki, Finland)
5 Siberian Rubythroat (first-winter female, Oct 1991, Norrskär, Finland)
6 Siberian Rubythroat (first-winter female, Oct 1991, Norrskär, Finland)
7 Siberian Rubythroat (first-winter male, Nov 1995*, Heligoland, Germany)
8 Siberian Rubythroat (first-winter male, Nov 1995*, Heligoland, Germany)

SIBERIAN BLUE ROBIN

Luscinia cyane L 13.5 cm (5.25 in)

DESCRIPTION Adult male deep blue above and white below, colours being sharply demarcated on lores, cheeks and breast sides by black line which merges into blue. Tone of upperparts brightest on head, dullest on wings and darkest on tail; white of underparts tinged with blue on sides of breast and flanks. Female rather nondescript brown above, paler and buffer below, with brown mottling on breast and white undertail-coverts; tail and rump often contrastingly bluish, and has pale eye-ring like female Red-flanked Bluetail. First-winters resemble female, but first-winter male often has at least some areas of upperparts toned blue. Bill dark, often pale at base of lower mandible; legs flesh-coloured and often startlingly pale. Short tail and wings and long legs give it a jizz unique among chats. Secretive and ground-dwelling; has characteristic habit of quivering tail when nervous.

VOICE Song varied and loud, comprising several repeated phrases. Alarm call given as *chuck-chuck-chuck*.

HABITAT Breeds in dense coniferous taiga with no undergrowth, often near rivers. In winter also frequents forested areas.

DISTRIBUTION Breeds from southern Siberia eastwards to northern China, Korea and Japan, wintering mainly in South-East Asia, Philippines and Indonesia.

EUROPEAN STATUS Extreme vagrant: one autumn record. Channel Islands (1: 27 Oct 1975).

RED-FLANKED BLUETAIL

Tarsiger cyanurus L 14 cm (5.5 in)

DESCRIPTION Adult male unmistakable, with cobalt-blue upperparts, white underparts and orangey flanks; upperparts browner after moult into fresh autumn plumage. Female and first-year male alike, with upperparts olive-brown instead of blue (though some young males may show traces of blue) and distinct pale eye-ring. Black bill is small and slightly upward-pointing; legs black. In all plumages has blue rump and tail (though may appear just dark in the field), unique among European passerines except for vagrant Siberian Blue Robin, which has shorter tail, longer and pale legs and no orange on flanks. Shy, but less inclined to skulk in ground cover like other rare chats, and may fly-catch like Redstart.

VOICE Song is short and Redstart-like, falling at the end. Call given as *weep* or, in the case of vagrants, a short *teck-teck*.

HABITAT Favours coniferous forests for breeding, though also in mixed forest and birch woods (especially in east of range), and sometimes at higher altitudes. May occur in more open areas on passage.

DISTRIBUTION Breeds from eastern Baltic region across Russia and Siberia to Japan and China, and in the Himalayas. Winters in southern China and South-East Asia.

EUROPEAN STATUS Breeds Finland (estimate of 200-400 territories based on extrapolation from sample; c 119 records 1949-94, with peak of 34 1969-73). Accidental elsewhere: Britain (15); Channel Islands (1: 31 Oct-2 Nov 1976); Denmark (2: May 1976; 6-9 Oct 1994); Estonia (2: May 1977; breeding pair May-June 1980); France (1: 27 Oct 1993); Germany (6); Italy (3: Nov 1879; 6 Dec 1967; 26 Apr 1978); Netherlands (2: 16 Oct 1967; Sept 1985); Norway (4: 31 May 1969; 9 Aug 1977; 5 Nov 1978; 25 Sept 1987); Sweden (11).

WHITE-THROATED ROBIN

Irania gutturalis L 16.5 cm (6.5 in)

DESCRIPTION Large, robust chat with shape and proportions recalling a thrush. Male is bluish-grey above, with black face bordered by thin white supercilium and neat white throat patch; breast and flanks warm orange, fading to pale grey on belly and undertail-coverts. Female less distinct, but size, structure and combination of brownish-grey upperparts, white throat, mottled greyish underparts and warm buffish tone to flanks are characteristic. First-winter male resembles adult male but is browner above, often with pale-tipped coverts, and has duller, less extensively orange underparts, with dark of face extending onto chest and becoming pale-fringed. Bill and legs black. Long tail, often held cocked, is black in all plumages. Generally shy and retiring.

VOICE Song is a short warble of rather harsh notes, given from perch or in flight. Call is a loud *tsee-chut*.

HABITAT Nests in thickets and scrub in ravines and on hillsides and mountains; occurs in broadly similar habitat in winter.

DISTRIBUTION Breeds from Turkey and (in small numbers) in Lebanon and Israel discontinuously eastwards to Kazakhstan. Migrates south to winter in Kenya and Tanzania.

EUROPEAN STATUS Very rare vagrant: 13 records, the majority in spring, with breeding recently reported. Britain (2: 22 June 1983; 27-30 May 1990); Greece (3: May 1966; 29 May 1991; 16 May 1994; subsequently proved to be breeding on Lesbos); Netherlands (1: 3-4 Nov 1986); Norway (2: 15 May 1981; 17 Aug 1989); Sweden (5: June-July 1971; 14 May 1977; 10 May 1981; 10-19 May 1986; 16-21 May 1989).

MOUSSIER'S REDSTART

Phoenicurus moussieri L 12 cm (4.75 in)

DESCRIPTION Adult male stunningly patterned black above and brick-red below, with broad white supercilia which extend forwards to meet across forehead and at rear broaden behind eye and run down neck sides into wider terminal wedge. Has prominent wing panel formed by white bases to inner primaries and secondaries. Female similar to female Redstart, but with more extensively reddish underparts, shorter tail and hint of male's pale wing panel. Both sexes share orangey-rufous rump and tail, latter with darker central feathers, and warm buff undertail-coverts. First-winters resemble adults of same sex, but elements of juvenile plumage retained, and in particular young male appears duller and browner than adult, with pale fringing above and below. Bill and legs black. Flickers tail like Redstart; typically observed on or near ground.

VOICE Song comprises a short warble. Call given as a loud *wheet*, often followed by a rasping *tr-rr-rr*.

HABITAT In breeding season frequents scrub and forest edges, often on hillsides and mountains. In winter in scrub, semi-deserts and open country down to sea level.

DISTRIBUTION Endemic to Morocco, Algeria and Tunisia, where mainly resident but subject to altitudinal and short-distance movements outside breeding season. Some winter in north-west Libya, where may have bred; has straggled to Malta on several occasions.

EUROPEAN STATUS Very rare vagrant: eight records, mostly in spring. Britain (1: 24 Apr 1988); France (1: 14 May 1993); Greece (2: 30 Mar 1988; 18 Sept 1994); Italy (3: 18 May 1906; 27 Feb 1987; 10 Nov 1993); Spain (1: 7 Apr 1988).

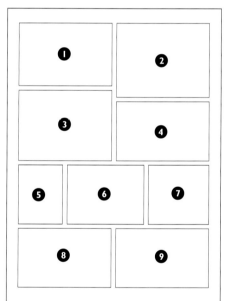

1 **Siberian Blue Robin** (first-winter female, Oct 1975, Sark, Channel Islands)
2 **Red-flanked Bluetail** (probably first-winter, Oct 1993, Winspit, Dorset, Britain)
3 **Red-flanked Bluetail** (male, Oct 1994, Landguard, Suffolk, Britain)
4 **Red-flanked Bluetail** (female or first-winter male, Oct 1994, Great Yarmouth, Norfolk, Britain)
5 **Red-flanked Bluetail** (first-winter, Sept 1993, Fair Isle, Shetland, Britain)
6 **White-throated Robin** (female, May 1990, Skokholm, Dyfed, Britain)
7 **White-throated Robin** (adult male, Nov 1986, Zuidholland, Netherlands)
8 **White-throated Robin** (adult male, Nov 1986, Zuidholland, Netherlands)
9 **Moussier's Redstart** (male, Apr 1988, Dinas Head, Dyfed, Britain)

ISABELLINE WHEATEAR

Oenanthe isabellina L 16.5 cm (6.5 in)
DESCRIPTION Large, upright wheatear, closely resembling female Northern Wheatear in winter plumage. Upperparts sandy-brown; head pattern like female Northern but in summer showing well-defined whitish supercilium and blackish lores. Wings brown but with extensive broad buffish edges, maintaining uniform appearance of upperparts; alula contrastingly dark. Whitish underwing, when discernible, is useful distinction from drab grey underwing of Northern. Unlike Northern, inverted T-pattern of black central tail much reduced and overall effect is close to even separation of white rump against black tail. In consequence, tail of Isabelline looks more extensively black and, in combination with sandy back, appearance in flight is tricoloured: sandy back, white rump, black tail. Underparts cream, buffer on throat and sandy-buff on breast and flanks. Rather strong, longish bill and legs black. Sexes similar; first-winter as adult. Structure subtly but distinctly different from Northern Wheatear's, with slightly larger head, broader wings, shorter tail, longer legs and erect posture imparting a different jizz; has tendency to run rather than hop.
VOICE Rich and varied song often delivered in flight. Calls include a loud, clear *cheep*, likened to that of domestic chick.
HABITAT Inhabits dry, stony open country and steppe with scattered bushes.
DISTRIBUTION Breeds from south-east Europe and Turkey eastwards across Central Asia to Mongolia. Winters from Pakistan and north-west India south-west through Arabia to north-east and sub-Saharan Africa.
EUROPEAN STATUS Breeds in Bulgaria and Greece (50 100 pairs), and regular on passage in Romania (has bred) and Italy (Sicily). Accidental elsewhere: Britain (9); Denmark (1: Sept 1989); Finland (6); France (6); Ireland (1: 10-17 Oct 1992); Norway (1: 29 Sept-18 Oct 1977); Poland (1: 29 May 1986); Spain (1: 29-30 Sept 1974); Sweden (2: 18-19 Oct 1980; 6 Apr 1994).

PIED WHEATEAR

Oenanthe pleschanka L 14.5 cm (5.75 in)
DESCRIPTION Small, slim wheatear. Adult male in summer plumage has white crown and nape, black face, throat and upper breast joined on neck sides to black mantle and wings, and white rump and underparts, latter with buffish tinge. Tail has narrower black terminal band than on Northern Wheatear, widest at corners and very like Black-eared. In fresh winter plumage pied appearance masked by extensive brown and buff fringing above and below. Female essentially dark brown above with indistinct pale supercilium, dusky on throat and whitish below; in winter also fringed paler above and buffer below, when especially like eastern female Black-eared, which usually has paler throat contrasting with darker breast (but sometimes inseparable in the field). First-winter

male variable, often recalling female but with blackish face and throat; first-year female very like non-breeding adult female. In very similar Cyprus Wheatear *O cypriaca* (formerly considered conspecific with Pied, not recorded Europe), sexes very similar; slightly smaller, darker adults have 'dirty' tinge to white crown and nape (extensively on females), shorter primary projection and less white in tail.
VOICE Variable song contains rattling and whistling notes and mimicry. Calls include a variable *zack*.
HABITAT Favours open stony areas and hillsides, often with cliffs and rocky outcrops.
DISTRIBUTION In summer occurs from south-easternmost Europe (where hybridises with Black-eared Wheatear) east across Central Asia to southern Siberia, Mongolia and northern China. Winters north-east Africa and south-western tip of Arabia.
EUROPEAN STATUS Breeds in Bulgaria and Romania, and regular on passage in Greece (has bred twice). Accidental elsewhere: Austria (1: 3 June 1983); Britain (31); Denmark (2: 13 June 1961; 27 Oct-1 Nov 1991); Finland (13); France (1: 25 Oct 1991); Germany (8); Hungary (8*); Ireland (3: 8-16 Nov 1980; 19-20 Nov 1983; 5-8 Nov 1988); Italy (9); Netherlands (4: 28 May 1988; 23-26 Oct 1992; 31 Oct-4 Nov 1992; 7-8 Oct 1993); Norway (2: 15 May 1976; 16-18 Nov 1986); Sweden (10); former Yugoslavia (bred in 1966).

DESERT WHEATEAR

Oenanthe deserti L 14-15 cm (5.5-6 in)
DESCRIPTION Has diagnostic black tail in all plumages. Adult male warm sandy-buff above, paler below, with black face mask extending onto throat and joined across neck sides to black wings, unlike black-throated form of Black-eared Wheatear. Mask edged above by indistinct whitish supercilium which is often more prominent behind eye. Wings black, with white innermost coverts forming bold pale line, and with pale or buffish fringes to greater coverts, tertials and inner secondaries; rump white. In winter, black areas (except tail) obscured by paler fringing, and upperparts greyer. Female rather uniform pale sandy-buff, with browner ear-coverts and, on some, blackish or dark brown on throat; wings dark brown, edged sandy-buff on coverts, tertials and secondaries. First-winter male resembles non-breeding adult male, but has pale tips obscuring mask and browner wings with broader pale fringing; first-winter female as adult female. Bill and legs black.
VOICE Song is a short, plaintive, descending trill. Call is a shrill *huiie*.
HABITAT Dry, open areas, barren and stony plains and semi-desert, often with scattered scrub.
DISTRIBUTION Breeds North Africa and the Middle East, and from the southern Caucasus and Iran east across Central Asia to Tibet and Mongolia. Winters chiefly from north-west India westwards through Arabia to north-east Africa; some North African birds resident,

others moving south into Sahara and Sahel.
EUROPEAN STATUS Frequent vagrant: most records are in autumn and early winter. Belgium (2: 5 Oct 1990; 13-15 Oct 1991); Britain (47); Channel Islands (1: 24-28 Nov 1991); Denmark (2: Oct 1987; Nov 1987); Estonia (2: 12 Apr 1985; 17 June 1986); Finland (7); France (10); Germany (6); Gibraltar (1: 3 Sept 1987); Greece (6-7); Hungary (1: 17-21 Nov 1991); Ireland (2: 11-21 Mar 1990; 27 Oct-2 Nov 1990); Italy (28+, but records under review); Netherlands (4: 23 Nov 1970; 24-26 Apr 1989; 8-9 Oct 1994; 6 Nov 1994); Norway (5: 15 Dec 1984; 27 Mar 1989; 8 May 1991; 3 Oct 1992; 10 Oct 1993); Spain (3: 25 Sept 1972; 3 Apr 1985; 15-17 Apr 1990); Sweden (17); Switzerland (1: 19-23 Dec 1992).

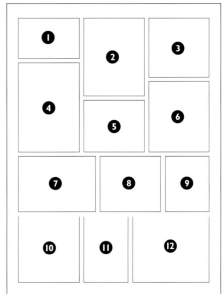

1 Isabelline Wheatear (Oct 1992, Mizen Head, Co Cork, Ireland)
2 Isabelline Wheatear (Oct 1990, Kilnsea, Humberside, Britain)
3 Isabelline Wheatear (Apr 1989, Helsinki, Finland)
4 Isabelline Wheatear (Oct 1991, Gugh, Isles of Scilly, Britain)
5 Pied Wheatear (first-winter male, Oct 1992, Hondsbosche, Zeewering, Netherlands)
6 Pied Wheatear (first-winter female, Oct 1994, Fagbury, Suffolk, Britain)
7 Pied Wheatear (first-summer male, June 1991, Scarborough, North Yorkshire, Britain)
8 Pied Wheatear (adult male, Nov 1991, Dodman Point, Cornwall, Britain)
9 Desert Wheatear (first-winter male, Oct 1992, Utsira, Rogaland, Norway)
10 Desert Wheatear (female, Nov 1991, Fleetwood, Lancashire, Britain)
11 Desert Wheatear (male, Oct 1994, Zandvoort, Netherlands)
12 Desert Wheatear (first-winter male, Nov 1994, Blackpool, Lancashire, Britain)

FINSCH'S WHEATEAR

Oenanthe finschii L 15 cm (6 in)

DESCRIPTION Breeding male recalls black-throated form of Black-eared Wheatear, with black mask and buffish-white crown, nape and mantle, but black of throat extends onto upper breast and broadly connects across neck sides with black of scapulars and wings, latter showing pale tips only to primary coverts and flight feathers. Underwing shows blackish coverts and contrasting silvery-grey flight feathers. Longish tail patterned like Northern Wheatear's, but terminal band narrower and of even width, with tips of outermost feathers white. Underparts creamy-white, becoming warmer-toned on undertail-coverts. In winter, upperparts greyer, underparts buffer and throat flecked paler. Female has grey or brownish-grey upperparts, rufous tone to cheeks and darker brown wings which are extensively fringed and tipped buffish; may show entirely pale throat or blackish mask, but underparts otherwise buff-white. First-winters like adult female, but with broader pale fringes to flight feathers. Bill and legs black. Barely larger than Black-eared Wheatear but more robustly built, with larger head and 'stronger' legs and feet. Rather shy.

VOICE Song is a short, scratchy warble. Calls include *tsak*, *zik* and *chek*.

HABITAT Found on dry, rocky mountainsides, foothills and stony plains.

DISTRIBUTION Breeds from Turkey eastwards through southern Caucasus to south-west Asia, wintering locally in southern parts of breeding range, west to Cyprus and south to Egypt, northern Saudi Arabia and Gulf coasts.

EUROPEAN STATUS Extreme vagrant, possibly colonising: about seven summer records. Bulgaria (c 6: breeding pair and singing male discovered in 1993; pair and possibly three singing males present in 1994); Greece (1: 10 June 1993).

WHITE-CROWNED BLACK WHEATEAR

Oenanthe leucopyga L 17 cm (6.75 in)

DESCRIPTION Large, elongated, predominantly black wheatear, in adult plumage typically with diagnostic white cap sitting high on crown above eye. Glossy, deep black coloration otherwise marked only by white lower back, rump and undertail-coverts (encircling rear end of body when wings raised) and by white tail which has black central feathers and, on some, black tips to outer feathers which broaden at corners. With juvenile and first-year birds, which lack white cap of most adults, latter is best distinction from very similar Black Wheatear, which has broader black tail band than Northern Wheatear (though note that young White-crowned Black can also show dark spots near tips of outer five tail feathers). Black Wheatear also has sootier plumage colour which extends further down belly than on White-crowned Black, is slightly larger and plumper with heavier bill,

and has black underwing-coverts contrasting with greyish-brown flight feathers (underwing all black on White-crowned Black Wheatear). As first-years approach adult plumage, crown shows variable pattern of black and white. Bill and legs black.

VOICE Varied song contains musical and scratchy notes and mimicry. Calls variously given as a quiet *trip-trip*, soft *hue* and *peeh-peeh*.

HABITAT Found around wadis, ravines and outcrops in desert or semi-desert.

DISTRIBUTION Largely sedentary, occurring from Morocco in west discontinuously through North Africa to Middle East and parts of Arabia.

EUROPEAN STATUS Extreme vagrant: four records of five birds, all in spring. Britain (1: 2-5 June 1982); Germany (1: 9-13 May 1986); Greece (1: 15 Apr 1993); Spain (1: 28 May 1977, two). Other records in Europe (eg in Britain and Ireland) also attributed either to this species or to extralimital Black Wheatear.

WHITE'S THRUSH

Zoothera dauma L 27 cm (10.75 in)

DESCRIPTION Size of Mistle Thrush but proportionately shorter-tailed, with larger head and heavier bill. Head, upperparts (except wings) and underparts golden-buff, unmistakably patterned with black crescentic markings which are boldest on breast and flanks. Chin, cheeks and belly have whiter ground colour underneath black scalloping; lores rather pale, and undertail-coverts unmarked whitish. Closed wing contrasts markedly with patterned body, appearing essentially golden-brown with blackish bases and tips to primaries, and with black coverts, medians with buff spotting and greater and primary coverts with buff edges; in strongly undulating flight reveals even more striking pattern of white underwing with black central-covert stripe and broad dusky trailing edge. Tail pattern also distinctive when flushed: has pale brown centre and darker outer feathers with bold white corners. Bill brown, with yellowish base to lower mandible; legs yellowish-brown. Very shy and secretive.

VOICE Song comprises a soft, drawn-out fluting whistle. Apparently silent outside breeding season.

HABITAT Breeds chiefly in coniferous taiga forest with dense undergrowth.

DISTRIBUTION In summer found in Urals and from central Siberia east to Japan and Korea; also breeds in Himalayas and China, southern India, South-East Asia and Indonesia. Northern migratory birds winter largely from north-east India east through much of South-East Asia to southern China.

EUROPEAN STATUS Frequent vagrant. Austria (3: 1844; autumn 1845; 1847); Belgium (16); Britain (44); Denmark (2: Apr 1909; Jan 1918); Faeroes (2: 9 Nov 1938; autumn 1974); Finland (2: 30 Sept 1961; 5 Oct 1988); France (10); Germany (c 38); Greece (2: autumn 1954; 3 Feb 1965); Iceland (3: 14 Oct 1939; 9 Oct 1982; 5-9 Nov 1982); Ireland (4: early Dec

1842; spring 1867; 9 Jan 1885; 16-20 Apr 1993); Italy (22); Netherlands (15); Norway (6); Poland (8); Romania (1: Sept 1981); Slovenia (1: 19 Nov 1973); Spain (2); Sweden (6).

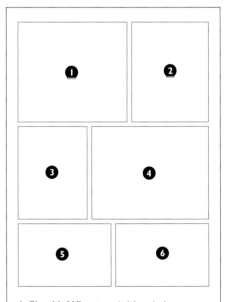

1 **Finch's Wheatear** (adult male, June, Turkmenistan)
2 **White-crowned Black Wheatear** (first-summer, June 1982, Kessingland, Suffolk, Britain)
3 **White-crowned Black Wheatear** (first-summer, June 1982, Kessingland, Suffolk, Britain)
4 **White's Thrush** (first-winter, Oct 1986, Katwijk, Netherlands)
5 **White's Thrush** (first-year, Apr 1993, Copeland Island, Co Down, Ireland)
6 **White's Thrush** (first-year, Apr 1993, Copeland Island, Co Down, Ireland)

SIBERIAN THRUSH

Zoothera sibirica L 22 cm (8.75 in)
DESCRIPTION Adult male unmistakable, with slate-grey head and body, conspicuous white supercilium extending almost to nape, whitish belly, grey-barred undertail-coverts and white corners to underside of tail. Tone of body darkest (almost black) on head, palest on flanks. In flight looks strikingly pied, showing white underwing with black central-covert stripe and broad dusky trailing edge, as on White's Thrush. Female has similar underwing pattern but black replaced by brown; upperparts grey-toned olive-brown, with long, broad buff-white supercilium flecked with brown at rear, brown eye-stripe, pale tips to median and greater coverts, whitish throat and belly, and buff-suffused whitish underparts heavily marked with dark brown spots on ear-coverts and neck sides and broader crescentic bars on breast and flanks. First-winters resemble adults, but young male is variably browner on head, with less distinct supercilium and paler throat. Size of Song Thrush, but has longer blackish-brown bill with pale base to lower mandible; legs yellow-brown or flesh. Very skulking.
VOICE Simple and variable fluty song ends in a twitter. Has Song Thrush-like *zit* flight call.
HABITAT Favours dense coniferous and broad-leaved taiga forest, often in moist areas.
DISTRIBUTION Breeds from western Siberia east to northern Japan and north-east China, wintering chiefly in India and South-East Asia.
EUROPEAN STATUS Very rare vagrant: 50 records. Austria (2: 1928/29; 26 Dec 1962); Belgium (3: Sept 1877; 18 Oct 1901; end Oct 1912); Britain (5: 1-4 Oct 1954; 25 Dec 1977; 13 Nov 1984; 1-8 Oct 1992; 18 Sept 1994); France (5: 1847; after 1859; 1861; 1870; 7 Jan 1982); Germany (11); Ireland (1: 18 Oct 1985); Italy (3: 27 Oct 1908; 13 Oct 1910; 11 Oct 1930); Netherlands (2: Sept 1853; 1 Oct 1856); Norway (7); Poland (10, including records of flocks); Sweden (1: 11 Sept 1990); Switzerland (1: 8 Dec 1978).

VARIED THRUSH

Zoothera naevia L 25 cm (10 in)
DESCRIPTION Fieldfare-sized thrush with strikingly patterned plumage. Adult male has blue-grey upperparts from head to tail, purest blue on rump and darker on crown; wings darker, extensively fringed bluish, but with orangey broad double wing-bars and patch at base of primaries. Underwing reveals typical *Zoothera* pattern of white with black central-covert stripe and broad dusky trailing edge. Face shows orange rear supercilium above black eye mask; lower cheeks, throat and breast also orange, latter divided by black breast band. Female has similar plumage pattern, but blue-grey and black of male's upperparts replaced by dark brown (though tail tinged bluish) and breast band indistinct. First-winters like respective adults, but young male has browner greater coverts and young female lacks bluish tinge to tail. Bill blackish, with

yellow base to lower mandible. Unlike many vagrant Nearctic thrushes, feeds in trees, spending less time on forest floor or skulking in undergrowth.
VOICE Simple song consists of high-pitched, drawn-out notes broken by pauses. Call is a soft *tuck*.
HABITAT Favours montane coniferous forest with undergrowth; in wider range of wooded habitats in winter, when also visits feeders.
DISTRIBUTION Breeds in Alaska, western Canada and western USA, wintering south to California. Regularly strays to eastern USA.
EUROPEAN STATUS Extreme vagrant: one autumn record. Britain (1: 14-23 Nov 1982).

WOOD THRUSH

Hylocichla mustelina L 19 cm (7.5 in)
DESCRIPTION In shape, character and boldly spotted underparts recalls small *Turdus* rather than large *Catharus* thrush. Adult has rufous-brown upperparts, warmest in orangey tone on crown and nape, less so on mantle and scapulars; wings and tail somewhat colder brown. Face shows prominent bold white ring around large, dark eye and white fore-supercilium above dark loral stripe, which combine to give impression of pale 'spectacle'. Ear-coverts intricately patterned with fine blackish streaks, and shows distinct black-spotted malar stripe. Underparts white, heavily marked with bold black spots from chin to flanks and belly; spots are largest on breast. First-winter distinguished from adult by pale tips to greater coverts, forming narrow wing-bar. Bill dark brown, with yellowish base to lower mandible; legs pink. Skulks less than *Catharus* thrushes, but still rather retiring and fond of feeding in undergrowth.
VOICE Song comprises loud varied whistles and trills. Calls include a sharp, staccato *whip-ip-ip-ip* in alarm.
HABITAT Frequents areas of contiguous mature deciduous or mixed forest and woodland.
DISTRIBUTION Breeds across eastern half of USA and just into south-east Canada, migrating to winter in Mexico and Central America.
EUROPEAN STATUS Extreme vagrant: two records in autumn. Britain (1: 7 Oct 1987); Iceland (1: 23 Oct 1967).

HERMIT THRUSH

Catharus guttatus L 17 cm (6.75 in)
DESCRIPTION Small Nearctic thrush, barely larger than Nightingale and with contrasting rufous tail recalling that species. Adult is grey-brown on crown, nape, mantle and wings, latter with rufous edges to primaries which may appear to form wing panel. Shares with other *Catharus* thrushes grey-and-buff underwing pattern recalling White's Thrush, though this character is difficult to see in the field. Rump, uppertail-coverts and tail warm rufous, contrasting noticeably with back and wings when viewed from rear; tail darker near tip. Face shows pale lores, complete narrow eye-ring and mottled olive-brown cheeks;

underparts whitish, washed buff on throat, breast and flanks and heavily spotted with black only on chest, becoming browner dappling on flanks. First-winter very like adult, but distinguished by triangular buffish tips to greater (and sometimes median) coverts. Bill dark brown, with pale flesh base to lower mandible; legs pale flesh. Often cocks and lowers tail; rather secretive.
VOICE Song is two short series of fluty notes, spaced by a pause, with the second at a different pitch. Commonest call is a Blackbird-like *chuck*; also a softer Bullfinch-like *huu*.
HABITAT Found in coniferous and mixed forests, often in vicinity of streams.
DISTRIBUTION Breeds in north-east USA, across much of Canada and Alaska except far north, and south through western USA to northernmost Mexico. Resident in far south-west USA, otherwise wintering from eastern and southern states south to El Salvador.
EUROPEAN STATUS Very rare vagrant: 17 records. Britain (4: 2 June 1975; 28 Oct 1984; 15-16 Oct 1987; 11 and 15-18 Oct 1993); Germany (4: 1 undated in 19th century; 1828; Oct 1836; 1851); Iceland (8); Sweden (1: 27 Apr 1988).

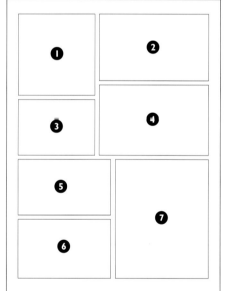

1 **Siberian Thrush** (first-winter female, Oct 1992, North Ronaldsay, Orkney, Britain)
2 **Siberian Thrush** (first-winter female, Oct 1992, North Ronaldsay, Orkney, Britain)
3 **Varied Thrush** (first-winter male with aberrant colouring, Nov 1982, Nanquidno, Cornwall, Britain)
4 **Varied Thrush** (first-winter male with aberrant colouring, Nov 1982, Nanquidno, Cornwall, Britain)
5 **Wood Thrush** *(Apr, Texas, USA)*
6 **Hermit Thrush** (Oct 1993, Tresco, Isles of Scilly, Britain)
7 **Hermit Thrush** (Oct 1993, Tresco, Isles of Scilly, Britain)

GREY-CHEEKED/BICKNELL'S THRUSH

Catharus minimus/bicknelli L 18 cm (7.25 in)
DESCRIPTION Very difficult-to-separate species pair. Adult Grey-cheeked Thrush is slightly larger than Hermit Thrush, with uniformly olive-grey-brown upperparts from crown to tail. Has greyish face with indistinct eye-ring mostly restricted to rear half of eye, pale lores and mottled cheeks. Underparts whitish, never appearing as extensively buffish on breast as on Swainson's Thrush; throat and breast spotted black, flanks suffused with grey. First-winter very like adult, but with buffish tips to greater coverts. Bill dark brown, with flesh or yellowish-flesh base to lower mandible; legs dusky flesh. Extremely similar Bicknell's Thrush, only recently split from Grey-cheeked Thrush and yet to be confirmed in Europe, is typically slightly smaller, with extensively bright yellow base to lower mandible, subtly warmer brown upperparts and contrastingly chestnut-toned tail. Both species are generally shy and skulking; tail never cocked like that of Hermit and Swainson's Thrushes.
VOICE Closing phrase to jumbled, squeaky song is claimed good distinction: Grey-cheeked Thrush has a louder, lower and descending *wheee-er*, Bicknell's has a thinner, higher *shre-e-e-e*. Calls similarly different, that for Grey-cheeked Thrush given as a lower *whe-err* and Bicknell's Thrush as a higher *cree-ee*.
HABITAT Breeds chiefly in coniferous forest, also willow and alder thickets with dense undergrowth.
DISTRIBUTION Grey-cheeked breeds in northern North America from Newfoundland west across Canada and northern Alaska into north-east Siberia, and further south in north-west Canada and in northern USA, wintering in northern South America. Bicknell's breeds in south-easternmost Canada and north-east USA, wintering in the Caribbean.
EUROPEAN STATUS Rare vagrant: October is the peak month. Totals given are for records accepted as Grey-cheeked Thrush; some occurrences may possibly relate to Bicknell's Thrush (results of investigation of possible occurrences of latter so far reported only in Britain, where no confirmed records). Britain (39); France (2: 20 Oct 1974; 22 Oct 1986); Germany (1: 18 Oct 1937); Iceland (2: most recent on 30 Oct 1983); Ireland (4: 19 Oct 1982; 9-12 Oct 1988; 6-7 Oct 1990; 12 Oct 1991); Norway (1: 28 and 30 Oct 1973).

SWAINSON'S THRUSH

Catharus ustulatus L 18 cm (7.25 in)
DESCRIPTION In many respects very like Grey-cheeked Thrush, with olive-brown upperparts and whitish underparts with black spotting on upper chest, but readily separated by distinctive head pattern. Swainson's has much bolder buff eye-ring which carries forward into buff supraloral stripe arcing towards base of upper mandible, quite unlike the duller head pattern with indistinct eye-ring of Grey-cheeked. Swainson's also has buffer ground colour to cheeks, throat and breast, somewhat recalling miniature Song Thrush, and has slightly more olive-toned upperparts. As with other *Catharus* thrushes, spotting on upper chest becomes indistinct grey dappling on lower breast and flanks, latter marginally less grey-toned than on Grey-cheeked Thrush. First-winters aged by pale tips to greater coverts. Bill dark brown, with buff-flesh base to lower mandible; legs grey-flesh. Occasionally raises tail in manner of Hermit Thrush; rather secretive.
VOICE Song is a short ascending series of fluty notes. Has distinctive *plip* call, like sound of water dripping into tin bucket, and, in flight, a high-pitched *heep*.
HABITAT Nests in coniferous forest and damp thickets.
DISTRIBUTION Breeds from central Alaska across Canada to Newfoundland and in northern USA, in east south along Appalachians and in west south to California and Colorado. Winters from Mexico to north-west Argentina.
EUROPEAN STATUS Very rare vagrant: 28 records. Austria (1: Mar 1878); Britain (16); Finland (2: 19 Oct 1974; 1 Nov 1981); France (2: 19th century; 17 Feb 1979); Germany (2: 2 Oct 1869; 1886); Iceland (1: 4 Oct 1978); Ireland (3: 26 May 1956; 14-16 Oct 1968; 8 Oct 1990); Norway (1: 20 Sept 1974).

VEERY

Catharus fuscescens L 17 cm (6.75 in)
DESCRIPTION Clearly separable from other vagrant *Catharus* thrushes by distinct rusty tone to upperparts. Crown, nape, mantle, wings and tail essentially plain warm cinnamon-brown, most intensely so on rump. Face lacks obvious eye-ring and has greyish lores. Underparts plainer than on other *Catharus* species, with dark spotting on buff-tinged throat and breast much fainter but converging towards bill as distinct malar stripe; belly and undertail-coverts white, flanks greyer and often obvious against cinnamon tone of upperparts and peachy wash to upper breast. Tail slightly longer than in congeners, but difference very subtle and difficult to appreciate in the field. Overall coloration may give rise to comparison with Nightingale or Thrush Nightingale, from which safely distinguished by bulkier, 'neckless' jizz, lack of obvious contrast between tail and upperparts, and pale buff throat showing malar stripe and indistinct spotting. Bill dark brown, with pale flesh base to lower mandible; legs pinkish. Habits much as other *Catharus* thrushes, but lacks frequent tail-cocking of Hermit Thrush.
VOICE Song is a descending series of *veery*-type notes. Characteristic call is a low, drawn-out *phew* or *whee-u*.
HABITAT Found in moist broad-leaved or mixed woodland and thickets with undergrowth.
DISTRIBUTION Breeds across southern Canada and northern USA, and southwards in Appalachians and Rockies. Long-distance migrant, wintering in northern South America.
EUROPEAN STATUS Extreme vagrant: three records in autumn. Britain (2: 6 Oct 1970; 10 Oct-11 Nov 1987); Sweden (1: 26 Sept 1978).

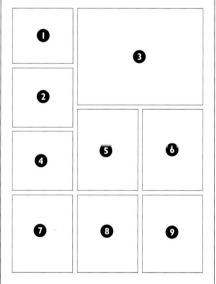

1 **Grey-cheeked Thrush** (Oct 1986, Tresco, Isles of Scilly, Britain)
2 **Grey-cheeked Thrush** (first-winter, Oct 1991, St Mary's, Isles of Scilly, Britain)
3 **Grey-cheeked Thrush** (first-winter, Oct 1991, St Mary's, Isles of Scilly, Britain)
4 **Swainson's Thrush** (Oct 1990, Fair Isle, Shetland, Britain)
5 **Swainson's Thrush** (Oct 1990, St Mary's, Isles of Scilly, Britain)
6 **Swainson's Thrush** (Oct 1990, St Mary's, Isles of Scilly, Britain)
7 **Veery** (first-winter, Oct 1987, Lundy, Devon, Britain)
8 **Veery** (first-winter, Oct 1987, Lundy, Devon, Britain)
9 **Veery** (first-winter, Oct 1987, Lundy, Devon, Britain)

EYEBROWED THRUSH

Turdus obscurus L 23 cm (9.25 in)

DESCRIPTION Subtly patterned, but unlikely to be misidentified. Adult male has grey head, throat and upper breast and black eye-stripe, with contrasting white supercilium, under-eye crescent and faintly streaked chin. Upperparts otherwise unmarked olive-brown except for indistinct white tips to outer tail feathers. Grey upper breast bordered below by apricot band which extends down flanks and around white lower breast and belly; undertail-coverts also white. Adult female similar but lacks 'grey-hooded' appearance, with crown and nape much as colour of mantle, white-streaked cheeks, obvious dark malar stripe and white throat. First-winters resemble adult female, but have pale tips to greater coverts forming narrow wing-bar; young male may show more grey on head and less white on throat than young female, but sexing difficult. Character and actions most like Redwing's.

VOICE Has a simple, rich song of trisyllabic ringing notes. Calls include *kek* in alarm and *dzeee* in flight, both recalling Redwing.

HABITAT Favours coniferous forests near water; in winter also in more open wooded habitats.

DISTRIBUTION Breeds largely in central Siberia, wintering from north-east India east through South-East Asia and Philippines to Taiwan and southern Japan.

EUROPEAN STATUS Rare vagrant. Belgium (6); Britain (15); Czech Republic (4: 2 before or in 1852; 1 Dec 1979; 15 Mar 1980); Finland (2: 11-12 June 1978; 1-14 Dec 1984); France (10); Germany (18, but only one documented record since 1900: 5 Oct 1994); Italy (c 20); Netherlands (6); Norway (3: 2 Nov 1961; 29 Dec 1978; 3 Oct 1981); Poland (7); Portugal (1: c 1991, shot*); Sweden (1: 28 Dec 1989)

NAUMANN'S/DUSKY THRUSH

Turdus naumanni naumanni/eunomus L 23 cm (9.25 in)

DESCRIPTION Siberian vagrant, with two distinct subspecies occurring in Europe. Adult male of nominate race (Naumann's) has grey-brown upperparts admixed with rufous, becoming bright rufous on rump and tail; wings dark brown, with rufous-grey fringing except on primaries and outer secondaries. Face shows pale buff or rufous supercilium, dark eye-stripe, brownish ear-coverts and blackish malar stripe; throat, breast and flanks dull reddish, latter especially mottled whiter. Adult male of race *eunomus* (Dusky) differs in darker brown head and back mottled with black and chestnut, chestnut (not rufous) rump, more blackish-brown tail, more extensively reddish fringes forming bolder wing panel, blackish ear-coverts, whiter supercilium, and creamy-white underparts with extensive blackish spotting, concentrated into band(s) on breast. Adult females resemble males of respective races but generally duller, with face pattern and other characters less contrasting. First-winters best aged by paler tips to greater coverts.

Intergrades showing characters of both subspecies have occurred in Europe. In all plumages shows reddish underwing, dark bill with yellowish base to lower mandible, and brown legs.

VOICE Song of both races is similar, a Redwing-like series of notes followed by a twitter. Calls include loud *cheeh-cheeh* (often repeated) when perched, *tchack-tchack* in alarm and a Redwing-like *shree* in flight.

HABITAT Occurs in open riverine woodland with undergrowth; in more open country in winter.

DISTRIBUTION Dusky breeds from central Siberia east to Kamchatka, wintering chiefly in southern Japan, southern China, northern South-East Asia and northern Indian region. Naumann's breeds to south of Dusky, but overlaps in west of range; winters largely in China and Korea.

EUROPEAN STATUS Rare vagrant: national totals are followed by those for *naumanni/eunomus* where identified to race. Austria (6: 3/3); Belgium (6: 1/5); Britain (9: 1/8); Czech Republic (3: 1836; 24 Mar 1963; 3 Nov 1964); Denmark (2: 0/2); Faeroes (1: 8 Dec 1947); Finland (4: 2 *naumanni*: 27 Apr 1988; 19-26 Nov 1994; 2 *eunomus*: 23 Oct 1980; 17 May 1983); France (12, including 3/5 and 1 intermediate); Germany (18: 8/10); Hungary (1 *naumanni*: winter 1820); Italy (26: 3/23); Netherlands (2 *eunomus*: 20 Nov 1899; 20 Feb 1955); Norway (6: 0/6); Poland (8: 6/2); former Yugoslavia.

RED-THROATED/ BLACK-THROATED THRUSH

Turdus ruficollis ruficollis/atrogularis L 25 cm (10 in)

DESCRIPTION Has two markedly dimorphic forms often collectively referred to as Dark-throated Thrush. Adult male of nominate Red-throated race has uniform grey-brown upperparts with dark-centred reddish tail; face, throat and upper breast dull red (fringed whitish in winter), rest of underparts off-white. Bill yellowish, with blackish culmen and tip; legs yellowish-brown. Adult female duller, with pale supercilium, and whiter underparts showing rufous tinge and darker spotting which may form breast band; also has moustache of dark spots. First-winters have pale tips to greater coverts, male usually with reddish face and throat broadly fringed paler. Adult and first-winter males of Black-throated race *atrogularis* have black instead of reddish face, throat and breast, wholly dark brown tail, dusky marks on flanks, paler bill and greyer legs. Females much as females of Red-throated, except for lack of rufous on breast and in tail, and duller bare parts. Races hybridise in overlap area of ranges. Actions rather as Blackbird's.

VOICE Song poorly described. Calls much as for Naumann's/Dusky Thrushes.

HABITAT Red-throated occurs in sparse montane forest and scrub; Black-throated in borders and clearings of variety of forest and taiga.

DISTRIBUTION Black-throated breeds from Urals east to Lake Baikal area, and in Caucasus; winters from the Himalayas west to Iran and locally in Arabia. Red-throated breeds chiefly in Lake Baikal region, wintering from Afghanistan east across northern Indian region and Burma to west and north China.

EUROPEAN STATUS Frequent vagrant: national totals are followed by those for *ruficollis/ atrogularis* where identified to race. Austria (9: 0/9); Belgium (4 *atrogularis*: autumn 1844; 15 Oct 1904; 21 Oct 1904; 17 Oct 1936); Britain (33: 1/32); Bulgaria (*atrogularis*); Czech Republic (1: between 1854 and 1870); Denmark (5, including at least 3 *atrogularis*); Estonia (1: 0/1); Finland (20, including at least 17 *atrogularis*); France (13: 10/2 and 1 intermediate); Germany (49: 9/40); Greece (1 *atrogularis*: 4 Mar 1956); Italy (19+: 1+/18); Latvia (3, including at least 2 *atrogularis*: 8 Dec 1909; 15 May 1981; 29 Oct 1991); Netherlands (2 *atrogularis*: Mar-Apr 1981; Oct 1982); Norway (17: 3/15); Poland (21+: c 5/16+); Romania; Sweden (14: 0/14).

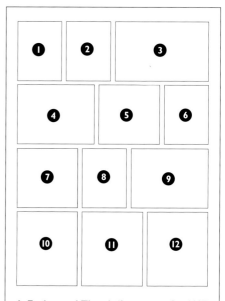

1 **Eyebrowed Thrush** (first-winter, Oct 1987, Fair Isle, Shetland, Britain)
2 **Eyebrowed Thrush** (first-winter, Oct 1993, St Mary's, Isles of Scilly, Britain)
3 **Eyebrowed Thrush** (first-winter, probably female, Oct 1991, St Mary's, Isles of Scilly, Britain)
4 **Eyebrowed Thrush** (first-winter, Oct 1993, St Mary's, Isles of Scilly, Britain)
5 **Naumann's Thrush** (first-winter male, Nov 1994, Helsinki, Finland)
6 **Naumann's Thrush** (male, Feb 1990, Chingford, Essex, Britain)
7 **Naumann's Thrush** (male, Feb 1990, Chingford, Essex, Britain)
8 **Dusky Thrush** (Nov 1975, Firth, Shetland, Britain)
9 **Red-throated Thrush** (first-winter male, Oct 1994, The Naze, Essex, Britain)
10 **Black-throated Thrush** (first-winter female, Mar 1994, Falsterbo, Sweden)
11 **Black-throated Thrush** (male winter, Feb 1976, Coltishall, Norfolk, Britain)
12 **Black-throated Thrush** (first-winter female, Oct 1993, St Martin's, Isles of Scilly, Britain)

AMERICAN ROBIN

Turdus migratorius L 25 cm (10 in)
DESCRIPTION In many ways the Nearctic equivalent of Blackbird, especially in size, shape, behaviour and calls. Adult male has blackish head with broken white eye-ring, olive-grey mantle, back and wings, purer grey rump and blackish tail with white-tipped corners. Chin and throat white with black streaking; breast, belly and flanks brick-red, latter with indistinct pale scaling in fresh plumage, and undertail-coverts white. Female similar but duller, with browner head, paler and browner upperparts, more orangey underparts and more distinct whitish scaling on flanks. First-winters similar to respective adults but typically paler, with more scaly flanks and with whitish tips to greater coverts forming narrow wing-bars. Bill yellowish-horn with dark culmen; legs black-brown.
VOICE Song is a loud, liquid series of clear notes of variable pitch. Calls include Blackbird-like *kwik-kwik-kwik* and *chut-chut-chut*.
HABITAT Occurs in wide variety of woodland, as well as parks, gardens and other similar habitat.
DISTRIBUTION Breeds across North America except in parts of extreme north, and south to Mexico. Mainly migratory, northern birds wintering from southernmost Canada south across USA (except some northern areas) to Guatemala.
EUROPEAN STATUS Very rare vagrant: most of the 50 records have occurred in autumn and winter. Austria (3: 1820; 1846; 1885); Belgium (1: Jan-7 Feb 1965); Britain (20); Czech Republic (1: between 1857 and 1874); Germany (10); Iceland (2); Ireland (10); Norway (1: 3 Oct 1983); Sweden (2: 24 Apr 1988; 10 Apr 1994).

PALLAS'S GRASSHOPPER WARBLER

Locustella certhiola L 13.5 cm (5.5 in)
DESCRIPTION Resembles a larger, more warmly-coloured Grasshopper Warbler. Upperparts almost rufous-brown, more heavily streaked than that species on greyer crown and on mantle and scapulars; rufous tone especially noticeable on unstreaked rump and lightly-streaked uppertail-coverts, which in combination with distinct pale supercilium, dark eye-stripe and dull ear-coverts can give appearance recalling Sedge Warbler. White tips to inner webs of tertials diagnostic when visible. Brown tail appears long and rounded, with diagnostic dark subterminal band and whitish tips (broadest on corners) on upperside, and dark underside. Underparts dull white, tinged buffish on breast, flanks and undertail-coverts; breast usually unstreaked or almost so. Some autumn vagrants in Europe have apparently still been in juvenile plumage, with paler crown, less distinct eye-stripe and yellowish underparts. Relatively long bill is blackish-brown, with pinkish base to lower mandible; legs flesh. Typically skulks in ground cover.

VOICE Song unlike typical reeling of *Locustella* warblers, with variable phrasing more recalling Sedge Warbler. Call of migrants typically *chir*, sometimes repeated.
HABITAT Favours marshes, swamps and damp meadows with weedy vegetation.
DISTRIBUTION Breeds in Central Asia, Siberia, Mongolia and north-east China, wintering from north-east India through South-East Asia to Indonesia.
EUROPEAN STATUS Very rare vagrant: 25 records, almost all in late September and early October. Belgium (1: 28 Sept 1989); Britain (13); France (1: 31 Aug 1987); Germany (1: 13 Aug 1856); Ireland (2: 28 Sept 1908, dead; 8 Oct 1990); Latvia (1: 15 Sept 1971); Netherlands (1: 5 Oct 1991); Norway (4: 28 Sept 1986; 15 Sept 1988; 7-8 Oct 1988; 14-15 Sept 1992); Poland (1: 12 Sept 1989).

LANCEOLATED WARBLER

Locustella lanceolata L 12 cm (4.75 in)
DESCRIPTION Very like Grasshopper Warbler, but separable on good views in the field when slightly smaller, shorter-tailed and more heavily-streaked appearance may be distinct. Upperparts dark brown (greyer on worn autumn adults), with dense rows of black streaks on crown, nape, mantle and scapulars, less so on rump and uppertail-coverts; on Grasshopper Warbler, streaks are more spot-shaped and less intense. Tertials have darker centres with narrower but better-defined pale edges than on Grasshopper. Underparts off-white, suffused buffish, with neat, heavy streaking on throat, breast and flanks; undertail-coverts have well-defined, drop-shaped streaks on Lanceolated Warbler (often only on inner feathers), and heavier, triangular streaks on Grasshopper (all feathers). First-winters are heavily streaked like adults, but juveniles showing much less streaking below have also been recorded in Europe. Rather secretive in habits, migrants often creeping around among ground cover, but can be very tame and confiding.
VOICE Reeling song similar to Grasshopper Warbler's, but higher-pitched and more metallic. Calls include a disyllabic *chir-chir*.
HABITAT Breeds in meadows and taiga clearings with thickets, bushy undergrowth and tall herbage or areas of grass or reed, often in damp situations. On passage and in winter in more open, grassy terrain.
DISTRIBUTION Breeds from European Russia eastwards across Siberia to Kamchatka, China and Japan. Winters from north-east India, south through much of South-East Asia and Indonesia to Philippines.
EUROPEAN STATUS Rare vagrant: most occur in September and October. Belgium (3: 10 Sept 1988; 5 Oct 1991; 14 Oct 1994); Britain (63); Denmark (4: Oct 1932; Oct 1935; Oct 1943; 7 Oct 1991); Finland (17, including 4 singing males in spring 1993); France (3: 15-16 Aug 1986; 11 Sept 1986, dead; 28 Oct 1990); Germany (4: 13 Oct 1909; 25 Sept 1920; 13 Oct 1979; 13 Oct 1993); Netherlands

(2: 11 Dec 1912; 20 Sept 1958); Norway (3: 29 Sept 1980; 6 Oct 1991; 3 Oct 1994; also 1 at sea, c 15 Sept 1982); Sweden (3: 13 Oct 1939, dead; 19 Oct 1987, dead; 22 June-10 July 1990); former Yugoslavia (1: Nov 1907).

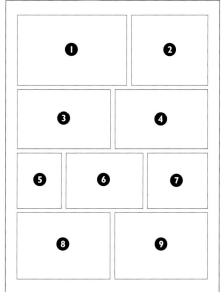

1 **American Robin** (first-winter male, Dec 1988, Inverbervie, Grampian, Britain)
2 **American Robin** (first-winter male, Dec 1988, Inverbervie, Grampian, Britain)
3 **American Robin** (first-winter male, Dec 1988, Inverbervie, Grampian, Britain)
4 **Pallas's Grasshopper Warbler** (first-winter, Sept 1992, North Ronaldsay, Orkney, Britain)
5 **Pallas's Grasshopper Warbler** (first-winter, Sept 1986, Fair Isle, Shetland, Britain)
6 **Lanceolated Warbler** (first-winter, Oct 1991, Utsira, Rogaland, Norway)
7 **Lanceolated Warbler** (male, July 1993, Hankasalm, Finland)
8 **Lanceolated Warbler** (Oct 1994, Zeebrugge, Belgium)
9 **Lanceolated Warbler** (probably juvenile, Sept 1990, Fair Isle, Shetland, Britain)

PADDYFIELD WARBLER

Acrocephalus agricola L 12.5 cm (5 in)
DESCRIPTION Unstreaked 'acro' similar to Reed Warbler in general appearance, but with well-marked head pattern of grey-brown crown, broad creamy supercilium bordered above by darkish smudge or stripe, and distinct dark eye-stripe recalling Sedge Warbler. Upperparts variably warm brown, darker than on Reed, but becoming paler with wear during breeding season, after which paleness can recall coloration of Booted Warbler; has subtle greyish collar vaguely reminiscent of Garden Warbler, and rump and uppertail-coverts contrastingly rufous-toned. Wings rather concolorous with mantle, but tertials show dark centres with clearly paler edges. Underparts whitish, with warm buff breast sides. First-winter very like adult, but slightly paler. Structure subtly different from Reed Warbler, with noticeably shorter primary projection and longer, more rounded tail which is often flicked, raised and fanned. Bill also slightly shorter, greyish with yellow base and extensive dark tip to lower mandible, unlike Booted; legs flesh-brown.
VOICE Song is a relaxed series of phrases, more melodious than Reed's and including some mimicry. Has distinctive, sharp *chik-chak* and softer *tack* call.
HABITAT Breeds chiefly in reedbeds, often in vicinity of scrubby undergrowth and drier ground.
DISTRIBUTION Summer range extends from south-easternmost Europe eastwards across Central Asia to Mongolia and north-east China. Winters chiefly in Indian subcontinent.
EUROPEAN STATUS Breeds Bulgaria and Romania. Accidental elsewhere, though has bred in the Baltic: Austria (1: 16 Aug 1992), Belgium (9); Britain (32); Channel Islands (1: 19 Aug 1993); Denmark (4: Sept 1987; 9 June 1991; 4 June 1992; 17 Sept 1992); Estonia (2: 15 July 1990; 11 Aug 1992); Faeroes (1: 13 Oct 1988); Finland (22: has bred); France (7); Germany (2: 12 June 1864; 5 Oct 1993); Greece (1: 16 Apr 1969); Hungary (2: 11 Aug 1978; 23 Sept 1992); Ireland (2: 3-4 Dec 1982; 13 Oct 1991, dead; also 1 at sea, 14 Sept 1993); Italy (5: 19 Sept 1993; 30 Sept 1993; 17 Dec 1993; 12 Mar 1994; 31 Aug 1994); Latvia (6: has possibly bred); Netherlands (7); Norway (2: 19 Oct 1990; 26 Sept 1992); Portugal (1: 12 Nov 1993); Slovenia (1: 29 Aug 1992); Sweden (14).

BLYTH'S REED WARBLER

Acrocephalus dumetorum L 13 cm (5.25 in)
DESCRIPTION Very like Reed and Marsh Warblers, and extremely difficult to separate in the field. Overall tone of upperparts is very subtly greyer and paler, with wings concolorous with mantle and rump, and lacking obvious rufous tone shown by many Reed Warblers; has shorter wing than Marsh Warbler, with only six primary tips visible (wing formula also distinctive in the hand). Underparts off-white, with grey-buff (rather

than warm buff) suffusion on breast sides, flanks and undertail-coverts. Forehead appears flatter than Marsh Warbler's, with face marked by distinct off-white fore-supercilium and pale eye-ring (sometimes combining to form 'spectacle') and dusky eye-stripe. First-winter often warmer-toned than adult. Long bill is dark greyish on upper mandible, paler on lower (especially at base); legs grey, often browner on first-years. Often holds head and frequently-flicked tail above line of body in distinctive concave 'banana' posture. Has hybridised with Marsh Warbler.
VOICE Varied song is slower than Marsh Warbler's, with well-spaced repeated phrases. Calls include a soft *chek* and grating *cherr*.
HABITAT Found in similar scrubby habitat to Marsh Warbler, but often in bushier and more wooded areas.
DISTRIBUTION Breeds from Baltic eastwards across Russia to central Siberia and south to southern Central Asia. Winters in Indian subcontinent and Burma.
EUROPEAN STATUS Breeding population increasing. Breeds Estonia (2,000-3,000 pairs), Finland (5,000-8,000 pairs), Latvia (5,000 pairs) and Lithuania (at least 10 pairs); also increasing Sweden (530 records: has bred). Accidental elsewhere: Belgium (4: 19 Sept 1988; 28 Sept 1992; 3 Oct 1992; 3 Oct 1992); Britain (27); Bulgaria (1); Denmark (19); Faeroes (1: Oct 1988); France (2: 26 Aug 1984; 23 Oct 1994); Germany (5: 10 Aug 1984; 20-28 June 1987; 15 Aug 1990; 6-27 June 1993; 14 June-3 July 1994*); Gibraltar (1: 24 Sept 1973); Ireland (1: 13-19 Oct 1969); Italy (1: 19 Sept 1969); Netherlands (1: 26 June 1990); Norway (16); Poland (22); Romania (13+); Slovenia (1: 16 Sept 1990); Spain (1: 24 Sept 1972).

THICK-BILLED WARBLER

Acrocephalus aedon L 18-19 cm (7.25-7.5 in)
DESCRIPTION Large unstreaked 'acro', almost size of similar Great Reed Warbler. Upperparts warm olive-brown, becoming more rufous on rump and uppertail-coverts; underparts whitish, buffer on breast and flanks. Rather rounded head lacks characteristic pale supercilium and dark eye-stripe of Great Reed, with dark eye, pale eye-ring and pale lores on otherwise plain face recalling Garden Warbler; sometimes raises crown feathers into a crest. Long, graduated and rounded tail often waved, cocked and fanned. Bill is rather short, thick and blunt-ended, notably less dagger-like than Great Reed's, with brown culmen to decurved upper mandible and yellow lower mandible; legs bluish-grey. Combination of size, heavy bill, short wings and long tail may almost give initial impression of a small shrike. Can be very secretive and skulking, but also perches in open.
VOICE Rather melodious, warbling song includes much mimicry. Commonest call is a loud, harsh *tschok-tschok*.
HABITAT Prefers dry rather than damp habitats, frequenting thickets and scrubby areas, often open forest and woodland with dense

undergrowth; in winter also in marshy and more treeless habitats.
DISTRIBUTION Breeds from southern Siberia and northern Mongolia east to Ussuriland, wintering from India east to southern China and Vietnam.
EUROPEAN STATUS Extreme vagrant: three autumn records. Britain (2: 6 Oct 1955; 23 Sept 1971); Finland (1: 11 Oct 1994).

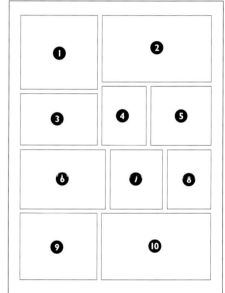

1 **Paddyfield Warbler** (first-winter, Dec 1993, Molentourgius, Sicily, Italy)
2 **Paddyfield Warbler** (Sept 1994, Quendale, Shetland, Britain)
3 **Paddyfield Warbler** (June 1992, Christansø, Denmark)
4 **Blyth's Reed Warbler** (June 1993, Karmøy, Rogaland, Norway)
5 **Blyth's Reed Warbler** (May 1994, Kergord, Shetland, Britain)
6 **Blyth's Reed Warbler** (June 1994, Christansø, Denmark)
7 **Blyth's Reed Warbler** (first-winter, Sept 1993, Landsort, Sweden)
8 **Thick-billed Warbler** (first-winter, Oct 1994, Norrskär, Finland)
9 **Thick-billed Warbler** (first-winter, Oct 1994, Norrskär, Finland)
10 **Thick-billed Warbler** (first-winter, Oct 1994, Norrskär, Finland)

BOOTED WARBLER

Hippolais caligata L 11.5 cm (4.5 in)
DESCRIPTION Small, slim *Hippolais* warbler with rather rounded head and (for its genus) short bill which can give an impression recalling a *Phylloscopus* warbler. Has subtle but distinct facial pattern comprising pale square-ended supercilium, bordered above by fine dark 'brow', and dark eye-stripe which is faint in front of eye. Upperparts of nominate race typically pale brownish-grey, often likened to colour of milky tea; wings slightly darker but with feathers broadly edged paler, and showing relatively short primary projection. Tail slightly darker than upperparts, with creamy edges to outermost feathers. Underparts creamy, suffused buffish on breast, flanks and undertail-coverts. Bill brownish-black, with pale base to lower mandible; legs flesh-brown. Birds of larger and greyer southern race *rama*, sometimes considered separate species (Sykes's Warbler), have longer bill and tail and closely resemble Olivaceous Warbler.
VOICE Song is a fast, monotonous chattering. Call is a short, harsh *tek* or *chet*.
HABITAT Inhabits bushes and scrub, thickets, tamarisks, open woodland and taiga. On migration, often feeds in weedy areas close to ground.
DISTRIBUTION Breeds from European Russia east to central Siberia and adjacent parts of China and Mongolia, and south to Iran, Afghanistan and south-east tip of Arabia. Winters in Indian subcontinent.
EUROPEAN STATUS Frequent vagrant: most records in autumn, though occasional in spring, especially in the Baltic. Belgium (5: 10 Sept 1988; 20 Sept 1993; 3 Oct 1993; 5 Oct 1993; 15 Sept 1994); Britain (57); Denmark (3: Sept 1988; Sept 1989; Sept 1989), Estonia (2: 5 June 1989, pair; 16 Aug 1989); Finland (23); France (4: 19 Sept 1984; 28 Sept 1984; 11 Oct 1985; 17 Sept 1988); Germany (3: 28 Sept 1851; 13 Sept 1987; 17 Sept 1990); Greece (2: 1 Apr 1978; 24 May 1992); Netherlands (4: Oct 1982; Oct 1986; Sept 1988; Sept 1990); Norway (3: 6 Oct 1978; 11 Sept 1983; 27 Aug 1989); Sweden (4: July 1971; 8-9 Sept 1990; 2 June 1991; 26-30 Aug 1993, *rama*).

TRISTRAM'S WARBLER

Sylvia deserticola L 12 cm (4.75 in)
DESCRIPTION Character somewhat reminiscent of Dartford Warbler. Breeding adult male slightly paler blue-grey above than that species (browner-toned on mantle in fresh plumage), with prominent white eye-ring around reddish inner ring and yellow eye; wings show contrasting panel formed by broad rufous fringes to black-centred tertials and median and greater coverts. White moustachial stripe (shorter and less prominent than on Subalpine Warbler) separates grey lores and cheeks from pinkish or vinous-brown throat, breast and flanks; chin whitish, with white flecking extending onto throat, and belly white. Non-breeding adult male buffer above and pinker

below, with more flecking on throat. Breeding adult female browner above, recalling Spectacled Warbler, but pinkish of underparts extends upwards onto throat (white on Spectacled); in winter, buffer still on upperparts and has paler, creamy underparts. First-years resemble adults, but upperparts paler. Longish blackish-brown tail (proportionately shorter than Dartford Warbler's) has white outer feathers and is often cocked. Dark brown bill has obvious yellow base; legs yellow-brown or flesh-brown. Rather skulking.
VOICE Rattling song recalls Subalpine Warbler's. Calls include *chit* or *chit-it* and *tchack tchack*.
HABITAT In summer found on hillsides with dense scrub and holm oaks; in winter descends to more open sandy areas, wadis and desert fringe.
DISTRIBUTION Breeding range restricted to north-west Africa, where found from Atlas Mountains of Morocco discontinuously eastwards through northern Algeria to western Tunisia. Altitudinal and short-distance migrant, usually wintering at lower levels to south of breeding range and east to south-west Libya. Has also straggled to Malta.
EUROPEAN STATUS Extreme vagrant: one record. Gibraltar (1: 10 Apr 1988).

RÜPPELL'S WARBLER

Sylvia rueppelli L 14 cm (5.5 in)
DESCRIPTION Large and relatively long-billed *Sylvia* warbler. Adult male diagnostically marked, with black forehead, chin and throat boldly divided by bright white moustachial stripe; has conspicuous red eye-ring like Sardinian Warbler. Upperparts slate-grey from nape to rump, wings blacker, with whitish fringes to tertials and greater coverts. Black tail contrasts with upperparts and has white outer feathers. Underparts cream, greyer on flanks and whiter on belly. Well-marked females patterned like male, but browner-toned above and buffer below, with black on face less extensive, often admixed with browner or paler feathers and appearing as mottling on throat; moustachial stripe also less distinct, and absent on more poorly-marked individuals which also lack black on throat. Wings duller brownish-black than male's, with buffish (not white) fringes. First-winter male has less solidly black face and browner upperparts than adult; first-year female also browner above and has white throat. Bill blackish, with pale grey-brown base to lower mandible; legs conspicuously reddish-brown.
VOICE Has monotonous, persistent 'gravelly' song. Calls include a hard *chrr*.
HABITAT Favours dry maquis and open oak woods with dense undergrowth.
DISTRIBUTION Breeding range confined entirely to southern Greece, southern and western Turkey and adjacent islands (excluding Cyprus). Whole population migrates south to winter in Chad and Sudan.
EUROPEAN STATUS Breeds Greece (3,000-10,000 pairs). Accidental elsewhere: Britain (4:

13 Aug-16 Sept 1977; 1-10 June 1979; 3-19 Oct 1990; 31 Aug-4 Sept 1992); Denmark (1: 7-8 May 1993); Faeroes (1: July 1974); Finland (2: 7-8 June 1962; 30 May 1985); France; Italy (c 35); Romania.

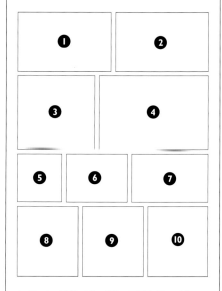

1 **Booted Warbler** (Oct 1995*, Maasvlakte, Netherlands)
2 **Booted Warbler** (June 1994, Paimio, Finland)
3 **Booted Warbler** (male, June 1992, Spurn, Humberside, Britain)
4 **Booted Warbler** (Sept 1991, Spurn, Humberside, Britain)
5 **Tristram's Warbler** *(December, Morocco)*
6 **Tristram's Warbler** *(December, Morocco)*
7 **Rüppell's Warbler** (male, Aug 1977, Boddam, Shetland, Britain)
8 **Rüppell's Warbler** (first-winter, Sept 1992, Holme, Norfolk, Britain)
9 **Rüppell's Warbler** (first-winter, Sept 1992, Holme, Norfolk, Britain)
10 **Rüppell's Warbler** (first-winter, Sept 1992, Holme, Norfolk, Britain)

DESERT WARBLER

Sylvia nana L 11.5 cm (4.5 in)

DESCRIPTION Small, somewhat secretive but unmistakable sandy-coloured warbler. Head and upperparts rather uniformly pale sandy-grey, contrasting with rufous rump and uppertail-coverts and browner, white-edged tail. Head marked only by pale greyish lores, very indistinct pale supercilium, white eye-ring and conspicuous yellow iris; underparts whitish, washed greyer on flanks. Wings darker than mantle, but with broad pale fringing on coverts and tertials offering little contrast. North African race *deserti* has paler, yellower upperparts, whiter underparts and less strongly rufous rump and tail than nominate *nana*, with more distinct whitish supercilium. Bill yellowish, with dark culmen and tip; legs yellowish. Generally unobtrusive, typically remaining in low vegetation or on the ground; in natural range habitually follows Desert and Red-tailed Wheatears.

VOICE Song is a simple, fast jingling warble. Calls include a harsh, rattling *chee-chee-chee-chee* and a weak *drrrrrrr*.

HABITAT Found in sand desert and steppe with scattered patches of grass and other vegetation, and also stonier areas and hillsides.

DISTRIBUTION Breeds from Black Sea eastwards across Central Asia, wintering from north-west India through Arabia to the Middle East and north-east Africa. Also breeds north-west Africa, where largely resident.

EUROPEAN STATUS Very rare vagrant: 36 records, with late autumn the peak period, but winter and spring records not unknown. Britain (10); Denmark (2: Nov 1989; 13 Nov 1994); Finland (9); Germany (1: 21 June-7 July 1981); Italy (1: 23 Apr 1988); Netherlands (2: Oct-Nov 1988; 8-9 Oct 1991), Sweden (11).

GREENISH WARBLER

Phylloscopus trochiloides L 11 cm (4.5 in)

DESCRIPTION Size of Chiffchaff but more brightly marked. European race *viridanus* is grey-toned olive-green on head and upperparts, with long, whitish supercilium, often wider behind eye and angled upwards on nape, and well-defined dark eye-stripe. Wings show distinct pale bar on outermost greater (and occasionally median) coverts and bright greenish fringes, but overall pattern of wing never as contrasting as on more compact Yellow-browed Warbler, which diagnostically has whitish fringes to tertials and dark bases to secondaries and greater coverts (all features lacking on Greenish and Arctic Warblers). Underparts whitish, with duskier flanks. Bill dark brown, with obvious yellow-orange base to lower mandible; legs grey-brown. Two other forms, sometimes treated as separate species, also recorded in Europe: south-west Central Asian *nitidus* (Green Warbler) has brighter yellowish-green upperparts, yellow suffusion to facial markings, larger bill, yellowish wing-bar in fresh plumage and, on some, a second wing-bar; eastern *plumbeitarsus* (Two-barred Greenish) is

darker above, and has broader bar on all greater coverts and obvious second bar on median coverts. For distinctions from Arctic Warbler, see that species.

VOICE Short, high-pitched song contains fast trills. Call is a disyllabic *chi-wee*.

HABITAT Favours open areas of deciduous and mixed woodland, often in canopy.

DISTRIBUTION Breeds from the Baltic eastwards in broad belt across Siberia to Mongolia and China, south to Himalayas and northern India, and in south-west Central Asia, Caucasus and Turkey. Winters from India and Sri Lanka east through South-East Asia to south China.

EUROPEAN STATUS Breeds Estonia (1,000-5,000 pairs), Finland (2,000-5,000 pairs), Latvia (1,000 pairs), Lithuania (over 1,000 pairs) and Sweden, and since 1992 regularly in Czech Republic (1-5 pairs). Range expanding westwards, and regular on passage in Denmark (has bred) and Poland (breeds irregularly). Accidental elsewhere, mainly August-September: Belgium (2: 1 Sept 1987; 18 Sept 1988); Britain (250); Channel Islands (1: Nov 1976); France (10); Germany (c 190; bred 1990); Ireland (10); Netherlands (13); Norway (39: bred 1991); Slovakia (has bred); Spain (1: 6 Sept 1988). Form *nitidus* recorded Britain (1: 26 Sept-4 Oct 1983) and Germany (1: 11 Oct 1867); *plumbeitarsus* recorded Britain (1: 21-27 Oct 1987), Netherlands (1: 17 Sept 1990) and Sweden (1: 5 July 1991).

ARCTIC WARBLER

Phylloscopus borealis L 12 cm (4.75 in)

DESCRIPTION Larger and more robust version of Greenish Warbler, but can be very difficult to separate in the field. General pattern and tone of plumage similar, chief differences from that species being as follows: longer, heavier bill; supercilium slightly longer behind eye; supercilium beginning above bill base, not (as on Greenish) at side of forehead; dark eye-stripe continuous on lores and reaching base of bill (Greenish has broken eye-stripe forming distinct dark spot in front of eye); strikingly plain tertials; and legs paler orange-brown to yellowish (not grey-brown). As well as larger size, differs from Greenish Warbler also in bulky but attenuated appearance, with slightly longer primary projection and longer undertail-coverts. First-winter is brighter green above and less white below than adult, with second wing-bar on median coverts. Call is most certain way to tell Arctic and Greenish apart, and most migrants are vocal.

VOICE Song is a fast, monotonous trill of loud repeated notes, likened to songs of both Bonelli's Warbler and Cirl Bunting. Call is a hard *tzik* with a Dipper-like quality, quite unlike Greenish Warbler's.

HABITAT Breeds in subarctic forest zone, especially in coniferous tracts but also in birch and other deciduous trees, and often near water.

DISTRIBUTION In summer occurs from north-east Scandinavia across northern Siberia to Alaska, and in east south to Japan. Winters in

South-East Asia, Indonesia and Philippines.

EUROPEAN STATUS Breeds Finland (3,000-5,000 pairs) and Norway (10-100 pairs). Accidental elsewhere, chiefly in autumn, but also spring in Scandinavia and Baltic outside breeding range: Britain (198); Denmark (1: 27 May 1988); Estonia (4: 29 May 1955; 14 June 1986; 9 Aug 1989; 8-10 June 1994); Faeroes (1: 13-15 Sept 1984); France (6); Germany (9); Gibraltar (1: 30 Oct 1984); Greece (3: Apr 1965; Apr 1967; 3 Oct 1993); Ireland (6); Italy (2: 22 Sept 1903; Oct 1917); Lithuania (1: 11 May 1994); Luxembourg (1); Netherlands (8); Poland (2: 11 Sept 1986; 14 May 1993); Sweden (c 200: has bred).

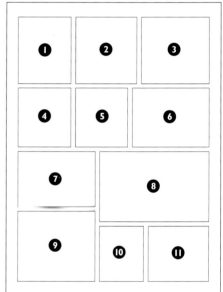

1 **Desert Warbler** (Oct 1994, Scheveningen, Netherlands)
2 **Desert Warbler** (Nov 1988, Zandvoort, Netherlands)
3 **Desert Warbler** (June 1993, Blakeney, Norfolk, Britain)
4 **Desert Warbler** (Oct 1987, Turku, Finland)
5 **Greenish Warbler** (spring 1985, Christansø, Denmark)
6 **Greenish Warbler** (first-winter of form *plumbeitarsus*, Two-barred Greenish Warbler, Oct 1987, Gugh, Isles of Scilly, Britain)
7 **Greenish Warbler** (first-winter, Aug 1994, Wells, Norfolk, Britain)
8 **Arctic Warbler** (first-winter male, Sept 1991, Bloemendaal, Netherlands)
9 **Arctic Warbler** (probably first-winter, Sept 1993, Blakeney, Norfolk, Britain)
10 **Arctic Warbler** (June 1989, Lakselv, Finnmark, Norway)
11 **Arctic Warbler** (Oct 1988, St Agnes, Isles of Scilly, Britain)

PALLAS'S WARBLER

Phylloscopus proregulus L 9 cm (3.5 in)
DESCRIPTION Very small, compact *'phyllosc'*, with almost *Regulus*-like jizz by virtue of tiny size, large head, 'bull' neck and short tail. Head diagnostically patterned with lemon-yellow median crown-stripe and supercilia extending from bill to nape, broad dark lateral crown-stripes and eye-stripe, and mottled cheeks. At rear, blackish eye-stripe encompasses larger area of ear-coverts than on Yellow-browed and contributes to more heavily striped head pattern. Upperparts olive-green, with conspicuous yellow rump and double wing-bars. Strength of yellow markings can vary from lemon-yellow (on most) to almost whitish on rump. Primaries and secondaries darker olive, fringed yellowish-green, with whiter tips to tertials. Underparts whitish, some having faint yellowish wash on flanks and undertail-coverts. Short bill dark brown or black; legs dirty pinkish to dark brown. Active and restless; often hovers when foraging.
VOICE Song surprisingly loud, rich and variable, and includes several Canary-like trills. Calls (infrequently uttered by migrants) include a husky *chweek* or *choing*, almost finch-like and rather incongruous for such a small warbler.
HABITAT Found in taiga forest with dense undergrowth and in more open woodland.
DISTRIBUTION Breeds in southern Siberia, northern Mongolia, Manchuria and the Himalayas, wintering in southern China, India and northern South-East Asia.
EUROPEAN STATUS Frequent vagrant: most occur from mid-October to November, with major influxes in some years. Belgium (33); Britain (770+); Channel Islands (3: 23 Oct 1971; 5 Nov 1991; 5 Oct 1994); Czech Republic (1: 18 Oct 1987); Denmark (100+), Estonia (15), Faeroes (4: 17 Oct 1987; three in 1993); Finland (315 to 1993); France (19); Germany (56); Ireland (13: also 1 at sea); Italy (1: 31 Oct 1994); Latvia (18); Lithuania (10+); Luxembourg (1: 19 Sept 1990); Netherlands (54+); Norway (48); Poland (16); Spain (1: 17 Apr 1987); Sweden (373).

YELLOW-BROWED WARBLER

Phylloscopus inornatus L 10 cm (4 in)
DESCRIPTION Slightly larger and less compact than Pallas's Warbler. Head and upperparts olive-green, with long yellowish-white supercilium, dark eye-stripe, double creamy wing-bars (latter with blackish bases which, along with similar pattern on greater coverts, form *Regulus*-like wing pattern common to this species and Pallas's), white fringes to blackish tertials, and white tips to yellowish-green-fringed primaries and secondaries; crown may have diffuse paler centre, but lacks clear yellow median stripe of Pallas's. Underparts dull white, variably suffused with pale yellow. Short, fine bill is brown, with yellowish base to lower mandible; legs brownish. The form *humei*, often considered separate species (Hume's or Hume's Yellow-browed Warbler) is duller, with more

greyish-brown upperparts and little or no yellow.
VOICE Song of nominate race short, plaintive and Goldcrest-like; call is a thin *weesp*, recalling Coal Tit. *Humei* has a different buzzing, drawn-out song and a disyllabic, sparrow-like call.
HABITAT Prefers open deciduous woodland, especially willows, but also in mixed and coniferous stands; migrants not infrequently in sycamores.
DISTRIBUTION Breeds from northern Urals eastwards across Siberia (*inornatus*) and in central China, wintering from South-East Asia west to Nepal and east to south-east China. *Humei* breeds in Central Asia south to north-west Himalayas, wintering chiefly in Indian subcontinent.
EUROPEAN STATUS Frequent vagrant/visitor: most arrive in September and October, but records in winter and spring increasing. Austria (4: autumn 1836; 26 Sept 1959; 29 Oct 1975; 29 Sept 1985); Belgium (c 242); Britain (many annually, eg 387 in 1993; max. 746 recorded 1988); Channel Islands (26+); Czech Republic (3: 30 Mar 1956; 24 Aug 1969; 19 Mar 1983); Denmark (270+); Estonia (34+); Finland (442); France (427); Faeroes (22); Germany (many, eg 370 birds on Heligoland alone in the period 1846-1994); Gibraltar (1: Oct 1984); Greece (3: 16 Apr 1976; 10 Aug 1991; 19 May 1992); Hungary (1: 8 Oct 1989); Iceland (49); Ireland (401+); Italy (15+); Latvia (119); Lithuania (30+); Luxembourg (1: 2 Oct 1990); Netherlands (many, with peak totals including 98 in 1985 and 105 in 1986); Norway (many); Poland (45); Portugal (2: 7 Nov 1987; 17-18 Oct 1992); Slovenia (1: 2 Oct 1991); Spain (10 records of 11 individuals); Sweden (504); Switzerland (5: 3 Oct 1961; 15-16 Oct 1979; 8 Oct 1985; 13 Sept 1988; 8 Oct 1992). Form *humei* also recorded in Europe, often later in autumn and in winter; Belgium; Britain (c 30 reports, including many confirmed sightings, under consideration); Denmark (5); Finland (7); France (2); Germany (3: 5-7 Nov 1990; 18 Feb-4 Apr 1992; 9-12 Nov 1994); Hungary (1: 9 Nov 1989); Iceland (49); Italy; Netherlands (11); Norway (1); Poland; Sweden (5 up to end 1992).

RADDE'S WARBLER

Phylloscopus schwarzi L 12 cm (4.75 in)
DESCRIPTION Almost size of Wood Warbler, with stocky build, large head and long, rather thick legs. Conspicuous buff supercilium is broadest in front of and around eye, extending almost to nape (where whiter) and bordered below by dark eye-stripe. Compared with Dusky Warbler, supercilium is diagnostically broad and diffuse in front of eye, with low-contrast darker eye-stripe across lores. Upperparts dark olive, slightly browner on head and greener on rump, with brighter olive-green fringes to flight feathers. Underparts vary from dirty white to buffish (more so on first-winters), with diffuse darker areas on breast sides occasionally joining across breast. Undertail-coverts warmer buff, even orangey. Deep-based bill is pale with darker culmen, noticeably blunt-

ended and rather stubby, combining with head pattern to give species distinctive, 'bull-headed' look. Legs appear long, strong and obviously pale. As with Dusky Warbler, very skulking and difficult to see; also less active in movements.
VOICE Song is a loud, rich and fast series of trilling warbles. Call is a quiet *tuc* or *tuc-tch*, less *Sylvia*-like than Dusky Warbler's.
HABITAT Found in thickets and mixed woodland with dense understorey; on passage and in winter also in more open habitats.
DISTRIBUTION Breeds in southern Siberia, northern Mongolia and north-east China, wintering in South-East Asia.
EUROPEAN STATUS Frequent vagrant: most occur in October. Belgium (6); Britain (141); Channel Islands (1: 5 Oct 1978); Czech Republic (1: 12 Oct 1991); Denmark (12); Finland (9); France (4: 12 Oct 1957; 28 Oct-2 Nov 1990; 18 Oct 1991; 9 Nov 1994); Germany (5: 18 Oct 1930; 12 Oct 1940; 3 Oct 1987; 4 Oct 1988; 8 Oct 1994); Ireland (7); Netherlands (6); Norway (3: 8 Oct 1981; 31 Oct 1987; 6 Oct 1991); Poland (1: 27 Sept 1976); Spain (1: 7 Nov 1966); Sweden (31).

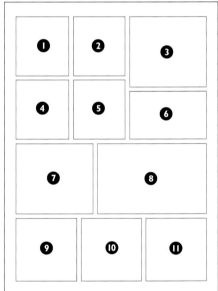

1 **Pallas's Warbler** (Oct 1991, Zeebrugge, Belgium)
2 **Pallas's Warbler** (Oct 1982, De Putten, Camperduin, Netherlands)
3 **Pallas's Warbler** (Oct 1988, Kilnsea, Humberside, Britain)
4 **Yellow-browed Warbler** (Nov 1995, Westkapelle, Netherlands)
5 **Hume's Yellow-browed Warbler** (Oct 1991, Heist, Belgium)
6 **Hume's Yellow-browed Warbler** (Dec 1990, Flevoland, Netherlands)
7 **Yellow-browed Warbler** (Oct 1994, Norrskär, Finland)
8 **Radde's Warbler** (Oct 1994, St Mary's, Isles of Scilly, Britain)
9 **Radde's Warbler** (Oct 1991, Landsort, Sweden)
10 **Radde's Warbler** (Oct 1988, Porthgwarra, Cornwall, Britain)
11 **Radde's Warbler** (Oct 1994, St Mary's, Isles of Scilly, Britain)

SEMI-COLLARED FLYCATCHER

Ficedula semitorquata L 13 cm (5.25 in)

DESCRIPTION Intermediate between Pied and Collared Flycatchers. Adult male in breeding plumage black above and white below, typically with divided white forehead patch (larger than on Pied Flycatcher), white of underparts extending onto neck sides as narrow 'half-collar' (though some very like Pied), whitish rump patch, white patch at base of primaries (usually larger than on Pied, smaller than on Collared), and Collared-like bold white wing patch on greater coverts and tertials; most also show distinctive narrow upper bar on median coverts. Tail typically has more extensively white outer feathers than on Collared, Pied or their hybrids, and is one of best distinctions from rather similar *iberiae* and *speculigera* races of Pied (occurring Spain and north-west Africa respectively). Summer adult female very like same plumages of Collared and Pied, but typically also with distinctive median-covert bar (though this character can also be shown by congeners) and medium-sized white patch at base of primaries, and with less white at bases of tertials. Non-breeding adults most closely resemble Collared; usually (but not always) best separated by median-covert bar, white primary patch and more white in outer tail feathers. First-winters aged by 'step-like' extension on central tertial; all three species, however, may show median-covert bar and all can have small white primary patch, so many individuals may be unidentifiable in the field.

VOICE Song recalls Collared Flycatcher's but is faster and less squeaky. Call is a relatively quiet, disyllabic *hueep*.

HABITAT Woodland, parks and mature gardens; on migration also in more open country.

DISTRIBUTION Breeds discontinuously from the Balkans and Turkey east to the Caucasus and southern Caspian Sea region, migrating chiefly through Middle East and Arabia to winter quarters in East Africa, where occurs from southern Sudan to Tanzania. Has straggled to Malta, Tunisia and Morocco; this species or an unidentified *Ficedula* flycatcher is said to breed alongside Pied in Algeria.

EUROPEAN STATUS Breeds Bulgaria (500-5,000 pairs), Greece (1,000-5,000 pairs) and possibly Albania. Accidental elsewhere: Italy (c 15, but records under review).

AZURE TIT

Parus cyanus L 13 cm (5.25 in)

DESCRIPTION Like a 'frosted' version of Blue Tit, but noticeably larger and longer-tailed. Head and underparts strikingly white, marked only by irregular blue-black ventral line and narrow black stripe running from eye into broader blue-black nape-collar. Upperparts powdery blue-grey, edged white and contrasting with darker blue wings which have broad white wing-bars, extensively white tertials and white fringes to flight feathers.

Dark blue tail is white at sides and tip, and more graduated than on Blue Tit. Juvenile greyer, especially on crown and upperparts. Occasionally hybridises with Blue Tit, with offspring known as 'Pleske's Tit'; some hybrids resemble Azure Tits more closely than others, but all usually show darker cap, greyer or yellower underparts and less white in tail.

VOICE Generally like Blue Tit's, though *tsirr* or *tsirrup* contact call recalls Long-tailed Tit.

HABITAT Prefers riverine thickets and cover near water, but also found in mixed and deciduous woodland. In winter also uses reedbeds.

DISTRIBUTION Breeds from Belarus (irregularly) and European Russia eastwards across southern Siberia to the Pacific coast and north-west China; in centre of range distribution extends south to Kazakhstan and the Altai Mountains. Largely sedentary, but periodically moves westwards, sometimes in numbers, after which hybridisation with Blue Tit is most likely to occur.

EUROPEAN STATUS Frequent vagrant. Austria (12); Czech Republic (25+); Estonia (14 records, including flock of 20-25 on 29 Dec 1985); Denmark (1: Jan 1964); Finland (19 records of 23 birds: has bred); France (1: winter 1907-08); Latvia (2: Jan 1901; 1915); Lithuania (5: all in 19th century); Poland (c 31); Romania; Slovakia (6 records of 22 birds); Sweden (2: 18th century; 12 Nov 1883); former Yugoslavia. Hybrids also recorded in Europe, including Belgium (1: Dec 1878) and Hungary (2: 26 Dec 1988; 28 Oct 1989).

RED-BREASTED NUTHATCH

Sitta canadensis L 11 cm (4.5 in)

DESCRIPTION Tit-sized nuthatch with striking head pattern and brightly-coloured underparts. Adult male has black crown and nape, long white supercilium reaching from forehead to upper mantle, black eye-stripe from bill to upper mantle (broadening at rear) and white cheeks and throat. Upperparts uniform mid blue-grey. Underparts rich cinnamon, on breast merging into white of throat. Adult female very similar, but sometimes with crown and eye-stripe tinged blue-grey, and underparts generally paler. Juveniles similar to respective adults, but head pattern duller and less well defined, on some with faint dark specks on pale areas of face, and sometimes paler tips to greater coverts; first-winters much as adults. Fine, pointed bill and legs grey-black. Often feeds in canopy or high up on trees, and unlike European Nuthatch frequently forages at tips of branches in active, rather tit-like manner; in natural range visits feeders in winter.

VOICE Call likened to the repeated sound of a toy trumpet or tin horn.

HABITAT Favours coniferous forest, but also found in mixed woods; in winter may frequent more open and deciduous woodland, orchards, parks and gardens.

DISTRIBUTION Breeds in much of central and southern Canada, south-east Alaska and

north-eastern and western USA. Northernmost birds migratory; in winter, occurs south throughout USA except Gulf coast and Florida, reaching these areas and northern Mexico only during periodic irruptions.

EUROPEAN STATUS Extreme vagrant: two records. Britain (1: 13 Oct 1989-6 May 1990); Iceland (1: 21 May 1970).

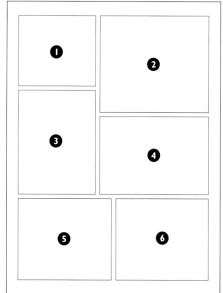

1 **Semi-collared Flycatcher** (male, Apr 1990, Montecristo Island, Italy)
2 **Azure Tit** (Apr 1992, Revonlaht, Finland)
3 **Azure Tit** (Mar 1996*, Åsele, Sweden)
4 **Red-breasted Nuthatch** (probably male, Jan 1990, Holkham, Norfolk, Britain)
5 **Red-breasted Nuthatch** (probably male, Jan 1990, Holkham, Norfolk, Britain)
6 **Red-breasted Nuthatch** (probably male, Jan 1990, Holkham, Norfolk, Britain)

BROWN SHRIKE

Lanius cristatus L 18-19.5 cm (7.25-7.75 in)
DESCRIPTION Distinctly larger and more stocky than Red-backed Shrike, with heavier bill, bigger head and 'bull' neck. In many respects adult male resembles western (darkest) race of Isabelline Shrike, but upperparts are a shade darker brown, black eye mask is solid from bill to ear-coverts, broader white supercilium widens into obvious patch on forehead, shows very little or no white at base of primaries, and slightly longer, more graduated rufous tail contrasts less with darker upperparts. Adult female very similar to male, differing chiefly in less solidly black lores and creamy tinge to supercilium and underparts, latter showing fine dusky 'chevrons'; therefore more easily separable from female Isabelline Shrike, which has, among other differences, more poorly-defined facial pattern. First-winter resembles female, but lacks pale forehead, has weaker supercilium and mask (especially in front of eye), is more heavily barred on underparts and has distinct black subterminal bands on retained juvenile greater coverts and tertials; differs from first-winter Isabelline and Red-backed Shrikes chiefly in plain or almost unbarred upperparts, more distinct facial pattern and structure. Bill black or lead-coloured, base of lower mandible paler on non-breeding birds; legs bluish-brown to black.
VOICE Call given as a loud *chr-r-r-r* or *shark*.
HABITAT Occupies a wide range of habitats, from montane plantations and woodland with dense undergrowth to scrub-covered grassy hillsides, semi-desert and steppe.
DISTRIBUTION Breeds from central Siberia eastwards to Mongolia, China and Japan, wintering chiefly in India and South-East Asia.
EUROPEAN STATUS Extreme vagrant: two autumn records. Britain (1: 30 Sept-2 Oct 1985); Denmark (1: 15 Oct 1988).

ISABELLINE SHRIKE

Lanius isabellinus L 17-18.5 in (6.75-7.5 in)
DESCRIPTION Recalls pale, slightly longer-tailed Red-backed Shrike. In all plumages essentially grey-brown or sandy-coloured with rufous tail. Adult male of western subspecies *phoenicuroides* (race often identified in Europe) has crown varying from greyish to rufous above white supercilium and black mask; on paler-crowned birds, mask often weaker and restricted to ear-coverts. Upperparts pale grey-brown, with darker wings showing broad pale fringes to coverts and narrower pale edges to blackish flight feathers; white patch at base of primaries shows as outer wing-bar in flight. Rufous rump and tail (latter with buff edges) contrast noticeably with rest of upperparts; from below, rufous of tail appears as light cinnamon, unlike Red-backed Shrike, which has grey underside to tail with white outer feathers. Underparts creamy-white, often buffish on flanks. Female similar but duller, with little or no white in wing, and with

crescentic barring on underparts; first-winter retains more extensive juvenile scaling above and below and usually has brown ear-covert patch rather than darker mask. Bill pale pink with small dark tip (Red-backed Shrike has dusky culmen, duller pink tone and more extensively dark tip); legs black or greyish. Character and actions much as Red-backed Shrike, with which *phoenicuroides* has hybridised; for differences from very similar Brown Shrike, see that species.
VOICE Calls as Red-backed Shrike's.
HABITAT Favours patches of tamarisk, scrub and scattered bushes in barren terrain such as steppe and semi-desert; also in grasslands and edges of cultivations.
DISTRIBUTION Breeds in Iran and from Caspian region east across Central Asia to north-west China, moving chiefly south-west to winter from north-west India, Afghanistan and southern Arabia to north-east Africa south of Egypt and west to Chad.
EUROPEAN STATUS Rare vagrant. Austria (1: 5-6 Oct 1994); Belgium (1: 23 Sept 1989); Britain (40); Denmark (1: 9 June 1994); Finland (4: 11-14 May 1980; 21-23 Oct 1980; 17 Oct 1987; 11 June 1989); France (4: 27 Sept 1982; 16 Aug 1986; 14 Sept 1987; 1 Nov 1991); Germany (5: 26 Oct 1854; 1-22 Sept 1980; 2-5 Oct 1993; 12-17 Nov 1993; 1 Nov 1994); Italy (4: 4 Aug 1985; 22 Sept 1988; 10 Oct 1992; 30 Oct 1992); Latvia (1: 5 Nov 1990); Netherlands (1: 21 Oct 1993); Norway (6); Poland (2: 8 Sept 1981; 18 Sept 1984); Sweden (8).

LONG-TAILED SHRIKE

Lanius schach L 22-23 cm (8.75-9.25 in)
DESCRIPTION Medium-sized shrike with conspicuously long, graduated tail and relatively short wings. Appearance of plumage recalls both Great Grey and Red-backed Shrikes, with grey crown and nape, black mask through eye and across forehead bordered above by narrow white supercilium, grey mantle merging into rufous scapulars, back, rump and uppertail-coverts, and long blackish tail with buff outer feathers and tip. Black wing shows white patch at base of primaries and pale tips to tertials. Underparts white on chin, throat and sides of neck, becoming progressively buffer on breast and flanks to rufous on undertail-coverts. Sexes very similar, though female slightly duller and with little or no white wing patch. First-winter is duller still, with remnants of crescentic barring on retained feathers from browner juvenile plumage. Strong bill is black, with pale base to lower mandible; legs also blackish. Typically shrike-like in actions, but long tail and short wings give distinctive silhouette both when perched and in flight.
VOICE Vocalisations include a harsh squealing.
HABITAT Found in open country with scattered trees, thickets, orchards and other similar terrain.
DISTRIBUTION Breeds from eastern Iran eastwards across southern Central Asia and India to China, South-East Asia and Indonesia.

Migratory northern birds winter in India and parts of South-East Asia. Has also straggled to Turkey and Israel.
EUROPEAN STATUS Extreme vagrant: one spring record. Hungary (1: 21 Apr 1979).

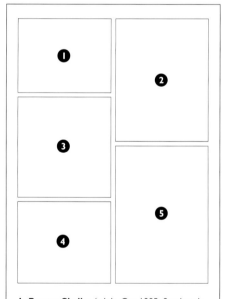

1 **Brown Shrike** (adult, Oct 1985, Sumburgh, Shetland, Britain)
2 **Isabelline Shrike** (first-winter, Sept 1989, Minehead, Somerset, Britain)
3 **Isabelline Shrike** (first-winter male, Oct 1993, Heligoland, Germany)
4 **Isabelline Shrike** (first-winter, Sept 1989, Heist, Belgium)
5 **Long-tailed Shrike** (*adult, Jan, India*)

DAURIAN JACKDAW

Corvus dauuricus L 32 cm (12.75 in)
DESCRIPTION Eastern counterpart of Jackdaw, with two distinct plumages. Adult ('pied phase') unmistakable, with whitish nape and half-collar linking with white underparts on otherwise all-black plumage; pattern recalls grey-and-black of Hooded Crow. Immature ('dark phase') closely resembles Jackdaw, with uniform blackish (rather than blackish-grey) body colour lacking white markings; separated from adult Jackdaw by darker grey nape, dark iris and hint of adult breast pattern, and from dark-eyed immature Jackdaw safely only by silvery streaks on ear-coverts. Immatures start to acquire pale collar on upper nape first, whereas Jackdaw is paler on lower nape. Size, structure and actions much as Jackdaw's; very sociable.
VOICE Flight call is a short *chak*, very like Jackdaw's.
HABITAT Occurs in meadows, steppes, plains and foothills, often with scattered trees; also found near human habitation.
DISTRIBUTION Breeding range begins where Jackdaw reaches eastern limit, at Lake Baikal. Extends eastwards across Siberia to Ussuriland, and south to Mongolia, Tibet and central China. Outside breeding season withdraws from northern part of range; also winters in Japan, Korea and south to southern China.
EUROPEAN STATUS Extreme vagrant: two spring records. Finland (1: early May 1883); Sweden (1: 26-28 Apr 1985).

DAURIAN STARLING

Sturnus sturninus L 18 cm (7.25 in)
DESCRIPTION Small, short-billed and boldly marked starling with pale head and underparts and striking wing pattern. Adult male is unmistakably patterned, appearing pale grey from forehead to belly, with variable dark purple hindcrown and nape-streaking merging into blackish upperparts which are glossed purple on mantle and green and purple on wings; latter also strikingly patterned, with broad whitish median-covert bar and narrower greater-covert bar, white on bases of primaries and secondaries, and also white on scapulars. Rump and undertail variable, ranging from blackish on some through grey-brown (often) and buff to white on others. Adult female similar but somewhat duller, with browner-toned upperparts, buffer underparts and more extensive, browner crown patch contributing to less striking appearance. First-winters resemble respective adults, but retain contrasting pale-edged brown inner secondaries from juvenile plumage. Has dark, beady eye appearing prominent on plain face; bill and legs blackish. In flight, appears pied above and pale on underwing, which has duskier tip. Actions and behaviour similar to Common Starling's.
VOICE Call given as a Common Starling-like, soft *chirrup*.

HABITAT Occurs in lowland farmland and river valleys with scattered trees, often in or near human settlements; breeds in holes in trees or in artificial structures.
DISTRIBUTION In summer found across central and eastern Asia, moving south to winter in southern China and parts of South-East Asia, including peninsular Malaysia, and Indonesia.
EUROPEAN STATUS Extreme vagrant: one record in autumn. Norway (1: 29 Sept 1985, shot). Additionally, one individual in Britain (7-28 May 1985) considered of uncertain origin and placed in category D.

ROSE-COLOURED STARLING

Sturnus roseus L 21 cm (8.5 in)
DESCRIPTION Adult is unmistakable in summer plumage, with bright pink body and black head, wings, tail and pink-tipped undertail-coverts. Breeding male has black areas glossed purplish, shaggy nape-crest (sometimes held flat against head) and bright pink, relatively short bill which appears slightly decurved towards tip; breeding female is usually less glossy and duller pink, with shorter nape feathers. In winter bill duller and pink areas much greyer in both sexes, when confusion is possible with partially albino or leucistic Common Starling (latter may have similar light-and-dark plumage, but distribution of light and dark colours only exceptionally matches Rose-coloured Starling closely, pale areas lack pinkish tones, has longer bill and no crest). Juvenile has sandy-brown head and body, dark eye on plain face (lores are pale), rump contrastingly paler against rest of plumage, browner wings and tail, and yellowish bill; separated on structure from occasional leucistic Common Starlings by bill shape (shorter, stockier), thicker legs and feet, and colour of bill and legs.
VOICE Calls include a loud, clear *ki-ki-ki* and a short *shrrr*, less harsh than voice of Common Starling.
HABITAT Steppes, plains, meadows and grassland, often with scattered trees and bushes; nests colonially in rock crevices and old buildings.
DISTRIBUTION Breeds from south-east Europe eastwards across steppes of Central Asia, migrating south-east to winter in easternmost Arabia and India. Prone to periodic westward irruptions, sometimes in large numbers and usually in late spring or summer, when may temporarily establish new breeding areas.
EUROPEAN STATUS In irruption years, sometimes seen in large numbers and/or may attempt breeding in Bulgaria, Greece (has bred at least six times since 1985), Hungary (eg c 15,000 pairs 1925, 500-600 pairs 1994), Romania, former Yugoslavia and possibly Albania (no data). Accidental elsewhere: Austria (c 40); Belgium (47+); Britain (341); Channel Islands (7); Czech Republic; Denmark (44); Estonia (8); Faeroes (7); Finland (c 45); France (49); Germany (c 170); Iceland (15); Ireland (86); Italy; Latvia; Lithuania (3: 20 May 1981; 16 July 1983; 23 May 1993, three); Luxembourg; Netherlands (38+); Norway (59);

Poland (8+ during 1950-94); Portugal (2: 28 Dec 1991; 23 Oct-27 Nov 1993); Slovakia; Slovenia (6 records of 48 birds); Spain (8+); Sweden (80 individuals); Switzerland (24).

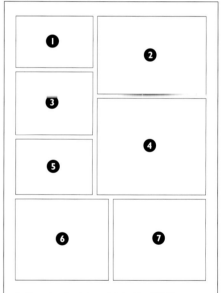

1 **Daurian Jackdaw** (adult, May 1995*, Katwijk, Netherlands)
2 **Daurian Jackdaw** (adult, May 1995*, Katwijk, Netherlands)
3 **Daurian Starling** (adult male, May 1985, Fair Isle, Shetland, Britain)
4 **Rose-coloured Starling** (adult summer male, July 1994, Anglesey, Britain)
5 **Rose-coloured Starling** (female or second-calendar-year male, June 1991, Särbisalo, Finland)
6 **Rose-coloured Starling** (juvenile, Oct 1995*, Texel, Netherlands)
7 **Rose-coloured Starling** (juvenile, Oct 1991, St Mary's, Isles of Scilly, Britain)

DEAD SEA SPARROW

Passer moabiticus L 12 cm (4.75 in)
DESCRIPTION Distinctly smaller than House Sparrow, with diagnostic head pattern in male plumages. Breeding male has grey forehead, crown, nape and ear-coverts contrasting with bicoloured supercilium (white in front, buffish at rear), black bill and bib, and white submoustachial stripe running into yellow neck patch; head pattern browner and bill much paler on non-breeding birds. Upperparts sandy-brown, streaked black, with blackish wing feathers edged pale buff and contrasting bright chestnut median and greater coverts; unstreaked rump grey, contrasting with darker tail. Underparts pale grey, becoming whiter on belly, with chestnut streaks on undertail-coverts. Coloration of male may recall obviously larger and pale-billed Dickcissel, also recorded once as vagrant in Europe. Female closely resembles a small, sandier-coloured female House Sparrow with faint yellow patch on neck sides. Gregarious, sometimes with other sparrows, but rather wary.
VOICE Song is a rhythmic and monotonous *chillung-chillung-chillung*. Otherwise often silent, but calls include *chet-chet-chet* and various *chirps* and *churrs*.
HABITAT Frequents tamarisks and scrub, often near water, and reedbeds; typically feeds in vegetation, but also in fields.
DISTRIBUTION Resident and partial migrant, distributed from Afghanistan westwards through Iran, Iraq and the Middle East to Turkey and Cyprus.
EUROPEAN STATUS Extreme vagrant: one autumn record. Greece (1: early Oct 1972, flock of c 20).

PHILADELPHIA VIREO

Vireo philadelphicus L 13 cm (5.25 in)
DESCRIPTION Recalls Red-eyed Vireo in general appearance, but smaller, more compact and weaker-billed, with less strikingly marked head pattern and underparts distinctly more yellowish. Typically has blue-grey tone to forehead, crown and (usually) nape, but lacks black lateral crown-stripes of larger species and has narrower, diffuse and less flared supercilium. Along with whitish crescent below eye, supercilium is most obvious as a bulge immediately over eye, giving distinctive 'quizzical' expression which is emphasised by dark eyestripe. Upperparts plain olive-green, with brighter green edges to darker flight feathers. Underparts extensively washed yellow, though belly or flanks may be whiter. All plumages similar in the field.
VOICE Song sounds rather like Red-eyed Vireo's, but is distinctly slower, weaker and higher-pitched.
HABITAT Deciduous forest, open woodland and riverside thickets, especially in willows and alders.
DISTRIBUTION Breeds mainly from south-central to south-eastern Canada and parts of New England, but uncommon through much of range. Migrates south to winter in Mexico and Central America south to Panama.
EUROPEAN STATUS Extreme vagrant: two autumn records. Britain (1: 10-13 Oct 1987); Ireland (1: 12-17 Oct 1985).

RED-EYED VIREO

Vireo olivaceus L 15 cm (6 in)
DESCRIPTION Distinctive Nearctic passerine, with characteristic head pattern of blue-grey forehead and crown, narrow black lateral crown-stripes, broad white supercilium flaring behind eye and black eye-stripe. Otherwise rather plain, with greenish upperparts fading to dingier tone on ear-coverts, neck and breast sides, and whitish underparts. First-winters and some adults are washed pale lemon-yellow on flanks and undertail-coverts. Bill is relatively long and stout, with slight hook at tip; legs blue-grey. All plumages similar, though in good views first-winters may be aged by browner iris colour and uniformly fresh flight feathers. Like other members of genus, has rather horizontal gait and heavy movements.
VOICE Call is a strong, nasal *mew* or *cher*. Song is a persistent series of short, repeated and variable phrases.
HABITAT Deciduous woodland, thickets and scrub.
DISTRIBUTION Breeds across much of central and southern Canada and eastern USA, migrating south to winter in the Neotropics. Currently increasing in numbers.
EUROPEAN STATUS Rare vagrant: 93 autumn records, chiefly between mid-September and mid-October. Britain (60); France (4: 19 Oct 1983; 17 Oct 1985; 10 Oct 1988; 12 Oct 1988); Germany (1: 4 Oct 1957); Iceland (5: 16 Sept 1951; 3 Nov 1960; 27 Sept 1973; 4 Oct 1984; 20 Oct 1985); Ireland (19); Netherlands (4: Oct 1985; Oct 1985; 24 Sept 1991; 2 Oct 1991).

YELLOW-THROATED VIREO

Vireo flavifrons L 14 cm (5.5 in)
DESCRIPTION Big-headed, boldy-plumaged vireo with unique combination of green, yellow, grey and white field marks. Most striking character is dark eye and loral line offset by bright yellow 'spectacles', throat and breast. Yellowish-green of crown, nape and mantle contrasts with grey scapulars and lesser coverts; wings otherwise black, with broad white tips to median and greater coverts forming two prominent wing-bars, and flight feathers edged white or yellowish. Rump grey, contrasting with black tail which has white outer feathers. Belly and undertail-coverts white. Greyish bill is rather broad and stout, with slight hook at tip; legs blue-grey. All plumages generally alike.
VOICE Song is a slow repetition of short phrases separated by long pauses, often ending on a higher double note.
HABITAT Deciduous and coniferous forest, riverside woodland.

DISTRIBUTION Fairly common breeder from central North America eastwards through the Great Lakes and south to the Gulf coast. Some winter from Florida west to Texas, but most migrate to eastern Mexico and the Neotropics beyond.
EUROPEAN STATUS Extreme vagrant: one autumn record. Britain (1: 20-27 Sept 1990).

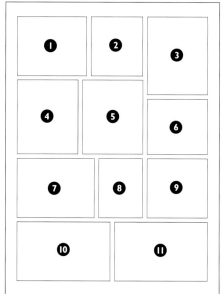

1 **Dead Sea Sparrow** *(female, Apr, Israel)*
2 **Dead Sea Sparrow** *(adult male, Apr, Israel)*
3 **Philadelphia Vireo** *(Oct 1987, Tresco, Isles of Scilly, Britain)*
4 **Philadelphia Vireo** *(Oct 1987, Tresco, Isles of Scilly, Britain)*
5 **Philadelphia Vireo** *(Oct 1987, Tresco, Isles of Scilly, Britain)*
6 **Red-eyed Vireo** *(Oct 1989, St Martin's, Isles of Scilly, Britain)*
7 **Red-eyed Vireo** *(Oct 1993, Gugh, Isles of Scilly, Britain)*
8 **Red-eyed Vireo** *(Oct 1991, Lizard, Cornwall, Britain)*
9 **Yellow-throated Vireo** *(Sept 1990, Kenidjack, Cornwall, Britain)*
10 **Yellow-throated Vireo** *(Sept 1990, Kenidjack, Cornwall, Britain)*
11 **Yellow-throated Vireo** *(Sept 1990, Kenidjack, Cornwall, Britain)*

RED-FRONTED SERIN

Serinus pusillus L 11-13 cm (4.5-5.25 in)
DESCRIPTION Uniquely patterned finch, in adult plumage with sooty-black head, upper breast and nape offset by red blaze on forehead. Darkness of upper body extends as streaks onto browner mantle and pale underparts, especially on more boldly-marked breeding males. Flight feathers browner with darker centres, contrasting with pale secondary edges and narrow double wing-bars. Can appear less striking in flight from underneath, when pale yellowish or white underparts and underwing-coverts help to mask dark-bodied impression. Juveniles have sooty forebody of adults replaced by brownish forehead, face and upper breast; dark streaking on paler mantle gives more contrasting appearance. Gregarious; often in family parties or small flocks outside breeding season, feeding on seed-heads or foraging on ground.
VOICE Song is like a softer version of European Serin's. Call, often given in flight, is a rapid trilling; also a ringing *ti-ihihihihi* and a soft *dueet* note.
HABITAT A montane finch, occurring in valleys, hillsides, plains and meadows, typically in open country but also at forest edge.
DISTRIBUTION Patchy breeding range extends from China and the Tien Shan range in the east, through Tibet, Pakistan, Afghanistan, Iran and the Caucasus, to central and southern Turkey in the west.
EUROPEAN STATUS Extreme vagrant: at least 10 records, though escapes also recorded (*eg* in Austria and Britain). Greece (10+ records, including several flocks).

ARCTIC REDPOLL

Carduelis hornemanni L 13-15 cm (5.25-6 in)
DESCRIPTION Large, bulky redpoll with two distinct races. Scandinavian/Russian subspecies *exilipes* closely resembles paler examples of large nominate *flammea* race of Common Redpoll ('Mealy' Redpoll). Upperparts generally greyish-white or buffish-white, paler than on typical Mealy, with pale head marked by red forehead, black lores and black chin, and whitish underparts; differences from Mealy include paler ear-coverts and nape, broader white double wing-bars and tertial fringes, unstreaked, extensively white rump, little or no flank streaking, unstreaked white undertail-coverts (or on some, a single narrow black streak along feather shaft), size (though overlap occurs) and smaller bill. Larger nominate race is even more bulky-looking than *exilipes*, with whiter ground colour to upperparts. Often fluffs out feathers. Frequently associates with Common Redpoll.
VOICE Song and call in essence similar to Common Redpoll's, though Arctic averages deeper in tone and volume of flight calls.
HABITAT A high arctic species, frequenting birch, spruce, willow thickets and shrubs on tundra or hillsides.
DISTRIBUTION Circumpolar in range, breeding from northernmost Scandinavia eastwards across northern Russia and Siberia, and in North America in Alaska and western and south-east Canada (*exilipes*); also north-easternmost Canada and Greenland (*hornemanni*). Winters in Europe largely in north-central Scandinavia, in Asia south through Siberia to Mongolia and north-west China, and in North America south to northern Michigan.
EUROPEAN STATUS Breeds Norway, Sweden (*c* 1,000 pairs) and Finland. Irregular or accidental elsewhere, typically from October to March, and great majority of race *exilipes*. Austria (1: 3 Dec 1977); Belgium (18); Britain (303); Czech Republic (20+); Denmark (many, *eg c* 50 in 1994); Estonia; Faeroes (2: 13 Apr 1945; 3 Oct 1984); France (9); Germany; Hungary (2: 3 Dec 1880; Jan 1894); Iceland (4+); Latvia; Lithuania (5+ records, including flock of 25 on 26 Feb 1989); Luxembourg; Netherlands (56+ individuals); Poland (62); Romania (15+); Slovakia (1: 31 Jan 1987, five); former Yugoslavia.

TWO-BARRED CROSSBILL

Loxia leucoptera L 15-17 cm (6-6.75 in)
DESCRIPTION Smaller and less stockily built than Common Crossbill, with weaker bill which is even more markedly crossed at tip. In all plumages shows broad double white bars on blackish wings, widest on adults but also prominent on juveniles (Common Crossbill can rarely show whitish wing-bars, but usually not so solidly marked); also has white tips to tertials (not buffish or off-white as on aberrant Common Crossbill). Males typically have pinker body colour than male Common Crossbill, with pale grey of lower flanks and belly fading to white on undertail-coverts. Females variably green above and yellowish-green below, with prominent paler yellow rump; immatures buffish-brown with dark streaking on upperparts. Vagrant Two-barreds are often found in flocks of Common Crossbills.
VOICE Song, given from tree-top or in song-flight, is varied series of trills and rattles recalling Siskin. Flight calls include a weaker, less metallic version of Common Crossbill's *glip-glip*, and a redpoll-like *chet-chet*.
HABITAT Shows marked preference for larches, but also occurs in spruces, firs and cedars; occasionally also feeds on berries.
DISTRIBUTION Occurs principally in northern conifer belts of Eurasia and North America. Range extends eastwards from Finnish/Russian border across Siberia to Manchuria, with birds wintering mainly within or just south of breeding areas, and from Alaska across Canada and in some adjacent US states, wintering south to North Carolina in east and Colorado in west. An isolated resident population exists on Hispaniola in the Caribbean. Periodically erupts south and west from normal range, in Europe chiefly into southern Scandinavia.
EUROPEAN STATUS Breeds Finland, and has bred Norway (scarce outside irruption years, *eg* 6 in 1993) and Sweden (total *c* 7,300 records). Irruptive vagrant outside breeding range: Austria (*c* 20); Belgium (*c* 35); Britain (113); Bulgaria; Czech Republic; Denmark (many); Estonia (irregular); Faeroes (6); France (9); Germany; Hungary (2: 12 Sept 1990, dead; 16 Dec 1990, dead); Ireland (4: 11 Jan 1802; *c* 1867; 17 Feb 1895; 2 Aug 1927); Italy (20+); Latvia; Lithuania; Luxembourg; Netherlands (56); Poland (14+ during 1950-94); Romania; Slovakia; Slovenia (2: 7 Jan 1985; 1 Oct 1985); Switzerland (3); former Yugoslavia.

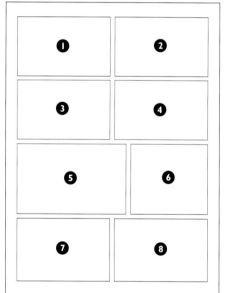

1 **Red-fronted Serin** *(adult male, July, Turkey)*
2 **Arctic Redpoll** (Nov 1988, Westenschauren, Netherlands)
3 **Arctic Redpoll** (Dec 1985, Turku, Finland)
4 **Arctic Redpoll** (Nov 1990, Zeebrugge, Belgium)
5 **Two-barred Crossbill** (female, Dec 1986, Turku, Finland)
6 **Two-barred Crossbill** (adult male, Oct 1990, Sandringham, Norfolk, Britain)
7 **Two-barred Crossbill** (juvenile, Sept 1990, Svenner, Vestfold, Norway)
8 **Two-barred Crossbill** (adult male, July 1990, Fair Isle, Shetland, Britain)

TRUMPETER FINCH

Bucanetes githagineus L 14-15 cm (5.5-6 in)
DESCRIPTION Chunky, pale, medium-sized finch with a stout, stubby bill. Breeding male is the most contrastingly marked, with pale greyish head, variable pinky tinge to face, breast and darker wings, and red bill. Otherwise adult plumages are plain sandy-grey with conspicuous dark eye and very faint pinkish tinges to wing and tail feathers; bill pale yellowish. Juvenile similar but lacks pink tinges; further distinguished from adult by overall bright clay-brown tone to plumage. Spends much time foraging on ground, but not averse to perching on fences, trees *etc*. Beware possible confusion with similar Mongolian Trumpeter Finch *B mongolicus* and with Desert Finch *Rhodospiza obsoleta* (neither recorded Europe), differences from both of which include lack of white on flight feathers.
VOICE Song is a distinctive buzzing wheeze. Call, often uttered in bounding flight, is a nasal *weechp*.
HABITAT Favours deserts, semi-deserts, steppe, hillsides and mountain slopes with sparse ground cover.
DISTRIBUTION Breeds from south-east Spain and Morocco south to Mauretania and discontinuously eastwards through Saharan North Africa to Sudan, parts of the Middle East, and Afghanistan and Central Asia eastwards to northern Pakistan. Has bred Turkey. Partial migrant, wintering elsewhere in Middle East and the Gulf states.
EUROPEAN STATUS Breeds southern Spain (100-300 pairs); irregular migrant Italy (records include flocks of 10 in May 1967 and c 20 in July 1967). Accidental elsewhere: Austria (2: autumn 1907; 12 May 1989); Britain (7); Channel Islands (1: Oct-Nov 1973); Denmark (1: June-July 1982); France (3: 26 Sept 1992; 19 Apr 1993; 30 June 1994); Germany (1: 26-27 July 1987); Gibraltar (4: most recent on 13 May 1989); Greece (7); Sweden (2: June 1966; 16 June 1971).

EVENING GROSBEAK

Hesperiphona vespertinus L 18-21 cm (7.25-8.5 in)
DESCRIPTION New World counterpart of Hawfinch, sharing that species' thickset build, large size and massive bill. Adult male has striking combination of golden-yellow body and blackish forecrown, lores and cheeks, becoming browner on nape, ear-coverts and throat, but with contrasting bright yellow supercilia meeting above black line on forehead. Mantle and breast variably yellow-brown, offset by black wings with striking white panels on tertials and inner secondaries; relatively short tail also black. Female has greyer body, with no obvious yellow, and black confined to wings and tail; in flight shows less white on secondaries than male, but also has white at base of inner primaries and white spots at base of white-tipped black tail. Juvenile resembles female but has duller tone to body and less pure white in wing. Bounding flight is like that of Hawfinch.

VOICE Song is a rambling, irregular jumble of notes, recalling Hawfinch's in pattern. Call is a loud *cleeip* or *cleer*.
HABITAT Forests, mixed woodland and copses; also parks and gardens, particularly in winter when attracted to feeders.
DISTRIBUTION Breeds from north-eastern USA and south-east Canada westwards in a narrow band across southern Canada to the Pacific coast, and south through the Rockies and parts of south-western USA to Mexico. Winters across United States except Gulf coast and Florida, but numbers erratic according to food supply.
EUROPEAN STATUS Extreme vagrant: four spring records. Britain (2: 26 March 1969; 10-25 March 1980); Norway (2: 2-9 May 1973; 17-26 May 1975).

BLACK-AND-WHITE WARBLER

Mniotilta varia L 13 cm (5.25 in)
DESCRIPTION 'Humbug-striped' wood-warbler, all plumages sharing white head with black lateral crown-stripes, white body variably streaked black or blackish above and below, black wings with bold white double wing-bars, streaked undertail-coverts and black tail. Adult male has black ear-coverts and lores, and dense black streaking on throat and underside in breeding plumage. Adult female has pale grey ear-coverts and lores, with less streaking on underparts. First-winter male like adult female, but usually more heavily streaked underneath; first-winter female indistinctly streaked on underparts, and often has buffish tint to white areas. Feeding behaviour recalls a nuthatch, running up and down trunks and along branches, searching for insects with relatively long, almost treecreeper-like bill.
VOICE Song is a Coal Tit-like *weesa-weesa-weesa*, in rhythmic pattern like bicycle wheel, and uttered throughout year. Calls include a sharp *tick* and a weaker *tzeet*.
HABITAT For breeding favours deciduous and mixed forest and woodlands, especially moist areas, but on migration found in wide variety of habitats with trees and scrub.
DISTRIBUTION Breeds in central, southern and south-eastern Canada, and in much of the eastern USA south towards the Gulf coast, with several isolated outposts further west. Winters from southern USA south to northern Peru.
EUROPEAN STATUS Very rare vagrant: 14 records, with September and October the peak months. Britain (9); Faeroes (1: 18-20 July 1984); Iceland (2: 1 Sept 1970; 19-20 Oct 1991); Ireland (2: 18 Oct 1978; 30 Sept-2 Oct 1984).

GOLDEN-WINGED WARBLER

Vermivora chrysoptera L 12 cm (4.75 in)
DESCRIPTION Male unmistakable, with golden-yellow wing patch, forehead and forecrown, black ear-coverts, and extensive black throat patch with white submoustachial area. Upperparts otherwise pearl-grey, contrasting with whitish underparts. Black bill is rather long and slender. Female patterned as male, but with

black areas distinctly greyer and yellow of crown and wing duller and more greenish. First-years much as adults, but tertials and inner secondaries show broad olive edges. All plumages show conspicuous white spots near tip of dark grey outer tail. In southern parts of range hybridises freely with Blue-winged Warbler *V pinus* (no records in Europe), producing offspring which usually show at least some yellow on underparts and/or whitish wing-bars. Feeds actively, often hanging upside-down on clumps of leaves when searching for insects.
VOICE Song is a drawn-out, buzzing *bee-bzz-bzz-bzz* with asthmatic quality. Call is a sharp *tchip*.
HABITAT Nests in open deciduous woodland with dense undergrowth, clearings and riverside thickets. On migration occurs in all kinds of wooded habitat.
DISTRIBUTION Has rather restricted breeding range from central North America east through the Great Lakes to New England, and south through the Appalachians; range expanding in north, but contracting in south. Migrates south-west to winter chiefly in Central America.
EUROPEAN STATUS Extreme vagrant: one record. Britain (1: 24 Jan-10 Apr 1989).

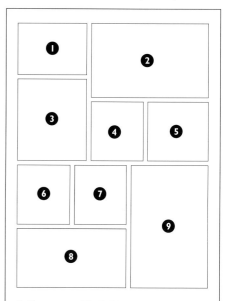

1 **Trumpeter Finch** (May 1984, Church Norton, West Sussex, Britain)
2 **Trumpeter Finch** (adult male, Mar, Israel)
3 **Evening Grosbeak** (adult male, June, Canada)
4 **Black-and-white Warbler** (probably first-winter male, Oct 1987, Prawle Point, Devon, Britain)
5 **Black-and-white Warbler** (probably first-winter male, Oct 1987, Prawle Point, Devon, Britain)
6 **Black-and-white Warbler** (probably first-winter male, Dec 1985, How Hill, Norfolk, Britain)
7 **Golden-winged Warbler** (male, Feb 1989, Larkfield, Kent, Britain)
8 **Golden-winged Warbler** (male, Feb 1989, Larkfield, Kent, Britain)
9 **Golden-winged Warbler** (male, Feb 1989, Larkfield, Kent, Britain)

TENNESSEE WARBLER

Vermivora peregrina L 12 cm (4.75 in)
DESCRIPTION Relatively compact, plump and short-tailed warbler, in all plumages showing short, pale supercilium, narrow, dark eye-stripe and white undertail-coverts. Breeding male has grey head contrasting with green upperparts and white underparts, which may give impression of a vireo; separated by more slender, pointed bill, less bulky jizz and black eye. Non-breeding males have more green-toned head and yellow-tinged underparts, like duller females; confusion then possible with *Phylloscopus* warblers, but note bill shape and colour, leg colour, subtly un-*phylloscopus* head pattern and, especially, purity of white undertail coverts and contrast of latter with remainder of underparts (as well as, in hand, nine primaries, not 10). Most show a narrow yellowish or white wing-bar, most obvious on fresh autumn individuals and least so on worn adults in summer, when may be absent altogether. Typically feeds high in trees, hanging upside-down to glean from leaves.
VOICE Song begins with several high-pitched notes, followed by a descending series of *sit* notes which run into a trill. Chief call is a soft *tsit*.
HABITAT Common breeder in northern coniferous, mixed and deciduous forests, occurring in more open woodland on migration and in winter.
DISTRIBUTION Breeds across much of Canada and in the USA in north-western Montana and New England. Migrates south to winter from southern Mexico to northern South America.
EUROPEAN STATUS Extreme vagrant: five autumn records. Britain (3: 6-20 Sept 1975; 24 Sept 1975; 5-7 Sept 1982); Faeroes (1: 22-29 Sept 1984); Iceland (1).

NORTHERN PARULA

Parula americana L 11 cm (4.5 in)
DESCRIPTION Small, dumpy and short-tailed warbler, unlikely to be confused with any other passerine occurring in Europe. In all plumages essentially blue-grey above, with variably yellow-green mantle and bold white double wing-bars, and pale below, with yellow on throat and breast and white belly. Males are brighter than females, with intensity of pattern strongest on adults (blackish lores, white eye-crescents and blue-grey edges to flight feathers, males also with narrow blue-grey and rufous breast bands), and weakest on first-years (face pattern plainer but with pale supercilium, males with weaker breast bands).
VOICE Song consists of a buzzy, rising trill ending in a lower, abrupt *zip* note. Chief call is a high-pitched *chip*.
HABITAT Open deciduous and coniferous forest, also wooded swamps and bogs.
DISTRIBUTION Occurs in summer from south-central to south-east Canada and New England, and in much of south-eastern USA, but not in intervening area. Some winter in southern states, but chief non-breeding range is from

Mexico south to Nicaragua and in the West Indies.
EUROPEAN STATUS Very rare vagrant: 23 records, chiefly in late September and October. Britain (13); France (1: 17-27 Oct 1987); Iceland (7); Ireland (2: 19-24 Oct 1983; 25 Sept 1989).

YELLOW WARBLER

Dendroica petechia L 13 cm (5.25 in)
DESCRIPTION A relatively plump and short-tailed warbler, readily identified by largely yellow or greenish-yellow plumage. Breeding male has strikingly bright yellow head and body, with beady black eye on plain, golden-tinged face and rufous streaking on breast and flanks; upperparts rather greener, wings darker with olive-yellow feather edges. Dark tail uniquely has extensive yellow in outer feathers and is yellow on underside. Female lacks brightness of male, with greener hue to head and neck and much fainter streaking on underparts. First-winters duller than respective adult plumages, with young females distinctly greyish-olive above and almost whitish on belly. Numerous races in North America have assorted plumage variations, and other distinct forms in which males have dark rufous head markings occur in Central America, northern South America and the West Indies.
VOICE Song, a variable series of *swee* notes followed by a warble, often transcribed as *sweet sweet sweet I'm so sweet*. Call is a loud *tship*.
HABITAT Frequents scrub, thickets (particularly alder and willow) and open woodland, often in damp terrain or near water.
DISTRIBUTION Breeds across much of North America except for the southern and south-eastern USA. Early migrant, leaving breeding grounds from mid July to winter chiefly from Central America to central South America; small numbers remain in southern USA in winter.
EUROPEAN STATUS Extreme vagrant: three autumn records. Britain (3: 29 Aug 1964; 3-4 Nov 1990; 24 Aug 1992).

CHESTNUT-SIDED WARBLER

Dendroica pensylvanica L 13 cm (5.25 in)
DESCRIPTION Distinctively marked wood-warbler in all plumages. Breeding males have unique pattern of yellow crown, white-bordered black eye-stripes meeting on nape, and black moustachial stripe running into elongated and irregular chestnut patch on breast sides and flanks; heavily streaked bright green upperparts and blackish wings with bold double wing-bars contrast with white underparts. Tail black, with white spots at tips of outermost feathers. Bill and legs blackish. Adult female similar to male, but head pattern dingier and chestnut on sides of breast and flanks much reduced. Non-breeding plumage (most likely in Europe) is very different, both sexes having unstreaked grape-green upperparts, pale eye-ring on grey face and grey underparts; wings much as on breeding adults,

though wing-bars often slightly yellower on young birds. First-winter males may have hint of chestnut on flanks.
VOICE Chief song is a series of loud whistles with an emphatic terminal flourish, often transcribed as *please please pleased to meetcha*. Has a sharp, rough *zeet* call.
HABITAT Open deciduous woodland, particularly second-growth stands and areas with young scattered trees.
DISTRIBUTION Distributed in summer from south-central Canada east through the Great Lakes region to south-east Canada, north-east USA and the Appalachians. Winters in Central America from Guatemala to Panama. One of the commonest eastern warblers.
EUROPEAN STATUS Extreme vagrant: one autumn record. Britain (1: 20 Sept 1985).

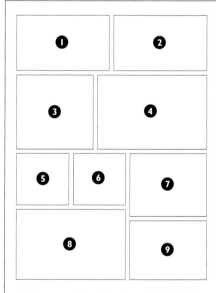

1 **Tennessee Warbler** (Sept 1995*, St Kilda, Western Isles, Britain)
2 **Tennessee Warbler** (Sept 1995*, St Kilda, Western Isles, Britain)
3 **Tennessee Warbler** (first-winter, Sept 1975, Fair Isle, Shetland, Britain)
4 **Northern Parula** (first-winter, Oct 1992, St Mary's, Isles of Scilly, Britain)
5 **Northern Parula** (female, probably first-winter, Oct 1988, Cot Valley, Cornwall, Britain)
6 **Northern Parula** (female, probably first-winter, Oct 1988, Cot Valley, Cornwall, Britain)
7 **Yellow Warbler** (first-winter male, probably of race *aestiva*, Nov 1990, Lerwick, Shetland, Britain)
8 **Chestnut-sided Warbler** *(first-year, Aug, USA)*
9 **Chestnut-sided Warbler** *(adult male, date unknown, Canada)*

BLACK-THROATED BLUE WARBLER

Dendroica caerulescens L 13 cm (5.25 in)
DESCRIPTION White patch at base of primaries on otherwise plain wing is diagnostic in all plumages. Upperparts of male plain dark blue from forehead to tail; wings and tail darker (latter with white spots in outer feathers), but with dark blue feather edges reinforcing otherwise uniform upperparts. Neat black of face extends from line through eye down across ear-coverts and throat and in irregular line down flanks, isolating narrow white 'shoulder'. First-year male like adult, but with variable greenish tinge to upperparts, darker flight feathers, and black on face and underparts less well defined. Female olive-brown above, with darker wings, smaller white primary patch, fine white supercilium and white crescent below eye, and buffish below, fading to white on belly and undertail-coverts; first-year female duller, with white areas less well defined. Bill black and legs brownish-pink in all plumages.
VOICE Song is usually a slow series of three or four rasping notes, the last one higher. Call is a single-note *stip*.
HABITAT Breeds in mixed and deciduous woodland with undergrowth, also clearings; often in more open habitat in winter.
DISTRIBUTION In summer, found commonly in North America from the Great Lakes region east to Nova Scotia, and south through New England and the Appalachians. Some winter in Florida, but vast majority continue south to the West Indies.
EUROPEAN STATUS Extreme vagrant: one autumn record. Iceland (1: 14-19 Sept 1988).

BLACKBURNIAN WARBLER

Dendroica fusca L 13 cm (5.25 in)
DESCRIPTION Male unmistakable, with black-patterned orange face and throat, blackish upperparts and bold white wing patch. In breeding plumage, orange is most intense fiery colour on throat; otherwise paler orange forehead, supercilium, eye-crescent and ear-covert surround, and black eye-stripe, crown and ear-coverts. Entire upperparts blackish except for white 'tramlines' on mantle, bold white patch on median and greater coverts, and white base to sides of tail. Underparts whitish with heavy black flank streaking, less so on non-breeding and first-year males, which are also paler orange on throat, greyer on upperparts and have less well-defined markings on face. Adult female resembles non-breeding male, but has upperparts olive-brown, streaked blackish, less extensive pale orange on crown, ear-coverts and throat, double white wing-bars rather than broad patch, and less streaking below; first-year female much drabber, with orange replaced by peachy-buff.
VOICE Song is a variable series of high-pitched *seet* notes followed by a trill. Chief call is *tsip*.
HABITAT Frequents mixed and coniferous forest in north of breeding range, and pine-oak in south; on migration in all kinds of woodland.
DISTRIBUTION Breeds in eastern North

America from south-central Canada east through upper Great Lakes region to Newfoundland and New England, and south through the Appalachians. Winters in southern Central America south through the Andes to Bolivia.
EUROPEAN STATUS Extreme vagrant: three autumn records. Britain (2: 5 Oct 1961; 7 Oct 1988); Iceland (1 at sea: Oct 1987).

CAPE MAY WARBLER

Dendroica tigrina L 13 cm (5.25 in)
DESCRIPTION Breeding male diagnostically patterned, with blackish crown, bright chestnut supercilium and ear-coverts divided by narrow blackish eye-stripe, orangey-yellow neck-collar and black-streaked breast and flanks. Upperparts olive with black streaking, tail and wing feathers blackish, edged olive; white on median coverts and edges of greater coverts forms bold wing patch. Female lacks chestnut on face and has supercilium, collar, throat, breast and rump washed much weaker yellow, less distinct breast streaking and a single white wing-bar. Non-breeding and first-year males similar to female, but with stronger yellow hue, more white in wing and heavier streaking below. Autumn immatures are dull, but always with yellowish rump and ghost pattern of yellow neck-collar, as well as indistinct streaking on underparts and whitish throat. Bill dark and finely pointed, with slightly decurved tip.
VOICE Song is a thin *zi zi zi zi*. Call is an equally weak, high-pitched *sip*.
HABITAT In summer inhabits coniferous forest, especially black spruce, and birch and hemlock woodland; uses wide variety of woodland on migration and in winter.
DISTRIBUTION Breeds from western Canada through Great Lakes region to Nova Scotia and northern New England, wintering chiefly in the West Indies, in small numbers in Florida and from eastern Mexico to northernmost South America.
EUROPEAN STATUS Extreme vagrant: one spring record. Britain (1: 17 June 1977).

MAGNOLIA WARBLER

Dendroica magnolia L 13 cm (5.25 in)
DESCRIPTION Easily recognised wood-warbler with distinctive yellow underparts and rump, white eye-ring or eye-crescent, and diagnostic broken white tail band across otherwise all-black tail. Breeding male has blue-grey crown and nape, broad white supercilium behind eye and black mask. Upperparts blackish, with bold white wing patch; underparts bright yellow, with black breast band and bold streaking along flanks, and white undertail-coverts. Female and non-breeding male duller, with olive upperparts lightly streaked darker on mantle, no black on face and paler or indistinct supercilium, double narrow white wing-bars and reduced streaking on underparts. First-winters like female, but with less streaking above and below, and readily identified by tail pattern and indistinct

greyish breast band. Bill blackish; legs brownish-black. Active species, frequently flicking tail to reveal white patches; fly-catches and hovers when feeding.
VOICE Song consists of series of variable musical notes, often given as *weety weety weeteo*. Commonest calls include harsh *tshekk* and soft *tship*.
HABITAT For breeding favours open mixed and coniferous forest, especially spruce and fir. On migration and in winter found in wider variety of woodland and more open terrain with trees.
DISTRIBUTION Breeds across much of Canada except far north and south-west, and in north-east USA from Great Lakes east to New England and northern Appalachians. Winters in Central America and in small numbers in the West Indies. Common, but declining steadily.
EUROPEAN STATUS Extreme vagrant: one autumn record. Britain (1: 27-28 Sept 1981).

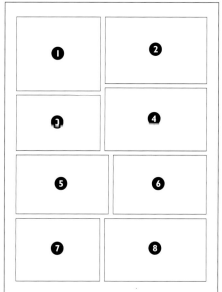

1 **Black-throated Blue Warbler** *(adult summer male, date unknown, New York, USA)*
2 **Black-throated Blue Warbler** *(adult summer male, Sept, New York, USA)*
3 **Blackburnian Warbler** *(adult summer male, date unknown, USA)*
4 **Blackburnian Warbler** *(adult summer male, date unknown, Ontario, Canada)*
5 **Cape May Warbler** *(adult summer male, May, Ontario, Canada)*
6 **Cape May Warbler** *(first-winter female, Oct, New York, USA)*
7 **Magnolia Warbler** *(first-year, Oct 1995*, Bakki, Iceland)*
8 **Magnolia Warbler** *(first-year, Oct 1995*, Seltjörn, Iceland)*

YELLOW-RUMPED WARBLER

Dendroica coronata L 14 cm (5.5 in)
DESCRIPTION Yellow rump is distinctive in all plumages. Adult male of nominate eastern form ('Myrtle Warbler') easily recognisable by blue-grey upperparts which are streaked blackish, white underparts with dense gorget of black streaks extending down flanks, black eye mask, double white wing-bars, and diagnostic yellow patches on crown and breast sides. Non-breeding male is considerably duller and browner with dirtier face and throat, but retains heavier streaking on mantle. Adult female is watered-down version of breeding male, with upperparts washed browner and with less distinctive streaking, duller mask, narrower white wing-bars, less intense black streaking on underparts, and duller, more restricted yellow crown and breast sides. First-year male very like adult female; first-year female similar but generally browner and duller, with indistinct streaking above and below, diffuse wing-bars and yellow on crown and breast sides much reduced or lacking. In all plumages has white oval-shaped spots near tips of outer tail, most prominent on adult male, least obvious on first-year female. Bill and legs blackish. Frequently feeds on ground during migration, in manner of pipits (with which vagrants have been known to loosely associate).
VOICE Song is a clear, slow trilling warble. Has distinctive, sharp *chek* or *chip* call.
HABITAT Occurs in coniferous, mixed and deciduous forest and woodland. On migration, frequents trees and bushy habitats.
DISTRIBUTION 'Myrtle Warbler' breeds from New England and south-east Canada north-westwards to Alaska, wintering chiefly in south-east USA, Caribbean and eastern Central America. Western form *auduboni* ('Audubon's Warbler', not recorded Europe) breeds throughout western North America and in western Central America, wintering mainly in south of breeding range.
EUROPEAN STATUS Very rare vagrant: 29 records, mostly in October, but at least two in spring and one instance of overwintering. Britain (12); Iceland (9); Ireland (8).

BLACKPOLL WARBLER

Dendroica striata L 13-14 cm (5.25-5.5 in)
DESCRIPTION The most frequently recorded American wood-warbler in Europe. Breeding male unmistakable, with black cap, white cheeks, boldly streaked greyish upperparts with double white wing-bars, and black malar stripe extending as bold streaks down breast sides and flanks. Breeding female lacks black cap and white cheeks, and has only fine, narrow streaking on breast sides and flanks. Non-breeding adults are olive-green above with whitish double wing-bars and tertial edges, and have dark eye-stripe, yellowish supercilium, throat and breast, and whitish belly; streaking on upperparts and underparts more prominent on male than on female. First-

winters very like non-breeding adult female, but with streaking even less distinct above and below. In all plumages has white spots in outer tail feathers. Bill grey, with flesh-coloured lower mandible; leg colour varies from orangey to flesh (darker on females and first-winters), with diagnostic yellow feet. In autumn, very similar Bay-breasted Warbler *D castanea* (one 1995 claim from Britain pending assessment) separated by paler, barely streaked upperparts, unstreaked underparts, brighter white double wing-bars and darker legs; diagnostically, feet are dark on Bay-breasted (as legs), whereas Blackpoll invariably has yellow feet even if legs appear dark (especially at sides).
VOICE Song comprises a rapid, high-pitched series of *si* notes. Typical call is a hard *chip*, occasionally given by migrants.
HABITAT Breeds in northern coniferous forest, especially favouring spruce, and in mixed woodland.
DISTRIBUTION In summer occurs across Canada and Alaska to northern tree limit, and in east south to northern New England. Has longest migration of all American wood-warblers, wintering in South America south to Bolivia.
EUROPEAN STATUS Very rare vagrant: 40 records, mainly from mid-September to October, and one in winter. Britain (27); Channel Islands (1: 26 Oct-4 Nov 1980); France (1: 15 Oct 1990); Iceland (6); Ireland (5: 6-10 Oct 1976; 24-30 Oct 1982; 6 Oct 1984; 3 Oct 1993).

AMERICAN REDSTART

Setophaga ruticilla L 13 cm (5.25 in)
DESCRIPTION Strikingly patterned flycatcher-like species, with distinctive tail markings in all plumages. Breeding male is glossy black with white belly, bright orange on 'shoulder' and bases of flight feathers, and extensively so on bases of outer feathers in relatively long, black tail. Orange markings replaced by yellow in female, which has pale grey head with white eye-ring and dark lores, plain olive-green upperparts, and white underparts from chin to undertail. First-winter male resembles adult female but has more orangey shoulder patch, and by first spring develops patchy black markings on throat. First-year female also like adult female, but yellow areas are duller and often lacking in wing. Bill and legs blackish. Very active, frequently fly-catching, drooping wings and raising and fanning tail to reveal diagnostic pattern.
VOICE Song is a variable, high-pitched series of *see* notes with a lower terminal note. Call is a sharp, hard *chip* or *tsip*.
HABITAT Favours open deciduous and mixed woodland, often in clearings or damper conditions.
DISTRIBUTION Breeds across southern Canada and much of USA except south-west and far west. Winters in Central America, northernmost South America and the West Indies.
EUROPEAN STATUS Extreme vagrant: nine

records, mainly mid-late autumn. Britain (5: 21 Oct 1967; 1 Nov 1982; 7 Nov-5 Dec 1982; 13-24 Oct 1983; 4-6 Oct 1985); France (1: 10 Oct 1961); Iceland (1); Ireland (2: 13-14 Oct 1968; 13-15 Oct 1985).

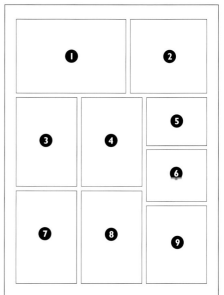

1 **Yellow-rumped Warbler** (probably first-year male, Nov 1994, Ramsey Island, Dyfed, Britain)
2 **Yellow-rumped Warbler** (first-year, Oct 1993, Cape Clear Island, Co Cork, Ireland)
3 **Yellow-rumped Warbler** (probably first-year male, Nov 1994, Ramsey Island, Dyfed, Britain)
4 **Yellow-rumped Warbler** (Nov 1994, Bristol, Britain)
5 **Blackpoll Warbler** (Oct 1990, St Mary's, Isles of Scilly, Britain)
6 **Blackpoll Warbler** (Sept 1991, Fair Isle, Shetland, Britain)
7 **Blackpoll Warbler** (Dec 1994, Bewl Water, East Sussex, Britain)
8 **American Redstart** (first-winter male, Oct 1983, Kenidjack, Cornwall, Britain)
9 **American Redstart** (first-winter, probably male, Nov 1982, Gibraltar Point, Lincolnshire, Britain)

OVENBIRD

Seiurus aurocapillus L 15 cm (6 in)
DESCRIPTION Rather large, plump warbler reminiscent of a short-tailed pipit, with distinctive open-faced expression, plain upperparts and boldly-streaked underparts. Has diagnostic orange crown-stripe with narrow black borders extending from forehead to nape, and white eye-ring; head and rest of upperparts otherwise plain olive-green. Underparts white, with bold black streaking on breast and flanks. Dark brown bill has pinkish base to lower mandible; legs bright pink. Sexes alike. Duller head pattern in autumn and on first-years, which have rusty edges to tertials. Unobtrusive, ground-dwelling species which bobs head and flicks tail constantly when walking.
VOICE Distinctive rising song is often transcribed as *teacher teacher teacher*. Chief call is a sharp *chip*.
HABITAT Frequents deciduous and mixed forests with dense undergrowth.
DISTRIBUTION In summer breeds across much of Canada from British Columbia to Newfoundland, and in USA chiefly in east except for Gulf coast states. Winters from Florida and Gulf coast south to northernmost South America and the West Indies. Apparently declining.
EUROPEAN STATUS Extreme vagrant: five records, but only two of live birds. Britain (2: 7-8 Oct 1973; 21 Oct 1985, dead; also a record of wing only, 4 Jan 1969); Ireland (2: 8 Dec 1977, dead; 24-25 Sept 1990).

NORTHERN WATERTHRUSH

Seiurus noveboracensis L 15 cm (6 in)
DESCRIPTION Upperparts uniform dark olive-brown, with obvious whitish supercilium (like Redwing), dark brown eye-stripe and slightly paler, mottled ear-coverts and neck sides. Underparts uniform pale buffy-white, with distinct blackish streaks extending more finely onto throat. Relatively short tail occasionally shows restricted white spots near tip. Bill dark brown, with pinker base to lower mandible; legs brownish-pink. Sexes alike and first-years as adults, though young birds have narrow buffish tertial edges in fresh plumage. Feeds on ground in horizontal posture, usually in damp areas, and pumps tail rhythmically at all times. Very similar Louisiana Waterthrush *S motacilla*, potential vagrant to Europe, has broader, whiter supercilium behind eye, buff suffusion on flanks contrasting with otherwise whitish underparts, brighter pink legs and pure white, unmarked throat.
VOICE Song is a loud, emphatic ditty reminiscent of Chaffinch. Call is a sharp *chink*, quite like that of Dipper.
HABITAT Requires swamps, thickets and woodlands near fresh water for breeding. On migration sometimes in drier areas; vagrants in Europe have also been seen on beaches.
DISTRIBUTION Common but declining across northern North America, breeding from Alaska

across Canada to the Atlantic coast, and in north-western and north-eastern USA. Winters from Mexico and the West Indies south to northern South America; some also winter in Florida.
EUROPEAN STATUS Very rare vagrant: eight records, of which seven in autumn (mainly September to mid-October) and one in spring. Britain (5: 30 Sept-12 Oct 1958; 3-8 Oct 1968; 29 Sept-4 Oct 1982; 22-23 Oct 1988; 29-30 Aug 1989); Channel Islands (1: 17 Apr 1977); France (1: 17 Sept 1955); Ireland (1: 10-11 Sept 1983).

COMMON YELLOWTHROAT

Geothlypis trichas L 13 cm (5.25 in)
DESCRIPTION Male readily identified by striking combination of black mask, yellow throat and olive-green upperparts; mask is bordered above by narrow greyish-white band. Plain dark olive-green above, contrasting with yellow of breast and undertail-coverts and whiter belly. Bill black; legs pinkish. Female lacks pale-bordered mask of male, instead showing olive crown, indistinct pale supercilium, and narrow dark eye-stripe with incomplete, broken eye-ring; otherwise similar to male, but often with less intense yellow throat and breast. First-winters of both sexes are like dull adult females, but young males often have traces of black feathering in mask area; yellow throat distinctive at all ages. Frequently feeds in thick cover but also perches in open, often with tail cocked.
VOICE Distinctive, rolling song frequently transcribed as *witchity witchity witchity witch*. Usual call is a hard tongue-clicking *chep*, like a loud *Sylvia* warbler.
HABITAT Frequents marshy vegetation, dense undergrowth in or near reedbeds and water, and damp meadows.
DISTRIBUTION Numerous across southern Canada from Atlantic to Pacific coasts, entire USA (though less common in south-west) and much of Mexico. Winters from southernmost USA south through Central America and West Indies to northernmost South America.
EUROPEAN STATUS Extreme vagrant: four records, with no seasonal pattern. Britain (4: 4 Nov 1954; 7-11 June 1984; 2-17 Oct 1984; 6 Jan-23 Apr 1989).

HOODED WARBLER

Wilsonia citrina L 13 cm (5.25 in)
DESCRIPTION Male has boldly-marked black and yellow head recalling face pattern of breeding male Pied Wagtail. Black on neck is neatly demarcated from olive-green upperparts and yellow underparts. Male shows same plumage year-round, and first-year male very like adult male in the field. Adult female resembles male but has weaker head pattern, appearing obvious on some but barely discernible on others. First-year females lack black in head, but dark lores and yellower cheeks aid separation from smaller female Wilson's Warbler; female Canada Warbler has grey cheeks and white

undertail-coverts. Bill blackish; legs pink. In all plumages shows extensive white in dark tail, which it constantly flicks and spreads; also frequently fly-catches.
VOICE Musical song consists of fast series of similar notes, ending in distinctive final note. Call is a loud, metallic *chink*.
HABITAT Occurs in mature deciduous forest, streams and ravine edges, thickets and swamps.
DISTRIBUTION Breeds in North America from south-east Great Lakes region south through eastern and south-eastern USA to Gulf coast, but absent from much of Florida. Migrates early, wintering in Central America and the West Indies.
EUROPEAN STATUS Extreme vagrant: two autumn records. Britain (2: 20-23 Sept 1970; 10 Sept 1992).

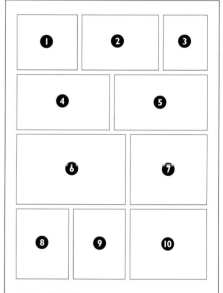

1 Ovenbird (first-winter, Sept 1990, Dursey Island, Co Cork, Ireland)
2 Ovenbird (first-winter, Sept 1990, Dursey Island, Co Cork, Ireland)
3 Northern Waterthrush (Aug 1989, St Agnes, Isles of Scilly, Britain)
4 Northern Waterthrush (Aug 1989, St Agnes, Isles of Scilly, Britain)
5 Northern Waterthrush (Apr 1977, Jersey, Channel Islands)
6 Common Yellowthroat (male, June 1984, Fetlar, Shetland, Britain)
7 Common Yellowthroat (male, June 1984, Fetlar, Shetland, Britain)
8 Common Yellowthroat (first-winter male, Oct 1984, Brhyer, Isles of Scilly, Britain)
9 Common Yellowthroat (first-winter male, Oct 1984, Brhyer, Isles of Scilly, Britain)
10 Hooded Warbler (adult male, May, New Jersey, USA)

WILSON'S WARBLER

Wilsonia pusilla L 12 cm (4.75 in)
DESCRIPTION Small, plump wood-warbler, with olive-green upperparts and yellow face and underparts in all plumages. Neat, glossy black cap of male distinctive; male has same plumage year-round, and adult and first-year males alike in the field. Adult female also shows some black on crown, but first-winter lacks this character. Female resembles female Hooded Warbler, but separated from that species by smaller size, shape, yellow lores and lack of white in dark tail. Bill blackish; legs pinkish. Feeds chiefly on insects in undergrowth, but will fly-catch.
VOICE Song is a descending series of *tsee* or *chip* notes, slurred in tone and accelerating towards end. Has a loud, low-pitched *chet* call.
HABITAT In breeding season shows preference for damp thickets, scrub and woodland, especially alongside streams. Winters in wider variety of wooded habitats and in more open areas.
DISTRIBUTION Breeding range extends from eastern Canada in broad swathe north of Great Lakes to the far west and Alaska, and south down west coast and Rockies to California and northern New Mexico. Winters from California south to Panama. More numerous in west of range than in east.
EUROPEAN STATUS Extreme vagrant: one autumn record. Britain (1: 13 Oct 1985).

CANADA WARBLER

Wilsonia canadensis L 13 cm (5.25 in)
DESCRIPTION Male rather uniform blue-grey above except for striking pattern of black forehead, fading to streaking on forecrown, black face with yellow fore-supercilium and throat, and white eye-ring. Has distinctive black necklace of streaks on yellow breast and white undertail-coverts. First-winter male similar, but with greyer upperparts and black areas on head and neck less well defined. Females much less boldly marked, with mid-grey head and upperparts lacking blue hues, and traces of male's black patterning faint or absent. Autumn immatures show olive-suffused grey upperparts and wholly yellow underparts, but with white undertail, obvious eye-ring and pale pink legs all useful features for separating from similar species. Usually forages in low undergrowth, but also fly-catches; often unobtrusive.
VOICE Song, beginning with at least one *chip* note, is a musical and variable warble not unlike Dunnock's. Calls include a sharp *chik* and softer *tsip*.
HABITAT Favours undergrowth in mixed and deciduous forests and woodland, often in or near bogs and riverside vegetation.
DISTRIBUTION Common but declining species, occurring in summer from southern Canada eastwards through Great Lakes region to Nova Scotia, New England and the Appalachians. Long-distance migrant, wintering mainly in northern South America.
EUROPEAN STATUS Extreme vagrant: one autumn record. Iceland (1: 29 Sept 1973).

SCARLET TANAGER

Piranga olivacea L 18 cm (7.25 in)
DESCRIPTION Large, finch-like but slender species. Adult male in breeding plumage unmistakable, with bright scarlet head and body and solidly black wings and tail; from late summer moults into olive and yellow winter plumage, during which displays peculiar patchy mix of red and greenish feathering. Adult female resembles winter male, with olive-green upperparts and yellower underparts, but greyish wings and tail have olive-green fringing (all black on male). First-winter male has wing coloration intermediate between adult male and female, with only some feather tracts appearing black; first-winter female very like adult female, differing chiefly in retained juvenile tertials which are worn and have whitish tips. In all plumages underwing-coverts are conspicuously white, unlike more colourful underwing of Summer Tanager (recorded once in Europe, see Appendix 1) – a constant character in separating females and immatures. Relatively short and pointed but deep-based bill is steely-grey on breeding male, paler in other plumages; legs grey.
VOICE Song somewhat recalls that of Mistle Thrush, though notes more slurred. Call is a distinctive, well-enunciated, two-note *chip-bur*.
HABITAT Frequents mature deciduous forest, especially stands of oak; in north of range also in mixed forests and pine woods.
DISTRIBUTION Breeds in south-easternmost Canada and much of eastern USA except southernmost states. Long-distance migrant, wintering chiefly in northern South America.
EUROPEAN STATUS Very rare vagrant: 11 records, all in autumn. Britain (4: 4 Oct 1970; 28 Sept-3 Oct 1975; 11 Oct 1981; 12-18 Oct 1982); Iceland (4: Nov or Dec 1936; 7-8 Oct 1967; 23 Oct 1967; 9 Nov 1992); Ireland (3: 12 Oct 1963; 12-14 Oct 1985; 18 Oct 1985).

EASTERN TOWHEE

Pipilo erythrophthalmus L 18-21 cm (7.25-8.5 in)
DESCRIPTION Chunky, relatively long-tailed passerine with large bill. Male is highly distinctive, with black head, upper breast and back, red eye, black wings with white patch at base of primaries and white edges to tertials, white-tipped black tail, whitish underparts, extensive orangey-rufous flanks and buff undertail. Female patterned as male, but black markings replaced by rufous-brown. First-years are very like adults but usually slightly browner, and with dark iris. Bill black, legs flesh-coloured. Western/southern forms, recently split as Spotted Towhee *P maculatus* (formerly lumped with Eastern as Rufous-sided Towhee) and unlikely to occur in Europe, often have white spotting on upperparts and two broad white wing-bars.
VOICE Song, usually delivered from prominent perch, is a variable two-note ditty followed by a higher-pitched series of notes. Normal call is *to-whee*, from which species gets its name.
HABITAT Found in thickets, wooded country with dense undergrowth, woodland edge, riverside groves, well-vegetated parks and gardens.
DISTRIBUTION Breeds mainly in south-east Canada and USA east of the Great Plains. Occurs throughout year in much of breeding range, though north-eastern areas vacated in winter.
EUROPEAN STATUS Extreme vagrant: one spring record. Britain (1: 7 June 1966). An additional record from Britain (5 Sept 1975-10 Jan 1976) involved a Spotted Towhee considered of uncertain origin and placed in category D.

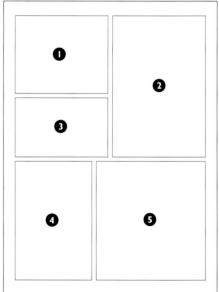

1 **Wilson's Warbler** (apparently adult male, Oct 1985, Rame Head, Cornwall, Britain)
2 **Canada Warbler** (adult male, June, USA)
3 **Canada Warbler** (female or immature, Aug, USA)
4 **Scarlet Tanager** (first-winter male, Oct 1975, Tresco, Isles of Scilly, Britain)
5 **Eastern Towhee** (male, date unknown, New York, USA)

SAVANNAH SPARROW

Passerculus sandwichensis L 14-16 cm (5.5-6.5 in)

DESCRIPTION Size, generally brown and buffish coloration and streaking above and below suggest a small Palearctic bunting (particularly Little Bunting), but lacks white in shortish, notched tail and has distinct yellow fore-supercilium. Plumage very variable, with up to 21 subspecies recognised. Nominate *sandwichensis* is one of larger northern races, with streaked dark brown crown showing pale median crown-stripe, brownish ear-coverts with darker borders above and below, whitish submoustachial stripe, dark malar stripe and buffish double wing-bars. Grey-brown upperparts streaked darker, heaviest on mantle; whitish underparts have narrow brownish streaks. Tail has pale grey outer feathers. Bill dark, with flesh-coloured lower mandible; legs flesh. Race *princeps* ('Ipswich Sparrow', also recorded in Europe) is larger and paler, with yellow fore-supercilium reduced or lacking and finer streaking on underparts. Sexes alike; first-years not reliably aged in the field. Relatively unobtrusive at all times; typically feeds on ground, especially on migration, and if disturbed often takes cover in long grass.
VOICE Song starts with short series of *chip* notes, followed by a long buzzy trill and ending with a shorter, lower trill. Calls include thin *seep* and a hard *tsep*.
HABITAT Occupies wide variety of primarily open habitats, including dune systems, saltmarsh, farmland, mountain pastures and tundra.
DISTRIBUTION Summer visitor to much of northern and central USA and across Canada and Alaska to north coast of mainland, and found year-round on Pacific coast south to Guatemala. Northern birds winter from southern USA and northern Central America to West Indies. Race *princeps* breeds only on Sable Island, Nova Scotia, wintering south to Georgia.
EUROPEAN STATUS Extreme vagrant: single records in spring and autumn. Britain (2: 11-16 Apr 1982; 30 Sept-1 Oct 1987).

LARK SPARROW

Chondestes grammacus L 17 cm (6.75 in)
DESCRIPTION Relatively large sparrow which is readily identified by distinctive head and tail patterns. In all plumages except juvenile (unlikely to occur in Europe), shows chestnut lateral crown-stripes (black in front of eye) and black-bordered ear-coverts offset by white median crown-stripe, supercilium, under-eye crescent and submoustachial stripe; eye-stripe and malar stripe also black. Upperparts pale greyish-brown, streaked darker except on rump. Wings largely blackish, with buffy feather edges and two indistinct white wing-bars. Underparts off-white, with prominent dark spot in centre of breast. Pattern of blackish tail is diagnostic,

with rounded corners which are boldly edged white (being obvious both at rest and particularly in flight). Bill greyish; legs flesh-coloured. Sexes alike. First-years resemble adults, with only a few retaining traces of juvenile streaking through to the following summer. Forms flocks in winter, sometimes with other sparrows; often quite approachable.
VOICE Song, given from a perch or in flight, is a melodious sequence of buzzes and trills following a two-note introduction. Call is a sharp *tsip* or *tink*, often repeated.
HABITAT Inhabits open country, farmland, prairies and woodland edge, with scattered trees and scrub; sometimes also found around towns and villages.
DISTRIBUTION Breeds in south-western Canada, across much of USA east to the Mississippi and locally on Atlantic coast, and south to northern Mexico. Northern birds move south to winter from southern part of breeding range south to El Salvador, Cuba and the Bahamas.
EUROPEAN STATUS Extreme vagrant: two spring records. Britain (2: 30 June-8 July 1981; 15-17 May 1991).

FOX SPARROW

Passerella iliaca L 18 cm (7.25 in)
DESCRIPTION Largest of the streaked North American sparrows to have occurred in Europe, but highly variable in plumage and 18 races described. In some respects adults of north-eastern nominate race recall chunky, outsized Song Sparrow, but plumage is even more rusty-toned and shows heavier rufous streaking on underparts. Head is densely streaked rufous on crown and has rufous-brown ear-coverts, with clear grey supercilium and neck sides. Greyish upperparts are also heavily streaked rufous, and blackish wings show broad rufous fringing on flight feathers and greater coverts, latter also with pale tips forming narrow wing-bar; rump and uppertail-coverts unstreaked rufous, with long tail browner-toned. White underparts show bold rufous malar stripe which continues as large blotchy streaks below, congregating to form conspicuous spot in centre of breast as on Song Sparrow. Strong, bicoloured bill is dark above and pale yellowish below; legs dark flesh. Sexes alike, and first-years not reliably aged in the field.
VOICE Has rich and melodious song, given from a perch, comprising several whistles followed by a series of variable short trills. Calls include a *chip* note.
HABITAT Found in a variety of woodland and wooded habitats which offer dense undergrowth.
DISTRIBUTION Breeds across much of northern Canada and Alaska except parts of far north and in western USA, wintering on Pacific coast and across southern USA east to Atlantic coast.
EUROPEAN STATUS Extreme vagrant: four records, three of which have occurred in

spring. Germany (2: May 1949; 24 Apr 1977; both individuals considered to be ship-assisted); Iceland (1: 5 Nov 1944); Ireland (1: 3-4 June 1961).

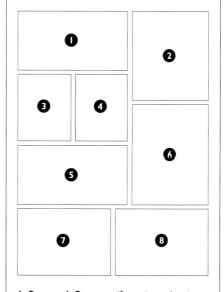

1 **Savannah Sparrow** (first-winter showing characteristics indicating subspecies *oblitus* or *labradorius*, Sept 1987, Fair Isle, Shetland, Britain)
2 **Savannah Sparrow** (showing characteristics of race *princeps*, Ipswich Sparrow, Apr 1982, Portland, Dorset, Britain)
3 **Savannah Sparrow** (first-winter showing characteristics indicating subspecies *oblitus* or *labradorius*, Sept 1987, Fair Isle, Shetland, Britain)
4 **Savannah Sparrow** (first-winter showing characteristics indicating subspecies *oblitus* or *labradorius*, Sept 1987, Fair Isle, Shetland, Britain)
5 **Lark Sparrow** (May 1991, Waxham, Norfolk, Britain)
6 **Lark Sparrow** (May 1991, Waxham, Norfolk, Britain)
7 **Lark Sparrow** (July 1981, Felixstowe, Suffolk, Britain)
8 **Fox Sparrow** (*nominate race, Nov, New York, USA*)

SONG SPARROW

Melospiza melodia L 15-18 cm (6-7.25 in)
DESCRIPTION Most likely to be confused with Savannah Sparrow, but has noticeably longer, more rounded tail, warmer, darker plumage and no yellow in supercilium. Like that species has many variable races in native Nearctic, but essentially identified by following characters: narrow pale greyish median crown-stripe flanked by broad rufous-brown lateral crown-stripes; whitish or pale grey supercilium; relatively pale grey-buff ear-coverts edged above and below by darker rufous borders; blackish-streaked grey-brown upperparts and whitish underparts with heavy dark streaking running up to blackish malar stripe, and often converging to form distinct dark spot in centre of breast. Wings show indistinct buffish bars on median and greater coverts. Long and rounded warm brown tail, pumped in flight, is distinctive in all races. Bill greyish, with paler lower mandible; legs pale flesh. Sexes alike, and first-years like adults. Birds become larger and darker in north-west North America, paler in south-west. Generally rather terrestrial.
VOICE Song, usually given from a perch, begins with several clear notes, followed by a buzzy phrase, then a trill. Calls include a House Sparrow-like *chirup* and a high-pitched *tsii* alarm note.
HABITAT Favours thickets, scrub, woodland edge, areas of cover in farmland, large gardens and other well-vegetated areas, but not forest; in west also on coasts and saltmarsh.
DISTRIBUTION Breeds across southern Canada and northern and western USA, on Pacific coast from Aleutians to Mexico and in central Mexico. Most northern birds vacate breeding areas, wintering south to Mexico, Gulf coast and Florida.
EUROPEAN STATUS Very rare vagrant: eight records, mainly in spring. Britain (7); Norway (1: 11 May 1975).

WHITE-CROWNED SPARROW

Zonotrichia leucophrys L 18 cm (7.25 in)
DESCRIPTION Rather slimline, long-tailed greyish sparrow with streaked upperparts and striking head pattern. Adult of nominate eastern race has white median crown-stripe and broad supercilium contrasting with bold black lateral crown-stripes and eyestripes which converge in front of eye; in other races (except northern *oriantha*) loral area is pale. Sides of head, nape and underparts otherwise rather uniformly grey, only slightly paler on throat, and entirely unstreaked. Upperparts grey with dark streaking, except on rump; wings blackish with rufous or buff edging, and white tips to greater and median coverts form two narrow wing-bars. Tail dark brown, with no white in outer feathers. Bill pinkish; legs dark flesh. Sexes similar; first-winter resembles adult, but has browner cast to grey plumage, especially on ear-coverts, and weaker and less contrasting striped head pattern.
VOICE Variable song consists of several whistling notes followed by a twittering trill, given from a prominent perch. Calls include *tsit* and a sharp *pzit*, likened to alarm note of Pied Flycatcher.
HABITAT Found in a variety of open and more wooded habitats with at least some undergrowth, often near water; in some parts of range occurs in towns.
DISTRIBUTION Breeds in Alaska, northern and western Canada and western USA. Also occurs on west coast of North America in winter, but most winter across southern USA to Atlantic coast except in south-east.
EUROPEAN STATUS Extreme vagrant: five records. Britain (2: 15-16 May 1977; 22 May 1977); France (1: 25 Aug 1965); Iceland (1: 4-6 Oct 1978); Netherlands (1: Dec 1981-Feb 1982). Additionally, one category D record from France (25 Aug 1965), and another from Germany relating to bird considered of doubtful provenance.

WHITE-THROATED SPARROW

Zonotrichia albicollis L 17 cm (6.75 in)
DESCRIPTION Appears somewhat stockier, less elongated and more round-headed than similarly-plumaged White-crowned Sparrow. Head pattern of adult recalls that species, with white median crown-stripe, black lateral crown-stripes and eye-stripe, and white supercilium, but latter is bright yellow, not white, in front of eye; in 'tan phase', head stripes are also grey-buff instead of white. Sides of neck and underparts are greyish, but throat is clearly demarcated and contrastingly white; underparts become paler on belly and sometimes show buffer and indistinctly streaked flanks. Browner, streaked upperparts are very similar in appearance to Dunnock. Relatively long tail is blackish-brown with pale edges, but has no white in outer feathers. Bill greyish-black, with paler lower mandible; legs flesh. Sexes alike, and first-winters similar to adults except in always showing tan-striped head pattern. In all respects behaviour is Dunnock-like; unlike White-crowned Sparrow, which is much more obliging and has character more like Reed Bunting, White-throated is a quiet, retiring species which is often hard to observe, retreating into cover when disturbed.
VOICE Song is a clear series of whistles, with first two notes higher-pitched. Has a lisping *tseet* call.
HABITAT Breeds in coniferous and mixed woodland with clearings, thickets, scrub and gardens in towns and cities. On migration in more bushy habitats than White-crowned Sparrow.
DISTRIBUTION In summer found across much of central, southern and eastern Canada and in north-eastern USA, where present year-round. Winter range includes eastern and southern USA west to Arizona, coastal California and northern Mexico.
EUROPEAN STATUS Very rare vagrant: 34 records, including some individuals which have taken up long stays of residence. Britain (17); Denmark (1: May 1976); Finland (2: 23 June-20 July 1967; 2 June 1972); Gibraltar (1: 18-25 May 1986); Iceland (6); Ireland (2: 3 Apr 1967; 1 Dec 1984-May 1985); Netherlands (4: Sept 1967; Oct 1967; Apr 1977; 10 June 1989); Sweden (1: 5 Dec 1963).

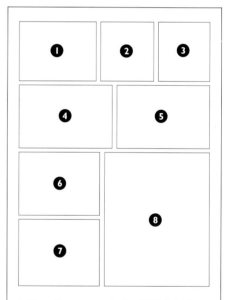

1 **Song Sparrow** (male, Apr 1989, Fair Isle, Shetland, Britain)
2 **Song Sparrow** (Oct 1994, Seaforth, Merseyside, Britain)
3 **Song Sparrow** (male, Apr 1979, Fair Isle, Shetland, Britain)
4 **White-crowned Sparrow** (first-winter, Oct 1995*, Seaforth, Merseyside, Britain)
5 **White-crowned Sparrow** (first-winter, Oct 1995*, Seaforth, Merseyside, Britain)
6 **White-throated Sparrow** (first-winter, Dec 1984, Belfast, Co Down, Ireland)
7 **White-throated Sparrow** (first-winter, Feb 1993, Market Rasen, Lincolnshire, Britain)
8 **White-throated Sparrow** (adult, June 1992, Trimley St Mary, Suffolk, Britain)

DARK-EYED JUNCO

Junco hyemalis L 14-16 cm (5.5-6.5 in)
DESCRIPTION Variable species occurring in a number of distinct plumages in its native North America. Individuals of vagrant nominate 'Slate-coloured' form are readily identifiable, with body entirely dusky or slate-grey except for white on belly, undertail-coverts and outer feathers of long tail. Adult male is greyest, adult female slightly paler and browner; first-winters correspond in general plumage coloration to respective adults, but usually have retained juvenile tertials (and occasionally some greater coverts) which have browner edges and often paler tips. In all plumages bill is ivory or pink, in winter with dark tip; legs usually pinkish or brownish. Rather tame; tail often held cocked and flicked when feeding on ground.
VOICE Song is a pleasant, bell-like trill on one pitch. Calls include a metallic *clink*, a *chek* alarm note and a twittering flight call.
HABITAT Breeds chiefly in coniferous forest, and also mixed woodland, favouring clearings and edge; in winter often found in more open areas.
DISTRIBUTION Nominate *hyemalis* breeds in Alaska, across much of Canada except far north and south-west, and in north-east USA, with most wintering south of breeding range. Other forms breed chiefly in western USA.
EUROPEAN STATUS Very rare vagrant: 24 records, mainly in winter and spring. Britain (16); Denmark (1: 13 Dec 1980, kept in captivity until died 18 Feb 1993); Gibraltar (1: 18-25 May 1986); Iceland (1: 6 Nov 1955); Ireland (1: 30 May 1905); Netherlands (1: Feb 1962); Norway (2: 4 Dec 1987, two; 18 May 1989); Poland (1: 4 May 1963). In addition, one record from Italy (28 Nov 1914) relates to bird of unknown origin.

BLACK-FACED BUNTING

Emberiza spodocephala L 14-16 cm (5.5-6.5 in)
DESCRIPTION Breeding male patterned with grey head and upper breast darkening to almost blackish on lores and throat, contrasting bicoloured bill with pink lower and blackish upper mandibles, and pale yellow underparts with narrow rufous streaking on flanks. Upperparts brown, streaked blackish on mantle, and blackish-brown wings edged rufous or brown, with pale tips to median and greater coverts forming double wing-bars; grey-brown rump is unstreaked, and relatively long, dark brown tail has white outer feathers. Female much more nondescript, lacking hooded appearance of male and usually with pale supercilium, submoustachial stripe and throat, and darker ear-coverts and malar stripe; some can show greyer tone on head and breast, but lores never blackish and underparts whiter than on male. First-winter male resembles female, but greyer crown and neck sides give Dunnock-like character to plumage; first-winter female lacks greyer tones and is rather featureless. Longish bill has straight culmen; legs pinkish-brown.

VOICE Song is a variable and short trilling sequence. Call is a sharp, thin *tzit*.
HABITAT Favours well-vegetated damp areas in the breeding season, and occurs in more open habitats, including cultivations, in winter.
DISTRIBUTION Breeds from central Siberia eastwards to Japan, Korea and north-eastern China, with separate population in central China. Winters chiefly from Nepal eastwards to south China, and also in Japan and Korea.
EUROPEAN STATUS Extreme vagrant: six records, two in spring and four in late autumn. Britain (1: 8 Mar-24 Apr 1994*); Finland (1: 2 Nov 1981); Germany (2: 5 Nov 1910; 23 May 1980); Netherlands (2: 16 Nov 1986; 28 Oct 1993).

PINE BUNTING

Emberiza leucocephalos L 17 cm (6.75 in)
DESCRIPTION Eastern counterpart of Yellowhammer. Males have diagnostic head pattern of white crown, black lateral crown-stripes and broad chestnut supercilium, lores, throat and moustachial area, latter continuing around neck sides and white ear-coverts to join supercilium at rear. Upperparts rufous-brown, streaked darker; wings essentially brownish-black, with narrow buff edges to primaries but otherwise edged rufous-brown, tipped paler on median and greater coverts. Longish tail is brown with white outer feathers. Underparts white with band of rufous mottling across breast and on flanks. Female very like drab, paler version of female Yellowhammer, differing chiefly in lack of yellow in plumage (Yellowhammer always has yellow on edges of outer tail feathers and outer primaries and on underwing-coverts), blacker-streaked crown (especially at sides), broader supercilium, streaked nape and whiter underparts. Bill dark brown on upper mandible, blue-grey on lower; legs flesh-brown. First-years very like respective adults, but young male has broader pale fringes on head. Hybridises with Yellowhammer in western Siberia, with offspring very occasionally reaching Europe; hybrids of both sexes usually show at least some yellow or obvious characters of both species.
VOICE Song and calls very like those of Yellowhammer.
HABITAT Breeds in open coniferous and mixed woodland and forest edge; in winter in more open habitat, often including arable land.
DISTRIBUTION Breeds in north-west China (where resident) and across Siberia west to the Urals. Winters northern China, parts of southern Central Asia and north-west India, and as far west as Israel; see also Italy (below).
EUROPEAN STATUS Rare but regular on passage and in winter in Italy. Accidental elsewhere: Austria (7+); Belgium (15); Britain (29); Bulgaria; Czech Republic (2: Oct 1889; 23 Oct 1962); Denmark (1: Nov-Dec 1973); Finland (4: 4 Nov 1968; 8-9 Nov 1986; 2-4 Apr 1988; 8 Oct 1994); France (14); Germany (6); Gibraltar (1: 2 May 1987, pair); Greece (4: Oct 1977; Nov 1980; Nov 1981; *c* 1986); Hungary

(1: Jan 1986); Iceland (1: 30 Oct 1944); Netherlands (26*); Norway (6); Poland (1: 16 May-24 June 1994, breeding with Yellowhammer); Slovenia (13+); Spain (3 records of 4 birds: most recent on 14 Nov 1989); Sweden (8); Switzerland (2: 5 Nov 1989; 12-18 July 1994).

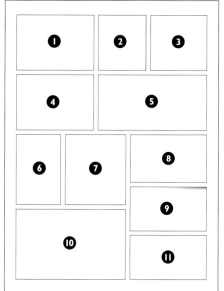

1 **Dark-eyed Junco** (male, Dec 1989, Portland, Dorset, Britain)
2 **Dark-eyed Junco** (male, Jan 1990, Portland, Dorset, Britain)
3 **Dark-eyed Junco** (male, Feb 1990, Church Crookham, Hampshire, Britain)
4 **Black-faced Bunting** (Jan 1987, Lekkerkerk, Netherlands)
5 **Black-faced Bunting** (first-winter male, Apr 1994, Pennington, Manchester, Britain)
6 **Black-faced Bunting** (Nov 1981, Vänö, Finland)
7 **Black-faced Bunting** (first-winter male, Apr 1994, Pennington, Manchester, Britain)
8 **Pine Bunting** (first-year male, Nov 1987, Bloemendaal, Netherlands)
9 **Pine Bunting** (adult summer male, June 1994, Biebrza Marshes, Poland)
10 **Pine Bunting** (female, Feb 1990, Big Waters, Northumberland, Britain)
11 **Pine Bunting** (male, Feb 1992, Dagenham, Essex, Britain)

CINEREOUS BUNTING

Emberiza cineracea L 16 cm (6.5 in)
DESCRIPTION Pale, plain and unobtrusive bunting. Breeding male of nominate western race has dull yellow-green head (brightest yellow on throat), grey mantle streaked dark brown, blackish-brown flight feathers edged paler, buff-tipped median and greater coverts forming two indistinct wing-bars, and unstreaked greyish underparts which fade to white on belly and undertail-coverts. Female drabber and more grey-brown above and below, with yellow wash on throat, faint malar stripe and indistinct streaking on breast and flanks. Breeding male of eastern race *semenowi* has brighter yellow head and yellow underparts, being greyish only on breast sides; female also yellow-washed below. First-winters of both races similar to respective females, but browner and more prominently streaked below. Has distinct pale eye-ring, unstreaked grey-brown rump and white tail corners in all plumages. Bill greyish; legs flesh-coloured.
VOICE Song said to resemble more ringing version of Ortolan Bunting's. Calls include a soft metallic *tsik* and a clear *tyeeh*.
HABITAT Frequents dry, rocky terrain with scattered scrub and occasional trees, often in hilly areas; on migration and in winter also on cultivated land and in semi-desert.
DISTRIBUTION Very restricted range, in summer occurring only in eastern Aegean and western Turkey (*cineracea*), and discontinuously from south-east Turkey to western Iran (*semenowi*). Migrates through Middle East and Persian Gulf to winter in north-east Sudan and Eritrea, and in south-west Saudi Arabia and Yemen. World population estimated within range of only 550-5,100 pairs.
EUROPEAN STATUS Breeds Greece, where known range confined to islands of Chios and Lesbos; at least three singing males on Corfu in June 1991 may indicate range expansion or possibility of other breeding sites in the region. Accidental elsewhere: Germany (1: 1-5 June 1877).

YELLOW-BROWED BUNTING

Emberiza chrysophrys L 15 cm (6 in)
DESCRIPTION Similar in structure to Reed Bunting but slightly stouter, with shorter tail. Most striking feature is boldly patterned head, with blackish lateral crown-stripes, eye-stripe and moustachial stripe offset by narrow white median crown-stripe (which broadens towards nape), white supercilium which is distinctly yellow in front of eye, blackish malar stripe and white submoustachial stripe and throat. Ear-coverts are brownish, bordered with black and with black and white spots at the rear. Upperparts brown with neat black streaking which extends onto rump; scapulars often with rufous fringes. Narrow but distinct double white wing-bars formed by pale tips to greater and median coverts; outer tail feathers also white. Underparts are off-white, with blackish streaking on breast extending down flanks, which may be suffused brownish. Relatively stout bill largely dark on upper mandible and pinkish on lower, with straight culmen; legs pink. Sexes similar; non-breeding adult and first-winter differ chiefly in weaker head pattern.
VOICE Song begins with a short, drawn-out phrase, followed by two high-pitched notes and a variable ending. Call is short *tic* or *tsip*, recalling Little Bunting.
HABITAT Occurs chiefly in clearings and edge of mixed forest in breeding season, and in more open areas in winter.
DISTRIBUTION Breeds central Siberia south to Lake Baikal, wintering in central and south-east China.
EUROPEAN STATUS Extreme vagrant: seven records. Belgium (1: 20 Oct 1966); Britain (4: 19 Oct 1975; 12-23 Oct 1980; 22-23 Sept 1992; 19-22 Oct 1994); France (1: *c* 1830); Luxembourg (1: spring 1863); Netherlands (1: 19 Oct 1982).

LITTLE BUNTING

Emberiza pusilla L 13 cm (5.25 in)
DESCRIPTION Small, compact and relatively short-tailed bunting, with characteristic head pattern in all plumages being the best distinction from Reed Bunting. Median crown-stripe, fore-supercilium and ear-coverts chestnut, latter with black surround, but on some whole face and throat suffused chestnut in breeding season; black lateral crown-stripes and pale eye-ring always distinctive, though whole head pattern somewhat paler in winter. As with Reed Bunting, black malar stripe reaches base of bill, but unlike that species black moustachial stripe stops short on side of cheek. Greyish-buff upperparts are heavily streaked darker, with greyish rump more diffusely streaked. Wings show whitish tips to median coverts and pale tips to greater coverts. Underparts whitish, finely streaked darker on breast and flanks. Pointed pinkish-grey bill has darker and straight culmen; legs flesh or reddish-brown. Sexes alike; first-winters much as non-breeding adults.
VOICE Rather variable short, buzzy song can recall Reed Bunting. Call is a Robin-like *tzik*.
HABITAT Breeds in damp open taiga forest with understorey of dwarf birch; in winter found in more open terrain, including arable land, woodland edge and marshes.
DISTRIBUTION Summer range extends from northern Scandinavia eastwards across northern Russia and Siberia to the Pacific coast. Winters in southern and eastern China and northern South-East Asia west to Nepal.
EUROPEAN STATUS Breeds Finland (5,000-10,000 pairs), but numbers in Scandinavia variable; probably breeds annually Norway and has bred Sweden (*c* 175 records in total). Accidental elsewhere, with records mainly in autumn, few in spring and occasional instances of overwintering: Austria (9); Belgium (30); Britain (many annually, eg 21 in 1992 and 53 in 1993: *c* 326 from 1984 to 1993); Bulgaria; Channel Islands (5); Czech Republic (1: 31 Jan 1981); Denmark (40); Estonia (5: most recent on 16 and 30 May 1992); Faeroes; France (54); Germany (many, eg 140 recorded Heligoland); Greece (1: 1 Feb 1964); Hungary (2: 7 Nov 1988; 22 Oct 1990); Iceland (5: 14 Nov 1965; 30 Oct 1980; 8 May 1988; 3 Oct 1992; 18 Nov 1994); Ireland (22); Italy; Latvia (2: 5 Oct 1972; 3 Oct 1984); Netherlands (63+); Poland (9); Portugal (1: 15 Nov 1991); Slovenia (6); Spain (9); Switzerland (12).

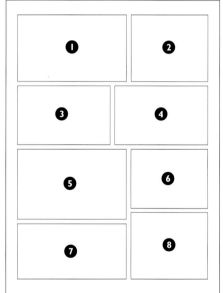

1 **Cinereous Bunting** *(Apr, Turkey)*
2 **Yellow-browed Bunting** (Oct 1994, St Agnes, Isles of Scilly, Britain)
3 **Yellow-browed Bunting** (Oct 1994, St Agnes, Isles of Scilly, Britain)
4 **Yellow-browed Bunting** (Oct 1994, St Agnes, Isles of Scilly, Britain)
5 **Little Bunting** (Nov 1993, Filey, North Yorkshire, Britain)
6 **Little Bunting** (Oct 1994, Heligoland, Germany)
7 **Little Bunting** (Jan 1988, Doel, Belgium)
8 **Little Bunting** (Apr 1992, Katwijk, Netherlands)

CHESTNUT BUNTING

Emberiza rutila L 14 cm (5.5 in)

DESCRIPTION Unique plumage of male instantly recognisable, with chestnut head, upperparts and upper breast contrasting sharply with pale yellow belly and white undertail-coverts. Plumage otherwise relieved only by pale eye-ring, brown flight feathers (pale-edged on primaries, chestnut-edged on secondaries), dark inner webs to tertials, brown tail and dusky flank streaking. In non-breeding plumage chestnut upperparts show pale fringing. Rather nondescript greyish-buff female, with streaked mantle, yellow belly and chestnut rump, recalls female Yellowhammer, but shows less heavy streaking on breast and flanks, shorter tail with little or no white in outer feathers, has different bill shape and never any yellow on throat. First-winters very like female, but young males usually show at least some trace of chestnut on head or breast. Rather conical bill is brownish or bluish-horn; legs pale brown.

VOICE Variable song has phrasing recalling Tree Pipit. Call is similar to *tzik* of Little Bunting.

HABITAT Frequents open forest with shrubby ground cover in the breeding season; in winter occurs in open woodland and arable land and other open ground with adjacent cover.

DISTRIBUTION Breeds in southern Siberia, northern Mongolia and northern China, wintering in south China and much of northern South-East Asia west to north-east India.

EUROPEAN STATUS Extreme vagrant: three records in autumn. Netherlands (1: 5 Nov 1937); Norway (1: 13-15 Oct 1974); Slovenia (1: 10 Oct 1987). Additional birds recorded in Belgium (1) and Britain (5, including 4 in June and a fifth on 2-5 Sept 1994) regarded as of uncertain origin.

YELLOW-BREASTED BUNTING

Emberiza aureola L 15 cm (6 in)

DESCRIPTION Boldly-patterned male unmistakable in breeding plumage, with black face and throat, chestnut crown, nape, upperparts and breast band, and bold white 'shoulder' patch above white-tipped chestnut greater coverts and darker flight feathers; bright yellow underparts divided on upper breast by breast band, with blackish streaking on flanks, whitish undertail-coverts and white in outer tail. In non-breeding plumage, has extensive pale fringing on darker areas and yellow throat. Breeding adult female much less striking, but still distinctive: essentially straw-coloured above, with darker lateral crown-stripes, broad pale supercilium, blackish border to ear-coverts, very indistinct malar stripe, narrow white wing-bar, dark streaking on upperparts and finer streaking on yellow-washed underparts. In non-breeding plumage unstreaked below and yellower. Autumn juveniles occurring in Europe are very like female, with streaked breast and, on some, a more distinct malar stripe. Bill has greyish upper mandible and pinkish lower mandible.

VOICE Song is a very variable jingle. Call is a metallic *tic*.

HABITAT Inhabits damp meadows with scattered trees and undergrowth in breeding season, moving to more open habitats, including arable land and rice fields, in winter.

DISTRIBUTION Breeding range extends from the Baltic in the west across northern Eurasia to Japan in the east, wintering in south China and much of South-East Asia west to Nepal.

EUROPEAN STATUS Breeds Finland (c 50 pairs 1995, declining). Accidental elsewhere: Belgium (1: 2 Sept 1928); Britain (162); Channel Islands (1: 14 Sept 1978); Czech Republic (2: 29 July 1931; 10 July 1984); Denmark (4: Aug 1984; 19 June 1990; 30 Aug 1991; 10 June 1993); Estonia (3: 13 June 1972, pair; 15 May 1977; 9 May 1984); France (5+); Germany (16); Greece (4: 15 Jan 1956; May 1961; 5 Sept 1974; 17 Sept 1976); Iceland (1: 22 Nov 1958); Ireland (3: 18 Sept 1959; 11-20 Sept 1983; 18 Sept 1985); Italy (c 20); Latvia (1: 8 June 1985); Netherlands (8); Norway (24); Poland (5: 7 Dec 1886; 25 Nov 1929; 30 Aug 1963; 30 Oct 1970; 18-19 July 1992); Spain (1: 7 Nov 1987); Sweden (30).

PALLAS'S REED BUNTING

Emberiza pallasi L 13 cm (5.25 in)

DESCRIPTION Smaller, paler version of Reed Bunting, which it resembles closely. Adult male in breeding plumage has all-black bill, same black head-and-throat pattern, with broadening white submoustachial stripe and white collar, but has whiter underparts with little or no streaking. Upperparts colder-toned than Reed Bunting's, appearing blackish with pale fringes and white 'tramlines', and with wear becoming even darker and contrasting strongly with greyish-white rump. Best distinction in all plumages from all races of Reed Bunting is diagnostic colour of lesser coverts (though often difficult to see): on Pallas's they are blue-grey (adult males) or grey-brown (females), on Reed always rufous. Non-breeding male and female paler and buffer than respective plumages of Reed, with wholly or largely unstreaked underparts, very pale rump and double wing-bars, less distinct supercilium, paler ear-coverts and two-toned bill showing pinkish (not bluish-grey) lower mandible. First-winters much as respective non-breeding adult, but young male has grey-brown lesser coverts. Legs flesh-brown.

VOICE Song is a shrill, repeated *srrie srrie srrie srrie srrie srrie*. Calls also distinct from Reed Bunting's, including Tree Sparrow-like *tsleep* and in flight a faint *preep*, recalling flight call of Richard's Pipit.

HABITAT Inhabits variety of open, often damp, habitats, from thickets and scrub in river valleys and wet meadows to tundra and steppe; in winter also in reedbeds, rice fields and arable land.

DISTRIBUTION Breeds chiefly from north-east European Russia eastwards across northern Siberia to Kamchatka, and in southern Siberia and northern Mongolia (and perhaps in intervening area). Winters largely in northern and eastern China, also western China, Ussuriland and Japan.

EUROPEAN STATUS Extreme vagrant: three autumn records. Britain (3: 29 Sept-11 Oct 1976; 17-18 Sept 1981; 17 Oct 1990).

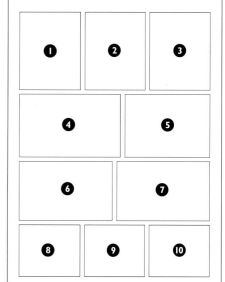

1 **Chestnut Bunting** (first-summer male, June 1986, Fair Isle, Shetland, Britain)
2 **Chestnut Bunting** (female, Sept 1994, Out Skerries, Shetland, Britain)
3 **Chestnut Bunting** (female, Sept 1994, Out Skerries, Shetland, Britain)
4 **Yellow-breasted Bunting** (first-winter female, Aug 1991, Westernschouwen, Netherlands)
5 **Yellow-breasted Bunting** (first-winter female, Sept 1993, Landguard, Suffolk, Britain)
6 **Yellow-breasted Bunting** (first-winter female, Sept 1991, Fair Isle, Shetland, Britain)
7 **Yellow-breasted Bunting** (first-winter female, Sept 1993, Portland, Dorset, Britain)
8 **Pallas's Reed Bunting** (first-winter male, Oct 1990, Icklesham, East Sussex, Britain)
9 **Pallas's Reed Bunting** (first-winter male, Oct 1990, Icklesham, East Sussex, Britain)
10 **Pallas's Reed Bunting** (first-winter female, Sept 1981, Fair Isle, Shetland, Britain)

DICKCISSEL

Spiza americana L 16 cm (6.5 in)
DESCRIPTION A large Nearctic seed-eater with distinctive head pattern. Breeding male has grey head, with yellowish supercilium, lores and eye-crescent forming prominent 'spectacles'; striking appearance completed by heavy bill, deep black bib with white chin and yellowish submoustachial stripes. Brown upperparts streaked darker, and blackish wing feathers edged brown except for rufous lesser and median coverts, forming contrasting 'shoulder' patch. Underparts pale yellow, greyer on flanks. Plumage of breeding male may recall much smaller Dead Sea Sparrow, which see for differences; in winter, black throat masked by paler feather edges. Female duller, with browner head faintly streaked on crown, less yellow in face pattern, no black on throat, smaller and duller 'shoulder' patch, and often fine streaking on yellowish flanks and breast; first-years more nondescript still, with little or no yellow on head and underparts and, on young females, less contrasting rufous wing-coverts and more streaking on underparts. Highly gregarious, especially on migration; in North America out-of-range migrants often associate with House Sparrows.
VOICE Species gets English name from its song, *dic dic sss-sss-sss*. Chief call, given in flight, is a buzzer-like *bzrrrt*, vaguely recalling a loud Long-tailed Tit.
HABITAT Typically occurs in open weedy fields, meadows, crops and prairies; visits feeders in winter.
DISTRIBUTION Breeds across central USA in some numbers, though local populations fluctuate and species is apparently declining east of Appalachians. Most migrate to winter in Mexico and Central America south to northern South America, though also recorded in winter on west and especially east North American coasts.
EUROPEAN STATUS Extreme vagrant: one record. Norway (1: 29 July 1981).

ROSE-BREASTED GROSBEAK

Pheucticus ludovicianus L 18-21 cm (7.25-8.5 in)
DESCRIPTION Size of Corn Bunting, but with heavier, triangular bill and longer tail. Adult male unmistakable, with black head and upperparts, pale bill, deep pink breast patch, white underparts and rump, and black wings and tail patterned with white. Equally striking in flight, with black-framed underwing flashing deep pink on coverts and white on bases of primaries. In autumn like pinker version of adult female, which is brown above and buffish-white below, streaked darker on mantle, breast and flanks; head pattern striking, with buff median crown-stripe, dark lateral crown-stripes and cheek patch, and broad off-white supercilium. Underwing-coverts yellow, often with some pink. First-winters (those occurring in Europe) are very like female, but with fresh coverts; these are blacker on young male, which, like adult male, shows bolder white

median-covert bar and pink underwing-coverts. In flight, shape and actions may recall Hawfinch.
VOICE Song is soft and melodious. Call is a far-carrying high-pitched *peek* or *kink*, likened to a creaking gate.
HABITAT Favours open mixed and deciduous woodland, especially clearings and edge, as well as parks and large gardens with tall trees; often in vicinity of water.
DISTRIBUTION Breeds in central and southern Canada, and in USA from Mid-West east to New England. Long-distance migrant, wintering in Central America and northernmost South America.
EUROPEAN STATUS Very rare vagrant: 31 records, chiefly in October but two in spring. Britain (16); Channel Islands (2: 26 Sept 1975; 10-13 Oct 1987); France (1: 15 Oct 1985); Ireland (7); Norway (2: 13-19 May 1977; Oct 1977); Spain (1: 17 Oct 1982); Slovenia (1: 29 Oct 1976); Sweden (1: 10 Oct 1988; another on 10-11 May 1992 considered to be an escape). Also, one in Germany (28 Sept 1993) considered to be an escape.

INDIGO BUNTING

Passerina cyanea L 12-13 cm (4.75-5.25 in)
DESCRIPTION Small, rather dainty Nearctic bunting. Deep blue plumage of breeding male unmistakable; in close views, dark centres to flight feathers, blackish lores and pattern of rather strong bill (blackish on upper mandible, paler on lower) are distinguishable, but at range or in poor light looks all dark. After moult in late summer male becomes much browner above and paler below, but some blue is always visible at least on flight feathers and tail, and increasing in extent with wear. Adult female is altogether plainer, essentially warm brown above and buffer below, but with buff-fringed darker wing feathers showing traces of dull blue on lesser coverts, primaries and secondaries, and also has some blue in tail; has subtly darker malar stripe, pinkish bill and diffuse breast streaking. First-winters much as adult female, but often with narrow white wing-bar and, on young male, darker malar stripe and some blue also on head and body feathering.
VOICE Song, often uttered late into season, comprises series of high-pitched phrases. Chief call is a sharp *pwit*.
HABITAT Occurs in woodland edge, clearings and overgrown areas with trees; outside breeding season sometimes in more open terrain.
DISTRIBUTION Breeds across eastern USA and in south-easternmost Canada, wintering chiefly in Central America, and in smaller numbers in southern Florida, the Caribbean and northernmost South America.
EUROPEAN STATUS Very rare vagrant: at least seven records, although also kept fairly commonly in captivity and occasional European records (eg in Britain, Finland, Germany and Sweden) considered to relate to birds of uncertain origin or probable escapes. Denmark

(1: 5 Aug 1987); Iceland (2: 27 Oct 1951; 20 Oct 1985); Ireland (1: 9-19 Oct 1985); Netherlands (2: June-July 1983; 10-23 Mar 1989); Poland (1: 26 June 1982).

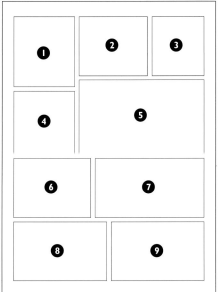

1 **Dickcissel** (*adult male, July, Iowa, USA*)
2 **Rose-breasted Grosbeak** (first-year female, Oct 1987, Cape Clear Island, Co Cork, Ireland)
3 **Rose-breasted Grosbeak** (first-year female, Oct 1987, Cape Clear Island, Co Cork, Ireland)
4 **Rose-breasted Grosbeak** (first-winter male, Oct 1993, Tresco, Isles of Scilly, Britain)
5 **Rose-breasted Grosbeak** (first-winter male, Oct 1993, Tresco, Isles of Scilly, Britain)
6 **Indigo Bunting** (adult winter male, Mar 1989, Amsterdam, Netherlands)
7 **Indigo Bunting** (adult winter male, Oct 1988*, Holkham, Norfolk, Britain)
8 **Indigo Bunting** (first-winter, Oct 1985, Cape Clear Island, Co Cork, Ireland)
9 **Indigo Bunting** (first-winter, Oct 1985, Cape Clear Island, Co Cork, Ireland)

BOBOLINK

Dolichonyx oryzivorus L 17-19 cm (6.75-7.5 in)
DESCRIPTION Breeding male strikingly marked, with black head and underparts, broad yellow-buff hindneck patch, black mantle and wings contrasting with elongated white 'shoulder' patches, and white lower back, rump and uppertail-coverts above black tail. Vagrants to Europe in autumn are in straw-coloured plumage with patterning recalling Aquatic Warbler, showing buffish median crown-stripe and black lateral crown-stripes, plain face with pale lores and blackish rear eye-stripe, pale braces on mantle and darker streaking on breast sides and flanks. Adults of both sexes are alike in autumn, but first-winter birds are typically buffer, often with hint of whitish median-covert bar. Deep-based but pointed bill is pinkish-brown with darker culmen in all plumages except breeding male, when may appear blackish; legs pinkish-brown. In size and shape often likened to slim-necked version of Corn Bunting. Diagnostically, all tail feathers are pointed at tips.
VOICE Loud, bubbling song, often given in flight, is origin of species' name. Has distinctive *enk* or *enghh* flight call, rather nasal and somewhat reminiscent of flight call of Brambling.
HABITAT Frequents prairies, meadows and grasslands in the breeding season, and also marshes and crop fields at other times. On migration, often hard to locate owing to unobtrusive habit of feeding among low vegetation.
DISTRIBUTION Breeds chiefly across plains of North America in broad band from Nova Scotia and New England west to the Rockies, with smaller populations further west. Long-distance migrant, wintering in South America south to northern Argentina.
EUROPEAN STATUS Very rare vagrant: 21 records. Britain (15); France (1: 15-16 Oct 1987); Gibraltar (1: 11-16 May 1984); Ireland (2: 12-14 Oct 1971; 13-24 Sept 1982); Italy (1: 18 Sept 1989); Norway (1: 6-8 Nov 1977). A further record from Germany is considered to have involved an escape from captivity.

BROWN-HEADED COWBIRD

Molothrus ater L 19 cm (7.5 in)
DESCRIPTION Reminiscent of a small Common Starling with an elongated, finch-like bill. Male looks all dark at range, but in closer views is distinctive with metallic green-black body and contrasting brown head. Female more nondescript, with rather uniform dark brown body, pale throat and indistinct streaking on underparts. Eye, bill and legs blackish in all plumages. Highly gregarious, often in large flocks; parasites nests of other species.
VOICE Calls include a variety of squeaky whistles and a harsh rattle. Song is a squeaky gurgling.
HABITAT Typically found in grassland, fields, thickets, woodland and forest edge, but also commonly in town parks and suburbs.
DISTRIBUTION Numerous breeder across much

of North America outside Arctic Circle, northernmost birds retiring south in winter. Population has expanded rapidly in recent decades, reaching pest proportions in some areas.
EUROPEAN STATUS Extreme vagrant: two spring records. Britain (1: 24 Apr 1988); Norway (1: 1 June 1987, dead).

YELLOW-HEADED BLACKBIRD

Xanthocephalus xanthocephalus L 20-27 cm (8-10.75 in)
DESCRIPTION Adult male unmistakable, with narrow black mask, bright yellow head and breast, white primary coverts forming prominent wing patch, and otherwise entirely black body. Smaller female is browner, with yellow restricted to throat and face (where may appear buffer), often contrasting with brownish cheeks and malar stripe; also has white streaking on belly and no white in wing. First-year birds resemble adult female, but both sexes show white tips to primary coverts; young male is usually larger and more extensively yellow than young female. Actions and shape recall a large starling more than a thrush, but heavier, deep-based bill and longer, rounded tail give bird a distinctive jizz of its own. Gregarious in its natural range.
VOICE Song comprises a range of grating, guttural notes, and a hoarse *krack* or *croak* call note.
HABITAT Favours reedbeds and marshes, but also occurs in open arable country, particularly crop fields.
DISTRIBUTION Breeds in North America west of the Great Lakes north to central Canada, wintering in south-western USA and Mexico. Regularly wanders to east coast and has straggled to Greenland.
EUROPEAN STATUS Extreme vagrant: three records. Denmark (1: Oct 1918); Iceland (1: 23-24 July 1983); Norway (1: 30 May 1979). Additionally, several records from Britain and one each from France and Sweden considered to relate to birds of uncertain origin.

BALTIMORE ORIOLE

Icterus galbula L 17-20 cm (6.75-8 in)
DESCRIPTION Size of Common Starling, with proportionately slimmer body, deeper-based conical bill and longer tail. Adult male unmistakable, with black hood and upperparts, bright orange underparts, 'shoulder' patch, rump and dark-centred tail, and broad single white wing-bar. Most occurring in Europe are in duller but still distinctive female/first-winter-type plumage, which is variably yellowish-green on head, breast, rump and tail, paler or whitish on belly, greyish-brown on upperparts with indistinct darker streaking, and with prominent double white wing-bars, and white tertial edges on otherwise dark grey flight feathers. In adult plumage, some well-marked females can approach male-type patterning and brightness. Formerly lumped with Bullock's Oriole *I bullocki* under Northern Oriole.

VOICE Has fluty song of irregular musical notes. Commonest call (occasionally given by vagrants) is a low churring rattle reminiscent of a quiet Magpie – a useful clue to presence of a bird hidden in cover.
HABITAT Frequents open mixed or deciduous woodland, clearings, orchards, leafy suburbs and other areas with scattered trees. On migration can occur in low bushy cover in exposed sites.
DISTRIBUTION Breeds in south-eastern Canada and much of the USA from the Great Plains eastwards, but absent in summer from south-eastern states. Migratory in much of range, wintering chiefly from Mexico south to north-western South America, but in increasing numbers in southern and eastern USA.
EUROPEAN STATUS Very rare vagrant: 23 records, mostly in autumn, but at least three in spring and two instances of overwintering. Britain (18); Iceland (3: 8 Nov 1955; 8 Oct 1956; 15 Oct 1971); Netherlands (1: 14-18 Oct 1987); Norway (1: 13 May 1986).

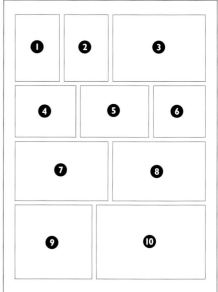

1 **Bobolink** (Oct 1991, St Mary's, Isles of Scilly, Britain)
2 **Bobolink** (Sept 1992, Portland, Dorset, Britain)
3 **Bobolink** (Sept 1991, Soar, Devon, Britain)
4 **Brown-headed Cowbird** (adult male, June, Manitoba, Canada)
5 **Yellow-headed Blackbird** (adult male, Apr 1990, Fair Isle, Shetland, Britain)
6 **Yellow-headed Blackbird** (adult male, May 1987, Yell, Shetland, Britain)
7 **Yellow-headed Blackbird** (adult male, Apr 1990, Fair Isle, Shetland, Britain)
8 **Baltimore Oriole** (first-winter male, Oct 1988, St Agnes, Isles of Scilly, Britain)
9 **Baltimore Oriole** (first-winter female, Apr 1989, Roch, Dyfed, Britain)
10 **Baltimore Oriole** (first-winter female, Apr 1989, Roch, Dyfed, Britain)

SPECIES RECORDED IN EUROPE BEFORE 1 JANUARY 1958 AND NOT SINCE

The following list gives records of those species recorded in Europe in a truly wild state before 1 January 1958 but not since (unless, for example, only at sea or as tideline corpses – see Appendix 3). This is not intended to be a complete list; in addition, some records are based on published reports and may not have been verified by the appropriate national rarities committee.

Black-capped Petrel *Pterodroma hasitata*
Britain (2: Mar or Apr 1850; 16 Dec 1984, dead).

Schrenk's Little Bittern *Ixobrychus eurhythmus*
Italy (1: 12 Nov 1912, caught).

Pallas's Fish Eagle *Haliaeetus leucoryphus*
Finland (2: c 1901; June 1926); Norway (1: 7 July 1949, shot); Poland (1: June 1943). In addition, a single recorded Germany, Denmark and the Netherlands (Sept-Oct 1976) may have been an escape.

Tawny Eagle *Aquila rapax*
Italy (2: 1876, 1898); Spain (1: winter 1877; perhaps at least one other subsequent record). Possibly also recorded Gibraltar.

Kittlitz's Plover *Charadrius pecuarius*
Norway (1: 14 May 1913, shot).

Eskimo Curlew *Numenius borealis*
Britain (6 records of 7 birds).

South Polar Skua *Catharacta maccormicki*
Faeroes (1: 24 Sept 1889, collected). A number of recent records from Britain remain under consideration.

White-eyed Gull *Larus leucophthalmus*
Greece (1: 19th century, collected).

Crested Auklet *Aethia cristatella*
Iceland (1: Aug 1912, collected at sea).

Parakeet Auklet *Cyclorrhynchus psittacula*
Sweden (1: Dec 1860, collected).

Spotted Sandgrouse *Pterocles senegallus*
Italy (1: 26 Apr 1909, two).

Chestnut-bellied Sandgrouse *Pterocles exustus*
Hungary (1: Aug 1863).

African Marsh Owl *Asio capensis*
Portugal; Spain.

Tickell's Thrush *Turdus unicolor*
Germany (1: 15 Oct 1932, collected).

Gray's Grasshopper Warbler *Locustella fasciolata*
Denmark (1: 25 Sept 1955); France (2: 26 Sept 1913; 17 Sept 1933).

Eastern Crowned Warbler *Phylloscopus coronatus*
Germany (1: 4 Oct 1843, collected).

Black-throated Green Warbler *Dendroica virens*
Germany (1: 19 Nov 1858); Iceland (1: 19 Sept 1984, dead on ship at sea).

Summer Tanager *Piranga rubra*
Britain (1: 11-25 September 1957).

ADDITIONAL RARE BREEDING BIRDS IN EUROPE

The following list details rare and generally sedentary species with a breeding population of less than 5,000 pairs in Europe which are not dealt with in the main systematic list, their countries of distribution (not including those where they may have been recorded as vagrants), and their total population range in the continent as estimated in Gibbons, Reid and Chapman (1993) or Tucker and Heath (1994),

Dalmatian Pelican *Pelecanus crispus*
Albania; Bulgaria; Greece; Romania. 450-560 pairs.

Eurasian Black Vulture *Aegypius monachus*
Greece; Spain. 910-1,014 pairs.

Barbary Partridge *Alectoris barbatus*
Gibraltar; Italy (Sardinia); Spain. 3,100-10,125 pairs.

Small Button-quail *Turnix sylvatica*
Spain. 5-10 pairs.

Purple Swamp-hen *Porphyrio porphyrio*
Italy; Portugal; Spain. 3,245-3,810 pairs.

Red-knobbed Coot *Fulica cristata*
Spain. 10-25 pairs.

Krüper's Nuthatch *Sitta krueperi*
Greece. 'Few hundred' pairs.

Corsican Nuthatch *Sitta whiteheadi*
France (Corsica). 2,000-3,000 pairs.

Scottish Crossbill *Loxia scotica*
Britain (Scotland). c 1,500 individuals.

CATEGORY D SPECIES AND ASSOCIATED RECORDS FROM EUROPE

The main systematic list of this book deals with those rare species which have been recorded in Europe since 1958 in a live and apparently wild state. Numerous other rare species have also occurred in Europe, but have been omitted from the main list for a variety of reasons. In addition to species recorded only prior to 1958 or as mainly sedentary breeding species – see Appendices 1 and 2 – there are a number of records which relate to species for which there is at least some likelihood that, despite the possibility of wild vagrancy, the individuals concerned may have been of captive origin (typically what are termed 'Category D' species – see Appendix 4 for definition in Britain). In addition to these species, there are those occurring only as dead birds or tideline corpses which may not have reached Europe while still alive, known ship-assisted or released vagrants which have benefitted from man's assistance, records for which insufficient documentation remains in existence, and those species recorded only in offshore waters.

The following list is not exhaustive, but includes many known or published occurrences (and not necessarily accepted category D records) of a number of species of uncertain origin recorded in various parts of Europe; those strongly suspected of having occurred only as escapes or from introduced populations are not listed. The species below are included in this appendix rather than the main systematic list solely for the purposes of this book, and no judgement of the veracity of the records or otherwise, or alteration to their status on national lists, should be inferred.

Cape Petrel *Daption capense*
Britain (1: 1879); France (1: Oct 1844, shot); Gibraltar (1: 20 June 1979); Ireland (1: Oct 1881); Italy (1: Sept 1964); Netherlands (1: 1930, skull only).

Red-billed Tropicbird *Phaethon aethereus*
Portugal (1: 13 Aug 1988, at sea). In addition, corpses have been found on a ship arriving in Britain, and in the Netherlands.

Pink-backed Pelican *Pelecanus rufescens*
France (12); Netherlands (2: Sept 1989; Oct 1990); Spain (4: 1-4 and 28-30 Aug 1990; 17 Feb-2 Mar 1991; 24 Apr 1991; 4 Aug and 10-28 Dec 1991).

Chinese Pond Heron *Ardeola bacchus*
Norway (1: autumn 1973, at sea).

Marabou Stork *Leptoptilos crumeniferus*
Spain (numerous records of perhaps 5 or 6 individuals).

African Spoonbill *Platelea alba*
France (15); Netherlands (1: Apr 1993); Spain (2: 1 May-24 Sept 1988; 20 Feb 1989).

Lesser Flamingo *Phoenicopterus minor*
France; Germany; Netherlands; Spain (4 records of 10 birds).

Fulvous Whistling Duck *Dendrocygna bicolor*
France (2: Apr 1929; Sept 1970); Spain (Sept 1971).

White-faced Whistling Duck *Dendrocygna viduata*
Spain.

Wood Duck *Aix sponsa*
Britain (several possible vagrants, but escapes and feral breeding birds also recorded); Iceland (4).

Bald Eagle *Haliaeetus leucocephalus*
Britain (1: 17 Oct 1978); Ireland (1: 18-25 Nov 1987, taken into captivity on latter date and transported to US).

Rüppell's Griffon Vulture *Gyps ruepellii*
Spain (3 records of 1 or 2 individuals: 7 April 1990; 1 June and 21-22 Oct 1992).

Lappet-faced Vulture *Torgos tracheliotus*
France (1: 19th century); Spain.

Common Bulbul *Pycnonotus barbatus*
France (1: 5 Oct 1992).

Güldenstädt's Redstart *Phoenicurus erythrogaster*
Finland (2: 28 Apr 1993; 11-20 Oct 1993).

Pale Thrush *Turdus pallidus*
Germany (1: 16 July 1986).

Mugimaki Flycatcher *Ficedula mugimaki*
Britain (1: 16-17 Nov 1991); Italy (1: 29 Oct 1957*).

Narcissus Flycatcher *Ficedula narcissina*
France (1).

Indian House Crow *Corvus splendens*
Gibraltar (1: 26 Mar-5 Apr 1991); Ireland (1: 3 Nov 1974); Netherlands (3: 10 Apr 1994-8 Apr 1996, two; 21 Nov 1994-26 Dec 1995).

American Goldfinch *Carduelis tristis*
Ireland (1: 6 Sept 1894, collected).

Palm Warbler *Dendroica palmarum*
Britain (1: 18 May 1976, dead on tideline).

Meadow Bunting *Emberiza cioides*
Finland (1: 20-27 May 1987); Italy (2: 1910; 1910); Spain (1: 3 Dec 1994)

House Bunting *Emberiza striolata*
Spain (1: June 1987).

Red-headed Bunting *Emberiza bruniceps*
Recorded from many European countries; commonly kept as a cagebird, though at least some occurrences may relate to wild individuals.

Blue Grosbeak *Guiraca caerulea*
Britain (4: 26 Aug 1970; 10-11 Mar 1972; 22 May 1977; 9 May 1986); Iceland (2: 1970; 22 Nov 1987); Norway (1).

Lazuli Bunting *Passerina amoena*
Britain (6+); Denmark (1: 11 Apr-7 Apr 1990); Netherlands (1: May 1985); Norway (2: 15 May 1988; 15 Aug 1990).

Painted Bunting *Passerina ciris*
Britain (7+).

Eastern Meadowlark *Sturnella magna*
Britain (4: Oct 1854; Mar 1860; 13 Oct 1876; before 1871).

Red-winged Blackbird *Agelaius phoenicus*
Britain (1: 27 Oct 1866); Netherlands (2: Sept 1975; June 1980, Apr 1981 and Mar 1982).

Rusty Blackbird *Euphragus carolinus*
Britain (1: 4 Oct 1881).

Common Grackle *Quiscalus quiscula*
Denmark (1: Mar-Apr 1970).

APPENDIX 4

NATIONAL LISTS OF EUROPEAN COUNTRIES

Every country in Europe has a system for maintaining a list of bird species recorded within its boundaries. Some use a process where species recorded are listed under one of four main categories, each denoted with the letters A-D. In Britain, for example, these are defined as follows (British Ornithologists' Union 1992):

● Category A: species which have been recorded in an apparently wild state in Britain or Ireland at least once since 1 January 1958.

● Category B: species which were recorded in an apparently wild state in Britain or Ireland at least once up to 31 December 1957, but have not been recorded subsequently.

● Category C: species which, although originally introduced by man, have now established a regular feral breeding stock which apparently maintains itself without necessary recourse to further introduction.

● Category D: species which would otherwise appear in categories A or B except that
(D1) there is a reasonable doubt that they have ever occurred in a wild state, or
(D2) they have certainly arrived with a

combination of ship and human assistance, including provision of food and shelter, or
(D3) they have only ever been found dead on the tideline;

also:

(D4) species that would otherwise appear in category C except that their feral populations may or may not be self-supporting.

In Britain, the 'main' national list is formed by categories A, B and C; category D is excluded from the total number of species regarded as having occurred. However, other countries do not necessarily use the same definitions, or even the same system; Norway and Spain, for example, have not yet established a separate category D, though their respective rarities committees still regard some species as of possible doubtful origin. On the other hand Austria and the Netherlands, for instance, do not include introduced species (category C in Britain) in their national list totals. Other matters, such as ship-assisted vagrancy, may also be treated in different ways in different countries.

National lists for European countries are

not, therefore, comparable on a direct basis. With that caveat acknowledged, the countries listed below had recorded the following totals of species as at 31 December 1994:

Austria	411
Belgium	415
Britain	544
Channel Islands (Jersey only)	297
Czech Republic	390
Estonia	332
Faeroes	257
Greece	422
Iceland	330
Ireland	413
Italy	439
Latvia	319
Lithuania	311
Luxembourg	281
Netherlands	438
Norway	454
Poland	415
Slovakia	333
Slovenia	369
Spain	494
Sweden	453
Switzerland	376

EUROPEAN RARE BIRDS COMMITTEES

Anyone finding a rare bird in Europe should report it to the appropriate national records committee or ornithological association at the addresses given below:

Austria
Avifaunistische Kommission (AFK), BirdLife Austria, Burgring 7, A-1014 Vienna

Belgium
Flanders: Belgische Avifaunistische Homologatic Commissic (BAHC), c/o Jan Pollet, Erfgoedlaan 8, B-9800 Deinze
Wallonia: Commission d'Homologation (CH), c/o Hugues Dufourny, 20 rue des Raimbaix, 7387 Honnelles

Britain
British Birds Rarities Committee, Mike Rogers, Secretary, 2 Churchtown Cottages, Towednack, St Ives, Cornwall TR26 3AZ

Bulgaria
Petar Jankov, Bulgarian Society for the Protection of Birds, 2 Gagarin Street, 1113 Sofia

Channel Islands
Guernsey: La Société Guernsiaise, Clyne, Rue de la Cheminée, Castel
Jersey: Société Jersiaise, 7 Pier Road, Saint Helier, Jersey JE2 4UW

Czech Republic
Czech Faunistic Committee, Správa CHKO Pálava, Námestí 32, 692 01 Mikulov

Denmark
Danish Rarities Committee, Dansk Ornitologisk Forening, Vesterbrogade 140, 1620 København V

Estonia
Eesti Linnuharulduste Komisjon, Eeril Liebak, Eestimaa Loodhuse Fond, 2 Struwe Str, 2400 Tartu

Finland
Pekka J Nikander, Kylänvanhimmantie 22 B 3, FIN-00640, Helsinki

France
CHN, La Corderie Royale, BP 263, 17305 Rochefort cedex

Germany
Deutsche Seltenheitenkommission – Dokumentationsstelle für seltene Vogelarten – Über dem Salzgraben 11, D-37574 Einbeck-Drüber

Gibraltar
Gibraltar Rare Birds Panel, c/o Gibraltar Ornithological and Natural History Society, Field Centre, Jews' Gate, Upper Rock Nature Reserve, P O 843

Greece
George I Handrinos, 44 El Venizelou St, 16675 Glyfada

Hungary
Hungarian Rarities Committee, Dr G Magyar, c/o MME, 1121 Budapest, Költo U 21

Iceland
Icelandic Rarities Committee, Gunnlaugur Thrainsson, Melbae 40, IS-110 Reykjavík

Ireland
Irish Rare Birds Committee, Patrick Smiddy, Ballykennealy, Ballymacoda, Co Cork

Italy
Fulvio Fraticelli, Comitato di Ornologazione Italiana, Museo Civico di Scienze Naturali, Via Ozanam 4-1, 25128 Brescia

Latvia
Latvijas Ornitofaunistikas Komisija, Mier 3, Salaspils, LV-2169

Lithuania
Petras Kurlavicius, Institute of Ecology, Academijos St 2, 2600 Vilnius

Luxembourg
Luxemburger Homologations Kommission, Tom Conzemius, 38 Kiischtewee, L-6113 Junglinster

Netherlands
Commissie Dwaalgasten Nederlandse Avifauna (CDNA), Postbus 45, 2080 AA Santpoort-Zuid

Norway
NSKF, Norsk Ornitologisk Forening, Seminarplassen 5, N-7060 Klaebu

Poland
Komisja Faunistyczna, Taduesz Stawarczyk, Sienkiewicza 21, 50-335 Wroclaw

Portugal
Portuguese Rarities Committee, SPEA, c/o Helder Costa, Rua da Vitoria, 53-4° Dt°, 1100 Lisboa

Romania
Societatea Ornitologica Româna, Str Republicii 48, RO-3400-Cluj

Slovakia
Dr Alfréd Trnka, Western Slovakian Museum, Muzejné námestie 3, 918 09 Trnava

Slovenia
Birdwatching and Bird Study Association of Slovenia, Andrej Sovinc, Pod Kostanji 44, SLO-61000 Ljubljana

Spain
Comité de Rarezas de la SEO, Eduardo de Juana, Facultad de Biologia, Planta 9, Ciudad Universitaria, 28040 Madrid

Sweden
Swedish Rarities Committee, c/o Christian Cederroth, Segerstads fyr, 38065 Degerhamn

Switzerland
Commission de l'Avifaune Suisse, c/o Schweizerische Vogelwarte, 6204 Sempach

There is also a body representing the collective interests of Europe's national rarities committees:

The Association of European Rarities Committees
Tom Conzemius
Secretary
D'Haus vun der Natur
L-1899 Kockelscheuer
Luxembourg

BIBLIOGRAPHY

Alström, P, with MacKay, A. 1995. Identification of Siberian, Black-throated, Radde's, Arabian and Brown Accentors. *Birding World* 8: 108-112.

Anon. 1996. Rare birds. *Ventes Ragas* 2: 34-36.

Beaman, M. 1994. *Palearctic Birds: a Checklist of the Birds of Europe, North Africa and Asia north of the foothills of the Himalayas.* Harrier Publications.

Birch, A. 1994. Yellow-throated Vireo: new to Britain and Ireland. *British Birds* 87: 362-365.

Bosy, R G, and Clarke, A W. 1993. Sjeldne fugler i Norge i 1991. *Vår Fuglefauna* 16: 205-225. Norsk Ornitologisk Forening.

Bradshaw, C, and Steele, J. 1994. Tests of patience. *Birdwatch* 27: 40-45.

Bradshaw, C, and Votier, S. 1993. Start with the legs ... *Birdwatch* 14: 44-48.

Bradshaw, C, and Votier, S. 1994. Mixed doubles. *Birdwatch* 19: 40-43.

Brazier, H, Dowdall, J F, Fitzharris, J E, and Grace, K. 1986. Thirty-third Irish Bird Report 1985. *Irish Birds* 3: 287-336.

British Ornithologists' Union. 1992. *Checklist of Birds of Britain and Ireland.* Sixth edition. BOU.

Brooks, R. 1995. *Birding in Lesbos.* Brookside Publications.

Byers, C, Olsson, U, and Curson, J. 1995. *Buntings and Sparrows.* Pica Press.

Chantler, P, and Driessens, G. 1995. *Swifts.* Pica Press.

Clement, P. 1987. Field identification of West Palearctic wheatears. *British Birds* 80: 137-157; 187-238.

Clement, P, Harris, A, and Davis, J. 1993. *Finches and Sparrows.* Christopher Helm.

Collar, N J, Crosby, M J, and Stattersfield, A J. 1994. *Birds to Watch 2: the World List of Threatened Birds.* BirdLife Conservation Series No. 4. BirdLife International.

Cortés, J E, Finlayson, J C, Mosquera, M A, and Garcia, E F J. 1980. *The Birds of Gibraltar.* The Gibraltar Bookshop.

Cramp, S, and Simmons, K E L (eds). 1977. *The Birds of the Western Palearctic.* Volume I. Oxford University Press.

Cramp, S, and Simmons, K E L (eds). 1980. *The Birds of the Western Palearctic.* Volume II. Oxford University Press.

Cramp, S, and Simmons, K E L (eds). 1983. *The Birds of the Western Palearctic.* Volume III. Oxford University Press.

Cramp, S (ed). 1985. *The Birds of the Western Palearctic. Volume IV.* Oxford University Press.

Cramp, S (ed). 1988. *The Birds of the Western Palearctic.* Volume V. Oxford University Press.

Cramp, S (ed). 1992. *The Birds of the Western Palearctic.* Volume VI. Oxford University Press.

Cramp, S, and Perrins, C M (eds). 1993. *The Birds of the Western Palearctic.* Volume VII. Oxford University Press.

Cramp, S, and Perrins, C M (eds). 1994. *The Birds of the Western Palearctic.* Volume VIII. Oxford University Press.

Cramp, S, and Perrins, C M (eds). 1994. *The Birds of the Western Palearctic.* Volume IX. Oxford University Press.

Curson, J, Quinn, D, and Beadle, D. 1995. *New World Warblers.* Christopher Helm.

De Juana, E. 1995. Observaciones homologadas de aves raras en España y Portugal informe de 1993. *Ardeola* 42: 97-113.

DeBenedictus, P A. 1996. Fortieth supplement to the *AOU Checklist. Birding* 28: 228-231.

del Hoyo, J, Elliott, A, and Sargatal, J (eds). 1992. *Handbook of the Birds of the World.* Vol 1. Lynx Edicions, Barcelona.

Delin, H, and Svensson, L. 1993. *Photographic Guide to the Birds of Britain and Europe.* Hamlyn.

Denton, M L. 1995. *Birds in the Yorkshire Museum.* Yorkshire Museum.

Dymond, J N, Fraser, P A, and Gantlett, S J M. 1989. *Rare Birds in Britain and Ireland.* T & A D Poyser.

Dymond, J N. 1991. *The Birds of Fair Isle.* Privately published.

Eischer, K. 1995. The Thick-billed Warbler in Finland. *Birding World* 8: 10-11.

Eldridge, M, and Harrop, A. Identification and status of Baikal Teal. *Birding World* 5: 417-423.

European Bird Report. *Birdwatch* 18: 60-61; 19: 60-61; 20: 60-61; 21: 60-61; 22: 60-61; 23: 60-61; 24: 60-61; 25: 60-61; 26: 60-61; 27: 60-61; 28: 60-61; 29: 60-61; 30: 60-61; 31: 60-61; 32: 60-61; 33: 60-61.

European News. *British Birds* 84: 1-12, 226-236; 85: 6-16, 443-463; 86: 36-47, 278-293; 87: 1-15; 88: 26-45, 288-290.

Evans, L G R. 1993. *Rare Birds in Britain 1992.* Privately published.

Evans, L G R. 1994. *Rare Birds in Britain 1800-1990.* Privately published.

Evans, L G R. 1995. *Rare Birds in Britain 1993.* Privately published.

Finlayson, J C, and Cortés, J E. 1987. The birds of the Strait of Gibraltar, its waters and northern shore. *Alectoris* 6: 1-74. The Gibraltar Ornithological and Natural History Society.

Finlayson, J C, and Tomlinson, D. 1993. *Birds of Iberia.* Mirador.

Finlayson, J C. 1992. *Birds of the Strait of Gibraltar.* T & A D Poyser.

Frich, A S, and Nordbjærg, L. 1994. Sjældne fugle i Danmark og Grønland 1992. *Dansk Ornitologisk Forenings Tidsskrift* 88: 99-110.

Frich, A S, and Nordbjærg, L. 1995. Sjældne fugle i Danmark og Grønland 1993. *Dansk Ornitologisk Forenings Tidsskrift* 89: 101-110.

Fry, C H, Fry, K, and Harris, A. 1992. *Kingfishers, Bee-eaters and Rollers.* Christopher Helm.

Gantlett, S. 1992. The Western Palearctic year. *Birding World* 5: 24-31.

Gantlett, S. 1993. The Western Palearctic year. *Birding World* 6: 16-27.

Gantlett, S. 1994. The Western Palearctic year. *Birding World* 7: 24-37.

Gantlett, S. 1995. The Western Palearctic year. *Birding World* 8: 22-39.

Garcia, E, and Paterson, A. 1994. *Where to Watch Birds in Southern Spain.* Helm.

Gaston, A J. 1992. *The Ancient Murrelet.* T & A D Poyser.

Gensbøl, B. 1984. *Birds of Prey of Britain and Europe.* Collins.

Golley, M, and Hough, J. 1992. Black-legged stints and peeps. *Birdwatch* 4: 18-20.

Golley, M. 1994. Great white hopes. *Birdwatch* 23: 42-45.

Gorman, G. 1996. *The Birds of Hungary.* Christopher Helm.

Grant, P J. 1986. *Gulls: a Guide to Identification.* Second edition. T & A D Poyser.

Gretton, A. 1991. *Conservation of the Slender-billed Curlew.* International Council for Bird Preservation.

Gustad, J R. 1994. Sjeldne fugler i Norge i 1992. *Vår Fuglefauna* 5: 259-276.

Handrinos, G, and Akriotis, A. 1996. *The Birds of Greece.* Christopher Helm.

Harrap, S, and Quinn, D. 1996. *Tits, Nuthatches and Treecreepers.* Christopher Helm.

Harris, A, Shirihai, H and Christie, D. 1996. *The Macmillan Birder's Guide to European and Middle Eastern Birds.* Macmillan.

Harrison, C. 1982. *An Atlas of Birds of the Western Palearctic.* Collins.

Harrison, P. 1985. *Seabirds: an Identification Guide.* Revised edition. Croom Helm.

Harrop, H. 1994. Welcome to the Hippodrome. *Birdwatch* 28: 40-44.

Harvey, P. 1992. The Brown Flycatcher on Fair Isle – a new British bird. *Birding World* 5: 252-255.

Heard, C. 1995. Unravelling the mystery. *Birdwatch* 41: 20-24.

Heinzel, H, Fitter, R, and Parslow, J. 1995. *Birds of Britain and Europe with North Africa and the Middle East.* HarperCollins.

Hill, P M. 1993. *A Checklist to the Birds of Mallorca.* Privately published.

Hockey, P. 1993. Jizz identification of sand plovers. *Birding World* 6: 369-372.

Hudec, K, Chytil, J, Stastny, K, and Bejcek, V. 1995. Ptáci Ceské Republiky. *Sylvia* 31: 97-149.

Humphreys, G R. 1937. *A List of Irish Birds showing the species contained in the National Collection.* The Stationery Office.

Jännes, H. 1995. Idänturturikyyhky – vieras aasiasta. *Alula* 1: 56-65.

Jonsson, L. 1992. *Birds of Europe with North Africa and the Middle East.* Christopher Helm.

Kapanen, M, and Lindroos, T. 1996. Marsh Sandpiper – its juvenile plumage and distribution. *Alula* 2: 56-62.

Kehoe, C, and Mitchell, D. 1993. Five star petrels. *Birdwatch* 15: 44-49.

Madge, S, and Burn, H. 1988. *Wildfowl: an Identification Guide to the Ducks, Geese and Swans of the World.* Christopher Helm.

Marr, T, and Porter, R. 1995. The White-winged Lark in Britain. *British Birds* 88: 365-371.

Maumary, L, and Volet, B. 1995. Oiseaux rares et observations inhabituelles en Suisse en 1993: rapport de la Commission de l'avifaune Suisse (CAvS). *Nos Oiseaux* 43: 95-112.

McGeehan, A. 1994. Enigma variations. *Birdwatch* 26: 42-45.

McGeehan, A. 1995. A little help. *Birdwatch* 39: 38-42.

McLaren, I A. 1995. Field identification and taxonomy of Bicknell's Thrush. *Birding* 27: 358-366.

Mild, K. 1993. Die Bestimmung der europäischen schwarzeiben Fliegenschnäpper Ficedula. *Limicola* 7: 221-276.

Millington, R. 1994. Pallas's Warblers in autumn 1994. *Birding World* 7: 438-439.

Mullarney, K. 1991. Identification of Semipalmated Plover: a new feature. *Birding World* 4: 254-258.

Muriset, J-C, and Maumary, L. 1994. Première apparition du Traquet du désert en Suisse. *Nos Oiseaux* 42: 329-333.

National Geographic Society. 1983. *Field Guide to the Birds of North America.* National Geographic Society.

O'Sullivan, O, and Smiddy, P. 1987. Thirty-fourth Irish Bird Report 1986. *Irish Birds* 3: 455-490.

O'Sullivan, O, and Smiddy, P. 1988. Thirty-fifth Irish Bird Report 1987. *Irish Birds* 3: 609-648.

O'Sullivan, O, and Smiddy, P. 1989. Thirty-sixth Irish Bird Report 1988. *Irish Birds* 4: 79-114.

O'Sullivan, O, and Smiddy, P. 1990. Thirty-seventh Irish Bird Report 1989. *Irish Birds* 4: 231-257.

O'Sullivan, O, and Smiddy, P. 1991. Thirty-eighth Irish Bird Report 1990. *Irish Birds* 4: 423-462.

O'Sullivan, O, and Smiddy, P. 1992. Thirty-ninth Irish Bird Report 1991. *Irish Birds* 4: 571-610.

Olsen, K M, and Larsson, H. 1995. *Terns of Europe and North America.* Christopher Helm.

Ornithologischer Jahresbericht Helgoland 1: 5-45; 2: 3-56; 3: 3-61; 4: 1-62.

Parmenter, T, and Byers, C. 1991. *A Guide to the Warblers of the Western Palearctic.* Bruce Coleman Books.

Preston, K. 1985. Thirty-second Irish Bird Report 1984. *Irish Birds* 3: 105-121.

Price, J, Droege, S, and Price, A. 1995. *The Summer Atlas of North American Birds.* Academic Press.

Richardson, C. 1990. *The Birds of the United Arab Emirates.* Hobby Publications.

Ristow, D, and Wink, M. 1994. Distribution of non-breeding Eleonora's Falcons. *Il-Merrill No 28, 1992-94.*

Rogers, M J, and the Rarities Committee, with comments by A R Dean and K E Vinicombe. 1985. Report on rare birds in Great Britain in 1984. *British Birds* 78: 529-589.

Rogers, M J, and the Rarities Committee, with comments by A R Dean and S J Gantlett. 1986. Report on rare birds in Great Britain in 1985. *British Birds* 79: 526-588.

Rogers, M J, and the Rarities Committee, with comments by S J Gantlett. 1987. Report on rare birds in Great Britain in 1986. *British Birds* 80: 516-571.

Rogers, M J, and the Rarities Committee, with comments by R A Hume. 1988. Report on rare birds in Great Britain in 1987. *British Birds* 81: 535-596.

Rogers, M J, and the Rarities Committee, with comments by R A Hume. 1989. Report on rare birds in Great Britain in 1988. *British Birds* 82: 505-563.

Rogers, M J, and the Rarities Committee, with comments by C D R Heard and R A Hume. 1990. Report on rare birds in Great Britain in 1989. *British Birds* 83: 439-496.

Rogers, M J, and the Rarities Committee, with comments by C D R Heard and R A Hume. 1991. Report on rare birds in Great Britain in 1990. *British Birds* 84: 449-505.

Rogers, M J, and the Rarities Committee, with comments by Colin Bradshaw and Peter Clement. 1992. Report on rare birds in Great Britain in 1991. *British Birds* 85: 507-554.

Rogers, M J, and the Rarities Committee, with comments by Colin Bradshaw and Peter Clement. 1993. Report on rare birds in Great Britain in 1992. *British Birds* 86: 447-540.

Rogers, M J, and the Rarities Committee, with comments by Graham P Catley and Michael J Rogers. 1994. Report on rare birds in Great Britain in 1993. *British Birds* 87: 503-571.

Rogers, M J, and the Rarities Committee, with comments by P M Ellis and A M Stoddart. 1995. Report on rare birds in Great Britain in 1994. *British Birds* 88: 493-558.

Seltene Vogelarten in der Bundersrepublik Deutschland 1990. *Limicola* 6: 153-177.

Shirihai, H, Christie, D A, and Harris, A. 1995. Field identification of Pine Bunting. *British Birds* 88: 621-626.

Shirihai, H. 1996. *The Birds of Israel.* Academic Press.

Smiddy, P, and O'Sullivan, O. 1993. Fortieth Irish Bird Report 1992. *Irish Birds* 5: 79-102.

Smiddy, P, and O'Sullivan, O. 1994. Forty-first Irish Bird Report 1993. *Irish Birds* 5: 209-230.

Smiddy, P, and O'Sullivan, O. 1995. Forty-second Irish Bird Report 1994. *Irish Birds* 5: 325-351.

Stipcevic, M. 1992. Crna komatna tekica ugotovljena na Hrvaskem. *Acrocephalus* XIII 55: 180-182.

Svensson, L. 1993. *Identification Guide to European Passerines.* Stockholm.

Trnka, A, et al. 1995. *Checklist of the Birds of Slovakia.*

Tucker, G M, and Heath, M F. 1994. *Birds in Europe: their Conservation Status.* BirdLife Conservation Series No. 3. BirdLife International.

van den Berg, A B, and Bosman, C A W. 1996. *Checklist of the Birds of the Netherlands.* Fifth edition. Santpoort-Zuid.

van den Berg, A B, de By, R A, and CDNA. 1992. Rare birds in the Netherlands in 1990. *Dutch Birding* 14: 73-90.

van den Berg, A B, de By, R A, and CDNA. 1993. Rare birds in the Netherlands in 1991. *Dutch Birding* 15: 145-159.

Votier, S, and Bradshaw, C. 1994. Three of a kind. *Birdwatch* 25: 42-45.

Wiegant, W M, Steinhaus, G H, and CDNA. 1994. Rare birds in the Netherlands in 1992. *Dutch Birding* 16: 133-147.

Wiegant, W M, Steinhaus, G H, and CDNA. 1995. Rare birds in the Netherlands in 1993. *Dutch Birding* 17: 89-101.

PHOTOGRAPHIC ACKNOWLEDGMENTS

Numbers in bold type in these acknowledgments refer to the page number and those in parentheses refer to the actual picture number. An asterisk indicates that the picture also appears on the dust cover.

Paul Archer **15**(5), **63**(1)
Nicola Baccetti **135**(1)
Alberto Badami **45**(5), **45**(6)
Theo Bakker **25**(3)
Mike Barratt **111**(9)
Leo Batten **55**(6)
Nigel Bean **87**(10), **149**(5)
Michael Bergman **55**(5), **55**(7), **121**(10)
Julian Bhalerao **19**(2), **21**(6), **23**(3), **27**(5), **53**(8), **113**(6), **129**(3), **129**(9)
Sarah Bhalerao **19**(4)
P. Boesman **85**(7), **85**(8)
Leo J. R. Boon **25**(9), **39**(6), **43**(6), **43**(7), **47**(3), **51**(4), **63**(2), **69**(6), **107**(9), **113**(11), **129**(1)
Colin Bradshaw **17**(9), **31**(9), **99**(6), **101**(7), **147**(8), **155**(3), **169**(4)
Kees Breek **35**(8), **47**(4)
M. Brosselin **71**(7)
Tony Broome **91**(2), **147**(3), **165**(10)
David W. Burns **53**(5)
Valerio Capello **73**(6)
Graham P. Catley **23**(2), **69**(7), **113**(2)
Robin Chittenden **21**(3), **21**(4), **29**(5), **33**(5), **37**(5), **37**(10), **51**(3), **59**(1), **75**(12), **79**(4), **89**(6), **89**(7), **103**(1), **103**(4), **111**(3), **119**(3), **123**(4), **135**(5), **141**(3), **161**(11), **165**(6), **167**(7)
Peter Clements **61**(1)
Peter Coe **169**(2)
Mark Coller **25**(5), **53**(7), **77**(9), **121**(4), **127**(9), **137**(2)
Tony Collinson **31**(3), **85**(3), **159**(7)
Paul Cook **99**(4), **155**(2)
Simon Cook **87**(9)
Bill Coster **35**(5)
David Cottridge **35**(7), **71**(4), **91**(8), **119**(9), **121**(7), **151**(9), **157**(7)
David Cottridge/Windrush **141**(1), **141**(2), **163**(1)
Dennis Coutts **13**(7), **29**(2), **61**(3), **67**(6), **75**(6), **79**(3), **89**(1), **89**(8), **95**(3), **105**(7), **111**(5), **121**(1), **121**(8), **123**(5), **125**(5), **127**(7), **133**(7), **137**(1), **139**(3), **147**(7), **151**(6), **153**(6), **153**(7), **157**(1), **159**(3), **165**(2), **169**(6)
Tony Croucher **53**(2), **65**(1), **71**(1), **71**(2), **71**(3), **117**(3), **117**(4), **145**(1), **151**(8), **157**(2)
Filip De Ruwe **67**(2), **123**(8), **143**(4)
Geoff Delve **63**(6), **75**(5)
Carl Derks **161**(9)
Wendy Dickson **35**(6)
Alan Dixon **23**(4), **23**(6)
Paul Doherty **23**(7), **63**(7)
Jack Donovan **111**(6)
Ken Douglas **147**(1), **147**(2)
Frank Dröge **27**(2), **27**(6), **35**(2)
Göran Ekström **95**(8)
Göran Ekström/Windrush **127**(5), **127**(6), **133**(4)
Patrik Engström **109**(2), **125**(7), **131**(9)
Tom Ennis **85**(6)
Jonathan Fairhurst **87**(8)
Ian Fisher **37**(7), **91**(6)
Thórhallur Frimansson **107**(7)
Vic Froome **23**(1)
Peter Gasson **83**(3), **119**(2), **141**(6)
Hans Gebuis/Aquila **27**(4), **27**(8), **35**(4), **43**(3), **43**(5), **47**(1), **47**(2), **59**(7), **71**(8), **81**(5), **127**(1), **139**(1), **163**(8), **167**(6)
D. J. Godfrey **107**(11)
Ricard Gutiérrez **85**(5)
John and Pam Hall **91**(7), **129**(6)
John Harriman **31**(8), **37**(9), **105**(5), **105**(6), **117**(1), **117**(2)

Hugh Harrop **125**(2), **165**(3)
Paul Harvey **65**(9), **65**(7), **133**(8), **133**(9), **143**(8), **159**(1)
Ren Hathway **61**(7), **107**(3), **141**(9)
Håkon Heggland **33**(4), **41**(3), **59**(3), **65**(6), **67**(4), **67**(7), **77**(4), **77**(5), **77**(6), **77**(7), **83**(1), **105**(1), **107**(2), **113**(9), **123**(6), **125**(4), **129**(10), **143**(7)
Andreas J. Helbig **75**(10)
Felix Heintzenberg **73**(7)*, **163**(6)
John Hewitt **49**(9), **73**(1), **115**(2)
Jóhan Óli Hilmarsson **31**(6), **33**(1), **37**(2), **39**(1), **39**(2), **75**(4), **77**(8), **83**(4), **89**(2)
W. R. Hirst **95**(9), **95**(10)
Don Hodgers **21**(1)
Brenda Holcombe/Windrush **21**(5)
Paul Hopkins **13**(6), **65**(5), **79**(2), **89**(3), **89**(4), **103**(10), **139**(7)
Eric Hosking **51**(7), **51**(8)
Julian Hough **99**(5)
Barry Howard **101**(1), **101**(2), **101**(3)
Markku Huhta-Koivisto **81**(7), **121**(5)
David Hunt **55**(1), **155**(4)
J. H. Johns **63**(8), **97**(4)
Adrian Jordi **33**(7)*
Kevin Karlson **19**(3)
Noel Kearns **123**(1), **123**(2), **123**(3)
Hannu Kettunen **35**(9), **45**(3), **51**(6), **69**(1), **103**(8), **125**(9), **129**(4), **131**(7), **135**(2)
Reston Kilgour **57**(4)
Jon King **15**(4), **17**(6), **17**(8), **17**(10)
Jan Kist **83**(7)
Yann Kolbeinsson **149**(7), **149**(8)
Pekka Komi **53**(1), **91**(1), **109**(3), **123**(7), **125**(8), **125**(10), **127**(2)
Aarne Lahti **103**(12)
Vagn Larsen **81**(4)
Sven Larsson **101**(8), **101**(9)
Henry Lehto **25**(6), **45**(2), **59**(2), **107**(4), **109**(4), **139**(5), **143**(3), **143**(5)
Jack Levene **37**(1), **67**(9), **93**(12), **95**(7), **103**(3), **119**(6), **141**(10)*
Vincenzo Loi **85**(4)
R. Long **109**(1), **153**(5)
Tim Loseby **21**(8), **41**(1), **47**(5), **49**(3), **55**(2), **73**(3), **79**(7), **87**(1), **93**(10), **97**(1), **101**(6), **115**(1), **119**(1), **141**(11), **157**(3)
Peter Loud **107**(8)
Peter Lyngs **93**(4), **93**(5), **93**(6), **97**(5), **125**(3), **125**(6), **129**(5)
George McCarthy **45**(4)
Mike McDonnell **117**(7)
Anthony McGeehan **13**(1), **31**(7), **47**(6)*, **61**(5), **69**(5), **99**(2), **99**(3), **113**(1), **151**(2), **153**(1), **153**(2), **159**(6), **167**(2), **167**(3), **167**(8), **167**(9)
Tony Marr **15**(2), **15**(3)
A. Marsden **111**(1)
D. Mason/Windrush **89**(5)
Karel Mauer **75**(7)
Barry Mitchell **169**(3)
Dave Morgan **83**(10)
Arthur Morris **69**(4)
A. Morris/Windrush **19**(1), **21**(9), **33**(3), **85**(1), **85**(2), **99**(1), **107**(10), **133**(5), **133**(6), **147**(9), **149**(1), **149**(2), **149**(4), **149**(6), **155**(5), **157**(8), **167**(1)
Pete Morris **145**(6)
J. P. Moulton **165**(8), **165**(9)
Killian Mullarney **31**(10), **115**(5), **115**(6)
A. J. Murphy **63**(5), **121**(11)
Howard Nicholls **15**(1)
Sergio Nissardi **123**(1)
Mikael Nord **135**(3)
Tappani Numminen **91**(3), **161**(6)
D. J. Odell **153**(3), **153**(4)
Kevin Osborn **133**(3), **157**(4), **165**(1), **169**(5), **169**(7)
Phil Palmer **103**(5)
Jim Pattinson **13**(5), **63**(4), **67**(1), **75**(2), **101**(4)

Keith Pellow **155**(1)
C. M. Perrins **15**(6)
Stefan Pfützke **17**(5), **25**(2), **41**(4), **41**(6), **109**(7), **109**(8), **143**(1), **145**(2)
René Pop **37**(3), **45**(1), **53**(3), **59**(6), **65**(7), **79**(5), **81**(1), **87**(2), **87**(4), **87**(5), **111**(7), **111**(8)
George Reszeter **33**(8), **41**(5), **91**(4), **101**(5), **105**(8), **105**(9), **119**(5), **121**(3), **121**(12), **127**(8), **129**(11), **133**(2), **137**(5), **145**(7), **145**(8), **147**(4), **163**(2), **167**(5), **169**(1)
Jouni Riihimäki **109**(5), **109**(6)
A. Sapsford **91**(5)
Alan J. Shearman **93**(7), **93**(8), **93**(9)
Dave Slater **153**(8), **153**(9)
R. G. Smith **21**(10), **71**(5), **71**(6), **117**(5), **145**(3), **161**(1)
Jostein Sørgård **13**(9), **13**(10)
Dave Stewart **165**(5)
Keith Stone **69**(2), **77**(10), **113**(10), **151**(4)
Bruno Sundin **43**(1), **43**(2)
Alan Tate **55**(4), **57**(1), **77**(2), **81**(3), **93**(2), **103**(2), **103**(9), **111**(4), **127**(10), **135**(6), **151**(5), **159**(2)
A. R. Taylor **85**(9)
Don Taylor **95**(1)
Steve Taylor **23**(5)
G. & V. Thompson/Windrush **19**(6)
Roger Tidman **41**(2), **149**(3)
David Tipling/Windrush **49**(2), **65**(4), **75**(1), **119**(4), **123**(9), **135**(4), **161**(12)
C. R. Tyler/Windrush **19**(5)
Magnus Ullman **25**(1), **49**(6), **59**(4)
Arnoud B. van den Berg **13**(2), **25**(4), **29**(6), **29**(7), **35**(3), **51**(2), **53**(9), **63**(3), **87**(7), **105**(2), **129**(2), **129**(8), **131**(6), **137**(3), **143**(2), **153**(10), **161**(4), **161**(8), **165**(4)
Jan van Holten **57**(6), **73**(4), **83**(5), **131**(4), **139**(6)
René van Rossum **61**(2), **61**(4), **73**(9), **83**(8), **103**(6), **113**(5), **115**(4), **131**(2), **139**(2)
Markus Vareswo **43**(4), **79**(1), **97**(2), **113**(3)
Luc Verroken **31**(5), **39**(7), **75**(8), **131**(1), **131**(5), **137**(4), **163**(7)
Will Wagstaffe **57**(5)
Nick Wall **93**(11), **95**(2), **119**(7)
Peter Walsh **29**(1), **79**(6), **113**(4), **113**(8), **131**(10), **141**(8), **147**(5), **147**(6)
Adrian Wander **17**(1), **17**(2), **17**(3), **17**(4)
Andy Webb **57**(2)
Barry Wells **67**(3)
Pete Wheeler **13**(3), **39**(3), **39**(5), **47**(7), **49**(1), **61**(6), **65**(3), **67**(8), **93**(3), **93**(1)*, **95**(4), **97**(6), **97**(7), **105**(1)0, **119**(8), **141**(4), **141**(5), **145**(9), **169**(8), **169**(9), **169**(10)*
R. C. Wilson **37**(6), **51**(1), **65**(2), **67**(6), **73**(8), **75**(11), **163**(4)
Pierre Yésou **49**(4), **49**(5)
Steve Young **13**(4), **13**(8), **21**(2), **21**(7), **25**(7), **25**(8), **27**(1), **27**(3), **27**(7), **29**(3), **29**(4), **31**(1), **31**(2), **31**(4), **33**(2), **33**(6), **35**(1)*, **37**(4), **37**(8), **39**(8), **49**(7), **49**(8), **49**(10), **51**(5), **53**(4), **53**(6), **55**(3), **57**(3), **57**(6), **57**(8), **59**(5), **65**(8), **69**(3), **73**(2), **73**(5), **75**(3), **77**(1), **77**(3), **81**(2), **81**(6), **83**(2), **83**(6)*, **83**(9), **87**(3), **87**(6), **95**(5), **96**(6), **103**(7), **103**(11), **105**(3), **105**(4)*, **107**(1), **107**(5), **107**(6), **111**(2), **113**(7), **113**(12), **117**(6), **121**(2), **121**(6), **121**(9), **127**(3), **127**(4), **129**(7), **131**(3), **131**(8), **131**(11), **133**(1), **139**(4), **141**(7), **143**(6), **145**(4), **145**(5), **151**(1), **151**(3)*, **151**(7), **157**(5) **157**(6), **159**(4), **159**(5), **159**(8), **161**(3), **161**(5), **161**(7), **161**(10), **163**(3), **163**(5), **165**(7), **167**(4)
Jeff Youngs **39**(4), **75**(9)

Despite every effort the following photographs were unable to be traced: **17**(7), **97**(3), **115**(3). All photographs on pages 1 to 13 were taken by Steve Young.

INDEX